OPERA

OPERA

The great composers and their masterworks

JOYCE BOURNE

Preface by
Lord Harewood

Foreword by
Bryn Terfel

MITCHELL BEAZLEY

OPERA

The great composers and their masterworks
by Joyce Bourne

First published in Great Britain in 2008 by Mitchell Beazley,
an imprint of Octopus Publishing Group Limited,
2–4 Heron Quays, London E14 4JP
An Hachette Livre UK Company
www.octopusbooks.co.uk

Distributed in the U.S. and Canada by Octopus Books USA:
c/o Hachette Book Group USA
237 Park Avenue
New York NY 10017
www.octopusbooksusa.com

A CIP catalogue record for this book is available from the British Library.

ISBN 978 1 84533 275 4

Set in Gillsans and Bembo

Colour reproduction by Fine Arts, China
Printed and bound Toppan, China

Commissioning Editors Anna Sanderson, Hannah Barnes-Murphy
Art Director Tim Foster
Art Editor Victoria Burley
Senior Editors Suzanne Arnold, Ruth Patrick, and Leanne Bryan
Editor Slaney Begley
Picture Research Manager Giulia Hetherington
Proofreader Howard Watson
Indexer Joyce Bourne
Production Controller Lucy Carter

TITLE PAGE **Interior view of L'Opéra Garnier, Paris, France**

Contents

Preface and Foreword

PREFACE BY LORD HAREWOOD

Opera is all things to all men – or, an overview such as this book presents sometimes suggests that it tries to be. We have it in its most popular form as romantic Italian opera; as comparably popular but differently aimed, the operas of Mozart; we have the grander and greatly challenging forms of Wagner; we have the airy delights of the Italian *ottocento* (Rossini, Bellini, Donizetti); we have the much loved but now also critically discussed operas of Verdi; and every now and then we have a new work that excites the imagination; and sometimes one that flops as a local disaster.

This book deals with every kind of opera that has ever been invented, from the first great masterpiece – Monteverdi's *La Favola d'Orfeo* – to Adès's *The Tempest*, and leaves the potential opera-goer to make a personal choice. What really matters is that some of these entries cover whatever area it is that fills us individually with excitement and brings us delight.

I have been going to opera for over 70 years, at first rather tentatively but gradually with more awareness of what it has to offer and eventually with a strong feeling that almost all of it is worthwhile. I have my own favourites and my own disaster areas, but I confess to the latter only to my closest friends.

Lord Harewood

FOREWORD BY BRYN TERFEL

I sat down to ponder: what could I possibly add as a foreword to this book? I had just arrived home from the Royal Opera House, Covent Garden, after the première of Puccini's *Gianni Schicchi*, a one-act opera that lasts a mere 55 minutes but is undoubtedly a masterpiece, lavishly scattered with jokes and tunes to die for – a real audience gem. I guess we performers are the lucky ones. We are the interpreters who carry the responsibility of breathing some essential life into the works of geniuses and we are ourselves, through hard work and dedication, consequently illuminated.

This book has a simple aim: to tell you about opera and its world, its highs and lows. It is certainly a marvellous and sometimes a magical world, a world of hopes and dreams. It is a world that many would like to enter and know and which, unfortunately, far too many people still do not appreciate.

Every piece of information that I beg, borrow, or steal from conductors, directors, singers, teachers, and writers, enriches me as an artist and performer on the stage. From the *cognoscente* to the real novice, from the stalls to the circle to the amphitheatre, this book can open windows that will help you find that final piece of the jigsaw which will make your visit to the opera an even more exciting, engrossing, and fabulous experience. It is also bound to impress your friends!

Bryn Terfel

Introduction

I have never been sure where my passion for music and especially opera arose. My parents were not musical but I learned to play the piano for two years in my early teens. The lessons cost 2s. 6d. (12½p) and took place in a room that was so cold that my teacher wore mittens while teaching. Our music teacher at school encouraged us to listen to music – scratchy 78rpm records on an old player. He also took us to hear the Yorkshire Symphony Orchestra conducted by Maurice Miles on their annual visit to Hull. The first live music I ever heard was the Prelude to Act III of Wagner's *Lohengrin* and I can still remember the frisson it gave me. This was long before the days of personal radios – there was one large radio in our home and I could listen to the Third Programme (as Radio 3 then was) only if the family was out. As soon as they came home, off went "that dreadful noise". Hull had a good repertory theatre and each year the Carl Rosa Opera came. I saw my first *Butterfly* and *Bohème* standing at the back of the theatre. As I wept for Cio-Cio-San or Mimì, it didn't matter that I couldn't afford a seat.

The main reason I chose Manchester University to study medicine was because Manchester had the Hallé Orchestra. New casements opened for me. I was lucky to be involved with various arts activities as a student. When the London opera companies came on tour they asked for students to sell programmes. Night after night I saw the operas while sitting on the stairs in the circle – no health and safety regulations in those days.

Later in life I have been fortunate in being married to a music critic and for a number of years we saw around 90 operas a year and were privileged to attend major opera festivals in the UK, Europe, America, and Australia. The performances were not always first-rate – but they were always worth seeing. The more one saw, the more one learned to judge quality. My love-affair with the human voice continues unabated to this day.

I have tried to cover a wide range of opera, mainly works that can be considered standard repertory, and have attempted to give some insight into the lives of the composers and the circumstances surrounding the composition of their operas. Hopefully, the chapter on voices and singers will help readers to appreciate the effort involved in becoming an opera singer – singers do not appear out of the blue, no matter what we might be told by the media about the latest new find. And we as listeners must also make some effort – there is no excuse for arriving at a theatre knowing nothing about the work one is about to see and hear. A little homework beforehand will repay one a hundredfold in understanding what is happening on the stage. Try to avoid it though I have, I'm sure my own likes and dislikes will show through and I do not apologize for this. You, too, I hope, will develop your likes and dislikes. Always remember: "elite" simply means "the best of its kind". Just give it a chance.

For help with many aspects of this book, I owe thanks to a number of people, not least my long-suffering husband, Michael Kennedy, who has encouraged me from the start, even though he has had to eat more ready-made meals than ever before in the past 30 years! I am grateful to Anna Sanderson, the editor who commissioned me, and to her successors at Mitchell Beazley, Suzanne Arnold and later Ruth Patrick, for their patience, enthusiasm, and friendly but firm prodding when things were sometimes getting tough. For their help and sense of humour, I thank the picture editor Giulia Hetherington for going to so much trouble to find all the right pictures and Victoria Burley for her skilful and attractive page design. I am grateful for the careful copy-editing of Slaney Begley and proof-reading of Howard Watson. I thank Hugh Canning for saving me from several howlers in the chapter on Baroque music and Rodney Milnes who assiduously and generously checked the whole manuscript for factual errors. For advice about voice production I very much appreciate the help of Barbara Robotham of the Royal Northern College of Music, Manchester. I am grateful to Charles Osborne and David Lloyd-Jones for permission to quote from their publications; to Louise Ringrose of DG/Archiv Production and Sally Groves of Schott's Music Publishers for the loan of librettos and scores; Christopher Underwood for help with French translation; Thea Musgrave for perusing and correcting her entry; and all those kindly opera press officers who responded to my numerous queries. I am indebted to the late Alan Blyth for his suggestions for listening in the chapter on voices and singers. I thank the Principal, Professor Edward Gregson, for giving me unlimited access to the library of the RNCM, and the chief librarian Anna Smart and her staff for all the help they have given me. Last, but not least, I thank Lord Harewood and Bryn Terfel for their willingness to write the forewords. Any remaining errors are entirely my responsibility and the opinions and musical judgments expressed are mine and mine alone.

Joyce Bourne

The Development of Opera through the Ages

"Opera" is the Italian word for "work", "action", "deed" (and also the plural of the Latin *opus* meaning "a work"). Opera is a dramatic work set to music, and is really short for *opera in musica*, a dramatic work in which the music is integral. In opera, the words of the "play" are sung by singers who are accompanied by instruments. The sung drama may be interrupted by dialogue, known as recitative (Italian = *recitativo*, often abbreviated to recit.), and this may or may not be accompanied by one or more instruments, so it can be *recitativo secco* (dry recitative, ie unaccompanied) or *recitativo accompagnato*. The sung part of the drama consists of solos (known as arias), ensembles for two or more singers, and choruses.

Dramatic works have always contained some form of music: Shakespeare's plays have songs, often accompanied by the actor himself on a lute. But this sort of music was incidental to the action, something different to keep the attention of the audience, and there are many examples of incidental music written specifically for plays (such as Mendelssohn's for *A Midsummer Night's Dream*). This type of composition has largely ceased with the disappearance of live theatre orchestras (but is still composed for use in films, which have full-scale scores accompanying the action, many of them classics of the genre).

Some of the earliest examples of opera are those written in Florence towards the end of the 16th century by a group of poets and musicians known as the Camerata ("society"). These included the musicians Jacopo Peri (1561–1633) and Giulio Caccini (1551–1618), both of whom had been associated with the Medici court in Florence. The Camerata met in the palace homes of Florentine aristocrats such as Count Giovanni de' Bardi (1534–1612) and Jacopo Corsi (1561–1602). The earliest known opera (or *dramma per musica*) is thought to be Peri's *Dafne* (1594–8), in a prologue and six scenes, but the music is now lost. In the works of this period the "spoken word", the *recitativo*, was the dominant feature.

Opera as we now know it developed rapidly with the Italian musician

Claudio Monteverdi (1567–1643). He served at the court of the Duke of Mantua as a viol player and madrigal singer. He heard and was influenced by the operas of the Camerata, especially by Peri's *Euridice* of 1600. Monteverdi's own first opera, *La favola d'Orfeo*, was produced in 1607 and was the first opera to be accompanied by a full (by the standards of that time) orchestra. His operas integrate madrigals and church music and encompass two major developments: the introduction of the aria as an important means of telling the story, and the portrayal of human characters, ie real people, rather than mythological beings. The interrelationships of these characters form the main theme of the drama. Three of Monteverdi's operas survive into the regular repertory today. An important contemporary of Monteverdi was Pietro Francesco Cavalli (1602–76), whose operas have had some modern revivals. The first composer to use (in 1685) instrumental accompaniment for recits is thought to have been the Italian Alessandro Scarlatti (1660–1725) in his *L'Olimpia vendicata*, but despite his having composed over 100 operas between 1679 and 1725 he is, like his son Domenico, remembered mainly as a composer of keyboard music. In France in the same period the pioneers in opera were Jean-Baptiste Lully (1632–87) and Jean-Philippe Rameau (1683–1764).

ABOVE LEFT **Opening page of a madrigal by the Florentine composer Francesco Landini (1325–97), showing an early form of notation**

ABOVE **Programme illustration from the Paris première of Debussy's *Pelléas et Mélisande*, with Jean Périer and Mary Garden in the title-roles, 1902**

After Monteverdi, the next great name in the history of opera was George Frideric Handel (1685–1759), a German who settled in England and composed most of his operas for London between 1711 and 1741. He wrote in Italian, with long display arias demanding brilliant techniques, many of them composed for the great castrati singers of that time (see p.37) or for equally talented sopranos. Handel's works have dramatic impact and his characters have involved relationships. His operas are long and he is famous for the *da capo* aria (*da capo* = from the head) in which the aria is introduced, expounded upon, and then the first part is repeated. These arias, glorious though many of them are, were thought by the next major opera composer, Christoph Willibald von Gluck (1714–87), to hold up the development of the plot, and it was Gluck who banished the *da capo* aria, insisting that the music should be used to express the drama and sentiments of the story.

Franz Joseph Haydn (1732–1809) had the misfortune to be in competition with Wolfgang Amadeus Mozart (1756–91) and his operas were almost totally eclipsed by those of his younger colleague. Great composer that Haydn was, his operas were not great and few have survived into the regular repertoire, although if well produced and well sung they can be very entertaining. Mozart's genius changed for ever the face of opera, bringing the orchestra into the foreground and introducing characters who have been known to opera-goers ever since they made their first appearance. His operas still made use of accompanied recits, but with Mozart the aria achieved its apotheosis. He was fortunate in having a company of singers who would perform his operas so he was able to tailor his music to the voices that were going to sing it.

After Mozart the beginning of the 19th century in Italy was dominated by Rossini (1792–1868), Donizetti (1797–1848), and Bellini (1801–35), who came to be known as the *bel canto* ("beautiful singing") school. Rossini in particular produced comic operas of wit and sparkle and a whole generation of truly great singers were given music worthy of them. In Germany the tradition of folklore and fantasy found its interpreter in Carl Maria von Weber (1786–1826), followed by the gigantic figure of Richard Wagner (1813–83). Wagner's early works followed the tradition of aria and recit., but as he matured he developed a style of "through-composed" operas – a seamless weaving of orchestra and singers in an almost symphonic way. He preferred the term "music-drama" and was the first of the great composers to write his own librettos. He disliked and reacted against the operas of his colleague Giacomo Meyerbeer (1791–1864) who, although German, spent most of his life in Paris outshining the more talented Hector Berlioz (1803–69), whose reputation has grown with the passage of time, as Meyerbeer's has diminished. Other French composers who had success at this time were Camille Saint-Saëns (1835–1921), Georges Bizet (1838–75), Charles Gounod (1818–93), and Jules Massenet (1842–1912). But the composer who had the most influence on music of this period – and not just on French music – was Claude Debussy (1862–1918), whose sole completed opera *Pelléas et Mélisande* remains a prime example of post-Wagnerian composition. Nevertheless, the greatest name in post-Wagnerian opera is Richard Strauss (1864–1949), who was particularly lucky in his librettist, the poet Hugo von Hofmannsthal. Later came the composers of the Second Viennese School, Arnold Schoenberg (1874–1951) and Alban Berg (1885–1935), and more recently Hans Werner Henze (b.1926).

As Richard Wagner dominated the German opera scene, so Giuseppe Verdi (1813–1901) rose in Italy. His early works owe much to the example of the *bel canto*

ABOVE The Austrian author, poet, and playwright Hugo von Hofmannsthal (1874–1929), who was the librettist for six of Richard Strauss's operas

composers (especially Donizetti), but he gradually developed his own style of drama while still keeping within the aria–recit. formula – this form had become known as numbers opera as opposed to the through-composed works of Wagner. At least 10 of Verdi's operas are in the regular repertory of the world's opera houses. After Verdi the next big development was the *verismo* school – "real life, true life" – whose followers composed works often derived from the same movement in literature, eg the novels of Émile Zola (1840–1902) and the plays of Victorien Sardou (1831–1908). Two prominent composers of this period are Ruggero Leoncavallo (1857–1919) and Pietro Mascagni (1863–1945), both of whom wrote several operas, only one of which has stayed the course – but what a triumph each has been, the former's *Pagliacci* and the latter's *Cavalleria rusticana*, both in one act and most often performed as a double bill known to opera-goers everywhere as "Cav. and Pag". Both these composers were eclipsed by the rise of Giacomo Puccini (1858–1924) in whose operas the music and the drama have equal appeal. Some of

Puccini's operas are, to this day, among the most frequently performed, the most moving, and the most popular with audiences (*Madama Butterfly*, *La bohème*, *Tosca*).

In Eastern Europe opera was a fairly late starter. *A Life for the Tsar* (1836) by the Russian Mikhail Glinka (1804–57) was probably the first of the truly nationalist operas. Of greater importance were *Prince Igor* by Alexander Borodin (1833–87) and *Boris Godunov* and *Khovanshchina* by Modest Musorgsky (1839–81). Pyotr Tchaikovsky (1840–93) was not a truly nationalist composer, but his two most

famous operas, *Eugene Onegin* and *The Queen of Spades*, are both based on poems by his compatriot Pushkin. The great Czech composer Antonín Dvořák (1841–1904) wrote operas, the best-known being *Rusalka*, and Bedřich Smetana (1824–84) achieved long-lasting success with *The Bartered Bride*; but the peak of Czech opera was reached by Leoš Janáček (1854–1928). Janáček's operas, amalgams of high drama, domesticity, romance, and tragedy, have an immediate dramatic appeal to audiences who are further moved by the glorious music, especially in the life-enhancing nature-opera *The Cunning Little Vixen*.

England was also slow in the opera stakes. Before the 19th century, only Henry Purcell (1659–95) can claim to have written anything resembling an opera (*Dido and Aeneas* and *The Fairy Queen*) though John Blow's *Venus and Adonis* (c.1682) and *The Beggar's Opera* of 1728, with words by John Gay and some music probably by the German-born J C Pepusch, are still revived. Arthur Sullivan (1842–1900) wanted to be seen as a serious opera composer and was very disappointed by the failure of his *Ivanhoe*, instead achieving fame through his collaboration with William S Gilbert (1836–1911) in the Savoy operettas that have retained their popularity. Frederick Delius (1862–1934) was born in Bradford in Yorkshire but spent most of this life abroad, first in Florida and then in France. He wrote five operas that have merits but have never reached repertory status. Ralph Vaughan Williams (1872–1958) wrote five operas that are still not considered standard but may be beginning to gain ground and are being shown to be more stageworthy than has been claimed by some writers.

ABOVE **Cyndia Sieden as Ariel in the première of Thomas Adès's Shakespeare opera *The Tempest*, Royal Opera House, Covent Garden, London, 10 February 2004**

But it was Benjamin Britten (1913–76) with *Peter Grimes*, which had its première at Sadler's Wells, London, in 1945, who showed that England could – and did – produce a natural opera composer. His operas are in every British company's repertoire and with increasing frequency are gaining ground in mainland Europe and the USA. Contemporary with Britten were William Walton (1902–83) and Michael Tippett (1905–98), and later still came Peter Maxwell Davies (b. 1934), Harrison Birtwistle (b. 1934), Judith Weir (b. 1954), Mark-Anthony Turnage (b. 1960), Thomas Adès (b. 1971), and others on whom it is too early to give a verdict.

If it took England a long time to enter the field, it took the USA even longer. George Gershwin's (1898–1937) *Porgy and Bess*, which had its première on Broadway in 1935, can claim to be the first truly successful American opera. Gershwin has been followed by Virgil Thomson (1896–1989), Samuel Barber (1910–81), the Italian-born Gian Carlo Menotti (1911–2007), Dominick Argento (b. 1927), and John Corigliano (b. 1938), all of whom have had some success, and the so-called minimalist composers Philip Glass (b. 1937) and John Adams (b. 1947), both of whom can be considered successful composers of opera. It is probably too early to make value judgments about the next generation of American opera composers, but in the past few years there has been quite a spate of new operas produced by major companies in the United States. Two names worth bearing in mind are Tobias Picker (b. 1954), whose *Thérèse Raquin* was produced in Dallas in 2000 and *An American Tragedy* at the Metropolitan Opera House in 2005; and Jake Heggie (b. 1961), whose *Dead Man Walking* was acclaimed after its première in San Francisco in 2000, and whose *The End of the Affair* was produced at Houston in 2004. Maybe after a late start the USA is rapidly catching up with the rest of the operatic world.

A few points of interest: many great composers have written no operas (Bach, Brahms, Bruckner, Mahler, Elgar, Ives); or operas which have not stood the test of time (Haydn, Schubert, Schumann); or only one opera of great significance (Beethoven, Debussy, Mascagni, Leoncavallo). And it is equally interesting to note how few composers have achieved greatness in opera and in other fields of music – only Handel, Mozart, Strauss, Janáček, and Britten come easily to mind.

ABOVE Lincoln Center for the Performing Arts: the Metropolitan Opera House in the centre; New York State Theater, home of NY City Opera on the left; and Avery Fisher Concert Hall on the right

Voices and Singers

What do we mean when we talk about singers' voices? Why do we like one voice and not another? And what do we mean by "like"? Of course there are *objective* judgements that can be made: if somebody is singing badly – out of tune, for instance, or phrasing in such a way that the words do not flow naturally – this is usually apparent even to the listener with little knowledge of the music they are hearing or of the technicalities of voice production. It just sounds wrong. But how a particular voice strikes a listener is also a very *subjective* thing. We may like or not like a voice without being able to say what it is that attracts or disturbs us. We have all had the experience of instantly recognizing the voice of a friend at the other end of a telephone. This is because some voices have a distinctive timbre, a tone-colour, that is difficult to describe. It is this timbre that distinguishes one singer from another and makes some voices at once recognizable. Maria Callas and Plácido Domingo are obvious examples – they each have a "sound" that makes it impossible to confuse them with any other singer.

The voice can be described as the oldest musical instrument. From a very young age children learn that the tone of voice they use can have different effects on adults. These different tones usually represent different emotions: anger, pleasure, frustration, distress, etc, and all these and other emotions have to be expressed by singers. At an early age we enjoy singing, with varying degrees of pleasure for the listener. But to use one's voice as a means of entertaining other people, and of thus earning a living is a different matter.

Singing teachers have to learn a considerable amount about the structure and function of the parts of the body used in vocal production: the articulating organs, resonating cavities, postural muscles, and the breathing and support muscles. We all have the anatomical necessities for the production of the voice. We have the larynx (voice box), which is at the top of the trachea (windpipe) and can be felt in the neck (more easily in men than women) as the

Adam's apple. Inside the larynx are the vocal cords, two thin pieces of cartilage that are drawn together and apart by a series of muscles. The vocal cords are set into vibration by air coming up from the lungs to create a sound. The sound that is made is amplified in the natural spaces of the throat, mouth, and head – the parts known as the resonators – and thus becomes the singing voice. When developed and trained, so that the sound emerging is controlled and energized by the breathing and support muscles, the voice can fill a large space such as an opera house and can give pleasure to the listener. Teachers must also encourage the individuality of a voice – young singers may want to sound like their favourite famous artist, but it is only through the use of their own natural instrument that they can convey an honest interpretation of the music.

We regularly hear on radio or television of a new singer introduced as "the great opera singer so-and-so". They usually have not sung in opera at all and, unless they are prepared to stop earning vast amounts of money as the latest sensation and knuckle down to serious study, they are unlikely ever to do so. The voice has not learned how to produce the effects necessary for an opera singer and will have only a short life. This untrained instrument, having been pushed too far, too quickly, and in the wrong direction, will have undeveloped vocal muscles and little stamina to protect it against the rigours of constant use and will rapidly deteriorate and the career will finish. The voice needs to be trained in the same way that an athlete has to train – just as an untrained athlete trying to run a four-minute mile would be very likely to injure himself, so will the untrained singer, often with serious and lasting consequences.

Of course there have been great singers who emerged with a beautiful voice having had little or no training and even less scientific knowledge of the voice. But even with this natural talent they all benefited from some form of training as their careers advanced. Because the instrument is the person, many things can affect the way a voice

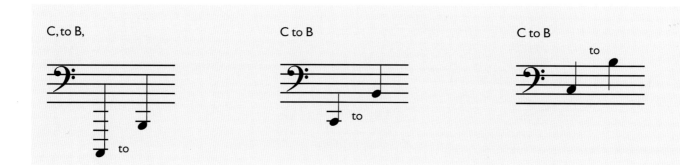

functions. Illness, tiredness, posture, poor footwear, emotional strain, can all take their toll. A pianist with a cold may be able to give a very good recital. A singer cannot.

Probably the earliest music to which our ancestors were exposed, was religious music: Gregorian chant, church chorales, cantors in synagogues. The singing was done by young boys and men, and in the 16th century, mainly in Italy, it was accepted practice to castrate boys aged between six and eight years in order to preserve their soprano voices. This continued well into the 19th century, one of the last of these castrati being Alessandro Moreschi (1858–1922) who sang in the Choir of the Sistine Chapel. Castrati were at their most popular in the operas of the 18th century, with famous singers such as Senesino (Francesco Bernardi, *c.*1680– 1759) and Farinelli (Carlo Broschi, 1705– 82). Handel wrote many leading roles for Senesino, who sang in 32 of his operas, the roles in modern times being sung by women (or occasionally countertenors, see p.23).

The singing voice is considered to have three main sections or *registers* – upper, middle, and lower – and these are accessed by employing a different muscular adjustment of the vocal cords and the use of appropriate resonating cavities. Thus according to which parts of the anatomy are primarily involved, singers learn to use a "head voice" or a "chest voice" as appropriate to the music they are interpreting, and must learn how to move smoothly from one register to another without an obvious – and ugly – join. Emotional effects rely considerably on the use of *vibrato*, a fluctuation in pitch that, if correctly controlled by the trained laryngeal muscles, should not affect intonation. If the fluctuation is too slow, the sound becomes a somewhat unpleasant wobble.

Opera singers these days have to master a number of styles of singing. Operas from the Baroque, Classical, Italian Romantic and *verismo*, German Romantic, and modern (from the 20th century onward) periods each demand a different vocal approach. Singers often specialize in a particular field (the German word is *Fach*, meaning a compartment or a pigeonhole). There is, of course, more than singing to being a good opera performer – clear and intelligent use of the text, a good memory, acting skill, and movement all play their part in making the total artist.

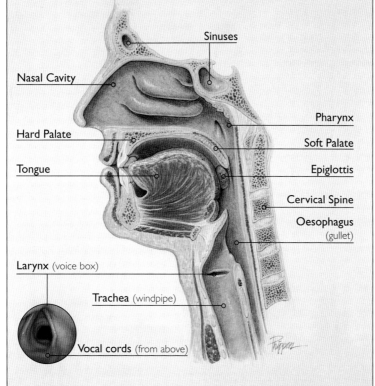

Sinuses
Nasal Cavity
Hard Palate
Tongue
Pharynx
Soft Palate
Epiglottis
Cervical Spine
Oesophagus (gullet)
Larynx (voice box)
Trachea (windpipe)
Vocal cords (from above)

middle c' to b'
to

c" to b"
to

c'" to c""
to

Notes of the scale As seen on the piano, in the centre of the keyboard is middle C (c')

RIGHT Back view of American soprano Grace
Bumbry (b. 1937) having a lesson in 1959 from
Lotte Lehmann (1888–1976)

SOPRANO

The highest female voice is the soprano, with a range of 2 to 2½ octaves from about middle C (*c'*) upwards to *b"* or even higher, up to *f"'* in some voices. There are different types of soprano voice. The one most easily recognized is the coloratura soprano, a high voice of great agility that can run up and down scales without apparent effort. One of the earliest coloratura sopranos was Henriette Sontag, a German soprano (real name Gertrud Walpurgis, 1806–54) who made her first public appearance at the age of 6 and her opera début aged 15. At the age of 23, at the composer's request, she created the title-role in Weber's *Euryanthe*. Among her roles were Mozart's Donna Anna in *Don Giovanni*, Rossini's Semiramide, and Donizetti's Lucrezia Borgia. Another name in this vocal mode is Jenny Lind (Sweden, 1820–87), who excelled in roles such as Amina in Bellini's *La sonnambula* and Marie in Donizetti's *La fille du régiment*, and was known as the Swedish Nightingale. Amelita Galli-Curci, an Italian soprano (1882–1963), was a famous exponent of Verdi's Gilda (*Rigoletto*) and Violetta (*La traviata*), and of Elvira in Bellini's *I puritani*. In more modern times there have been Beverly Sills, an American soprano (1929–2007), and the Australian Joan Sutherland (b. 1926) who can be described as a dramatic coloratura. She burst on the operatic scene in 1959 when she sang Lucia in Donizetti's opera at Covent Garden and was an instant success. This type of voice is less common today, as opera has moved into a more natural mode, but a great example is the French soprano Natalie Dessay (b. 1965), a celebrated Queen of Night in Mozart's *Die Zauberflöte* and Fiakermilli in Strauss's *Arabella*.

Possibly the commonest form of the soprano voice is the lyric soprano, singing such roles as Pamina in Mozart's *Die Zauberflöte*, Massenet's Manon, Agathe in Weber's *Der Freischütz*, and the Marschallin in Strauss's *Der Rosenkavalier*. A good example of this type of voice early in the 20th century was the Czech soprano Emmy Destinn (1878–1930). She was Senta in the first Bayreuth performance of Wagner's *Der fliegende Holländer* in 1901 and created Minnie in Puccini's *La fanciulla del West* in 1910. In modern times there are many great exponents of this type of voice: Kiri te Kanawa (Countess in Mozart's *Figaro*), Felicity Lott (Governess in Britten's *The Turn of the Screw*), Elisabeth Söderström (Janáček's *Jenůfa*), Carol Vaness (Vitellia in Mozart's *La clemenza di Tito*), and Amanda Roocroft (*Desdemona* in Verdi's *Otello*) to name but a few.

The dramatic soprano had to develop with the advent of the heavier roles and larger orchestras of the mid-19th-century composers – Wagner and Verdi prominent among them – the lighter lyric or coloratura voices being unsuitable. The German soprano Lotte Lehmann (1888–1976) started out singing lyric roles but over the years her voice became more dramatic and, as her voice changed, she was the first soprano to sing all three leading roles in Strauss's *Der Rosenkavalier* – Sophie, Octavian, and the Marschallin. She sang at Bayreuth as Elsa in *Lohengrin*, Eva in *Die Meistersinger*, Elisabeth in *Tannhäuser*, and Sieglinde in *Die Walküre*, but was not a true *Heldensopran* and did not sing Brünnhilde or Isolde. Kirsten Flagstad (Norwegian, 1895–1962) is one of the most famous dramatic sopranos and one of the greatest Wagnerian singers. She began her career in operetta and first sang at Bayreuth in 1933 in small

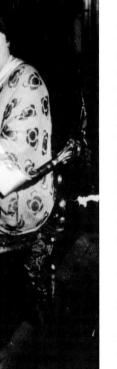

ABOVE Czech soprano Emmy Destinn (1878–1930),
aged 50, a soprano who in 1910 in New York
created Minnie in Puccini's *La fanciulla del West*

RIGHT Legendary Norwegian *Heldensopran*, Kirsten Flagstad, as Isolde in the United States in 1937. She gave the first performance of Strauss's *Vier letzte Lieder* in London in 1950

roles, returning in 1934 to sing Gutrune (*Götterdämmerung*) and Sieglinde (*Die Walküre*). She was outstanding as Isolde and Brünnhilde and was also a great *Fidelio* Leonore. Birgit Nilsson (Sweden, 1918–2005) was acknowledged as Flagstad's natural successor at Bayreuth. She was also preeminent in Strauss, a famous Salome, Elektra, and Färberin (Barak's Wife in *Die Frau ohne Schatten*). She was equally good as Puccini's Turandot, a role in which another dramatic soprano, the English Eva Turner (1892–1990), excelled. (She was also a famous Brünnhilde.) Another English Brünnhilde was Rita Hunter (1933–2001) and, from Wales, Gwyneth Jones (b. 1936) who sang the role at Bayreuth. Moving further into the 20th and 21st centuries one can name Deborah Polaski, Anne Evans, Susan Bullock, and Christine Brewer as worthy successors.

The name most easily recognized in the dramatic soprano category is surely Maria Callas (1923–77). Born in the USA of Greek parents, she became probably the best-known singer of the 20th century (partly through her private life, played out in front of the press cameras). Not everyone liked the voice and opera buffs are divided in their opinion of her greatness. The voice was not conventionally beautiful and at times she made some ugly sounds, but for those who responded to her very special timbre, her interpretations, her stage presence, and her fearless determination to produce the notes as the composer wrote them, she was the dramatic soprano of the century and they believe that her Norma (Bellini), Anna Bolena (Donizetti), Violetta (*La traviata*), and Medea (Cherubini) will rarely be equalled.

ABOVE Back-stage interval: Birgit Nilsson (1918–2005) as the Dyer's Wife and Leonie Rysanek (1926–98) as the Empress in Strauss's *Die Frau ohne Schatten*, San Francisco, 1980

MEZZO-SOPRANO

Literally, in Italian, "half-soprano", this is midway between the soprano and the contralto (see below) and the usual range is *a* to *g*", but this is extended at both ends of the range. In practical terms, mezzo-sopranos at the high end of their range can often sing roles written for or usually sung by sopranos (such as the Composer in Strauss's *Ariadne auf Naxos* or Cherubino in Mozart's *Le nozze di Figaro*). If the voice is at the other end of the scale, they can also tackle roles that some years ago would have been described as contralto parts. The term "mezzo-soprano" was not used very much until the 19th century, the voices in that range previously being regarded as sopranos with a deeper downward extension. As castrati became obsolete, mezzos came into their own, the two having similar ranges. Roles that encompass this are Bellini's Romeo, and Mozart's Cherubino and Dorabella (*Così fan tutte*). Later composers wrote specifically for this type of voice and the term became more common. Roles such as Eboli in Verdi's *Don Carlos*, Kundry in Wagner's *Parsifal*, and Santuzza in Mascagni's *Cavalleria rusticana* can also be sung by dramatic sopranos. Some roles, however, such as Bizet's Carmen, and Mozart's Dorabella, are better suited to mezzos. It can be difficult to categorize accurately, and the terms mezzo-soprano and contralto become interchangeable and examples of these voices are discussed together later.

CONTRALTO (Alto)

This is the lowest range of the female voice, the range being about *g* to *e*". The voice is often dark and rich and before the 19th century female voices were considered either

sopranos or contraltos. With the introduction of the mezzo-soprano, the true contralto has become rare and few modern composers write for this voice. There are relatively few operatic roles that demand the deep contralto voice, exceptions being the fortune-teller Ulrica in Verdi's *Un ballo in maschera*, and Erda the earth-goddess in Wagner's *Das Rheingold*. Carmen, Saint-Saëns's Delilah, and Verdi's Azucena (*Il trovatore*) used to be sung by contraltos, but are now more often than not given to mezzos. It is worth noting that in the Gilbert and Sullivan operettas, the comic and formidable ladies such as Katisha in *The Mikado*, are designated as contralto roles and are best personified by this deep rich voice.

As mentioned earlier, many of the roles for the lower female voice are interchangeable between mezzos and contraltos. Among the most famous early mezzos were the French-born Spanish sisters Maria Malibran (1808–36) and Pauline Viardot (1821–1910). Malibran's roles ranged from Rossini's Angelina (*La Cenerentola*) to Bellini's Norma and even Beethoven's Leonore, whilst Viardot made her London début as Desdemona in Rossini's *Otello*, designated for a soprano. Both sisters had remarkable and flexible voices, superbly trained by their father Manuel García, and were able to encompass a wide repertoire. One contralto with an enormous vocal range was

Ernestine Schumann-Heink (Prague-born American, 1861–1936), who was the first Klytämnestra in Strauss's *Elektra* and a regular interpreter of Wagner's contralto/ mezzo roles: Erda (the *Ring* cycle), Ortrud (*Lohengrin*), Brangäne (*Tristan und Isolde*), and Fricka (*Das Rheingold*).

Janet Baker (English, b. 1933) is one of the best-known mezzos of the 20th century, the major part of her career having been in recital and concert, but with a bigger opera repertoire than is often realized: Gluck's Orfeo, Monteverdi's Penelope (*Il ritorno d'Ulisse in patria*), Donizetti's Maria Stuarda, Mozart's Dorabella, and Strauss's Composer and Octavian. Her immediate predecessor, Kathleen Ferrier (English, 1912–53), a famous Orfeo, was a true contralto as was the earlier Clara Butt (English, 1872–1936) who also sang Orfeo but specialized more

in oratorio and recitals. Ann Murray (Irish, b. 1949), usually described as a mezzo, is well-known for her interpretation of *travesti* roles (ie male characters sung by a female singer), such as Handel's Xerxes, Ariodante, Giulio Cesare, and Ruggiero (*Alcina*), and Strauss's Octavian and Composer. She has also portrayed Berlioz's Béatrice, Donizetti's Maria Stuarda, and Wagner's Waltraute (*Götterdämmerung*), as well as singing Mozart's Despina (*Così*), a role as often sung by a lyric soprano. In Germany there have been Christa Ludwig (b. 1928), a famous Eboli, Octavian, and Klytämnestra, who also sang the soprano roles of the Marschallin and the *Fidelio* Leonore; and Brigitte Fassbaender (b. 1939), a specialist in *travesti* roles and a memorable Amme in Strauss's *Die Frau ohne Schatten*, Klytämnestra in *Elektra*, and an amusing Clairon in his *Capriccio*. Starting life as a mezzo and singing such roles as Cherubino is Waltraud Meier (German, b. 1956), but she graduated to the true dramatic soprano repertoire and became an outstanding Isolde.

The Americans have produced many superb singers in this voice range: Grace Bumbry (b. 1937) sang soprano roles such as Tosca later in her career, but earlier sang Cassandra in Berlioz's *Les troyens* at the opening of the Paris Opéra Bastille; Shirley Verrett (b.1931) was a famous Carmen (and was another mezzo who sang soprano roles later in her career, such as Norma and Lady Macbeth); Marilyn Horne (b. 1934) sang Isabella in Rossini's *L'italiana in Algeri*, Carmen, and mezzo/contralto roles from Handel to Wagner; and Frederica von Stade (b.1945), a lovely Mélisande in Debussy's opera and Penelope in Monteverdi's *Il ritorno d'Ulisse in patria*, was also an exceptional Cherubino and Octavian. Outstanding among the newer generation of Americans, Susan Graham

RIGHT Winner of the 1997 Cardiff Singer of the World competition, Chinese mezzo Guang Yang as Rosina in Rossini's *Il barbiere di Siviglia*, WNO, 2000

(b. 1960) sings all the famous mezzo parts: Strauss's Octavian and Composer, Erica (Barber's *Vanessa*), Mozart's Dorabella and Cherubino, Massenet's Chérubin, Monteverdi's Poppea, and Verdi's Meg Page in *Falstaff*. Sweden's Anne Sofie von Otter (b. 1955) is a very successful mezzo, a good Handel and Monteverdi singer, and also a lively Carmen, Cherubino, and Octavian.

The greater "weightiness" of the mezzo makes the voice less suited to light florid passages, but it would be remiss not to mention the charismatic Italian Cecilia Bartoli (b. 1966) – truly a coloratura mezzo. She sings the major Rossini roles but also has made a speciality of Baroque music. Famous among previous generations of Italian mezzos were Ebe Stignani (1903–74), engaged by Toscanini to sing at La Scala, Milan, where her mezzo roles were considered the best of her day, including Amneris (*Aida*) and Azucena (*Il trovatore*); Fiorenza Cossotto (b. 1935), who sang in the first performance of Poulenc's *Dialogues des Carmélites* in 1957 and was Adalgisa in performances of *Norma* with Maria Callas, as were Giulietta Simionato (b. 1910) and the above-mentioned Stignani. A young Chinese mezzo-soprano coming to the fore is Guang Yang (b. 1970), the winner in 1997 of the Cardiff Singer of the World

competition. She has an agile mezzo voice with a very wide range. She is able to sing Suzuki (*Madama Butterfly*) and Wagner's Waltraute, as well as Santuzza (which verges on the dramatic soprano), and Eboli, which demands high notes and considerable agility in fast passages.

From the above, it can be seen that although one can designate different female voice ranges, the distinction between them is frequently blurred. Voices also change with age, and as has been indicated earlier, sopranos can become mezzos as they get older, just as the transposition can be made the other way. It is not necessary or advisable to be too pedantic.

Broadly speaking, just as female voices divide into soprano (upper), mezzo (middle), and contralto (lower), so do male voices divide into tenor, baritone (including bass-baritone), and bass.

TENOR

The highest male voice (the countertenor will be discussed later) usually has a range of around c to b' or sometimes up to c''. Like the soprano voice, tenors can roughly divide into three categories: light or lyric, dramatic lyric, and *spinto* ("driven" or "pushed") or heroic tenor (the German *Heldentenor*). But beware – different experts use different classifications and subdivisions, so this should be considered a guide rather than a strict classification. Each of these types of tenor is suited to singing different music although, once again, the boundaries are blurred. In early music (say pre-17th century), most solos were given to tenors and in early operas such as Monteverdi's *Orfeo*, the leading role was commonly written for this voice range. The castrati gradually took over these roles and tenors were used for smaller, often comic, roles and even played women. As the 18th century moved on, so did the roles given to tenors. Handel, as well as writing many castrato leading roles, also wrote significant roles for tenors (Bajazet in *Tamerlano*, Grimoaldo in *Rodelinda*, and Lurcanio in *Ariodante,* for example). In Mozart's operas the tenor started to come into his own, often being assigned the part of a king.

Light lyric tenors usually have less power and weight but more flexibility and are often expected to sing in a

ABOVE Kathleen Ferrier (1912–53), a great English contralto whose career was cut short by her early death from cancer

LEFT Most elegant of lyric tenors, Alfredo Kraus (1927–99), as Tonio in Donizetti's *La fille du régiment*, Metropolitan Opera, NY, 1983

coloratura manner, with florid decorations. They are well suited to Handel and to Rossini roles such as Almaviva in *Il barbiere di Siviglia*. The creator of Almaviva (in 1816) was the Spanish tenor and teacher Manuel García (1775–1832), the father of the mezzos Maria Malibran and Pauline Viardot and also of his namesake son Manuel García (1805–1906), the bass who became a renowned singing teacher. García *père* sang Otello in Rossini's opera, taking the part for the first London performance. A famous light tenor of this era was the Italian Giovanni-Battista Rubini (1794–1854), who created several roles for Donizetti (Riccardo in *Anna Bolena*) and Bellini (Gualtiero in *Il pirata*, Elvino in *La sonnambula*, and Arturo in *I puritani*). Later in his career he occasionally sang Don Ottavio in Mozart's *Don Giovanni*. In the early part of his career, the Italian Luciano Pavarotti (1935–2007) could be described as a lyric tenor and certainly sang Edgardo in Donizetti's *Lucia*, but he soon graduated to the more lyrico-dramatic roles. The Welshman Ryland Davies (b. 1943) is a classic example of the light tenor, making his début as Almaviva in 1964. The Englishman Peter Pears (1910–86) made his reputation primarily as the first interpreter of the leading tenor roles in the operas of Britten, written with his voice in mind. Earlier in his career he was a delightful Vašek in Smetana's *The Bartered Bride* and also appeared as Ferrando (*Così*) and Alfredo (*La traviata*). Maybe the light lyric tenor *par excellence* of modern times was Alfredo Kraus (1927–99). Spanish-born of Austrian descent, he was an elegant and stylish singer, an ideal Alfredo (*La traviata*), Almaviva (*Il barbiere di Siviglia*), Don Ottavio (*Don Giovanni*), Des Grieux (Massenet's *Manon*), and Hoffmann (Offenbach, *Les contes d'Hoffmann*), a role he last sang in 1991 when he was 64, the voice maybe no longer pristine, but still remarkable. The best-known light tenor since then is the Sicilian Roberto Alagna (b. 1964), delightful in such roles as Roméo in Gounod's *Roméo et Juliette* and Ruggero in Puccini's *La rondine*, but now venturing into a heavier repertoire such as Don Carlos, Manrico, and Cavaradossi. Rising stars in this field are the Mexican Rolando Villazón (b. 1972), who has made an impression as Alfredo in *La traviata*, Rodolfo in *La bohème*, and Offenbach's Hoffmann, and the Peruvian Juan

Diego Flórez (b. 1973), who has been especially noted in the *bel canto* repertory singing such roles as Rossini's Almaviva, Ernesto in Donizetti's *Don Pasquale*, and Arturo in Bellini's *I puritani*. The dramatic lyric tenor overlaps the above category and many light tenors sing more dramatic parts – often to the detriment of the quality of their voice. Wise is the singer who knows what he's good at and sticks to it. The more dramatic roles may need a heavier voice but they still require a degree of flexibility. Many lyric tenors had to adapt their voices to be able to sing the early operas of Verdi. This is the commonest type of tenor voice and is personified in such roles as Don José in Bizet's *Carmen*, Rodolfo in Puccini's *La bohème*, Alfredo in Verdi's *La traviata*, and the Duke of Mantua in his *Rigoletto*. An outstanding Italian tenor at the turn of the century was Francesco Tamagno (1850–1905) who sang the title-role in Verdi's *Don Carlos* and was chosen by the composer to create his Otello, a role he sang worldwide, including Covent Garden and the New York Metropolitan Opera House. Otello is the Everest of dramatic tenor roles, ideally suited to a tenor with a baritonal quality. Most dramatic tenors are ill-advised to attempt it in the early parts of their career, but it is not a true *Heldentenor* role. Many great tenors have encompassed the part, from the Polish Jean de Reszke (1850–1925), to the Italian Giovanni Martinelli (1885–1969), and the Chilean Ramón Vinay (1912–96), and, in more recent times, the American James McCracken

ABOVE Making his mark among the present generation of tenors is the Mexican Rolando Villazón (b. 1972), seen here as Massenet's melancholy poet Werther, Nice Opera, 2006

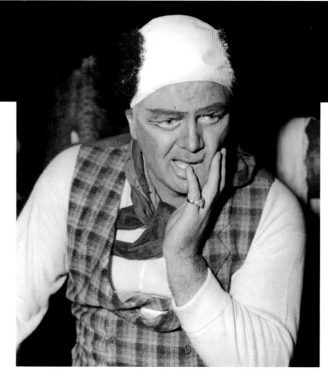

(1926–88), the great Canadian tenor Jon Vickers (b. 1926), the Welshman Dennis O'Neill (b. 1948), and, of course, the Spaniard Plácido Domingo (b. 1941) who, notwithstanding previous reservations, sang the role for the first time at the age of 34 and does not seem to have come to any harm.

As the later Verdi and Wagner operas emerged, the *Heldentenor* had to develop. While some of those mentioned in the preceding paragraph could certainly sing Wagner characters such as Lohengrin, Parsifal, Siegmund, and even Walther in *Die Meistersinger*, the true *Heldentenor* roles, such as Siegfried and Tristan, are in a class apart. An outstanding Siegfried in the first half of the 20th century was Danish-born Lauritz Melchior (1890–1973). Others have been Set Svanholm (Sweden, 1904–64), Wolfgang Windgassen (German, 1914–74), Alberto Remedios (England, b. 1935), and Siegfried Jerusalem (German, b. 1940). True *Heldentenors* do not grow on trees and there have been times when they have been very thin on the ground, the 1950s being one such period and the late 20th and early 21st centuries being another. Doubtless another *Heldentenor* generation will emerge – the Canadian Ben Heppner (b. 1956), for instance, is beginning to dip his toes in this repertoire.

BARITONE (and Bass-baritone)

This is the middle range of male voice, equivalent to the mezzo in women's voices. The range is about A to f'. It is not only between the tenor and the bass in range, but also in depth of tone. Certain operatic parts written in the 18th century and then described as "bass", eg roles by Handel and many by Mozart (Count in *Figaro*, Don Giovanni, and Papageno in *Die Zauberflöte*), are today nearly always sung by baritones. This is another voice category that had to develop as the demands of the repertoire increased during the 19th century. Verdi wrote many important roles for baritones, including the title-roles in *Nabucco*, *Simon Boccanegra*, *Rigoletto*, and *Falstaff* and notable in several Verdi operas are duets between baritone and soprano – often father/daughter duets. The role can lie high in the register and baritones may learn to extend their range upward – they need to be able to encompass elements of the tenor voice at one end and the bass at the other. Several well-known tenors have either started out or finished up as baritones. Strauss certainly wrote leading and demanding roles for baritone, a voice he favoured over the tenor, as did Puccini and several contemporary composers.

One of the earliest of true baritones was the Frenchman Henri-Bernard Dabadie (1797–1853) who created roles in various Rossini operas, such as Raimbaud in *Le Comte Ory* and William Tell. He was also the first Belcore in Donizetti's *L'elisir d'amore* in 1832. The latter was a favourite role of one of the greatest baritones of the early 19th century, Antonio Tamburini (Italian, 1800–76), who was described by composers and critics of the day as a bass, but we would now recognize him as a baritone. He created several Donizetti roles, including Malatesta in *Don Pasquale*, and was outstanding in Bellini. An early Verdi baritone was Giorgio Ronconi (1810–90). He was already a success in many roles in Donizetti's less well-known operas, but had his greatest triumphs in Verdi. He created the title-role in *Nabucco* and was the first London Rigoletto. He sang Don Carlo in *Ernani* and was a renowned Macbeth. A most gifted interpreter of Verdi was the French baritone Victor Maurel (1848–1923), who created Iago in *Otello* and the title-role in *Falstaff*, and sang Posa in Naples at the Italian première of *Don Carlos*. He was also the first singer of Tonio in Leoncavallo's *Pagliacci* as well as singing Wagner's Wolfram in *Tannhäuser* and Telramund in *Lohengrin* (both sung in Italian) at their London premières. One thing these roles have in common is the need for good acting, and this is a common feature of baritone roles. A German baritone, Karl Perron (1858–1928), created Jochanaan in Strauss's *Salome* in 1905, Orestes in *Elektra* in 1909, and Baron Ochs in *Der Rosenkavalier* in 1911. He also sang Escamillo (*Carmen*) and Mozart's Don Giovanni and the *Figaro* Count. He sang at Bayreuth between 1889 and 1904 in

RIGHT A great *Lieder* exponent, Dietrich Fischer-Dieskau (b. 1925), sang a wide range of operatic roles from Mozart to Wagner to contemporary works by Berg, Henze, and Reimann

roles such as Amfortas in *Parsifal* and Daland in *Der fliegende Holländer*. He also sang Wotan and it may be better to call him a bass-baritone, like another Baron Ochs, the Austrian Richard Mayr (1877–1935) – certainly the low notes in Ochs's music would test any baritone. Which brings us to Hans Hotter (German, 1909–2003) who started his career as a high baritone and ended it, some 60 years later, as a bass. In 1942 he created Olivier in Strauss's *Capriccio* and Jupiter in *Die Liebe der Danae* in 1944. He progressed to the Wagner bass-baritone roles (Amfortas in *Parsifal*, Sachs in *Die Meistersinger*) and was the most eminent Wotan of his day. He later sang the bass roles that will be referred to later. There have been many good American baritones, such as Leonard Warren (1911–60), Robert Merrill (1917–98), and Sherrill Milnes (b. 1935), and there was the Australian John Brownlee (1901–69) who was a famous Don Giovanni. Excelling in Verdi and Puccini in the early part of the 20th century was Tito Gobbi (Italian, 1913–84). He was not only a great comic actor but also played major tragic roles such as Berg's Wozzeck, which he sang at the opera's Italian première. But he was best-known for such Verdi roles as Posa, Iago, Boccanegra, and Falstaff and, perhaps his most famous role, Scarpia in Puccini's *Tosca*, which he sang on more than one occasion opposite Callas. When he sang Mozart's Count or Don Giovanni, he often had as his Figaro or Leporello the Welsh baritone Geraint Evans (1922–92), who was also a great interpreter of Falstaff, Papageno, and Wagner's Beckmesser (*Die Meistersinger*). Evans created roles in 20th-century works: Mr Flint in Britten's *Billy Budd* in 1951 and Mountjoy in the same composer's *Gloriana* in 1953. Another great baritone who sang contemporary roles was Dietrich Fischer-Dieskau (German, b. 1925). He was one of the world's leading singers, famous in a wide range of roles from Mozart's Count and Don Giovanni to Strauss's Mandryka (*Arabella*), Wagner's Hans Sachs (*Die Meistersinger*), and Verdi's Falstaff. He created the title-role in Reimann's *Lear* (Munich, 1978) and Mittenhofer in Henze's *Elegy for Young Lovers* (1961), as well as singing Berg's Wozzeck and Dr Schön (*Lulu*). And he was an outstanding *Lieder* interpreter. The Englishman Thomas Allen (b. 1944) has had an international career in such varied roles as Mozart's Count Almaviva, Don Giovanni, and Don Alfonso (*Così fan tutte*), Ulisse in Monteverdi's *Il ritorno d'Ulisse in patria*, Thomas's Hamlet, the Forester in Janáček's *The Cunning Little Vixen*, the Music Master in Strauss's *Ariadne auf Naxos*, and Beckmesser in *Die Meistersinger*. He was also one of the best interpreters of Britten's Billy Budd. At the time of writing there is a spate of very good baritones: the Russian Sergei Leiferkus (b. 1946), the English Simon Keenlyside (b. 1959), the Canadian Gerald Finley (b. 1960), and the Romanian Alexandru Agache (b. 1955) all warrant consideration, as they all sing leading roles worldwide. And there is Bryn Terfel (Welsh, b. 1965), a bass-baritone of outstanding merit and international renown. His interpretations of Strauss's Jochanaan; Mozart's Guglielmo, Leporello, Don Giovanni, and Count Almaviva; Puccini's Scarpia; Stravinsky's Nick Shadow (*The Rake's Progress*); Verdi's Falstaff; Britten's Balstrode (*Peter Grimes*); and Wagner's Wotan have all been widely and rightly acclaimed.

BASS

The usual range for this lowest male voice is *F* to *e'* with extension in either direction. It is the least complicated of the male voices with little division into different "types" of bass, the only terms commonly used being *basso buffo* to describe the comic roles often undertaken by bass singers and *basso profundo* for the serious characters. Monteverdi (1567–1643) was the first composer to write seriously for this voice, all three of his surviving operas having an important bass part – Pluto (and also Charon) in *Orfeo*, Neptune in *Il ritorno d'Ulisse in patria*, and the sage Seneca in *Il coronazione di Poppea*. Most other composers around this time limited themselves to writing bass parts for comic roles such as servants or drunks, and they were given quite florid lines to sing with much staccato patter. Handel's low-voice male roles were designated as bass parts, often for kings (many of these now sung by baritones) or for villains

ABOVE Italian baritone Tito Gobbi (1913–84) is pictured in 1964 in one of his most famous roles: Scarpia in Puccini's *Tosca*

BELOW Two great artists of the present-day: Bryn Terfel (bass-baritone) as Méphistophélès and Simon Keenlyside (baritone) as Valentin in Gounod's *Faust*, Royal Opera House, London, 2004

such as Garibaldo in *Rodelinda*, the dark tone of the voice adding to the atmosphere of evil. Gluck (1714–87) wrote some important roles for basses in his French operas, examples being Calchas in *Iphigénie en Aulide* and Hercules in *Alceste*. As with Handel, many of the roles designated bass by Mozart are now sung by baritones (see above), but there are two undisputed bass parts of importance – the High Priest Sarastro in *Die Zauberflöte* and the violent but comic supervisor Osmin in *Die Entführung aus dem Serail*, as well as smaller roles (the Commendatore in *Don Giovanni*, for instance) and others that are equally well or better sung by basses than bass-baritones, such as Leporello and Don Giovanni. But, as always, it seems, the distinctions become blurred and a bass with a good upward extension may sing Don Alfonso (*Così fan tutte*) although there are times when he will sweat to reach the topmost notes!

As the 19th century progressed and the opera repertory grew, composers felt less restricted in their writing. Hitherto roles had nearly always been composed with a particular voice in mind (a composer having a company of regular singers on whom he could call), whereas now composers were starting to write operas just because they liked the subject and wanted to compose the music. The lowest male voice developed into a more distinct category as the baritone and bass-baritone emerged at about this time and the bass found himself being given certain types of roles to which the deep and sombre tones were most suited, frequently of older characters of authority. In Debussy's *Pelléas et Mélisande* (1893–5), old King Arkel is a bass and in Verdi's *Don Carlos* both the elderly King Philip and the Grand Inquisitor are sung by basses, the High Priest Zaccaria in *Nabucco* is a bass, as are the King and the High Priest in *Aida*. Wagner's most notable bass role is Gurnemanz in *Parsifal* and Puccini cast the blind ancient King Timur as a bass in *Turandot*. In more recent times, Britten wrote the part of Claggart, the evil Master-at-Arms in *Billy Budd*, for a deep bass, Walton (1902–83) gave the role of the High Priest Calkas to a bass, and Tippett (1905–98) used the same voice for the He-Ancient, the Priest of the Temple, in *The Midsummer Marriage*.

Early bass singers were often expected to have voices almost as flexible as sopranos. Rossini wrote many roles for the agile bass of Filippo Galli (Italian, 1783–1853), including Mustafa in *L'italiana in Algeri* and Assur in *Semiramide*. Galli also created Henry VIII in Donizetti's *Anna Bolena* and sang Guglielmo in *Così fan tutte* (a role sung these days by a bass-baritone). The eminent Italian bass Luigi Lablache (1794–1858) made his début as Dandini in Rossini's *La Cenerentola*. He created many roles for Donizetti, including Don Pasquale, and for Bellini (eg Giorgio in *I puritani*). A principal bass at the Mariinsky Theatre in St Petersburg was Fyodor Stravinsky (1843–1902), father of the composer Igor Stravinsky. He sang Rodolfo in *La sonnambula* and even as a student was Basilio in *Il barbiere*. He created several roles in operas by Rimsky-Korsakov and Tchaikovsky. The Polish Edouard de Reszke (1853–1917), brother of the famous tenor Jean, was Fiesco in the revised version of Verdi's *Simon Boccanegra*,

Méphistophélès in Gounod's *Faust*, and Friar Lawrence in the same composer's *Roméo et Juliette*. He was also a renowned Wagner bass, singing King Mark in *Tristan*, Pogner in *Die Meistersinger*, Hunding in *Das Rheingold*, and the Wanderer in *Siegfried*.

Another great Russian bass was Fyodor Chaliapin (1873–1938). He joined his first opera company in 1890, having had very little training, but by 1899 was a member of the Bolshoi Company in Moscow. The role with which he was most often associated was Boris Godunov in Musorgsky's opera, but he also sang in French opera, creating the title-role in Massenet's *Don Quichotte*.

The 20th century saw some outstanding basses. Richard Mayr, discussed earlier, was the most lauded Baron Ochs of his time. His other Strauss roles included Barak in *Die Frau ohne Schatten*, which he created in 1919, and the heroine's father, Count Waldner, in *Arabella*. He also sang at Salzburg as Mozart's Sarastro, Figaro, and Leporello, and at Bayreuth where he portrayed Hagen, Pogner, and Gurnemanz. Ezio Pinza (Italian, 1892–1957) was a Wagnerian who sang Gurnemanz, Pogner, and King Mark and also sang *bel canto* roles such as Oroveso in Bellini's *Norma* and Rodolfo in *La sonnambula*. He sang for over 20 seasons at the New York Metropolitan Opera, mainly the French and Italian repertoire, dominating in bass roles such as Don Basilio, Figaro, Don Giovanni, Dulcamara, and Fiesco. He was also a very good actor. The next generation of Italian basses included Cesare Siepi (b. 1923), a memorable Don Giovanni. Alexander Kipnis (1891–1978) was yet another leading Russian singer both at Bayreuth and Salzburg in the standard bass roles. He appeared at Glyndebourne as Sarastro.

Many careers were interrupted by the Second World War, but after it several German basses emerged: Gottlob Frick (1906–94) had a particularly dark voice, well suited to the Wagner repertoire and was a leading Gurnemanz, Hagen, and Hunding, who performed well into his 60s, singing Gurnemanz at Covent Garden as late as 1971; Kurt Böhme (1908–89)

created two Strauss roles, Dominik in *Arabella* in 1933 and Vanuzzi in *Die schweigsame Frau* in 1935, his best role being Ochs, but he also sang the Wagner bass roles; Ludwig Weber (1899–1974) appeared worldwide in the Strauss and Wagner bass roles and was equally at home in Mozart.

Moving further into the century, several other basses come to mind, two of them Bulgarians: Boris Christoff (1914–93) and Nicolai Ghiaurov (1929–2004), both outstanding as Boris Godunov. Three excellent Finnish basses should be mentioned: Kim Borg (1919–2000), Martti Talvela (1935–89), and Matti Salminen (b. 1945), all of whom had international careers. Later still came the Italian Ruggero Raimondi (b. 1941), who sang the famous bass roles at all the major opera houses, and the Englishman John Tomlinson (b. 1946), variously described as a bass or a bass-baritone. He began his career as Colline in Puccini's *La bohème* and as Masetto and the Commendatore (*Don Giovanni*), and has encompassed throughout his career a wide variety of characters such as Figaro, Leporello, Verdi's Sparafucile (*Rigoletto*), Fiesco (*Simon Boccanegra*), Ramfis (*Aida*), both Pimen and the title-role in *Boris Godunov*, Britten's Claggart, and Bartók's Bluebeard, a role in which he excels. He has had a spectacular career, especially as Wotan, which he has sung round the world including two different productions at Bayreuth. He is a superb interpreter of Hans Sachs in *Die Meistersinger* (but possibly the voice is better suited to the lower-lying Pogner, which he also sings), Fasolt (*Das Rheingold*), and one of his best roles is that of Gurnemanz (*Parsifal*).

Yet more male voices

There are two other voice types not yet discussed: the *countertenor* and the special voice associated with the singing of French music, the *haute-contre*, both of these being male vocal categories. Before describing these any further, it will be helpful to consider the word *falsetto*. This is a technique used in voice production (male or female) to enable a singer to sing high notes that are outside his or her natural vocal range. It uses part of the vocal chords, but mainly uses the resonant spaces in the head and neck (such as the sinuses and pharynx) rather than in the chest. It is not a "fake" voice, but a musical addition to the normal voice.

ABOVE LEFT Italian Ezio Pinza (1892–1957) in one of the best-known bass parts, the title-role in Musorgsky's *Boris Godunov*

ABOVE One of the greatest basses of all time, the Russian Fyodor Chaliapin (1873–1938), a famous Boris Godunov, but seen here as Prince Igor in Borodin's opera

Any singer can make use of it, and many do, especially male pop singers, many of whom use it all the time.

A **countertenor** does use a falsetto voice, but one that has been highly trained to sing in the (usually female) alto or even soprano range. It is almost entirely a head voice, not using the chest mechanism. The range varies from singer to singer, as it does in all voice categories. There are, and have been, several very good and famous countertenors, maybe the most notable of all being the English Alfred Deller (1912–79). From 1947 he had a full-time career, forming the Deller Consort in 1950. He was almost single-handedly responsible for the revival of the countertenor voice and its use in the authentic performance of Baroque music. He created the role of Oberon in Britten's *A Midsummer Night's Dream*. His son, Mark Deller, is also a countertenor. Among other well-known singers in this voice category are James Bowman, Michael Chance, Christopher Robson, Robin Blaze, and Paul Esswood (all British), the Americans David Daniels, Brian Asawa, Bejun Mehta, and David Walker, and the Germans Jochen Kowalski and Andreas Scholl.

Related to the countertenor, but different, is the **haute-contre**, especially, but not exclusively, associated with the French repertoire. France did not approve of castration as a means of preserving the high male voice, written for so prolifically by Handel. So the French Baroque composers did not write music for castrati, but there developed the *haute-contre*, really a very high tenor voice. It uses both the chest and the head voice and sometimes falsetto also, but singers using this technique are usually so well trained that they move from one to the other with no audible change of gear.

It should be emphasized that castrati did not need to use falsetto. Their voices, both singing and speaking, had never been allowed to drop to the normal male range, so they used their chest voices and muscles in a natural manner, the sound having an almost ethereal quality, neither male nor female.

Whilst attempting to give an over-all picture of the various types of voice, one must always remember that no two voices are the same, not even when they are similarly categorized. That is, after all, what makes any particular voice recognizable and distinguishable from any other voice. But, as was said at the beginning of this chapter, exactly what "that" is, how it is produced, why we "like" one voice and not another, is inexplicable, and it is that which makes the singing voice, one of the miracles of the human body, so attractive and endlessly fascinating.

SUGGESTED LISTENING

The choice is limitless and is complicated by the rapidity with which CDs come in and out of the catalogues. The CDs recommended here cover different composers and singers and will give a flavour of the variety of music available in opera. There are numerous other compilations discs, many of historical performances, which will give great pleasure as long as the listener is able to ignore the crackles and clicks that even excellent modern techniques are not always able to eliminate in transferring from the original very old recordings to CD. There are also many superb videos and DVDs, two of which are recommended. But nothing can compare with the thrill of live opera in the theatre.

CDs
World of Opera Favourites. Decca 448-053 - 2DWO
Duets and Arias. Decca 467-488 - 2DFQ
The Original Opera Album. EMI 873 5712
Four Great Italian Basses. Preiser 89960
Great Sopranos of the 20th century. HM5 740 34-2
Opera Love Songs. Decca (ADD) 458 201 - 2

Video/DVD
Metropolitan Opera Gala. DG VHS 072 451-3
The Art of Singing. Teldec DVD 0630 15896-2

The Baroque Era

1600 to the mid-18th century

The French word Baroque translates as "bizarre". It was originally a term applied to the ornate German and Austrian architecture of the 17th and 18th centuries. Similarly, Rococo, from the French *rocaille*, meaning "fancy rock-work" in architecture. Both these words have been borrowed to describe music: Rococo for the decorative styles of François Couperin (1668–1733) and Jean-Philippe Rameau (1683–1764) of France and Johann Christian Bach (1735–82) of Germany, and Baroque to describe music from about 1600 to the mid-18th century – roughly to the deaths of Johann Sebastian Bach (1685–1750) and George Frideric Handel (1685–1759).

During the Baroque period, the emphasis in music changed. It developed more contrast of texture, pace, and volume, and more complex harmony. In church music, for instance, there was more contrast between solo voices, chorus, and orchestra.

FEATURED OPERAS

MONTEVERDI
La favola d'Orfeo *1607*
Il ritorno d'Ulisse in patria *1640*
L'incoronazione di Poppea *1642*

CAVALLI
L'Ormindo *1644*
La Calisto *1651*

PURCELL
Dido and Aeneas *c.1684*

RAMEAU
Hippolyte et Aricie *1733*
Castor et Pollux *1737*

HANDEL
Giulio Cesare *1723–4*
Tamerlano *1724, 1731*
Rodelinda *1725*
Orlando *1733*
Ariodante *1735*
Alcina *1735*
Serse *1738*
Semele *1744*

LEFT **Detail from** *The Concert* **(c.1626) by the Dutch artist Hendrick ter Brugghen (1588-1629), National Gallery, London**

The Baroque Era

In instrumental music, the suite (the precursor of the classical symphony), the sonata, and the concerto grosso (the earlier form of the classical concerto) developed, especially in the music of Corelli, Vivaldi, Bach, and Handel. In opera the aria became more important than the recitatives. The use of *basso continuo* developed as accompaniment to recitatives. This is a configuration provided by the composer indicating the sort of chords he feels would make an appropriate accompaniment, but leaving the interpretation of them to the continuo. It may be helpful at this point to explain that the continuo is not a specific instrument. In full, the term is "continuo player" and is the player who interprets the *basso continuo* as an accompaniment to the recitatives. Most often this was played on the harpsichord, but other keyboard instruments have been used and also the cello or older stringed instruments such as the theorbo or chitarrone (both larger than the lute and used to provide stronger bass notes).

The most famous name in Baroque music is Johann Sebastian Bach (1685–1750), a prolific composer of orchestral, instrumental, and keyboard works and a great deal of vocal music in the shape of secular and sacred cantatas and oratorios. He composed no opera. He produced 7 children in his first marriage and a further 13 in his second marriage (to Anna Magdalena) and several of his sons became composers. The term "Baroque" does not strictly apply to the younger sons or to the later works of some of the others, but they are all described here for the sake of completing the Bach family history. Wilhelm Friedemann (1710–84), the second child and eldest son, was heralded as a composer but was a failure as such, and spent most of his life as an organist and teacher in Germany. Carl Philipp Emanuel (1714–88), the third son and fifth child, composed many keyboard sonatas, early concertos, and sinfonias but, like his father, no operas. Johann Christoph Friedrich (1732–95), the 9th son and 16th child, composed a number of orchestral and instrumental works, cantatas, and songs, but again no operas. Johann Christian (1735–82), the 18th child, was known as the "English Bach" because he settled in England as an opera composer at the King's Theatre,

London (and in the orchestral parts of his first operas, clarinets were used for the first time in England). Of the 11 operas he composed few have been revived in modern times. He died a poor man and was buried in a mass grave in St Pancras churchyard, London. However, his works caught the ear of the boy Mozart, who is known to have met him in London in 1764. They had what has been described as a warm relationship and Bach had a considerable influence on the young Mozart who, whilst in London on tour with his father, would have been able to see a Bach opera (*Adriano in Siria*) having its première in that city.

Other composers of this period whose works did include operas were Georg Philipp Telemann, George Frideric Handel, and Johann Hasse in Germany; Claudio Monteverdi, Pietro Francesco Cavalli, Alessandro Scarlatti, Antonio Vivaldi, and Giovanni Battista Pergolesi in Italy; Jean-Baptiste Lully and Jean-Philippe Rameau in France; and Henry Purcell and Thomas Linley (*père*) in England. The name of John Gay crops up but he was a poet, playwright and theatre manager (and built the first Covent Garden theatre) who wrote librettos for operas by others. The major figures in this list – as far as opera is concerned – are Monteverdi, Cavalli, Rameau, Purcell, and Handel, and they and their works will be discussed in some detail. The others were less successful as opera composers, or it might be fairer to say that they had greater success in other genres.

The Italian-born Frenchman Jean-Baptiste Lully (1632–87) collaborated with the Paris-born playwright, actor and director Molière, pen name of Jean-Baptiste Poquelin (1622–73), in a number of comedy-ballets, forerunners of French opera. The best-known of these is *Le bourgeois gentilhomme*, written for the court of Louis XIV. Lully wrote about 20 operas and ballets, produced and conducted them, and was important in the development of accompanied recitative, as opposed to the spoken, dry (*secco*) form which predominated until now. He made opera popular in France. Since the 1980s the rise of specialized French Baroque conductors has given his works a new lease of life.

ABOVE **Alessandro Scarlatti**, credited with the invention of the *da capo* aria but, like his son Domenico, better known for his keyboard works

In Italy Alessandro Scarlatti (1660–1725) spent most of his life living between Rome and Naples, composing operas for both cities, all but one of his 115 operas (64 survive) being on serious subjects. He is credited with the invention of the *da capo* aria adopted so successfully by Handel. Scarlatti had to battle with the church's objections to this frivolous form of music but, especially in his later years in Rome, he stimulated the Italian enthusiasm for opera. Occasional revivals have shown his operas to be well constructed and of quite advanced invention. The best-

known is his last, *La Griselda* (1721). Another Italian, Giovanni Battista Pergolesi (1710–36) is most famous for *La serva padrona* (*The Maid as Mistress*) of 1733, a two-act intermezzo and the only part of his opera *Il prigioniero superbo* to have survived. The Venetian Antonio Vivaldi (1678–1741) was a prolific composer of instrumental music but also wrote nearly 100 operas, of which fewer than 50 survive. He was quite an impresario in Venice and conducted and played the violin in many performances. His genius as an opera composer has been recognized in modern times, a revival that owes something to the enthusiasm and voice of the Italian mezzo-soprano Cecilia Bartoli (b. 1966) who has championed his vocal works in recitals and recordings. His operas are now beginning to gain ground.

As music director of the opera in Hamburg, Georg Philipp Telemann (1681–1767) wrote about 40 operas. More successful in Germany but less well remembered was Johann Hasse (1699–1783). He sang as an operatic tenor in Brunswick and in Hamburg between 1718 and 1721 and his first opera was produced in 1721. He went to Naples three years later, married the famous mezzo-soprano Faustina Bordoni in 1730 and was director of the Dresden court opera from 1731 to 1763. He composed operas to nearly all the texts of Metastasio (1698–1782), the Italian poet and librettist whose texts were set by many composers, including Handel, Gluck, and Mozart. He wrote over 100 operas, but in 1771, on hearing *Ascanio in Alba*, the opera composed by Mozart at the age of 15, Hasse prophesied: "This boy will cause us all to be forgotten".

In England, apart from Henry Purcell (1659–95), there was little opera to talk about. John Gay (1685–1732), whose name is known in connection with *The Beggar's Opera* and its sequel *Polly*, was not, as has already been mentioned, a composer. Thomas Linley senior (1733–95) wrote music for plays, songs, and madrigals and together with his son Thomas Linley (1756–78) was the composer of *The Duenna*, to the play by Richard Brinsley Sheridan (1751–1816), which was first performed at Covent Garden on 21 November 1775 and was the most successful ballad-opera of the 18th century, outshining even *The Beggar's Opera*.

Before we look more closely at the five composers whose works have survived and whose genius as opera composers cannot be gainsaid, it is important to understand that the classification of voices has changed since their works were composed. In Baroque opera, the deep male roles would all be designated as bass parts, the baritone voice not yet being considered as a separate category. Similarly, the deep female parts were designated alto (contralto), the lowest female voice, and these roles are now mainly sung by mezzo-sopranos. Even some roles called "soprano" are sung by mezzos. The choice of voice will vary from production to production and will also depend on the range of any particular artist.

ABOVE **The only surviving part of Pergolesi's opera** *Il prigioniero superbo*, this two-act Intermezzo is still performed (title-page from first edition, 1752)

ABOVE **King's Theatre, in the Haymarket, London,** designed by Sir John Vanbrugh, where many of Handel's operas had their première

27

Monteverdi

Claudio Monteverdi
(1567–1643)

WHERE TO START
L'incoronazione di Poppea
Il ritorno d'Ulisse in patria

WHERE TO GO NEXT
La favola d'Orfeo

The Italian Claudio Monteverdi is generally acknowledged as the first composer of opera as we now perceive it. He was born in Cremona where he became a chorister at the cathedral and, by the age of 16, was a good organist and viol player and had published some madrigals. He was employed by the Duke of Mantua as a singer and viol player and, in his early 30s, travelled with the Duke on military campaigns in Flanders and the Danube. He heard the operas of the Camerata composers of Florence and was particularly impressed by the work of Jacopo Peri (1561–1633), who is credited with composition of the first opera or music-theatre, *Dafne* of 1594–8. Monteverdi heard Peri's *Euridice* in 1600 and wrote his own first opera, *Orfeo*, based on the same subject, and it was produced in 1607. In this work, for the first time, the accompaniment was for full orchestra (such as it then was). The following year his second opera, *Arianna*, was produced in Mantua, but only the famous and beautiful Lament survives. When the Duke died in 1612, Monteverdi left Cremona and the following year became Master of Music at St Mark's, Venice. For the next 25 years his compositions were mainly sacred works for St Mark's and in 1632 he was admitted to holy orders. The first public opera house in Venice, the San Cassiano, opened in 1637 and Monteverdi's interest in opera was rekindled. By this time 12 of his operas had been lost when Mantua was sacked by Austrian troops in 1630. In the last 16 years of his life he composed many more operas, but only two survive. His tomb is in a chapel in a beautiful church in Venice, the Santa Maria

Gloriosa dei Frari, and no matter when one visits it, there are always flowers thrown into the chapel by visitors.

Monteverdi was the first composer to transform the face of music in every genre in which he worked (a feat not achieved again, in my opinion, until the works of Beethoven 200 years later). He was not a total revolutionary, but he did introduce into his music all the then available styles, especially instrumental accompaniments. The dramatic nature of his madrigals makes them the forerunner of operatic recitatives, so much so that his *Il ballo delle ingrate* and *Il Combattimento di Tancredi e Clorinda* have been semi-staged as "operas" but are from his eighth book of madrigals. His sacred *Vespers* of 1610 are also coloured by the drama of his secular madrigals and by what he learned from Italian and French opera composers. His three best-known and most often performed

operas make use of an early type of leitmotiv (a form brought to fruition many years later by Richard Wagner, see p.91) though these are in the form of orchestral interludes that return at various key points in the drama. In *L'incoronazione di Poppea* we have the earliest music-drama in which the characters are real people rather than mythological. It has been said that Monteverdi was an opera composer way ahead of his time and the advanced harmonic experiment of his operas has caused many musicological arguments that have been solved in various editions over the past century.

LA FAVOLA D'ORFEO
(*The Fable of Orfeo*), 1607

This work represented a considerable advance in style on Monteverdi's earlier vocal works and can be credited as the first great opera. It is based on the Greek mythological story, but with some differences (the story is followed more closely in Gluck's opera on the same subject, see p.47).

SYNOPSIS Orfeo (ten), believing his beloved Euridice (sop) dead from a snakebite (1), attempts to rescue her from Hades. He is refused permission to cross the river Styx by Charon (bass) (2). Orfeo plays his lute (3) and lulls Charon to sleep (4). He takes the boat across the river himself. Inscribed on the rock at the entrance to Hades are Dante's words: *Lasciate ogni speranza voi ch'entrate* (Abandon

hope, all ye that enter here). Pluto's wife Proserpine (sop) begs her husband to allow Orfeo to rescue Euridice **(5)**. Pluto (bass), king of the underworld, agrees **(6)** but on condition that Orfeo does not look at Euridice until they have left Hades **(7)**. When Euridice at last appears, Orfeo is overcome by emotion and unable to keep his promise. He looks at her **(8)** and she dies **(9)**. The distraught Orfeo is consoled by his father Apollo (ten) **(10)** and they return together to heaven where Orfeo can see Euridice in the stars **(11)**.

> **MUSIC** (1) Orfeo: *Tu se' morta, mia vita – You are dead, my life*; (2) Charon: *O tu ch' innanzi morte a queste rive – Ho, you who dare approach these shores*; (3) Orfeo: *Possente spirto e formidabil Nume – Powerful spirit, awe-inspiring presence*; (4) Orfeo: *Ahi, sventurato amante – Alas, unfortunate lover that I am*; (5) Proserpine: *Signor quell' infelice – My lord, the unhappy man* (6) Pluto: *Benche severo e immutabil fato – Although a harsh and immutable law*; (7) Orfeo: *Ma mentre io canto (ohimé) chi m'assicura – But as I sing (alas!) can I be sure she's behind me?*; (8) Orfeo: *O dolcissimi lumi io pur vi veggio – O sweetest eyes, I see you indeed*; (9) Euridice: *Ahi vista troppo dolce e troppo amara – Ah, sight too sweet and too bitter*; (10) Apollo: *Perch'a lo sdegno et al dolor impreda. . . – Why have you given way, my son. . . ?*; (11) Orfeo/Apollo duet: *Saliam cantand' al cielo – We rise with song towards the sky.*

IL RITORNO D'ULISSE IN PATRIA

(The Return of Ulysses to his Homeland), 1640
An opera in 3 acts, it is based on Homer's *Odyssey* and was Monteverdi's first new opera written for the Teatro SS Giovanni e Paolo in Venice. It was produced there in its year of composition, receiving ten performances before being transferred to Bologna, but it had to wait until the 20th century to be widely heard and

seen in Europe and the USA. In 1925 there was a concert performance (of a much-reduced score) in Brussels, and it was seen in Paris in the same year. It was first heard in England in a BBC broadcast in 1928. Florence staged it in 1942, Wuppertal in 1959, London in 1965, Vienna in 1971, Glyndebourne in 1972, Washington in 1974, and Salzburg in 1985 – all of these productions were in different editions.

SYNOPSIS In a prologue set in legendary Ithica (Ithaca), an island in the Ionian Sea, after the Trojan War, Il Tempo (Time, bass), La Fortuna (Fortune, sop), and Amore (Cupid, sop) discuss their domination of L'Humana Fragilità (Human Frailty, sop). This will be proven in the opera which follows. Ulisse (Ulysses, bar/ten) went to fight in the Trojan War, leaving behind his young wife Penelope (mez/cont) **(1)** and their son Telemaco (Telemachus, ten). Despite the efforts of various suitors, Penelope has remained faithful to her husband for over 20 years. She is unaware that Ulisse has been rescued by Phaeacians and has been brought back to Ithica **(2)**. The goddess Minerva (sop) disguises Ulisse as a very old man **(3)** so he can return unrecognized to his palace. He finds his servant Eumete (Eumaeus, ten), who

recognizes him **(4)** and tells his old master of his wife's enduring faithfulness. Ulisse is reunited with his son Telemaco **(5)**, whom he sends off to Penelope, promising to follow soon in disguise.

Three suitors are trying to win the hand of Penelope, who resists them **(6)** and they plot to kill her son who is his father's rightful heir. Penelope promises to marry whichever of them can succeed in stringing Ulisse's great bow. The suitors agree to this, but none of them has the strength to manage it and they all fail the test. Meanwhile, Ulisse has arrived at the palace and had a fight with the glutton Iro (Irus, ten) **(7)**, a tragi-comic character who provides some light relief (but eventually kills himself). Ulisse soundly thrashes Iro. He then observes the suitors' efforts, and asks to be allowed to string the bow **(8)**. He, of course, succeeds, and fires arrows at the suitors and kills them. Iro bemoans the loss of the suitors **(9)**. Penelope cannot believe that this old beggar is her husband, even when he throws off his disguise, fearing it is some kind of plot to take over her palace. Only when Ulisse describes accurately the embroidered quilt on their marriage bed **(10)**, which nobody else can have seen, is Penelope convinced that this is indeed her husband and they are united in a joyous love duet **(11)**.

RIGHT Nerone's costume, designed by Joyce Conwy-Evans, for the 1962 production at Glyndebourne of *L'incoronazione di Poppea*

RIGHT **Nerone's costume, designed by Joyce Conwy-Evans, for the 1962 production at Glyndebourne of** *L'incoronazione di Poppea*

MUSIC (1) Penelope: *Di misera regina… – The grievous sorrows of a hapless Queen*; **(2)** Ulisse: *Dormo ancora o son desto? – Do I still sleep or am I awake?*; **(3)** Minerva: *Incognito sarai – You shall remain unknown*; **(4)** Eumete: *Ulisse generoso – Noble Ulysses*; **(5)** Ulisse/Telemaco duet: *O padre sospirato/O figlio desiato – O sighed-for father/O longed-for son*; **(6)** Penelope: *Non voglio amor no, no – I do not wish to love, no, no*; **(7)** Iro: *Partità, movi il piè – Go, if you have come to eat*; **(8)** Ulisse: *Gioventute superba – Proud youth*; **(9)** Iro: *O dolor, o martir – O pain, o torment*; **(10)** Ulisse: *Del tuo casto pensiero – I know the habits of your chaste thoughts*; **(11)** Ulisse/Penelope duet: *Sospirato mio sole – My longed-for sun.*

L'INCORONAZIONE DI POPPEA
(*The Coronation of Poppea*), 1642

Written in a prologue similar to that in his previous opera, and three acts, this is the first opera based on historical figures. It was Monteverdi's last opera, produced in Venice the year after its composition and in Naples eight years later. It reached the USA and England earlier than its predecessor, being produced in Massachusetts in 1926 and Oxford in 1927. There had been a concert version in Paris in 1905 and it was staged there in 1913. It has received many productions in modern times, again in various editions. *Poppea* can be considered the first modern opera, treating human emotions and personalities. It is generally accepted that some sections of the music were written by other composers, the major part being the final duet, most likely composed by Benedetto Ferrari (*c.*1603–81), and there is also some music probably by Cavalli (see p.31).

SYNOPSIS Rome, about AD 65. In the prologue, Amore (Cupid, sop) sets out to prove his superiority over Fortuna (sop) and Virtù (sop). Ottone (mez/counterten, orig. castrato) is suspicious of his beloved Poppea's relationship with Emperor Nerone (sop/ten).

Poppea (sop) is indeed in love with Nerone **(1)**, who is married to Ottavia (sop/mez). Poppea's nurse Arnalta (cont/ten) warns her of the trouble that will ensue because of her ambition to become empress **(2)** and Ottavia expresses her own humiliation **(3)**. Nerone's tutor, the sage Seneca (bass), tries to reason with his former pupil **(4)**. Angry at this interference, Nerone orders Seneca to kill himself **(5)**. The empress's lady-in-waiting, Drusilla (sop), helps Ottone disguise himself as a woman, lending him some of her clothes **(6)**. At the insistence of Nerone's wife Ottavia, he attempts to kill Poppea, but is prevented by the intervention of Amore. Ottone is mistaken for the maid; Drusilla is arrested as the supposed assassin and Nerone sentences her to death. Ottone saves her by confessing his own guilt and is banished by Nerone. The emperor is now able to divorce Ottavia and marry Poppea. Ottavia says farewell to Rome **(7)** and Nerone proclaims Poppea as empress **(8)**. Love (Amore) has won through.

One of the interesting aspects of this human drama is the way in which the "baddies", Poppea and Nero, who not only have an extramarital affair but plot murder, are the ones who triumph.

MUSIC (1) Poppea: *Signor, sempre mi vedi – My lord, you always see me*; **(2)** Arnalta: *Ahi figlia, voglia il cielo… – Oh daughter, may heaven grant…*; **(3)** Ottavia: *Disprezzata regina – Humiliated queen*; **(4)** Seneca: *Signor, nel fondo alla maggior dolcezza – Sire, at the bottom of great sweetness often lies regret*; **(5)** Seneca: *Nerone a me t'invia – Nero sends you to me*; **(6)** Ottone: *Eccomi trasformato – Here I am, changed*; **(7)** Ottavia: *Addio, Roma – Farewell, Rome*; **(8)** Nerone: *Ascendi, o mia diletta – Ascend, o my beloved.*

ABOVE **Alice Coote (Poppea) and David Walker (Nerone) in Steven Pimlott's production conducted by Harry Christophers, ENO, 2000**

Cavalli

(Pietro) Francesco Cavalli
(1602–76)

WHERE TO START
La Calisto
L'Ormindo

WHERE TO GO NEXT
L'Egisto

Francesco Cavalli, born in Crema, Italy, but resident in Venice from the age of 14, may have been a pupil of Monteverdi. He was in the choir of St Mark's and was one of its organists during the time Monteverdi was director of music in Venice. Cavalli composed his first opera in 1639 and in the next 35 years composed another 32. After Monteverdi's death in 1643, Cavalli was the leading opera composer in Venice. During his time there, opera was staged for the first time for the general public rather than for court occasions. Most of his manuscript scores survive in the library in Venice. He visited Paris and one of his operas was performed in the Louvre in 1660 as part of the wedding celebrations of Louis XIV.

Several of Cavalli's operas have been revived in modern times, but have not entered the regular repertoire of opera companies. They are notable for their highly dramatic content and for their use of comic possibilities – prior to this, only Monteverdi's glutton Iro in *Ulisse* and Arnalta in *Poppea* were deliberately comic characters. They are worth the occasional airing and when well produced can be very amusing, as two of them, *L'Ormindo* (in 1967) and *La Calisto* (in 1970), proved to be at Glyndebourne in editions by the conductor and Baroque scholar Raymond Leppard. These editions, or realizations, have since been much criticized as being un-authentic, and this may well be true. But there is no doubt that Leppard brought the work of Cavalli to the attention of modern audiences and musicians and it is possible that, had he not done so, further editions (by Jane Glover and by René Jacobs, for instance) may not have appeared.

L'ORMINDO, 1644

This has become a quite popular Baroque opera since its Glyndebourne revival in 1967. At the time of its composition, however, it was just one of many operas that were written, performed for a short season, and then disappeared. The librettist was the poet and impresario Giovanni Faustini, with whom Cavalli wrote nine operas. All his operas contain a high proportion of recitative, although the importance of arias was gaining ground at this period.

SYNOPSIS Prince Ormindo (ten/alto) is the long-lost son of King Hariadeno (bass) of Mauritania. He returns to his homeland and falls in love with Erisbe (mez), the king's young wife (1). Not knowing his true identity, she reciprocates his love. This distresses Ormindo's friend Amida (ten) (2), who is also in love with Erisbe, and also distresses Amida's former love Sicle (sop) (3). Erisbe, who is comforted by her old nurse Erice (ten) (4) announces that she cannot love her husband, as he is too old, and that she loves both Amida and Ormindo (5). Sicle disguises herself as a gipsy and reads Amida's palm, telling Erisbe of his past unfaithfulness. Erisbe, disenchanted, departs in a boat with Ormindo (6). The king orders his captain Osman (ten) to pursue them and kill them. When Hariadeno realizes that Ormindo is his son, he regrets his decision to poison them (7). Fortunately,

ABOVE **A rare image of the Baroque composer Francesco Cavalli**

RIGHT The goddess Diana, sung by Louise Winter in the Berlin Staatsoper 2002 production of Cavalli's *La Calisto*

Osman has substituted a sleeping-draught for the poison he was supposed to give the lovers. The king is so relieved that he cedes both his wife and his throne to his son (**8**).

MUSIC (**1**) Ormindo: *Miracolo d'amore – Oh, marvellous power of love!*; (**2**) Amida: *Ma non consenta Giove… – But Jove has no intention…*; (**3**) Sicle: *Perfidissimo, Amida – False and faithless Amida*; (**4**) Erice: *Verginella infelice – Most unhappy young virgin*; (**5**) Erisbe: *Ti giuro, io gelerei… O principi diletti – You can imagine… O Princes twain*; (**6**) Erisbe/Ormindo duet: *Oh mia speme – O my blessing*; (**7**) Hariadeno: *Io sono umano al fine – After all, I am human*; (**8**) Hariadeno: *Dormano? Oh ne le vite loro ravvivato, Adriano – Sleeping? Oh, Adriano lives again through their lives.*

LA CALISTO

(*Callisto*), 1651

As is the case with the preceding opera, *La Calisto* owes its popularity to Leppard's Glyndebourne revival in 1970. It was Cavalli's 15th opera and was not a success at its première. The librettist is again Faustini, who died during the initial run of performances.

SYNOPSIS In legendary Greece, Callisto (sop) is a follower of the chaste goddess Diana (mez/sop). Jove (Jupiter, bar) and Mercury (ten) come to earth and see Callisto lamenting the drying up of the springs (**1**). Diana is loved by the ruler of the pastoral world, Pan (bass), but is in love with the shepherd Endymion (cont/counterten, orig. castrato) (**2**). Jove follows the advice of Mercury and comes to earth disguised as Diana (**3**) in an attempt to win Callisto for himself. Pan captures Endymion. Jove's wife Juno (sop), jealous of her husband's love for Callisto, turns her rival into a little bear (**4**). Diana rescues Endymion (**5**), but Jove is unable to reverse Juno's spell. He places Callisto among the stars as the constellation Ursa minor (the Little Bear) (**6**).

MUSIC (**1**) Callisto: *Piante ombrose – Cool shades*; (**2**) Endymion: *Improvvisi stupori – O, breath-taking wonder!*; (**3**) Jove/Callisto duet: *Esprimerti non posso – I cannot tell you*; (**4**) Juno: *Da le sponde tartaree a questo luce – Jealousy, a veritable Fury*; (**5**) Diana/Endymion duet: *Dolcissimo baci – Sweet kisses*; (**6**) Jove: *Questi alberghi stellati – These stellar spaces.*

Among Cavalli's other operas, *L'Egisto* (another Faustini libretto), *Giasone*, *Didone*, *Xerse*, and *L'Erismena* are occasionally performed. They were all successful in their day, *Giasone* (*Jason*) being possibly the most popular opera of the 17th century. Handel used a revision of the *Xerse* libretto for his *Serse* (see p.41) and learned much from his predecessor which he incorporated into his version of the story.

Purcell

Henry Purcell
(1659–95)

WHERE TO START
Dido and Aeneas

WHERE TO GO NEXT
King Arthur
The Fairy Queen

Believed to be the son of Thomas Purcell, one of Charles II's musicians, Henry was a boy chorister of the Chapel Royal, the body of clergy and musicians that arranged and sang music for the divine services attended by the king. At 18 he became "composer-in-ordinary to the King's violins", a band of 24 string players, and organist at Westminster Abbey in 1679. He composed many official choral pieces and in 1680 wrote his first music for the London theatre. He composed the anthem *My heart is inditing* for the coronation of James II in 1685 and also music for the coronation of William and Mary four years later.

It was thought for a long time that in 1689 he wrote his first opera, *Dido and Aeneas*, which was said to have had its first performance at a boarding school for girls in Chelsea, but it is now thought likely that he wrote the opera at

least five years earlier. He wrote several other works described as "semi-operas" – these are more like Restoration dramas containing musical episodes performed by some of the subsidiary characters.

Purcell is usually considered the only English opera composer of note before the 20th century, yet he wrote only one true opera, *Dido and Aeneas*. For the last five years of his life, he and many of his colleagues had to earn a living outside the court, as William and Mary reduced considerably their need for royal music. He composed much for the stage at this time including the music, in 1690, for *The Prophetess, or The History of Dioclesian*, an adaptation by the actor Thomas Betterton from a Jacobean tragi-comedy. The resultant semi-opera *Dioclesian* was an artistic and financial success – Dryden was so impressed

by it that he offered the composer his *King Arthur* libretto. This was followed by lavish and successful productions of *The Fairy Queen,* an anonymous adaptation from Shakespeare's *A Midsummer Night's Dream.* Purcell died before finishing the music for *The Indian Queen,* which was completed by his younger brother Daniel.

DIDO AND AENEAS, *c.*1684

The libretto was by Nahum Tate (1652–1715), who was to become Poet Laureate in 1692. It was based on his own play *Brutus of Alba* (1678) and Virgil's *Aeneid* and was modelled on John Blow's opera *Venus and Adonis.* The first recorded performance was in 1689, but recent scholarship indicates that there was probably an earlier London hearing in 1683 or 1684. It was staged twice more in London, in *c.*1700 and in 1704, but then languished until the London Royal College of Music performed it in 1895. Its first performance in New York was in 1924. There are several versions of the score extant, but the original is thought to be the one kept at St Michael's College, Tenbury Wells.

SYNOPSIS The setting is Carthage in the 13th century BC, after the Greeks have defeated the Trojans. The Trojan Prince Aeneas (ten/high bar) is sailing to Italy to found a new Troy (Rome). Blown off course, he lands at Carthage. There he meets Queen Dido (sop/mez) and falls in love with her and she, encouraged by her confidante Belinda (sop) (1), reciprocates his feelings, to the approval of her court. A Sorceress (mez/bass-bar), determined to bring about Dido's downfall (2), sends her elf, disguised as Mercury, to remind Aeneas that he must continue his journey to Italy (3). When he departs, Dido cannot live without him and, before she dies, sings the justly famous Lament (4).

> **MUSIC** (1) Belinda: *Fear no danger;*
> (2) Sorceress: *Wayward sister;* (3)
> Mercury: *Stay, Prince;* (4) Dido: *When
> I am laid in earth.*

ABOVE **Bernard Miles used a Shakespeare stage modelled on his own Mermaid Theatre in London for this Oslo 1953 production with Kirsten Flagstad (Dido) and Bjarne Buntz (Aeneas)**

Rameau

Jean-Philippe Rameau
(1683–1764)

WHERE TO START
Hippolyte et Aricie
Castor et Pollux

WHERE TO GO NEXT
Les Boréades

**TRAITÉ
DE
L'HARMONIE**
Reduite à ses Principes naturels;
DIVISÉ EN QUATRE LIVRES.
LIVRE I. Du rapport des Raisons & Proportions Har-
moniques.
LIVRE II. De la nature & de la proprieté des Accords;
Et de tout ce qui peut servir à rendre une
Musique parfaite.
LIVRE III. Principes de Composition.
LIVRE IV. Principes d'Accompagnement.
*Par Monsieur R A M E A U, Organiste de la Cathedrale
de Clermont en Auvergne.*

DE L'IMPRIMERIE
De JEAN-BAPTISTE-CHRISTOPHE BALLARD, Seul
Imprimeur du Roy pour la Musique. A Paris, ruë Saint Jean-
de-Beauvais, au Mont-Parnasse.
M. DCC. XXII.
AVEC PRIVILEGE DU ROY.

LEFT Title-page of the first Paris edition of
Rameau's important treatise on harmony, 1722

The leading 18th-century composer of
France, Rameau was primarily self-taught.
Aged 20 he was organist at the cathedral in
Clermont-Ferrand and held similar posts for
the next 20 years. He published an important
and much respected treatise on harmony in
1722, about the time that he settled in Paris
as a teacher of the harpsichord and a prolific
composer of keyboard music. He came late
to opera, being 50 when he published his
first, *Hippolyte et Aricie*, which was initially a
failure. Nothing daunted, he wrote a further
20 operas (or opera-ballets), using bold
harmonies, colourful orchestration, and

making use of recitatives. His intensely
dramatic style of writing was compared
unfavourably to the more traditional works
of Jean-Baptiste Lully (1632–87) and at the
Paris Opéra two factions soon formed, with
Rameau's supporters known as the Ramistes,
as opposed to the Lullistes. There was
further controversy in the *Querelle des
Bouffons* (War of the Comedians) which
raged in a series of published pamphlets and
letters, from 1752 to 1754. It involved the
supporters of serious French works and the
champions of the Italian composer Giovanni
Battista Pergolesi (1710–36) whose comic
opera, *La serva padrona*, was brought to Paris
by an Italian troupe popularly known as the
"Bouffons". But gradually Rameau overcame
the opposition, his works were accepted, and
he was appointed court composer to the
king (Louis XV) in which post he remained
until his death.

Rameau's operas were almost completely
neglected following his death, having not
survived the arrival of Gluck's works in the
1770s. But in the past 25 years, maybe in
relation to the rise of interest in authentic
performance, there has been a renewed
interest in the Baroque period generally,
and performances of Rameau's operas have
taken place throughout Europe, with many
recordings following.

HIPPOLYTE ET ARICIE, 1733

In the libretto by Simon-Joseph Pellegrin,
the story is retold of the incestuous love
of Phèdre for her stepson Hippolyte. The
orchestral score is complicated and during
the composer's lifetime it was drastically cut

ABOVE LEFT Jean-Philippe Rameau, c.1728, French
composer and theorist (portrait attributed to
Joseph Aved, 1702–66)

in performance, which led to its being very
undervalued. It is a moving love story.

SYNOPSIS Thésée (Theseus, bass) has
massacred his enemies, the Pallantids. The last
of the line, the captured Aricie (sop), is obliged
to take the vow of chastity in the Temple of
Diana (1) and Phèdre (mez) comes to make
sure she does so. But Aricie and Hippolyte
(ten) have fallen in love and the goddess
Diana (sop) has sworn to protect them (2).
Hippolyte is the son of Thésée and stepson
of Phèdre, who is in love with him and
determined to prevent his union with Aricie.
Phèdre, believing Thésée to be dead, offers
herself to Hippolyte, together with the throne,
and when he rejects her she demands that he
kill her (3), which he refuses to do. Thésée
appears, and seeing his wife and his son
wrestling with Hippolyte's sword, thinks
his son is about to rape or kill Phèdre, and
banishes him. Aricie's offer to follow Hippolyte
into exile is refused and he is carried off
by a sea monster, apparently dead. Phèdre
confesses her part in the misunderstanding
(4), and Diana returns Hippolyte to be reunited with Aricie.

MUSIC (1) Aricie: *Temple sacré, séjour
tranquille – Holy temple, tranquil abode*;
(2) Diana: *Ne vous alarmez – Do not be
alarmed*; **(3)** Phèdre: *Étouffe dans mon
sang un amour que j'abhorre – Stifle in my
blood a love I abhor*; **(4)** Phèdre: *Non, sa
mort est mon seul ouvrage – No, his death
is my sole doing.*

CASTOR ET POLLUX, 1737

The story of the brotherly love of Castor and
Pollux was a contrast to the usual romantic
love stories told in French operas of the time.
It was coolly received at its first performance
in 1737, but after revivals in 1754 and 1764
came to be highly regarded.

SYNOPSIS The action takes place in Sparta
and the Elysian Fields. Castor (ten) has been
killed in battle. Telaira (sop), daughter of the

BELOW Snakes and daggers on the 18th-century design of a Fury costume in *Hippolyte et Aricie*

Sun, weeps for her lost lover (1) and asks his twin brother Pollux (bass) to beseech his father Jupiter (bass) to bring Castor back to life. Jupiter agrees to do this (2), but only on condition that Pollux takes his brother's place in Hades. Because Pollux also loves Telaira, he agrees to his father's bidding. Castor cannot accept his brother's sacrifice. He agrees to change places with Pollux for one day only (3) to enable him to see Telaira again. Jupiter, impressed by the selflessness of the twins, restores them both to life and grants them immortality (4).

> **MUSIC** (1) Telaira: *Au pied de ce tombeau laissez couler mes pleurs –* At the foot of the tomb let my tears flow; (2) Jupiter: *Mon amour s'intéresse à ces tendres alarmes –* My love is moved by these gentle alarms; (3) Castor: *Oui, je cède enfin à tes voeux –* Yes, then finally I yield to your wishes; (4) Jupiter: *Les Destins sont contents, ton sort est arrêté –* The Fates are satisfied, your lot has been decreed.

Other operas of note

There are too many to mention, but other Rameau operas include *Les Indes galantes* (1735), *Dardanus* (1739), *Les fêtes d'Hébé* (1739), *Platée* (1745), *Zoroastre* (1749), *Les Paladins* (1760), and *Les Boréades* (*The Sons of Boreas*) of 1762–3. This final work in the list was Rameau's last opera and was not performed during his lifetime. It was thought to be in rehearsal at the Paris Opéra at the time of the composer's death, but it has been shown that this is a misconception – it was rehearsed about a year earlier but for reasons not known it was not performed. Possibly it was considered too difficult, and musical tastes were changing about this time. It has been suggested that some elements in the libretto could be construed as having Masonic overtones, which might have been considered politically undesirable. But this is mostly conjecture. Suffice it to say that it was not fully staged until 1982 at the Aix-en-Provence festival, although it had been broadcast and had occasional previous concert performances.

With the revival of interest in operas of this period, and the advent of specialist conductors and orchestras, several of Rameau's operas continue to receive occasional performances and recordings, including *Platée*, which was commissioned to celebrate the wedding at Versailles in 1745 of the Dauphin and the apparently very unattractive Spanish Princess Maria Teresa. The opera incorporates a comical mock wedding between Jupiter and an ugly nymph. This may be thought to be a not very tactful episode to set before the Dauphin under the circumstances, but it was reported to have been well received at its première. Nevertheless, the libretto was modified before its next production, at the Paris Opéra four years later, and it became one of Rameau's most popular works. There have been productions of *Platée* in the 20th and 21st centuries in Europe and the USA. Some Baroque specialists consider it to be Rameau's masterpiece.

ABOVE RIGHT **A character from *Hippolyte et Aricie*, sung by Mme Caro Lucas, probably in about 1908**

Handel

George Frideric Handel
(1685–1759)

WHERE TO START
Serse
Semele
Alcina
Giulio Cesare

WHERE TO GO NEXT
Rodelinda
Tamerlano
Orlando
Ariodante

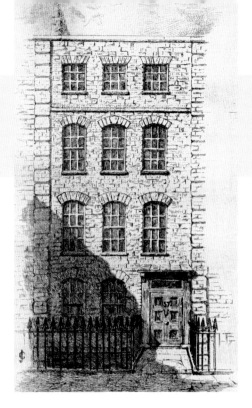

LEFT **25 Brook Street, London, where in 1741 Handel composed *Messiah* for Dublin**

Born in Halle, Germany, George Frideric Handel is probably the greatest opera composer of the Baroque era. He studied law at Halle University, his father opposing music as a career, though allowing him to have some lessons from the local church organist. After his father's death in 1697 Handel turned to music full-time and in 1703, aged 18, he joined the second violins in the orchestra of the Hamburg Opera House, soon rising to become accompanist on the keyboard. The orchestra was directed by the composer Reinhard Keiser (1674–1739), who was once

regarded as Germany's greatest composer of operas – he wrote 100 for Hamburg alone. Handel was impressed by Keiser's florid arias and instrumentation, features he was to emulate in his own operas. Handel's first opera was written to a libretto that had been given to Keiser who lost interest in it. This was *Almira*, produced in Hamburg in 1705 and rapidly followed by three more operas the same year. A year later he went to Italy, where he met the composers Arcangelo Corelli and the father and son Alessandro and Domenico Scarlatti, and quickly learned the Italian style of composition. *Rodrigo* was performed in Florence in 1707 and *Agrippina* in Venice in 1709. He was already being hailed as a genius. In 1710 he moved to Hanover as court conductor, but on a visit to London to attend performances of his music, he decided to stay in England permanently.

By 1712 he received an annual pension of £200 from Queen Anne. King George I, who had been his employer in Hanover, increased this to £600 when he succeeded to the British throne in 1714. It was for King George, in 1717, that Handel wrote his *Water Music,* although it is not known for what occasion. And for the coronation of George II in 1727, he composed the anthem *Zadok the Priest* which has been sung at every subsequent British coronation.

From 1719 Handel was director of the Royal Academy of Music, where he worked with various Italian composers. This was not a

ABOVE LEFT **George Frideric Handel, an early 18th-century portrait by Jan van der Banck**

teaching college, as is the present-day London establishment of that name, but a business venture formed to enable them to perform Italian operas. It survived for ten years, but closed through lack of support (a story which will be familiar to many arts establishments in Britain to this day). But in that period Handel composed another 14 operas, including three masterpieces: *Giulio Cesare* (1723–4), *Tamerlano* (1724), and *Rodelinda* (1725). Over the next few years Handel often travelled to Italy to engage singers and to listen to operas by his contemporary Italian composers. He moved in 1734 to the new Covent Garden theatre and for there he wrote two of his greatest operas, *Ariodante* and *Alcina*, both produced in 1735. Realizing that the appeal of Italian opera was waning, he developed the genre of dramatic-oratorio, using the choir and orchestra in a more dramatic way than hitherto and adding stage directions into the scores.

He continued to write operas, but without much public success and his health began to suffer. He had a stroke, but recovered enough to compose the oratorio *Messiah* for Dublin in 1742, the work by which he is probably best known. Despite going blind about 1752, he continued to conduct oratorios and, with the assistance of a friend, to revise many of his scores. He never married and died in 1759.

Handel bestrode the world of Baroque opera in the same way that Mozart would dominate the Classical period. He usually set adaptations of librettos that had been written for and set by other composers, but occasionally had one written specifically for his own use. His skilled composition and knowledge of the stage brought the aria to its peak, developed the *da capo* aria (first used by Scarlatti) to its full capacity, drew the characters and their emotions to a dramatic level previously unseen, and raised *opera seria* to its highest level.

From about 1920 onwards performances of his operas have gradually increased in number. Produced in England at first by the London-based Handel Opera Society and smaller opera companies, many of his operas have now been taken into the regular repertoire of European and American companies. This revival has coincided with the rise of interest in "authenticity" in music, ensembles having been formed to play on original instruments for performances of Baroque operas, and several conductors having made a speciality of this period. It is difficult to know which is cause and which effect, but it has enabled a new generation of opera-goers to experience these works for the first time. At the time of their composition, many roles were sung by Italian castrati (see p.13), and Handel, whose works were written to be performed in Italian, wrote specifically for some of the

greatest of these, especially Senesino, who sang in 32 of his operas. These roles are now most often sung by mezzo-sopranos or countertenors, but occasionally by tenors. As the great Italian castrati created some of the Handel roles, so have equally great mezzo-sopranos sung these roles in the past 50 or more years. Several other roles, such as Sesto in *Giulio Cesare*, were actually *written* as *travesti* roles, ie male characters to be sung by women from the start.

GIULIO CESARE
(Julius Caesar), 1723–4
This is one of the longest of Handel's operas and is on an elaborate scale. The libretto was adapted by Nicola Haym, not from

Shakespeare's play but from Bussani's *Giulio Cesare in Egitto*. It was written in London during Handel's time with the Royal Academy of Music and was first performed in London in 1724 (in the USA not until 1927 in Northampton, Massachusetts). The title-role is one of several written by Handel for the alto castrato Francesco Bernardi, known by his stage name of Senesino, one of the most famous of all the Italian castrati. Handel gave him eight arias in this opera.

SYNOPSIS In 48 BC, Giulio Cesare (cont, orig. castrato) has returned to Egypt after defeating Pompey in Greece. Pompey's wife Cornelia (cont) and son Sesto (sop/ten) have arrived at a settlement with Cesare so that they can all live in peace. But the king of Egypt,

ABOVE **Countertenor David Daniels in the Senesino title-role of Giulio Cesare, with soprano Elizabeth Futral as Cleopatra, in Handel's opera, Los Angeles Opera, 2001**

Tolomeo (Ptolemy) (cont, orig. castrato), who reigns with his sister Cleopatra (sop) as his queen, has Pompey beheaded. Sesto swears to avenge his father. Cleopatra, disgusted by her brother's action, wants to join Cesare to defeat Tolomeo. Cesare is attracted to Cleopatra, without knowing who she is (1). Tolomeo has Sesto arrested and sends Cornelia to the king's harem. Tolomeo's general Achilla (bass) offers to release her and rescue her son in return for marriage, an offer she refuses. Cleopatra reveals her identity to Cesare and urges him to leave Egypt, where war is being declared. He refuses and she begs the gods to have pity on her (2). Believing Cesare to be dead, Cleopatra flees to the Romans who are going to fight against Tolomeo. Achilla claims Cornelia as his bride as a reward for killing Cesare, but Tolomeo refuses him and Achilla leads his army against the king's, during which battle Cleopatra is taken prisoner by Tolomeo's soldiers. She bemoans her fate (3). But Cesare is not dead, and he prays for help (4). He rescues Cleopatra, Tolomeo is killed by Sesto in a duel, and Sesto and Cornelia are welcomed to live peacefully in Egypt, while Cesare and Cleopatra declare their love for each other (5).

> **MUSIC** (1) Cesare: *Non è si vago e bello – Not so fair and lovely*; (2) Cleopatra: *Se pietà di me non senti – Just heaven, if for me you feel no pity*; (3) Cleopatra: *Piangerò la sorte mia – I will lament my lot*; (4) Cesare: *Aure, deh, per pietà – Ye breezes, in pity*; (5) Cesare/Cleopatra duet: *Caro! / Bella! – My dear!/ My fair one!*

TAMERLANO, 1724, revised 1731

The librettist was Nicola Haym. Senesino sang Andronico and the title-role was sung by another castrato, Andrea Pacini (c.1690–1764). Another leading role, that of his opponent the Turkish Emperor Bajazet, was sung by a tenor, Francesco Borosini (c.1690–after 1747). Borosini may well have been responsible for supplying Handel with the score and libretto of the 1719 revision of the same opera written (originally in 1710) by the Italian composer Francesco Gasparini (1668–1727) under the title of *Il Bajazet*. This resulted in Handel revising his own work, incorporating new scenes based on this 1719 version.

SYNOPSIS In Prusa, the capital of Bithynia, in about 1402, the Tartar leader Tamerlano (Tamburlaine, cont, orig. castrato) has defeated and captured the Turkish Emperor Bajazet (ten) together with his daughter Asteria (sop), with whom Tamerlano falls in love. Unknown to Tamerlano, she loves, and is loved by, his friend and ally, the Greek Prince Andronico (cont, orig. castrato). Bajazet contemplates suicide, but is persuaded by Andronico against leaving Asteria an orphan (1). Tamerlano promises Andronico the throne and his own fiancée, Princess Irene of Trebizond (cont), if Andronico helps him win Asteria, as Bajazet refuses to allow Tamerlano to marry his daughter. Tamerlano orders the death of Asteria and her father. Andronico realizes he can save Bajazet's life only by hiding his love for Asteria (2). Andronico and Asteria declare their love for each other (3). Asteria poisons Tamerlano's drink, but Irene intervenes.

Bajazet poisons himself, cursing Tamerlano as he dies. Tamerlano, acknowledging that there has been sufficient bloodshed (4), agrees to marry Irene, and Asteria and Andronico are free to be together.

> **MUSIC** (1) Bajazet: *Forte e lieto – Resolutely and gently*; (2) Andronico: *Benchè mi sprezzi – Even though the idol I adore despises me*; (3) Andronico/ Asteria duet: *Vivo in te – I live in you*; (4) Tamerlano: *Arresto! – Stay your hand!*

RODELINDA, 1725

Rodelinda was first performed in London less than a month after the score was completed. Haym was again the librettist. It was written with the same singers in mind as those who created the leads in *Tamerlano*: Senesino, Borosini, and the soprano Francesca Cuzzoni.

SYNOPSIS The scene is 7th-century Milan. Bertarido (cont, orig. castrato, a Senesino role), King of Lombardy, is married to Rodelinda (sop) and they have a son Flavio (a silent role). The king is reputed to have been killed in battle and his arch enemy, Grimoaldo (ten), Duke of Benevento, decides to marry the widowed queen and thus inherit the throne. She is distressed at this suggestion (1). His friend Garibaldo, Duke of Turin (bass), would like to inherit the king's wealth and he proposes to Bertarido's sister Eduige (cont) (2). But Eduige loves Grimoaldo, who has rejected her. Rodelinda tells Grimoaldo she can only marry him if he first kills her son, heir to his father's throne – she cannot reign with a new husband, a tyrant, whilst at the same time being mother to the rightful heir. Observed by Bertarido, who is in disguise, Grimoaldo cannot bring himself to kill the child. Unulfo (cont, orig. castrato) is an old friend of Bertarido, and also counsellor to Grimoaldo. Bertarido, hiding in the woods, awaits Unulfo (3) (made famous in an English rendition by Kathleen Ferrier as "Art thou troubled?"). He assures Bertarido that Rodelinda has been faithful to him and brings about a reunion between king and queen (**4**). They are interrupted by Grimoaldo, who arrests Bertarido and sentences him to death. Unulfo, aided by Eduige, helps Bertarido escape and leads him to freedom but Rodelinda thinks him dead (**5**). Garibaldo tries to kill Grimoaldo but Bertarido, who has been watching, intervenes and kills Garibaldo. Grimoaldo decides to renounce all claims to the throne and to Bertarido's inheritance and to marry Eduige.

> **MUSIC** (**1**) Rodelinda: *L'empio rigor del fato – The cruel harshness of fate*; (**2**) Eduige: *E tu dice d'amarmi? – You claim you love me?*; (**3**) Bertarido: *Dove sei? – Where are you?*; (**4**) Bertarido/Rodelinda duet: *Io t'abbraccio – I embrace you*; (**5**) Rodelinda: *Se'l mio duol non è si forte – If my grief is not bitter enough.*

ORLANDO, 1733

Although Handel wrote another dozen operas in the six or seven years after *Rodelinda*, the next one to achieve a regular place in the repertoire was *Orlando*, based on Ariosto's epic of 1516, *Orlando furioso*. Premièred in London in 1733 (it waited until 1981 for its USA première), no time or place is specified in this opera, unlike most of the operas Handel had written in the previous 20 years. It is yet another opera with a leading role for Senesino, who sang the errant knight of the title. At the end of the season, Senesino left Handel to join a rival company, and Handel never revived *Orlando*.

SYNOPSIS Orlando (cont/counterten, orig. castrato) is in love with the Queen of Cathay, Angelica (sop), who is in turn in love with Medoro (cont), an African prince. Medoro is also loved by the shepherdess Dorinda (sop), who is very jealous of his relationship with Angelica. She informs Orlando of the betrothal of Medoro and Angelica. Orlando, jealous of Medoro and of Angelica's love for him (**1**), loses his reason (**2**). Dorinda tells Angelica of Orlando's sorry state and comments on what love can do to you (**3**) A magician, Zoroastro (bass), changes the scene to a large cave (**4**). Dorinda tells Orlando that he has murdered Angelica and Medoro. Overcome with remorse, Orlando vows to kill himself. Zoroastro releases Orlando from the bonds of love and restores his sanity. He then saves the young lovers and brings them to Orlando who, greatly relieved that he has overcome his own desire for revenge, blesses their unions (**5**).

> **MUSIC** (**1**) Orlando: *Ah, Stigie larve! – Ah, Stygian monsters!*; (**2**) Orlando: *Cielo! Se tu il consenti – Heaven! If this is your decree*; (**3**) Dorinda: *Amor è qual vento – Love is a blast*; (**4**) Zoroastro: *Sorge infausta una procella – Pernicious tempests often rise*; (**5**) Orlando: *Trionfa oggi 'l mio cor – My heart now triumphs over each care.*

ARIODANTE, 1735

Again based on Ariosto, and set in medieval Scotland, *Ariodante* was produced for the first time at London's Covent Garden, where Handel had set up his opera company having been driven out of the Haymarket theatre (then London's main opera house) by another company, Opera of the Nobility. Of his leading singers, only the soprano Anna Maria Strada (del Pò) went with him and he had to find a new cast for his next work. He managed to persuade the castrato Giovanni Carestini to join him from Italy (even Senesino had defected to the other company), as well as the Negri sisters (Maria Caterina, cont, and Maria Rosa, sop). The soprano Margherita Durastanti, for whom he had composed some of his finest solo cantatas and who had sung with him previously (she created the title-role in

ABOVE **The German countertenor Jochen Kowalski sang Andronico in** *Tamerlano* **(Germany 2002), one of many Handel roles created by Senesino**

BELOW **Renée Fleming as the sorceress of the title
and Susan Graham in the travesti role of Ruggiero,
Handel's *Alcina*, Paris Opera, 1999**

Agrippina), returned to his company. A later
addition was a young English tenor, John Beard,
who became an important Handel soloist,
especially in his oratorios. An advantage of the
new venue was that he was able to employ a
chorus regularly, instead of the choruses being
sung only by the combined soloists. He also
engaged a dance troupe to help counter the
defection of some of his star singers.

SYNOPSIS In Edinburgh Ginevra (sop),
daughter of the King of Scotland (bass),
awaits the arrival of the man she loves, Prince
Ariodante (sop/mez, orig. castrato). Ginevra
has rejected the love of Polinesso (cont),
Duke of Albany, who wants to marry her **(1)**.
The king has consented to her marriage to
Ariodante who is overwhelmed by his love
for her **(2)**. Ginevra's maid Dalinda (sop) is
attracted to Polinesso. She is also loved by
Ariodante's brother Lurcanio (ten). Polinesso
takes advantage of Dalinda's feelings to get his
own back on Ginevra **(3)**, using Dalinda to
convince Ariodante that Ginevra has been
unfaithful. The mortified and furious Ariodante
is so distraught at this news that he swears to
end his own life, until he learns from Dalinda
(4) that Polinesso has deceived him, which
Polinesso admits before Lurcanio kills him.
Ariodante proves Ginevra's innocence, in
return for which the king pardons Dalinda her
part in the plot, much to Ariodante's relief **(5)**.
Dalinda agrees to marry the faithful Lurcanio.
The king declares Ariodante to be his heir and
Ariodante and Ginevra celebrate their union **(6)**.

MUSIC (1) Ginevra: *Orrida agli occhi miei
– Nothing is more hateful to my sight;*
(2) Ariodante: *Con l'ali di costanza – Love
takes its flight;* **(3)** Polinesso: *Se l'inganno
sortisce felice – If deception proves
successful;* **(4)** Ariodante: *Cieca notte,
infidi sguardi – Dark night, duped sight;* **(5)**
Ariodante: *Dopo notte, atra e funesta –
After black and gloomy night;* **(6)** Ariodante/
Ginevra duet: *Bramo aver mille vite/cori –
I long to have a thousand lives/hearts.*

ALCINA, 1735

Alcina was the last of Handel's operas to be
based on Ariosto. Its première was at Covent
Garden where it had a run of 18 successful
performances. It was one of the first of his
operas to re-enter the modern repertoire.
The first American performance was not until
1960 in Dallas.

SYNOPSIS The action takes place on a
magic island ruled by the Sorceress Alcina
(sop). She is in love with the knight Ruggiero
(sop, orig. castrato) and has cast a spell on
him. Ruggiero's fiancée Bradamante (mez,
orig. castrato) disguises herself as a man and
presents herself as "Ricciardo". She arrives on
the island together with her guardian Melisso
(bass), determined to rescue Ruggiero. Also
visiting the island is young Oberto (sop),
looking for his father, whom Alcina has turned
into a lion. Ruggiero, under Alcina's spell, does
not recognize Bradamante – the only lover he
knows is Alcina **(1)** and he tries to persuade
her/him and Melisso to leave the island.
Alcina's sister Morgana (sop), previous lover of
Oronte (ten), the leader of Alcina's soldiers,
finds she is attracted to "Ricciardo" **(2)**. Melisso
gives Ruggiero a magic ring which will restore
him to his normal self. He comes to his senses
and determines to escape from the island with
Bradamante. At the same time, he is saddened
to think of how the beauty of the island will
diminish as Alcina's power fades **(3)**. Morgana
intervenes to prevent the angry Alcina from
turning Ruggiero into a beast or a stream –
the usual fate of her ex-lovers **(4)**. Alcina
realizes that, with the ring's protection, she will
not be able to keep Ruggiero on her island
(5). Before he departs, Ruggiero uses the ring
to restore to normality Alcina's other captives.

MUSIC (1) Ruggiero: *Di te mi rido – I
scorn you;* **(2)** Morgana: *Ama, sospira –
He loves, he sighs;* **(3)** Ruggiero: *Verdi
prati – Green meadows;* **(4)** Alcina: *Ombre
pallide – You pale shadows;* **(5)** Aleina: *Mi
restano le lagrime – Only tears remain to me.*

SERSE (*Xerxes*), 1738

In 1737 the Opera of the Nobility played its last season and Handel returned to the Haymarket theatre. Carestini left London and Handel had to start with a new leading castrato, Gaetano Majorano, known as Caffarelli. Elisabeth Duparc (pseudonym La Francesina) had sung with the rival company in its last season and now became Handel's leading lady. *Serse* is, for the most part, a comic opera, with one frank comic character, the servant Elviro. The most famous music from this opera is that known in its instrumental form as "Handel's *Largo*". In the opera it is marked *larghetto* and is sung, at the beginning of the first act, by Serse in praise of a tree that gives him shade from the sun.

SYNOPSIS In Persia, King Serse (mez, orig. castrato) is in his garden in the shade of a plane tree (1). He is engaged to Amastre (cont) but falls in love with Romilda (sop), fiancée of his

ABOVE **In a revival of *Xerxes*, ENO, 2002, soprano Rebecca Evans was the enchanting Romilda**

brother Arsamene (mez/counterten). She is one of the daughters of Ariodate (bass), Serse's army commander. Serse orders his brother to convey his feelings to Romilda. When he does so, Romilda's sister Atalanta (sop), herself in love with Arsamene, overhears the conversation and Romilda's rejection of Serse's love. Serse tries to persuade Arsamene to marry Atalanta. Amastre, made aware by Arsamene's servant Elviro (bass) of all this intrigue, dresses up as a man in an attempt to thwart the king's intentions and overhears Serse declare his love for Romilda (2). Atalanta tells Romilda, falsely, that Arsamene has been unfaithful to her and Romilda states that she cannot love him if this is true (3). Ariodate, believing he is carrying out the king's wishes, marries Romilda to Arsamene. When Serse discovers this he, the king, orders his brother to kill his new wife. Amastre throws off her disguise and Serse repents his betrayal and wickedness and is reconciled with her, at the same time approving the union of Romilda and Arsamene (4).

> **MUSIC** (1) Serse: *Ombra mai fù – Never was nature's own shade*; (2) Serse: *Piu che penso alle fiamme del core – The more I think of the flames in my heart*; (3) Romilda: *Se l'idol mio – If you intend to take my love*; (4) Romilda: *Caro voi siete all'alma – What kindness to out souls*.

SEMELE, 1744

This was first given in a concert performance in London. It was billed as "*The Story of Semele, performed after the manner of an oratorio*" rather than an opera, and composed to a text adapted from Congreve's libretto written for an opera composed by John Eccles in 1706. It is now considered a "near opera" and in the past 50 years has been produced by several opera companies. It concerns Semele's love for Jupiter. It was written in English and contains two famous arias: "O Sleep, why dost thou leave me?" and "Where'er you walk".

SYNOPSIS Semele (sop) and Ino (cont) are the daughters of Cadmus (bass), King of Thebes. Semele is about to marry Athamas (cont), Prince of Boeotia, but does not love him. He is loved by her sister Ino. Semele asks the gods to save her from this loveless marriage (1) and Jupiter (ten) intervenes and falls in love with her. The wedding is abandoned and Jupiter and Semele are together (2). Jupiter's wife Juno (cont) is furious and calls on the god of sleep, Somnus (bass), for help. Semele awakens in her palace (3). She is only too conscious of being a mere mortal and worries about holding on to her relationship with the god Jupiter. Jupiter transforms the scene so they are in Arcadia (4) and brings her sister Ino to her for company. At Juno's request, Somnus puts Ino to sleep so that Juno can disguise herself as Ino and visit Semele, to whom she gives a mirror to admire her human form (5). Juno persuades Semele to ask Jupiter to appear to her in his full glory as a god – she knows that the mortal Semele will not be able to survive Jupiter's divine power. When faced with Jupiter as he truly is, Semele is consumed by his fire and dies. Ino, back in the mortal world, is able to marry Athamas. In the clouds overhead, Apollo (ten) appears. He foresees the creation of Bacchus: "From Semele's ashes a Phoenix shall rise".

> **MUSIC** (1) Semele: *O Jove! In pity teach me which to choose*; (2) Semele: *Endless pleasure, endless love*; (3) Semele: *O sleep why dost thou leave me?*; (4) Jupiter: *Where'er you walk*; (5) Semele: *Myself I shall adore*.

Other operas of note

Among these are *Agrippina*, *Rinaldo*, *Radamisto*, *Teseo*, *Amadigi*, and *Berenice* – and many more too numerous to list. The first three mentioned are quite often staged today, many more receive occasional production, and they all have some music worth hearing. Those described in some detail above are, at the present time, the ones most often available in the theatre.

The Classical Era

Mid-18th to mid-19th century

The period implied by the term Classical is roughly the years from 1750 to 1850. It was an era of great technological advance. The Industrial Revolution, which spread throughout Europe from its origins in Great Britain, led to an age of social upheaval as Western civilization experienced previously unimagined wealth. Travel became easier with the development of steam power and life changed for much of the population. As is usual, development in the arts echoed the pattern of social and industrial development. In the world of music, the advance of printing methods made it possible for ordinary people, as well as musicians, to possess sheet music from which they could study and learn. Music critics made their first appearance, reporting on concerts in printed journals.

FEATURED OPERAS

GLUCK
Orfeo ed Euridice 1762
Alceste 1766–7
Iphigénie en Aulide 1774
Armide 1776–7
Iphigénie en Tauride 1778

MOZART
Idomeneo 1780–1

Die Entführung aus dem Serail
    1781–2
Le nozze di Figaro 1785–6
Il dissoluto punito, ossia Il
    Don Giovanni 1787
Così fan tutte 1789
Die Zauberflöte 1790–1
La clemenza di Tito 1791

BEETHOVEN
Fidelio 1805–14

LEFT *The Sacrifice of Iphigenia* at Aulis, the subject of Gluck's opera, as painted by Francis Harding (fl.1730–66)

The Classical Era

The price of musical instruments dropped significantly as manufacturing methods improved, and most prosperous households had at least a piano in the drawing-room. It was considered normal for people to acquire a certain degree of skill in playing an instrument and for families to make music together as a means of home entertainment – there was no radio or television.

The word "Classical" has been applied to all aspects of the arts from many different cultures – literature, painting and sculpture, architecture, and music. It came to mean works with two main components: a formal discipline and a standard of excellence by which other works can be measured. It also acquired other inferences, such as works of ancient Greece and Rome and those which were the opposite of "Romantic", the latter being considered less well formed and more rambling. In the case of music, which is our primary consideration, the formal discipline and standard of excellence are the most important. Another definition is also significant: a Classical work of music should gain from repeated hearing and analysis.

Musical construction underwent considerable change when sonata-form developed, leading to the symphony and concerto. Compositions became simpler than those of the Baroque era, with the emphasis on melody and harmony – Classical composers were supposed to be more detached, more intellectual, and less inclined to ornate decoration. Christoph Willibald von Gluck (1714–87) can be considered the first of the Classical composers. In his operas his emphasis was on the interpretation of the text and the telling of the story, and to this end he reduced the amount of florid decoration that singers, especially sopranos, expected in order to show off their coloratura technique. At the same time, he increased the importance of the chorus and the orchestra. There was less use of the harpsichord and more use of strings, and the orchestra was developing into something resembling the present-day ensemble, but with many fewer players than in a modern orchestra. One of the most famous Classical orchestras was the Mannheim Orchestra in Germany, which was one of the earliest to develop its own "sound", but even this orchestra had only about 50 players and that was large for its day.

By the 1830s, Classical music was beginning to mean the Viennese classics of Haydn (1732–1809), Mozart (1756–91), and Beethoven (1770–1827). Of these three, only Mozart was fully Austrian, being born in Salzburg. Haydn, though Austrian-born, was of German stock and Beethoven was born in Bonn. They all died in Vienna. It is the music of these three composers which is referred to by writers using the term "Classical music" or, more accurately, music of the "Classical period". (There is also, of course, the use of the term "Classical music" to distinguish it from "popular music", the more ephemeral music of its day. Care needs to be taken in using these terms – much "popular" music can become "classics" of their time, but this is a different use of the word to that being discussed here.)

Whilst discussing the Classical composers, it is relevant to remember that the Romantic period in music dates from about 1830, and thus overlaps the later Classical era. Some writers have included the works of Schubert (1797–1828), who died only a year after Beethoven, in the

ABOVE **The Estates Theatre, Prague, where Mozart's *Don Giovanni* had its première in 1787, when it was called the National Theatre**

BELOW Stage design for the Act II graveyard scene in *Don Giovanni* at Munich 1789. The statue of the Commendatore can be seen in the left foreground

Classical period, and others consider the late works of Beethoven to demonstrate the disintegration of the Classical form. Haydn's role in the defining of the Classical style is central. By the 1770s he had put behind him the earlier forms of dance, and was a master of counterpoint, his music being extremely tuneful. Mozart followed Haydn's style in composing his quartets and symphonies, even dedicating a group of his quartets to the older composer from whom he learned much. They were both using harmony, rhythm, dynamics, and orchestral colours to produce long arches of sound, with tensions building and relaxing. The use of humour in their music, especially by Haydn, was frowned upon by some of the north German critics. With the printing of music becoming easier, Haydn's works were being widely played throughout Europe. Both Haydn and Mozart were happy to stay within certain frameworks that they knew pleased the public who listened to their music. They produced vast amounts of music in every genre – keyboard, chamber, instrumental, concertos, symphonies, vocal, choral, and opera. In fact, one could say that Mozart was the last great composer to have mastered every genre.

And where does Beethoven fit into this picture? Initially he was happy to please the public, especially in his keyboard works, which he performed himself to great acclaim. His orchestral music to a certain extent took up where Haydn left off, but he was also influenced by the early ideals of *liberté, égalité, et fraternité* coming from Revolutionary France, as became increasingly apparent from about the time of his third (*Eroica*) symphony. Arguments will

continue as to whether Beethoven was a Classical or a Romantic composer. Certainly his lifestyle was that of a Romantic – extravagant, isolated, with lots of romantic relationships with women. The onset of deafness before he was 30 led to him becoming increasingly inward-looking and in his last years he became less concerned about the ease of communication in his compositions (one of the reasons some people consider him a Romantic, rather than a Classical composer, for whom ease of communication was essential). It was important to Beethoven for his works to be original, to be the result of a personal struggle, in contrast to Mozart who stressed the virtues of moderation, of music easily understood by the listener.

Music had come a long way: early music had been written for the church and was primarily vocal. Later, into the Baroque period, musicians were employed by royalty and noblemen and their music was written for king and court. Now, in the Classical era, it was being written for the interest and enjoyment of the more general public. Maybe we can consider this as an early demonstration of that modern, over-used word, "accessibility".

ABOVE Title-page of Mozart's *Le nozze di Figaro*, published 1788

Gluck

Christoph Willibald von Gluck
(1714–87)

BELOW **View of old Prague as it was when Gluck was a student there,** *c.*1731

WHERE TO START
Orfeo ed Euridice
Alceste

WHERE TO GO NEXT
Iphigénie en Aulide
Iphigénie en Tauride
Armide

The son of a forester in Bohemia, Gluck was born in Erasbach and his native language was Czech. He went at the age of 14 to Prague and from 18 attended the university, where he studied philosophy and music, earned money as an organist, and learned to play the cello. Leaving the university after three years, he went to Vienna, supported by Prince Lobkowitz, and joined the private orchestra of Prince Melzi, who engaged him to play in his orchestra in Milan. There he wrote eight operas (in Italian) between 1741 and 1744. The following year he travelled to London, meeting Handel, composing two more operas and giving two concerts as performer on the glass armonica (glasses filled with

water to varying heights and played by rubbing the finger round the edge of the glass to produce the notes). In 1754 he was appointed by Empress Maria Theresa as *Kapellmeister* (literally "chorus master" but in practical terms, conductor) at the court theatre in Vienna. The post required him to compose works in the style of the fashionable French *opéra-comique*. This was a more lively and flexible way of composing and Gluck was responsible for important operatic reforms in which the drama took pride of place and the singers had to subjugate their performances to this end. He introduced accompanied recitative to replace the more formal *recitativo secco*, or "dry" recitative, ie unaccompanied. His operas henceforth embodied these ideas, the first being *Orfeo ed Euridice* of 1762. By the time he composed *Alceste* in 1766–7 he was, without knowing it, anticipating by more than half a century the "through-composed" music-dramas of Richard Wagner.

In 1773 Gluck moved to Paris, having been contracted to write a work for the Opéra, *Iphigénie en Aulide*, produced in 1774. He revised his own *Orfeo* for Paris and, in 1776, his *Alceste* was performed with a French

libretto. Gluck's success in Paris led to a manipulated quarrel with the Italian composer Niccolò Piccinni, who was asked to set the same libretto on which Gluck was working. As a result, Gluck destroyed his composition sketches and composed instead *Armide* (1776–7) and *Iphigénie en Tauride* (1778). He returned to Vienna in 1779, living in a grand style and dying in 1787 from an excess of alcohol. Apart from his sublime music, his intense sense of drama has helped to ensure the survival of many of his stage works.

Among the other operas Gluck wrote are *La clemenza di Tito* (to the Metastasio text that would be set by Mozart almost 40 years later) and *Le cinesi* (*The Chinese Ladies*), to another Metastasio text. The latter was given in London in 1977 by the Royal Danish Academy of Music at Sadler's Wells and again in 1984 and in 1995 by small British companies – not exactly frequent performances, but not totally neglected either. But neither of these works, nor many of Gluck's other operas, are very likely to reach a modern audience on a regular basis. However, the five operas discussed below are, whilst not standard repertory, produced frequently enough by many major opera companies to warrant consideration.

ABOVE LEFT **Christoph Willibald von Gluck,** *c.*1775 (bust by Jean-Antoine Houdon)

ORFEO ED EURIDICE, 1762

The three-act libretto by Ranieri de' Calzabigi (1714–95) is based on the mythological legend of Orfeo and Euridice. The opera is often defined as a "theatrical-action to music", an early form of music-drama. It was first performed in Vienna in 1762, in London in 1770, and in New York in 1863 (but not at the Metropolitan Opera until 1891). At the Vienna première, the role of Orfeo was sung by an alto castrato (Gaetano Guadagni), who had sung in Handel's *Messiah* in England in 1750. In the French version (*Orphée et Eurydice*), which Gluck re-wrote for Paris in 1774 using the librettist Pierre-Louis Moline, Orfeo was sung by a high tenor (see p. 17), but nowadays it is usually performed by a mezzo-soprano, though occasionally by a countertenor or even a high baritone. Famous singers of this role have included Pauline Viardot (Paris, 1859), Kathleen Ferrier (Covent Garden, 1953), and Janet Baker (Glyndebourne, 1982).

SYNOPSIS Set in mythological Greece, the dead Euridice (sop) is mourned by her distraught husband Orfeo (cont/ten, orig. castrato). Near her tomb, he sings of his grief (1). The god of love, Amore (Cupid) (sop), tells Orfeo he may go to Hades to seek Euridice, but he must not look at her until they have crossed the Styx (2). If he disobeys this order, or even tries to explain his behaviour to her, she will die. Orfeo plays his lute as he enters the underworld. At first the Furies refuse him entry, but they are moved by the sweetness of his song, and when they see how distressed he is they allow him through to search for his wife. In Elysium, Orfeo comments on the beauty surrounding him (3). Euridice is brought to him, blindfolded, and he leads her by the hand from Hades, refusing to look at her. She, unable to understand his actions, is distressed and tells him that death was better than this, life is so miserable (4). Eventually he gives in to her pleading and embraces her. At once she dies. Orfeo sings his beautiful and justly famous lament, known in English as

RIGHT **Title-page of the Paris edition, 1764, of Gluck's best-known opera, *Orfeo ed Euridice***

Euridice amor ti rende.   atto. 11. Sec. 11.

"What is life for me without thee?" (5). Amore is so touched by the beauty of his singing and the depth of his grief that he restores Euridice to life so they can be together on earth. They all join in a celebratory chorus (6).

MUSIC (1) Orfeo: *Chiamo il mio ben così – Thus I call to my beloved*; (2) Amore: *Gli sguardi trattieni – Withhold thy looks*; (3) Orfeo: *Che puro ciel! Che chiaro sol! – How pure the sky! How clear the sun!*; (4) Euridice: *Che fiero momento – What a cruel moment*; (5) Orfeo: *Che farò senza Euridice? – What shall I do without Euridice?*; (6) Orfeo/Euridice/Amore/Chorus: *Trionfi Amore, e il mondo intiero – Let love be triumphant for ever.*

ALCESTE, 1766–7

Written for Vienna, *Alceste* continues the mythological theme of Gluck's earlier operas. For the first time, Gluck did not write a part for a castrato. He made a much-revised French version for Paris in 1776 with F L Leblanc du Roullet (described below). There are many differences in the plots of the two versions. The story is based on Euripides's *Alkestis*, a tragi-comedy. In the original (Italian) version, the librettist Ranieri de' Calzabigi concentrated on the tragic aspects, possibly because he dedicated the libretto to the recently widowed Empress Maria Theresa. It made for a very miserable evening in the theatre. Nevertheless the work made a deep impression on the 11-year-old Mozart who attended a performance with his father.

SYNOPSIS Alceste (sop) is the wife of Admète (ten). Apollon (bar) has decreed that Admète must die and Alceste is already mourning his loss (1). Apollon announces that the only thing that can save him is for somebody else to be sacrificed in his place. Alceste offers herself to save her husband (2), but points out it is not to be considered a sacrifice. She tells the gods not to pity her as this is an act of love (3). Admète recovers, but the people are horrified when they realize that Alceste will die in his place and she bids life farewell (4). Admète begs her to change her mind and let him die (5), but she refuses. In the Italian version of the opera, she is restored to life by Apollon; in the French verison, she is rescued from the underworld by Hercules (bass).

> **MUSIC** (1) Alceste: *Grands dieux! Du destin qui m'accable – Dear gods! Destiny is depressing*; (2) Alceste: *Non, ce n'est point un sacrifice – No, it is not a sacrifice*; (3) Alceste: *Divinités du Styx – Gods of the Eternal Night*; (4) Alceste: *Ah, malgré moi – Ah, in spite of myself*; (5) Admète: *Alceste, au nom des dieux – Alceste, in the gods' names.*

IPHIGÉNIE EN AULIDE, 1774

This is the first opera Gluck wrote for Paris, to a libretto by F L Leblanc du Roullet, based on Euripides. It is set in the Greek port Aulis on the eve of the Trojan War. Gluck caused a sensation at the Paris Opéra because of his insistence that the principals (including some of France's most eminent singers) and the chorus should act their parts and it was reported that he had to be very authoritarian in order to persuade them to do so – hitherto, the vocal pyrotechnics were the most important aspect of their performances.

SYNOPSIS Iphigénie (sop) is the daughter of Clitemnestre (sop) and Agamemnon (bar). The Greeks are in Aulis waiting for favourable wind so that they can sail onward to Troy. The goddess Diana (sop) has decreed that Iphigénie must be sacrificed before the Greeks can be allowed to continue to Troy. Agamemnon is reluctant to sacrifice his daughter (1), but is urged on by the High Priest Calchas (bass) and the Greek soldiers. Iphigénie agrees to her father's wishes to appease the troops, but Achille (ten), who wants to marry her, protests and tries to rescue her, even if this means a fight with Agamemnon (2). Agamemnon at first insists on carrying out the sacrifice (3). Just in time, Calchas, who has been encouraging the sacrifice, relents and announces that the gods will provide the winds necessary to enable them to sail to Troy, thus avoiding any bloodshed.

> **MUSIC** (1) Agamemnon: *Peuvent-ils ordonner – In vain do you demand of me*; (2) Agamemnon/Achille duet: *De votre audace téméraire – Of your rash audacity*; (3) Agamemnon: *O toi, l'objet le plus aimable – O you, the most lovable object.*

ABOVE **Gluck** being handed his wig by a singer during a rehearsal of his opera *Iphigénie en Aulide*, Paris, 1774

LEFT The outstanding English mezzo Dame Janet Baker in the title-role of Gluck's *Alceste* at ROH, Covent Garden, in 1981.

ARMIDE, 1776–7

Gluck set this five-act opera, to a libretto by Philippe Quinault, in Damascus in 1099 during the First Crusade. (The same text had already been set by Lully 90 years earlier and it was altered very little for use by Gluck.) It was the fifth of seven operas Gluck wrote for Paris.

SYNOPSIS The sorceress Armide (sop) has succeeded in seducing many knights, but not yet the one she most wants to conquer, Renaud (ten) (1), whom she pretends to hate in order to disguise her true feelings (2). She vows to kill him rather than be rejected by him, but cannot bring herself to do so (3). She carries him off to her enchanted palace and eventually does succeed in making him love her, with the help of her uncle, the magician Hidraot (bar), King of Damascus. He puts a spell on Renaud, who then falls in love with Armide. But Armide knows his love for her depends on magic and she summons Hate (cont) to try to rid herself of her feelings for him (4). Hate is dismissed after warning Armide that Renaud will leave her (5). Ubalde (bar) and a Danish Knight (bar) rescue Renaud (6), and he leaves with them. In a fury, Armide destroys her magic palace and all its contents (7).

> **MUSIC** (1) Armide: *Je ne triomphe pas du plus vaillant de tous! – I do not triumph over the most valiant of all!*; (2) Armide: *Les enfers ont prédit cent fois… – Hell has foretold a hundred times…*; (3) Armide: *Enfin, il est en ma puissance – At last he is in my power*; (4) Armide: *Il m'aime? Quel amour! – He loves me? What love!*; (5) Hate: *Suis l'amour, qui te guide dans un abîme affreux – Follow Love, who is leading you into a dreadful abyss*; (6) Ubalde: *Notre général vous appelle – Our general calls you*; (7) Armide: *Quand le barbare était en ma puissance – When the barbarian was in my power.*

IPHIGÉNIE EN TAURIDE, 1778

This is the last important opera Gluck wrote for Paris before he returned to Vienna and retired. It had its first British performance in London in 1796 and in New York (in a version by Richard Strauss) in 1916. Again the text was based on Euripides and again it was a triumph. Berlioz was so impressed by it that he persuaded Charles Hallé to give a performance of it in Manchester in 1860. It is still one of Gluck's most often revived operas.

SYNOPSIS The action takes place after the Trojan War, on the peninsular of Tauris (the Crimea). Iphigénie (sop) has become a priestess of the goddess Diana/Artemis (sop). She has had a dream in which her mother, Clitemnestre, killed her own husband, Agamemnon; their son, Oreste (bar), killed his mother to avenge his father (see *Elektra*, p.138); finally, Iphigénie herself killed Oreste, her brother. Tormented by the dream, she prays to Diana (1). The cruel King Thoas (bass) has serious forebodings (2). He demands the sacrifice of two strangers – Oreste (whom Iphigénie has yet to recognize) and his friend Pylades (ten, orig. *haute-contre*) – who have been washed ashore during a storm. Iphigénie asks Oreste about himself and his family and he ends his story by announcing his own forthcoming death (3). Iphigénie prays to be released from her obligation to kill Oreste (4). As they stand at the altar ready for the act, Iphigénie recognizes Oreste. King Thoas is furious when she fails to kill Oreste and is about to do so himself when Pylades arrives and kills Thoas. Diana appears, pardons Oreste, and sends him to be King of Mycenae.

> **MUSIC** (1) Iphigénie: *O toi, qui prolongeas mes jours – O you, who extended my days*; (2) Thoas: *De noirs pressentiments – With black forebodings*; (3) Iphigénie: *O malheureuse Iphigénie – O, unhappy Iphigenia*; (4) Iphigénie: *Je l'implore et je tremble – Trembling I implore thee.*

ABOVE RIGHT **Katerina Karneus**, winner of the Cardiff Singer of the World Competition 1995, as Clitemnestre in Gluck's *Iphigénie en Aulide*, Glyndebourne Festival Opera, 2002

Mozart

Wolfgang Amadeus Mozart
(1756–91)

WHERE TO START
Le nozze di Figaro
Così fan tutte
Don Giovanni
Die Zauberflöte

WHERE TO GO NEXT
Die Entführung aus dem Serail
Idomeneo
La clemenza di Tito

LEFT **Mozart at the piano during the composition of** *Don Giovanni*

Mozart was born in Salzburg, Austria, and died in Vienna only 35 years later. He was the son of Leopold Mozart, deputy *Kapellmeister* (choirmaster) to the Prince-Archbishop of Salzburg. Wolfgang played the keyboard at three and wrote his first compositions when he was five. His older sister Maria Anna (1751–1829), known as Nannerl, was also a brilliant keyboard player and Leopold decided in 1762 to show off his children's talents to various European courts. The two children performed in Munich and Vienna. A year later a second and wider tour was arranged, during which they spent two weeks at Versailles at the court of Louis XV. In April 1764 they were received by King George III in London. In 1769 Leopold took the young composer to Italy where, in 1770, the 14-year-old Mozart wrote his opera *Mitridate, re di Ponto*, for Milan. This initiated a decade as a travelling prodigy until the Elector of Bavaria commissioned *Idomeneo, re di Creta*, to a libretto by Giambattista Varesco, produced in Munich in January 1781. It is the first of seven great operas which Mozart wrote over the next 10 years. During this period he also composed his last seven symphonies as well as 17 piano concertos; the clarinet concerto; his last 10 string quartets; a dozen piano sonatas; and many other instrumental and vocal works.

After the success of *Idomeneo*, Mozart resigned as *Konzertmeister* at the Salzburg court and settled in Vienna where, in August

1782, he married Constanze Weber. The wedding took place shortly after the première of his next major opera, *Die Entführung aus dem Serail*, written during the previous year. Between then and 1785 he wrote three operas of less importance and then, in the autumn of 1785, he began work on *Le nozze di Figaro*, the first of three operas Mozart composed to texts by the Italian poet and librettist Lorenzo da Ponte (1749–1838), who based this libretto on Beaumarchais's comedy *La folle journée, ou Le mariage de Figaro*. The main characters have entered the hearts of generations of opera-goers ever since the first performance in Vienna in May 1786. In December that year, *Figaro* enjoyed a great success in Prague, which then commissioned an opera from Mozart for the following autumn. This opera, *Don Giovanni*, also had the libretto written by da Ponte, based on the Don Juan legend as told in a libretto by Giovanni Bertati (1735–c.1818). It was composed in a few months in 1787 and was well received in Prague that year but less enthusiastically in Vienna in 1788.

During 1789, Mozart's finances were so poor that he had to earn a living by performing, and he travelled to Dresden, Berlin, and Leipzig. Whilst in Berlin he received a commission for six string quartets from King Friedrich Wilhelm II (but he only wrote three of them). In the autumn Emperor Joseph II of Austria commissioned a comic opera. *Così fan tutte* had its first performance early in 1790. It is the

third and last of the three Mozart–da Ponte operas and on this occasion da Ponte wrote an original libretto. The comedy may be obvious, but the underlying seriousness and anguish are there if one looks for them. *Così fan tutte* was written in 1789 and first produced in Vienna the following year.

Emanuel Schikaneder (1751–1812), an actor, singer, and theatre manager and, like Mozart, a Freemason, asked the composer in 1791 to write the music for a fairy-tale opera for which he had concocted a libretto. It was based on a story, "Lulu, or the Magic Flute", by Jacob August Liebeskind, published between 1786 and 1789 in a collection of oriental fairy-tales, *Dschinnistan*, edited by Christoph Martin Wieland (1733–1813). Most of the music for the opera, called *Die Zauberflöte*, was written by July that year and it had its first performance in Vienna later the same year, only 10 weeks before Mozart's death, with Schikaneder singing one of the leading roles (Papageno). They made no secret of the fact that Sarastro's brotherhood in the opera represented the Freemasons.

Mozart by now had begun work on what was to be his final opera, written to celebrate

ABOVE **The soprano Constanze Weber, who married Mozart in 1782, and is buried in Salzburg**

BELOW A place of pilgrimage, visited by thousands every year: Mozart's birthplace in the Getreidegasse, Salzburg

the coronation of Emperor Leopold II as king of Bohemia. *La clemenza di Tito* was adapted from an existing libretto by the poet Metastasio (1698–1782). The composer supervised its first performance in Prague in September and then returned to Vienna to conduct the première of *Die Zauberflöte*. He then resumed work on a requiem which had been commissioned by an anonymous patron (Count F. von Walsegg, who was going to pretend he had written it himself).

By now Mozart's health, which had been deteriorating for some time, worsened and he died on 5 December 1791. The *Requiem* was left unfinished and was later completed by his pupil Franz Süssmayr (1766–1803) and others. There has been much speculation about the cause of Mozart's death and the circumstances surrounding it, and of the circumstances of his funeral – to this day the location of his burial place remains unknown. There has never been any reliable evidence to support any of the rumours of murder. Efforts to incriminate rival composer Antonio Salieri (1750–1825) as a poisoner have all been discredited. Mozart was buried in a mass grave, along with others who had died at the same time, which was not a sign of poverty but was in accordance with the emperor's regulations of 1784.

IDOMENEO, 1780–1

Idomeneo is the earliest of the seven operas regarded as Mozart's masterpieces of the genre. Through his correspondence with his father, who joined him in Munich a few days before the opera's première, it is possible to follow many of the problems, both interesting and amusing, of the creative process. For instance, he described the singers of Idomeneo (the 67-year-old tenor Anton Raaff) and Idamante (Vincenzo dal Prato, a castrato) as "the two worst actors any stage has ever borne" and their limitations, both vocally and histrionically, influenced the music he wrote for them.

SYNOPSIS After the Trojan War, the King of Crete, Idomeneo (ten), has sent home to Crete Ilia (sop), daughter of King Priam of Troy. Ilia is in love with Idomeneo's son Idamante (mez/ten), who is also loved by Elettra (sop), the Greek princess, daughter of Agamemnon. She is jealous of Ilia's influence over Idamante (**1**). Idomeneo's confidant, the elderly Arbace (ten), announces the sinking of Idomeneo's ship. But Neptune has saved Idomeneo's life, and in return the king has promised to sacrifice the first person he meets when he returns to the shore. To his horror, this turns out to be Idamante, who eventually recognizes his father (**2**). In an attempt to avoid the promised sacrifice, Idomeneo rejects his son (**3**), sending him away in the company of Elettra, leaving behind the distraught Ilia.

Neptune, furious at Idomeneo's attempt to avoid the fulfilment of his promise, sends a huge sea monster in a storm, which wreaks havoc and terrifies the people (**4**). In the royal garden Ilia sings to the breezes (**5**) and confesses to Idamante her love for him. He, upset by his father's rejection of him, sets sail to defeat the monster. When he learns the true reason for his father's refusal to acknowledge him, he returns, offering to be sacrificed in order to placate Neptune. Ilia offers to save him by taking his place. Neptune is so impressed by this demonstration of love, that he agrees to release Idomeneo from his promise, on condition that the king will hand over his throne to Ilia and Idamante. The only person not happy with this solution is, of course, Elettra (**6**).

> **MUSIC** (**1**) Elettra: *Tutte nel cor vi sento – In my heart I feel you all*; (**2**) Idamante: *Il padre adorato – My beloved father*; (**3**) Idomeneo: *Fuor del mar – Saved from the sea*; (**4**) Chorus: *Corriamo, fuggiamo – Let us run, let us flee*; (**5**) Ilia: *Zeffiretti lusinghieri – Gentle breezes*; (**6**) Elettra: *O smania! – Oh madness!*

DIE ENTFÜHRUNG AUS DEM SERAIL
(*The Abduction from the Harem*), 1781–2

This opera was commissioned for a *Singspiel* company directed by Gottlieb Stephanie, who wrote the libretto based on Christoph Friedrich Bretzner's *Belmonte und Constanze* (1780). Its composition took Mozart longer than was usual for him and is again well chronicled in letters to his father. It had its première in Vienna about a month before the composer's marriage. The work was a success and was performed in 40 cities during Mozart's lifetime.

SYNOPSIS *The Abduction from the Harem* is set in Turkey. A Spanish lady, Constanze (sop), has been kidnapped by pirates together with her maid Blondchen (sop) and taken to the home of Pasha Selim (spoken role). A

Spanish nobleman, Belmonte (ten), is in love with Constanze and his servant Pedrillo (ten) is in love with Blondchen. The two men try to enter Pasha Selim's house to rescue their ladies. They first encounter Osmin (bass), the keeper of the Pasha's harem, a bloodthirsty but comic character who has fallen in love with Blondchen (1). The Pasha tries to woo Constanze, but she firmly tells him she is in love with another man. Blondchen rejects Osmin (2). The Pasha threatens Constanze with torture, but she replies defiantly (3). Pedrillo drugs Osmin and, when he has fallen asleep, he and Belmonte enter the palace and learn that their ladies are still alive (4). They find them and Blondchen anticipates their escape (5). Constanze is reunited with Belmonte (6). The men attempt to rescue their ladies by climbing down a ladder which they have conveniently placed outside a window. But a guard has removed the ladder, preventing their escape. Pasha Selim, an apparently severe man, now shows his gentler side by forgiving them and allowing the four lovers to leave his palace and return home together.

> **MUSIC** (1) Osmin: *Wer ein Liebchen hat gefunden – He who has found a sweetheart*; (2) Blondchen: *Durch Zärtlichkeit und Schmeicheln – With tenderness and pretty words*; (3) Constanze: *Martern aller Arten mögen meiner warten – Tortures of every kind may await me*; (4) Belmonte: *Konstanze! Dich wiederzusehen – Constanze, to see you again*; (5) Blondchen: *Welche Wonne, welche Lust – What bliss, what delight*; (6) Belmonte: *Wenn der Freude Tränen fliessen – When the tears of joy flow.*

LE NOZZE DI FIGARO

(*The Marriage of Figaro*), 1785–6

Very little is known about the composition of *Figaro*. None of Mozart's letters from the period leading up to its first performance survive. In his memoirs of 1823–7, the Italian librettist Lorenzo da Ponte took much of the credit unto himself, but even he admitted that it was Mozart's idea to set the play of Beaumarchais, which had been banned as "subversive". It was written about five years before the French Revolution when social mores were changing – in it, the servants teach the aristocracy a lesson in clemency. There is much humour in the opera, but an equal amount of melancholy. The cast included 12-year-old Anna Gottlieb as Barbarina – she later created Pamina in *Die Zauberflöte*.

SYNOPSIS In the Almavivas' château near Seville, the Count's valet Figaro (bar) and the Countess's maid Susanna (sop) are measuring up the room they have been allotted for their use after their forthcoming marriage. Count Almaviva (bar) plans to seduce Susanna and does his best to delay the wedding. At the same time he is suspicious of Cherubino (mez/sop), a page obsessed with the Countess (sop) (1). To get Cherubino out of his hair, the Count sends him off to war and Figaro teases the youngster about the difficulties of army life (2), scotching his attempts to woo the Countess. The Countess's former guardian Dr Bartolo (bass) is helping the Almavivas' elderly housekeeper Marcellina (mez/sop) in her attempts to persuade Figaro to marry her in order to pay off a debt he owes. (Figaro is later revealed as the long-lost son of Bartolo and Marcellina.) The music master Basilio (ten) does his best to cause trouble between the various couples.

The Countess, lonely and neglected by her husband, is trying to find a way to return to their days of love and happiness (3). Cherubino, before departing for war, calls to see the Countess and sings to her (4), accompanied by Susanna on a guitar. The Countess, Susanna, and Figaro plot to teach the Count a lesson by catching him in an illicit assignation. To this end, they send him a note purporting to come from Susanna and asking him to meet her in the garden that night after dark. The note is delivered by Barbarina (sop), daughter of the gardener Antonio (bass) and Susanna's cousin. (It is always worth taking note of Barbarina –

it is a small part, but many a well-known soprano has made her début in this role.) The Countess muses on their plan and the humiliation to which she has been reduced in order to win again her husband's love **(5)**. In the garden that evening she and Susanna exchange clothes and as they await the Count's arrival Susanna sings her wonderful aria **(6)**. The watching Count sees, apparently, "his wife" in an embrace with Figaro (who has had no trouble seeing through Susanna's disguise) and accuses her of being unfaithful, behaviour which he cannot possibly forgive. The Countess enters and removes her veil. Realizing his mistake and his misjudgment of his wife, his plea for forgiveness, "Contessa, perdono!" ("Forgive me, Countess"), is one of the most tender moments in the opera. The Countess, of course, agrees to do so **(7)** – pointing out that she has a kinder heart than her husband.

MUSIC (1) Cherubino: *Non so più cosa son – I no longer know what I am*; **(2)** Figaro: *Non più andrai, farfallone amoroso – No more, you amorous butterfly*; **(3)** Countess: *Porgi amor. . . – Grant love. . .*; **(4)** Cherubino: *Voi che sapete che cosa è amor – You ladies who know what love is*; **(5)** Countess: *Dove sono i bei momenti – Where are they, those happy moments?*; **(6)** Susanna: *Deh, vieni, non tardar, oh gioia bella – Come, do not delay, oh bliss*; **(7)** Countess: *Più docile io sono, e dico di sì – I am kinder than you, and I will say "Yes".*

IL DISSOLUTO PUNITO, OSSIA IL DON GIOVANNI

(The Rake Punished, or Don Giovanni), 1787
Don Giovanni is the second of the three operas which Mozart wrote with da Ponte as librettist. Da Ponte was seven years older than the composer, had written only three librettos, but understood what Mozart wanted and was able to write lines that the composer found ideal in length and metre for setting to music

as recitatives and arias. The libertine Don Juan has been the source of more works than can be remembered – including two operas by minor composers before Mozart's – since he first appeared in the play *El burlador de Sevilla y convidado de piedra*, written by a monk in around 1630. *Don Giovanni* received its first performance in the Bohemian capital, having been commissioned for Prague after the successful performances there of *Figaro* in December 1786. It was a triumph. For *Don Giovanni*'s Viennese première in 1788 Mozart added an extra aria for Elvira ("Mi tradì"), gave a simpler aria to Ottavio ("Dalla sua pace"), and made various other changes.

SYNOPSIS In 17th-century Seville a masked Don Giovanni (bar/bass-bar) is trying to seduce the noblewoman Donna Anna (sop), daughter of the Commendatore (bass). Giovanni's servant Leporello (bass), acting as a

look-out, sees his master fight and kill the Commendatore who was trying to catch the man who was assaulting his daughter. Giovanni escapes unrecognized; Anna and her fiancé, Don Ottavio (ten), find her father's body and she swears vengeance. A past conquest of Giovanni, Donna Elvira (sop), comes searching for him and Leporello tells her of Giovanni's unfaithfulness, reading her the long list of his conquests and their countries of origin in the Catalogue Aria **(1)**. He suggests that Elvira gives up the chase. A peasant-girl, Zerlina (sop), is to marry Masetto (bass). Giovanni plans to seduce Zerlina, and offers to host their celebrations at his castle. Zerlina is flattered by Giovanni's attentions and would have succumbed **(2)**, but Elvira comes to her rescue. In the subsequent imbroglio, Anna recognizes Giovanni's voice as that of her attacker and her father's killer and begs

ABOVE **Donna Elvira (Giselle Allen) and Donna Anna (Susannah Glanville) at the masked ball given by Don Giovanni (Roderick Williams), Opera North, Leeds, 2005**

RIGHT *Così fan tutte*, English Touring Opera, 2004: Leslie John Flanagan (Guglielmo), Amy Freston (Despina), and Gardar Thor Cortes (Ferrando)

Ottavio to help her revenge him, to which he agrees **(3)**. (This aria is sometimes omitted.) Zerlina meanwhile begs Masetto to forgive her for flirting with the Don **(4)**. At a masked ball given by Giovanni for the local peasants ("Fin ch'han dal vino" – "Now prepare a great feast"), Elvira, Anna, and Ottavio arrive, disguised. They remove their masks and accuse Giovanni of murder, but he escapes. Ottavio asks his friends to console Anna **(5)**. Elvira describes her feelings for Giovanni **(6)**. Giovanni meets Leporello in the local cemetery and laughs as he boasts that he has seduced his servant's wife. A mysterious voice tells him he will not laugh tomorrow. Giovanni and Leporello find a statue of the Commendatore bearing an inscription threatening vengeance. Giovanni insists that Leporello must invite the statue to supper. Anna explains to Ottavio that she does love him but cannot contemplate marriage whilst mourning for her father **(7)**. As Giovanni dines, waited on by Leporello, the statue enters and tells him to repent his ways and lead a better life. Giovanni refuses, and takes the statue's hand. He is pulled into the flames of hell. The rest of the characters vow to carry on with their own lives, Elvira to a convent, Ottavio continuing his wooing of Anna, Zerlina and Masetto settling down together – and Leporello goes off to seek a new master.

MUSIC (1) Leporello: *Madamina, il catalogo è questo – Little lady, here is the list*; **(2)** Zerlina/Giovanni duet: *Là ci darem la mano – There will I take your hand*; **(3)** Don Ottavio: *Dalla sua pace – On her peace of mind*; **(4)** Zerlina: *Batti, batti, o bel Masetto – Beat me, beat me, dear Masetto*; **(5)** Don Ottavio: *Il mio tesoro – My dearest one*; **(6)** Elvira: *Mi tradì… – I was betrayed…*; **(7)** Donna Anna: *Non mi dir, bell'idol mio – Say not, my beloved*.

COSÌ FAN TUTTE, OSSIA LA SCUOLA DEGLI AMANTI

(*Thus are all Women, or The School for Lovers*), 1789

Even less is known about the creation of this, the last of the three great Mozart–da Ponte operas, than about *Figaro*. It is assumed that it was commissioned for Vienna after a successful revival there of *Figaro* in August 1789. It had been a difficult year for Mozart and his wife, Constanze: she was seriously ill during her fifth pregnancy and the baby girl died within an hour of her birth in November. Mozart himself had a period of illness and was unable to work. But the year saw the completion of the first Prussian quartet (he composed a group of three, commissioned by King Friedrich Wilhelm II of Prussia), the clarinet quintet, one of his most sublime

works, and a large piano sonata (K576) as well as this opera. For many years *Così fan tutte* was regarded as a frivolous comedy, but it is now recognized as a comedy with a savage and painful undercurrent. The comedy may be there in the words, but the tenderness and beauty of the music lift the opera to another plane.

SYNOPSIS The action takes place in the Bay of Naples at the time of composition. The sisters Fiordiligi (sop) and Dorabella (sop/mez) are engaged to, respectively, Guglielmo (bass-bar) and Ferrando (ten). The men boast to their friend Don Alfonso (bar/bass) of their fiancées' unshakeable faithfulness. Alfonso assures them that all women can be unfaithful and sets about proving this to them, with the innocent help of their maid Despina (sop). He tells the young ladies that the men have been ordered to join their regiment immediately, and tears follow as Alfonso and the sisters wave farewell **(1)**. After their departure, the girls are in despair, Dorabella explaining how she feels **(2)**, refusing to be cheered up by Despina, who tries to tell them there are plenty more fish in the sea and they should enjoy themselves in their fiancés' absence **(3)**. Enter two handsome Albanians, "friends of Don Alfonso" – really Guglielmo and Ferrando in disguise. They set about wooing the ladies. At first the sisters are able to resist the men's advances, especially Fiordiligi **(4)**, which greatly boosts Ferrando's

ABOVE LEFT **Two great baritones of the 20th century: Tito Gobbi as Don Giovanni (left) and Geraint Evans as Leporello at the Royal Opera House, Covent Garden, 1963**

confidence (**5**), but gradually they weaken. The first to capitulate is Dorabella, who decides she will "take the dark one" – Guglielmo, her sister's fiancé. Soon Fiordiligi is also won over – by Ferrando, but at the same time she feels guilty about betraying Guglielmo (**6**). The two men, of course, are distressed to realize that their faithful fiancées can be seduced in their apparent absence and they will have to admit that Alfonso was right about them. A double wedding is arranged and a notary summoned to carry out the ceremony. The notary is Despina in disguise. Amidst the celebrations after the marriage contracts have been signed, a band is heard playing on the shore announcing the return of the regiment. The new bridegrooms are hastily hidden – and come back a few minutes later as themselves, returning from battle to reclaim their faithful loved ones. Alfonso makes sure the men see the marriage contracts and the girls, overcome with remorse and embarrassment, try to explain what has happened. Guglielmo and Ferrando draw their swords and set off to find their rivals, to return wearing part of their Albanian costumes. All is revealed. Alfonso has been proved right. Despina is mortified to realize she has been lured into helping to deceive her mistresses. And the four young lovers? How will they now pair off? Will each girl return to her original fiancé? Will she want to, knowing how she has been deceived?

ABOVE **The Three Boys on their triple cycle in Welsh National Opera's production of** *Die Zauberflöte*, **2005, designed by Julian Crouch**

Producers of this opera have to decide which ending they prefer. Sometimes they do not make the decision – all four lovers leave the stage separately and the audience is left to decide for itself.

MUSIC (**1**) Don Alfonso/Fiordiligi/Dorabella trio: *Soave sia il vento – May the breezes blow gently*; (**2**) Dorabella: *Smanie implacabili – May those terrible pangs*; (**3**) Despina: *In uomini, in soldati – In men, in soldiers*; (**4**) Fiordiligi: *Come scoglio – Like a rock*; (**5**) Ferrando: *Un'aura amorosa – A breath of love*; (**6**) Fiordiligi: *Per pietà – Have pity on me*.

DIE ZAUBERFLÖTE
(*The Magic Flute*), 1790–1

The genesis of this opera remains as obscure as that of his previous works as discussed above. The librettist was Emanuel Schikaneder, an actor, singer, composer, and theatre manager in Vienna, whom Mozart had known for about 10 years since they met in Salzburg whilst Schikaneder's company was on tour. Composer and librettist worked on the opera together. Like Mozart, Schikaneder was a Freemason and in the opera the Freemasons are represented by the Temple's brotherhood. The first performance was quite a "family affair": Schikaneder played Papageno, Benedikt Schack, a singer and also a composer, was

Tamino, and the Queen of Night was Mozart's sister-in-law, Josepha Hofer, who was a member of Schikaneder's company. It was an immediate success: in the two years after its composition, *Die Zauberflöte* had nearly 200 performances – but the composer died only 10 weeks after completing the score.

SYNOPSIS Tamino (ten), a prince of debatable nationality, is chased by a snake and falls unconscious. He is found by Three Ladies (sop, sop, mez) who kill the snake and depart to tell their mistress the Queen of Night (sop) what has happened. As Tamino awakens, the birdcatcher Papageno (bar) enters (**1**) and claims to have killed the snake himself. His lie is overheard by the Three Ladies, who padlock his mouth. They give Tamino a portrait of the Queen of Night's daughter Pamina (sop), with whom he immediately falls in love (**2**). The Queen will agree to their marriage if he rescues Pamina (**3**), who is being held prisoner by the High Priest Sarastro (bass). The Three Ladies give Tamino a magic flute and Papageno a set of magic bells. These instruments will always protect them as they set out to rescue Pamina and to prove Tamino's worthiness to be her husband. The two men are guided on their way by Three Boys (boy sops/sops). The moor Monostatos (ten) tries to seduce Pamina, but is frightened away by the arrival of the strange-looking Papageno. The birdcatcher explains to Pamina that Tamino loves her (**4**).

Tamino plays his flute and wild animals come to listen to him. Papageno brings Pamina to meet Tamino, but Monostatos chases them and Papageno uses his magic bells which bewitch Monostatos and his slaves. Sarastro arrives with his priests and demands to know why Pamina is trying to escape. She explains, and then sees Tamino for the first time. The couple embrace. Sarastro and his priests **(5)** tell Tamino he must undergo trials of water and fire before he can be admitted to the brotherhood and marry Pamina. He must remain silent throughout. Papageno finds this impossible, and chats to an old crone, who tells him she has a boyfriend called Papageno – and she then disappears. Pamina cannot understand Tamino's refusal to speak to her **(6)**. Nevertheless, she joins him in his trials and they succeed in passing the tests, guided by the magic flute. Papageno is filled with thoughts of love **(7)**. The old crone reappears and turns into the beautiful Papagena (sop), whilst Tamino and Pamina are united before Sarastro.

> **MUSIC** (1) Papageno: *Der Vogelfänger bin ich ja – I am the birdcatcher*; **(2)** Tamino: *Dies Bildnis ist bezaubernd schön – This portrait is more beautiful*; **(3)** Queen of Night: *O zittre nicht – Have no fear*; **(4)** Papageno/Pamina: *Bei Männern, welche Liebe fühlen – Men who feel the call of love*; **(5)** Sarastro and his priests: *O Isis und Osiris*; **(6)** Pamina: *Ach ich fühl's – Ah, I feel it*; **(7)** Papageno: *Ein Mädchen oder Weibchen – A little maid or wife*.

LA CLEMENZA DI TITO
(*The clemency of Titus*), 1791

For the coronation of Emperor Leopold II as King of Bohemia, Prague asked Salieri to compose an opera. Only when he made it clear that he was too busy to accept the commission was Mozart approached, in July 1791 while he was still writing *Die Zauberflöte*. This left him only about six weeks in which to write the opera, but it is known that some of the music was composed – and performed in

concert – some months earlier than that and by the time he arrived in Prague at the end of August that year, he had almost completed the score. This was the first *opera seria* Mozart had written since *Idomeneo* more than 10 years earlier. Caterino Mazzolà, the Dresden court poet who had recently replaced da Ponte in Vienna, adapted the libretto from Metastasio's text. This was a wise choice: as a result of Leopold's enlightened rule whilst Grand Duke of Tuscany, including the abolition of torture, he

was known as "the German Titus" and was widely identified with the opera's eponymous hero. Titus is the only historical character to have a role in the opera, which is more static than any of Mozart's previous operas. There is little interaction between the characters, who in their arias express their inner thoughts and feelings.

SYNOPSIS Mozart's last opera is set in Rome, AD 79–81. The Emperor Tito (ten) is planning to marry Berenice, daughter of Agrippa of Judea, much to the distress of Vitellia (sop), daughter of the deposed Emperor Vitellius. Helped by Sesto (mez), a young Roman nobleman who is in love with her, Vitellia plots to assassinate Tito (1). Sesto's friend Annio (mez) is in love with Servilia (sop), Sesto's sister. But Tito has changed his mind and has decided he no longer wants to marry Berenice. He wants to marry Servilia instead (2). She tells him of her love for Annio and the Emperor gives them his blessing and switches his attentions to Vitellia. Unaware of his change of heart, she has continued with her plot to kill him, promising to marry Sesto if he will murder Tito. As he reluctantly sets off to do so (3), Annio and Publio (bass), the Captain of the Guard, come to tell Vitellia she has been chosen as the future Empress. Sesto cannot anyway bring himself to murder his beloved Emperor and Vitellia, delighted to be the future Empress, prevents him confessing her part in the plot. Publio arrests Sesto, who has admitted his involvement but is determined not to reveal Vitellia's part in the assassination plot and he confesses his anguish to Tito (4). Annio pleads for Tito to show mercy to his friend. Servilia begs Vitellia to save Sesto. Tito, keen to be seen by his people as a compassionate ruler (5), tears up Sesto's death warrant. Vitellia, anxious to help this man who has not betrayed her, tells Tito of her guilt (6) and is also forgiven. Thus Tito demonstrates his clemency, and announces that he will devote the rest of his life to the service of Rome.

> **MUSIC** (1) Sesto/Vitellia duet: *Come ti piace imponi – Command me as you will*; (2) Tito: *Del più sublime soglio – From the most splendid of thrones*; (3) Sesto: *Parto, ma tu, ben mio – I go, but, my dearest*; (4) Sesto: *Deh, per questo istante solo – Ah, for this one moment*; (5) Tito: *Se all'impero – If it is necessary for a ruler to have a hard heart*; (6) Vitellia: *Non più di fiore – No more shall the flowers*.

Other operas of note

Four further operas by Mozart, whilst not considered as important as the seven described above, are occasionally produced by major companies or at opera festivals. The first of these is *La finta giardiniera* (*The Feigned Gardener*), composed in 1774 when he was 18. It was produced in Munich the following year, in New York in 1927, and in London in 1930. Since then it has appeared sporadically. It is a light-hearted comedy, with music easy on the ear but without any memorable arias or

ABOVE Sarah Connolly sings the *travesti* role of Sesto in English National Opera's 2005 production by David McVicar of *La clemenza di Tito*

ensembles. *Mitridate, re di Ponto* was an even earlier composition, written in 1770 when Mozart was just 14. A *dramma per musica* in three acts, it was produced in Milan the same year and Salzburg the following year. It did not reach London until 1979 or New York until 1985 (both in concert versions), but has since been staged both in England and the USA. It was produced at Covent Garden in 1992 and showed that, when well sung and with spectacular designs and costumes, it is worth the occasional staging. *Lucio Silla* was composed in 1772 and had its first performance that year in Milan. It waited until 1967 for its London première and 1968 for its first production in the USA (in Baltimore). It is a long work, very much in the Baroque mould, and is unlikely to enter the regular repertory of opera companies. (The same drama was also set to music by other composers, including J C Bach in 1775.) *Il re pastore* (*The Shepherd King*), usually described as a "Serenata", has a text by Metastasio that had been set many times before, usually in honour of Habsburg princes. The first performance was in 1775 in the Archbishop's Palace, Salzburg having no theatre or operatic tradition. It was given as a cantata, with minimum scenery. The music shares several themes with instrumental music that Mozart was composing at the same time, but it is not a very dramatic work. After this unsatisfactory performance, it was five years before Mozart's next opera was produced.

In 2006 Salzburg honoured its most famous son on the 250th anniversary of his birth by wall-to-wall productions of his operas, the first time this has ever been undertaken. In addition to those discussed above, a further 12 works could be seen and heard, including all his teenage operas and even those that were unfinished. It is an undertaking that only a festival of Salzburg's eminence and financial backing could even consider, and whether it was worth the effort is debatable.

LEFT Pamina and Tamino face Sarastro in San Francisco Opera's 1987 production by John Cox of *Die Zauberflöte,* designed by David Hockney

Beethoven

Ludwig van Beethoven
(1770–1827)

WHERE TO START – AND FINISH
Fidelio (Beethoven's only opera)

Ludwig van Beethoven is one of the very few composers who changed the face of every musical form in which he worked (as did Monteverdi, Wagner, and Schoenberg). He was born in Bonn in 1770, his father's family having emigrated from Belgium – hence the Flemish *van* rather than the German *von.* Young Ludwig was taught piano mainly by his father and some uninspiring teachers. He made his first visit to Vienna at the age of 16 and it is thought he played for Mozart. In 1792 he was invited to study there with Haydn, who was impressed by some of his compositions. Despite his uncouth manner, he was soon patronized by the aristocracy, who recognized his genius both as a pianist and later as a composer, and for his first two years in Vienna he stayed in the home of Prince Karl von Lichnowsky.

Beethoven lived for the rest of his life in Vienna, composing music for the next 30 years in every genre. His first major appearance on the platform as composer as well as performer was in 1795 when he played his B♭ Piano Concerto (No.2 op.19). His First Symphony was premièred in 1800 and between then and his death he produced another eight symphonies, four more piano concertos, a violin concerto, the Triple Concerto (for piano, violin and cello), 32 piano sonatas, 16 string quartets, piano trios, choral works, songs, and many other orchestral and instrumental works, the majority of which are still in the regular repertoire of orchestras, ensembles, and soloists worldwide. And, of most importance to this book, his only opera, *Fidelio.*

Although much of Beethoven's music may have been considered difficult and been misunderstood in his lifetime, it was never neglected and his major works were all performed within a very short time of their composition. His tragedy was the onset, as early as 1798, of deafness. This steadily worsened, bringing an early end to his career as a virtuoso. By 1819 it was possible to have a conversation with him only by writing in his "conversation books", which have been preserved and published. The distress that the deafness caused him led him to contemplate suicide, feelings that he expressed in the Heiligenstadt Testament, a document written in October 1802, addressed to his brothers and found after his death. In it he said "how could I possibly admit an infirmity in the one sense which ought to be more perfect in me than in others?". He never married, though he had many female friends. Mystery still surrounds the identity of the woman he addressed as his "Immortal Beloved" in passionate letters of 1812 that were found after his death. He was made a Freeman of the City of Vienna in 1815 and when he died in 1827 his funeral was a national occasion, with some 20,000 people lining the streets of Vienna.

FIDELIO, ODER DER TRIUMPH DER EHELICHEN LIEBE
(*Fidelio, or The Triumph of Married Love*), 1805–14
Beethoven's only opera is in two acts to a libretto by Josef von Sonnleithner (1766–1835), based on *Léonore, ou l'Amour conjugal* by the French librettist Jean-Nicolas Bouilly (1763–1842). It had been set by the French composer and tenor Pierre Gaveaux and the same plot was set in 1804 as the opera *Leonore* by the Italian Ferdinando Paer (1771–1839). The heroine is Leonore, known as Fidelio when she is disguised as a man. The opera had a long and complicated gestation. It was first performed in three acts in Vienna in 1805, conducted by the composer. Beethoven's friend Stephan von Breuning (1774–1827) reduced it to two acts, in which version it was given again in Vienna the following year, 1806. The libretto was then revised by Georg Friedrich Treitschke (1776–1842), further revision of the music took place and it received its third Vienna "première" in 1814. It was produced in London in 1832 and in New York in 1839. The original three-act version of 1805 has occasionally been produced in modern times. *Fidelio* is the best-known example of a "rescue opera", a genre of opera dating from the time of the French Revolution, where the hero or heroine is rescued at the eleventh hour by an act of great heroism or sacrifice. The heroine here is Leonore, who rescues her imprisoned husband Florestan just in time to prevent him being killed by Pizarro.

The overtures for the opera, of which there are four, deserve discussion. Three of them bear the name of the heroine (*Leonore No.1, No.2,* and *No.3*), the fourth the name of the opera. The last of these, *Fidelio,* was composed for the 1814 version (but was not ready in time) and is the one usually used in opera houses and described below. The three *Leonore* overtures are really tone-poems and are too long for use before the opera begins. *Leonore No.3* (1806) is often played as an entr'acte between the two scenes of Act 2

of the opera. *Leonore No.2* was probably composed in 1804 or 1805 for the première, and *No.1* in 1807 for a Prague performance which never materialized. All three are played in concert-halls and contain the famous off-stage trumpet call announcing the arrival of Don Fernando.

SYNOPSIS In a prison near 18th-century Seville, a Spanish nobleman Florestan (ten) has been imprisoned by his political enemy, Pizarro, (bar) who plans to murder him before the king's minister, Don Fernando (bass), an old friend and supporter of Florestan, arrives to inspect the prison. Florestan is guarded by the chief gaoler Rocco (bass), whose assistant Jaquino (ten) is in love with Rocco's daughter, Marzelline (sop). But Marzelline has become attracted to her father's new assistant Fidelio, who is Florestan's wife Leonore (sop), disguised as a man. Leonore suspects that her husband is in the prison's death-cell and has taken the job in order to rescue him.

Pizarro tries to bribe Rocco to kill Florestan, but Rocco will only agree to dig the grave in an old well in the dungeons – he stops short of murder. Pizarro orders that a trumpet be sounded in warning on the arrival of Don Fernando. Fidelio/Leonore overhears this conversation and sings her most difficult aria (1). After Pizarro has departed, she persuades

Rocco to allow all the prisoners out into the sunshine for a short while, where they sing one of opera's most famous choruses (2). When Leonore proves to be a hard-worker and physically strong, Rocco allows her to accompany him into the dungeons to dig the grave for the condemned prisoner, who is first heard as he sings about the darkness down there (3). When Leonore sees the prisoner and hears him speak, her suspicion is confirmed – it is Florestan who is manacled there. She persuades Rocco to allow him some water and bread. Pizarro has heard that Don Fernando is approaching the prison and descends to the dungeon to kill Florestan. As he raises his dagger, Leonore places herself between Pizarro and the prisoner, declaring "First kill his wife!" Pizarro would murder them both, but Leonore takes out a pistol. A trumpet is heard announcing Fernando's arrival. Pizarro flees and Florestan and Leonore are reunited (4). Don Fernando recognizes his old friend (5), whom he believed dead, and insists that the brave wife should be the one to unlock her husband's chains and set him free. The other prisoners are also released and joined by their families to listen to Don Fernando's address. As they all sing of their joy (6), poor Marzelline has to accept that the "man" she loves is, in fact, Florestan's wife.

MUSIC (1) Leonore: *Abscheulicher! – Abominable devil!*; (2) Prisoners' chorus: *O welche Lust, in freier Luft – Oh what joy to breathe freely in the open air*; (3) Florestan: *Gott! Welch' Dunkel hier! – God, how dark it is here!*; (4) Florestan/Leonore duet: *O namenlose Freude! – O nameless joy!*; (5) Don Fernando: *Des besten Königs Wink und Wille – At the wish and suggestion of the best of kings*; (6) Ensemble: *O Gott, welch' ein Augenblick – O God, what a moment.*

ABOVE RIGHT **A matchless Florestan, Canadian tenor Jon Vickers at Covent Garden, 1983**

Haydn and the Rest

Apart from the three composers whose operas have been discussed in detail, and who can be regarded as Classical composers in every sense of the word, other composers of this period did write operas with varying degrees of success. C P E Bach and J C Bach (p.26) have been discussed, as has the Italian Giovanni Pergolesi (p.26). The most prolific composer of operas in the Classical period was the Austrian-born **FRANZ JOSEPH HAYDN (1732–1809)**, who wrote 20. Some of them are lost, but 15 are extant and were composed in the 25-year period from 1766 to 1791. Haydn had been sent to Vienna at the age of eight as a choirboy at St Stephen's Cathedral. When his voice broke at the age of 17 he had to earn a living and became a teacher and accompanist for the Italian composer and singing teacher Nicola

Porpora (1686–1768), who had among his private pupils the two castrati Farinelli and Caffarelli – Farinelli made his début in one of Porpora's operas in 1720. In the 1750s Haydn worked for two aristocrats until, in 1761, he was employed as *Vice-Kapellmeister* at Eisenstadt, Hungary, by Prince Paul Esterházy, a great music lover. Prince Nikolaus Esterházy, who succeeded his brother, was equally passionate about music. He built the palace of Eszterháza, modelled on Versailles, in an isolated area of Hungary on the banks of the Neusiedlersee. Haydn remained with the household as court composer for 30 years and it was for performances at the Esterházy court that he wrote his operas. Some of these are occasionally produced, often at opera festivals. Most are based on mythical stories and several use the same stories as those used by Handel (*Orlando paladino*) or Gluck (*Armida, Orfeo ed Euridice*). Haydn's Orfeo opera is often produced under its original title of *L'anima del filosofo* (*The Spirit of Philosophy*). Composed in 1791 (his last opera), it did not receive its première until 1951 at the Maggio Musicale in Florence, with Maria Callas as Euridice and Boris Christoff as her father Creonte. In good productions, well sung, several of Haydn's operas are worth an airing and can be quite amusing, as has been shown in England by Garsington Opera Festival, where six of his operas have been produced to considerable acclaim, including *Il mondo della luna* and *La fedeltà premiata*. But Haydn's genius lay in his orchestral, choral, and chamber music.

FRANZ SCHUBERT (1797–1828) was born in Vienna, the son of a schoolmaster who was his first teacher. At 11 he became a chorister in the imperial chapel, learned the violin, and became a pupil of Salieri. When his voice broke in 1813 he became an assistant teacher to his father, but he had already that year composed his first symphony. He attended many opera performances in Vienna and wrote his first true opera, *Der Teufels*

Lustschloss (*The Devil's Pleasure House*), in 1814. He wrote several more operas, as well as music for dramas and ballets, and the influence of Mozart and of Beethoven's *Fidelio* can be heard in the music. In 1815 he collaborated for the first time with the poet Johann Mayrhofer in an unsuccessful two-act *Singspiel, Die Freunde von Salamanka* (*The Friends from Salamanca*), the dialogue of which is lost, possibly destroyed by the poet himself. Schubert compensated for this disappointment by successfully setting 47 of Mayrhofer's poems. Two of his operas, *Die Zwillingsbrüder* (*The Twin Brothers*) and *Die Zauberharfe* (*The Magic Harp*), brought his works to public attention in 1820 without being regarded as great successes, although the former had the famous Austrian baritone Michael Vogl singing as both the twins. His best opera, *Fierrabras*, composed in 1823, has had several modern productions in Britain and in the USA. It is long, and neither the drama nor, it must be said, the music are great enough to hold the attention of the listener. None of his operas was successful, his fame – and his genius – lying in other musical genres. Musically they are not in the same class as his orchestral or vocal compositions.

ABOVE LEFT Haydn's *L'anima del filosofo*, staged at Covent Garden in 2001 for Cecilia Bartoli (as Euridice)

ABOVE Domenico Cimarosa (1749–1801)

LEFT Detail of the Italian composer Luigi Cherubini (1760–1842) and his muse, painted by one of the greatest portraitists of the time, Jean-Auguste-Dominique Ingres (1780–1867)

GIACOMO MEYERBEER (1791–1864) was the German-born son of a rich Jewish merchant, his mother being from a wealthy banking family. He spent most of his life in France, as did the Cologne-born **JACQUES OFFENBACH** (1819–80). Their major compositions fall more naturally into the Romantic period and they will be discussed with the French Romantics (see p.64), with whom they have most in common.

Among Italian opera composers of the late Classical period is **DOMENICO CIMAROSA** (1749–1801), known primarily for one opera, which receives a considerable number of performances in a year without being classifiable as regular repertory. Cimarosa was a popular composer in the late 18th century who wrote over 80 operas. He spent some time (1787–91) at the Russian court of Empress Catherine but was happier when he moved to Vienna where, in 1792, his wrote his very successful *Il matrimonio segreto* (*The secret marriage*). It was so popular that it was translated into several languages and widely performed in Europe. It is a real *opera buffa,* highly regarded by Verdi and by the German critic Eduard Hanslick (the man who later pilloried Wagner, but who was an intelligent and deep-thinking critic). Soon after, Cimarosa returned to Italy

where, in Naples in 1799, he was imprisoned for involvement with a short-lived political movement. He was released after four months and exiled to Venice where he eventually died.

Born in Florence, **LUIGI CHERUBINI** (1760–1842) was from a musical background and was composing music of considerable facility by the time he reached his middle teens. He visited England where some of his early operas were performed without much success. Encouraged by his friend the violinist and composer Giovanni Battista Viotti (1755–1824, who later became director of the Italian opera in Paris), Cherubini moved in 1787 to the French capital and lived there for the rest of his life. His *Les deux journées* of 1800 (known in English as *The Watercarrier*) is an early "rescue opera", with good tunes, which was popular in France and Germany into the 20th century, but lost ground after that. Cherubini arrived in the French capital at the time of the battles between the rival supporters of Piccinni and Gluck and, like many of the latter's pre-revolutionary works, Cherubini's masterpiece, the three-act *Médée* written in 1797, uses a Classical story of Médée's hatred of Jason and her love of her children. It is an intense work both dramatically and musically. It was not too well received at

its première, but soon gained ground and was admired by Beethoven, Weber, and Wagner. *Médée* (which in many ways is a Romantic rather than a Classical opera) was revived for Maria Callas in Florence in 1953, and she subsequently sang it in Venice, Rome, Milan, Dallas, and London.

GASPARE SPONTINI (1774–1851) was another Italian composer who found his feet in Paris, where he achieved overnight success with *La vestale* (*The Vestal Virgin*), composed in 1807. Spontini was a great melodist and an imaginative and often experimental orchestrator. He was also an early user of the metronome. In 1819 he moved to Berlin, but the works he produced in Germany were never of the same quality as those written during his time in Paris, where he was much respected by the musical fraternity, including Berlioz. Spontini's works did not survive long after his death, with only *La vestale* having the occasional airing.

As can be deduced from the above paragraphs, music was already showing signs of moving towards more dramatic subjects and more emotional music. In other words, the Classical is giving way to the Romantic era, which will be discussed in the following pages.

ABOVE RIGHT Rosa Ponselle, a great *bel canto* soprano of the early 20th century, as Giulia in Spontini's *La vestale*

As romantic as it comes: Detail from Turner's *Venice, the Bridge of Sighs* connecting the Prison (left) and the Doges' Palace (right)

The Romantic Era

around 1830 to 1900

Although there are elements of the romantic in music of all periods, the term is generally applied to music written from about 1830 to 1900, and is also applied to other art forms. In literature the term covers a shorter period, the 20 years from 1830 to 1850. In European literature it found its expression in the romantic novels and nature-poetry of Wordsworth, Byron, Balzac, Hugo, Heine, Goethe, and others. Pushkin in Russia and Poe in America reflected a similar movement.

FEATURED OPERAS

ROSSINI
Il barbiere di Siviglia *1816*
La Cenerentola *1817*

DONIZETTI
Anna Bolena *1830*
L'elisir d'amore *1832*
Maria Stuarda *1834*
Lucia di Lammermoor *1835*
Don Pasquale *1843*

BELLINI
I Capuleti e i Montecchi *1830*
La sonnambula *1831*
Norma *1831*
I puritani *1834–5*

VERDI
Nabucco *1841, 1842*
Rigoletto *1851*
Il trovatore *1853*
La traviata *1853*
Simon Boccanegra *1857, 1881*
Un ballo in maschera *1859*
Don Carlos *1867, 1884*
Aida *1870–1*
Otello *1884–6, 1887*
Falstaff *1893*

WEBER
Der Freischütz *1817–21*

WAGNER
Der fliegende Holländer *1840–1*
**Tannhäuser und der Sängerkrieg
  auf Wartburg** *1843–5 and rev.;
  1859–61*
Lohengrin *1845–8*

Der Ring des Nibelungen
  Das Rheingold *1853–4*
  Die Walküre *1854–6*
  Siegfried *1856–7, 1869–71*
  Götterdämmerung *1869–74*
Tristan und Isolde *1856–9*
Die Meistersinger von Nürnberg
  1845–67
Parsifal *1865–82*

OFFENBACH
Les contes d'Hoffmann *1877–80*

BERLIOZ
Les troyens *1856–8, 1859–60*
Béatrice et Bénédict *1860–2, 1863*

GOUNOD
Faust *1856–9, 1868–9*
Roméo et Juliette *1865–7*

SAINT-SAËNS
Samson et Dalila *1868–77*

BIZET
Carmen *1873–5*

MASSENET
Manon *1882–3*
Werther *1885–7*

MUSORGSKY
Boris Godunov *1867–9, 1871–2*

TCHAIKOVSKY
Eugene Onegin *1877–8*
The Queen of Spades *1890*

SMETANA
The Bartered Bride *1863–6,
  1869–70*

The Romantic Era

In the visual arts in England, Romanticism was reflected in the paintings of Turner, Constable, and the Pre-Raphaelites. In both literature and the visual arts there developed at the same time a taste for the gruesome and the macabre, with the writing of horror novels and the portraying in pictures of scenes of violent death and madness. After the middle of the century, literature and art moved away from Romanticism into a period of realism, with the novels of writers such as Émile Zola, George Sand, and the Brontë sisters and the predominance of the French Impressionists.

In music, the Romantic period encompassed almost exclusively European composers. Although the number of American states was expanding, there was no classical music tradition and composers there were usually European immigrants. A few native composers were beginning to emerge, but it was not until the turn of the 19th to 20th century that the first truly American composer was recognized internationally in the shape of Charles Ives. Russia mirrored Europe, although their talented musicians were mostly educated abroad. In addition, nationalism played an even greater part in Russia than in Europe and in 1834–6 Glinka (see p.113) composed what can be considered the first genuinely Russian opera, *A Life for the Tsar*. He, like his fellow composers, was influenced by Pushkin's writings.

The Romantic composers considered the expression of emotions in music to be more important than the strictness of form in composition so important to the Classical composers. The new and the sensational gained in importance, as did experimentation. This led to two main developments: firstly of new musical forms such as the large tone-poem, the miniature nocturne, the art-song often with words by some of the poets already mentioned, and large-scale opera; and secondly, the rise of the virtuoso instrumentalists who in turn inspired composers to write yet more difficult music for them to play.

Opera became even more "grand", sometimes featuring the supernatural (as in Weber's *Der Freischütz*), or having political themes, tales of aggression, and fights for freedom.

The lead for this had been given by Beethoven's *Fidelio* (see pp.58–9) with its political prisoners and heroic wife saving her condemned husband – an obvious example of the "rescue opera". It is debatable whether Beethoven should be classed as a Classical or a Romantic composer – he could be said to have started as the former and ended as the latter. Nationalism, as has been mentioned, loomed large in the new Russian operas, and continued to do so well into the 20th century – think no further than Prokofiev's *War and Peace*. But not only in Russia. The same can be said of Polish and Bohemian composers. And the two greatest names in Romantic opera, the Italian Verdi and the German Wagner, both born in 1813 and whose careers ran parallel, had links to the nationalist movements in their countries that were reflected in their works. The natural successor to Wagner was Richard Strauss who was born in 1864 and lived until 1949. Is he a Romantic or a 20th-century composer? The same question can be asked about the Englishman Ralph Vaughan Williams and of several others whose composing lives continued well into the 20th century. The answer is they were both, and will be discussed in the next section as what we may call the "late-Romantics". It is never easy, and often not desirable, to categorize too severely. The music can speak for itself.

The first major opera composers to be classed as Romantic are the Italians Rossini, Donizetti, Bellini, and the German Weber. The first three of these developed the lighter side of Italian opera, but with a fair share of tragedy and drama. Their works were just as popular in France, where the native-born Massenet, Berlioz, Saint-Saëns, Bizet, and Gounod made their mark in opera, and where the German-born Meyerbeer and Offenbach flourished as French composers in style if not by nationality. In Russia, Glinka, Borodin, Musorgsky, Rimsky-Korsakov, and Tchaikovsky were Romantic – and nationalist – composers, and Eastern Europe entered the picture in the shape of Smetana. Weber, the first of the German Romantics, has already been mentioned, as has Wagner, and all these composers will be discussed in some detail. But the hotbed of full-blooded Romanticism in opera was surely Italy.

ABOVE **Brünnhilde on the rock, one of the 1911–12 illustrations by Arthur Rackham (1867–1939) for Margaret Armour's translations of the librettos of Wagner's *Ring***

RIGHT Engraving of a supernatural scene from
Weber's *Der Freischütz*

As so often, art mirrors life and in post-Napoleonic Italy a new society was emerging that needed the emotional and spiritual stimulus of the arts. Verdi reigned supreme in 19th-century Italian opera – and not only in Italy – parallelled only by Wagner in Germany, the twin operatic giants of the Romantic era.

The composers of that era, starting around the time of Giovanni Paisiello (1740–1816) and finishing with early Verdi, included Cherubini, Spontini (both of whom have been discussed among the Classical composers, see p.61), Giovanni Pacini (1796–1867), Saverio Mercadante (1795–1870), and many more, but three Italian composers born at the turn of the 18th to 19th centuries, Rossini, Donizetti, and Bellini, are generally acknowledged as the great *bel canto* composers. The literal translation of the Italian term *bel canto* is "beautiful singing" and we might suppose that this is a prerequisite for any opera performer. It is a term open to a variety of interpretations and has even been used by some early 20th-century musicologists, mainly in Germany, to describe the lyrical singing of the early Baroque era. But generally it has come to be associated with the special qualities of the elegant Italian singers of the late 18th and early 19th centuries. It implies performance in a lyrical rather than a declamatory style, where beauty of tone, *legato* phrasing, and a faultless technique are paramount. According to Rossini, *bel canto*

singing required a naturally beautiful voice, effortless delivery that could only be the result of a high degree of training, and a mastery of style that could not be taught but was instinctive and was further "absorbed" by listening to the best Italian singers of the day. This style of singing, and therefore these operas, had almost disappeared by the middle of the 19th century (Rossini is reported to have said in Paris in 1858: "…we have lost our *bel canto*"). But in the mid-20th century they began to be revived, largely due to the emergence of several singers, mainly female, but some male, with the voice and technique to perform them in the style that their composers intended. Some of the biggest names in this connection were the sopranos Maria Callas, Joan Sutherland, and Beverly Sills, the mezzo Marilyn Horne, and the tenors Nicolai Gedda (b. 1925) and Alfredo Kraus. Succeeding generations of singers have continued to perform these works, with artists such as Cecilia Bartoli leading the way.

The Romantic composers will be discussed geographically rather than chronologically. There are characteristics common to each nationality, such as the nationalism of the Russian and East European composers, which makes this a more logical way of looking at them. Starting with the Italian composers of the period, let us begin with the *bel canto* composers mentioned above.

ABOVE A gathering of Italian composers in the 19th century: (left to right) Bellini, Donizetti, Verdi, and Rossini

Rossini

Gioachino Rossini
(1792–1868)

LEFT **Gioachino Rossini (1792–1868)**

WHERE TO START
Il barbiere di Siviglia
La Cenerentola

WHERE TO GO NEXT
L'italiana in Algeri
Guillaume Tell

Born in Pesaro, the Italian town which, since 1980, holds an annual opera festival bearing his name, Rossini was the son of a soprano and a trumpeter and horn player. As a boy he sang in churches and played the harpsichord, piano, viola, cello, and horn, the last with his father as teacher. He wrote his first opera, *Demetrio e Polibio*, in 1806 whilst studying at the Bologna Liceo Musicale. He left the Liceo and moved to Venice in 1810 at the invitation of friends of his parents who ran a small opera company. He soon composed for them his first comic opera, *La cambiale di matrimonio* (*The Bill of Marriage*), which was quite successful and has occasionally been revived.

Two operas produced in Venice in 1813 established Rossini's reputation: his first serious opera (*opera seria*), *Tancredi*, based on Voltaire's tragedy of 1760; and another comic opera (*opera buffa*) *L'italiana in Algeri* (*The Italian Girl in Algiers*). In 1814, at the invitation of the impresario Domenico Barbaia, he became music director of the San Carlo opera house in Naples, where he remained for the next eight years. For this company he wrote several operas, but the one most familiar to opera-lovers, *Il barbiere di Siviglia* (*The Barber of Seville*) of 1816 and still one of the best-loved of comic operas, was written for Rome where it was premièred in February that year. In the same year he wrote *Otello* and this was followed by *La Cenerentola* (*Cinderella*) and *La gazza ladra* (*The Thieving Magpie*) in 1817. His last two operas were the comedy *Le Comte Ory* (1828) and the dramatic *Guillaume Tell* of 1829, both of which were premièred in Paris, where he then lived.

Rossini was fortunate to be able to call on many talented singers based in the Naples company, most significantly the soprano Isabella Colbran who created several of his roles between 1815 and 1823. Colbran, seven years older than Rossini, had worked in Naples from 1811, where she had become the mistress of Barbaia whom she left in 1815 in order to live with Rossini. They married in 1822 but formally separated in 1837.

Rossini settled in Paris in 1824, as director of the Théâtre-Italien. In the early 1830s he became close to the courtesan Olympe Pélissier, who had been the mistress of the painter Émile Vernet (1789–1863). In 1836 Rossini and Olympe returned to Italy. For the next 20 years he suffered almost constant physical and mental ill-health, and during this time he composed only three religious works and some smaller pieces. Isabella Colbran died in 1845, and the following year Rossini married Olympe. They settled once again in Paris in 1855, where Olympe was an outstanding society hostess. Rossini lived in Paris for the rest of his life and was at the city's artistic centre. He wrote no operas after 1829. Rossini died in 1868 and was buried in Paris (he was re-interred in Florence in 1887), many of the greatest singers of the day taking part in his funeral service.

Had he written nothing else, Rossini's reputation would be safe in the hands of *Il barbiere di Siviglia,* which has held its place ever since its early success and is a model of comic opera composition. In 1898, no less a judge than Verdi declared that "for abundance of ideas, comic verve, and truth of

ABOVE **Act 3 of Beaumarchais's play** *The Barber of Seville*, from which Rossini composed his most famous opera

RIGHT *Il barbiere di Siviglia*: Diana Damrau (Rosina), Peter Mattei (Figaro), and Juan Diego Flórez (Almaviva), Metropolitan Opera, NY, 2006

declamation, *Il barbiere di Siviglia* is the most beautiful *opera buffa* in existence." Despite all that has been composed since that date, I see little reason to argue with Verdi.

IL BARBIERE DI SIVIGLIA
(*The Barber of Seville*), 1816

Rossini's opera deals with the same major characters as Mozart's *Le nozze di Figaro* (see pp.52–3), but at an earlier stage in their lives. It was written for and premièred in Rome.

SYNOPSIS In 18th-century Seville Count Almaviva (ten) is unmarried and is wooing Rosina (mez, Mozart's Countess), ward of Dr Bartolo (bass), himself romantically interested in her. The Count's barber is Figaro (bar) and Rosina's singing teacher is Don Basilio (bass). The housekeeper Berta (sop) and Almaviva's servant Fiorello (bass) complete the cast.

At dawn, Almaviva is serenading beneath Rosina's window (**1**). Figaro enters, with his famous aria "Figaro here, Figaro there" (**2**). He tells Almaviva that Rosina is the ward of Dr Bartolo, who wants to marry her and keeps her locked in the house. Almaviva pretends to be a poor student called Lindoro. He bribes Figaro to help him enter the house. Rosina, attracted by the young "student", has written a letter to him (**3**) – there are many famous "letter songs" in opera. Don Basilio announces that the Count is in town in search of Rosina and suggests they spread gossip about him (**4**). Bartolo, suspicious of Rosina's behaviour, warns her not to try to fool him (**5**). Soldiers arrive to arrest the drunken Lindoro, but he shows them his official papers and to everyone's amazement they treat him with great respect as they depart. Rosina, Bartolo, Basilio, Berta, Almaviva, and Figaro express their confusion in a delightful ensemble (**6**), which brings the first act to an end.

Almaviva next poses as a pupil of Basilio, come to give Rosina a singing lesson. During the lesson Bartolo falls asleep and the young couple admit their love (**7**). Figaro manages to gain the key to the balcony window in order to help Rosina and "Lindoro" escape. When their plans are frustrated, Lindoro reveals his true identity to her. Bartolo admits defeat and gives their marriage his blessing.

MUSIC (**1**) Almaviva: *Ecco ridente in cielo – Lo in the smiling sky*; (**2**) Figaro: *Largo al factotum – Make way for the factotum*; (**3**) Rosina: *Una voce poco fa – The voice I heard a while ago*; (**4**) Don Basilio: *La calunnia – Calumny*; (**5**) Dr Bartolo: *A un dottor della mia sorte – When you try to fool the doctor*; (**6**) Sextet (Act 1 finale): *Freddo ed immobile – Frozen with fright and fear*; (**7**) Almaviva/ Rosina duet: *Contro un cor che accende amore – Who can stay the power of love.*

LA CENERENTOLA, OSSIA LA BONTÀ IN TRIONFO
(*Cinderella, or Goodness Triumphant*), 1817

This opera is loosely based on the classical fairy-tale. The libretto was by Rossini's friend Jacopo Ferretti who adapted it from earlier librettos written for Paris and Milan. In doing so, many of the features of the original fairy-tale were lost or altered – for instance, the glass slipper became a bracelet. Rossini borrowed the overture from one of his earlier operas, *La gazzetta* (1816), and much of the recitative and some arias were written by Luca Agolini, a young musician from Rome.

SYNOPSIS Angelina (mez), known as Cenerentola, is cruelly treated by her stepfather, Don Magnifico (bass), and her two stepsisters Tisbe (mez) and Clorinda (sop). In the kitchen of their house, Cinderella muses on her position and her dreams (**1**). A beggar enters and Cinderella gives him food and drink. She does not know that he is Alidoro (bass), tutor of Prince Ramiro (ten). It is announced that the prince himself will soon be arriving, searching for the most beautiful woman in the land to be his bride. Magnifico envisages his life when one of his daughters is on the throne (**2**). The prince arrives, disguised as his own valet Dandini (bass), and Cinderella and he admire each other (**3**). Dandini enters, acting as the prince, and invites the two sisters to a ball. Cinderella begs to go too, but Magnifico refuses. Alidoro asks for the third sister named on the census, but is told by Magnifico that she is dead.

RIGHT *La Cenerentola,* Luciano di Pasquale as Don Magnifico, Glyndebourne, 2002

After they have all left, Alidoro arrives to take Cinderella to the ball (**4**). Everyone, including Ramiro, admires the strangely familiar masked lady who has arrived – this is, of course, the beautifully attired Cinderella. She refuses the "prince's" advances as she is in love with "his valet". When he overhears this Ramiro is overjoyed; to test his sincerity Cinderella leaves, first giving Ramiro one of a pair of bracelets, and tells him that if he finds her again then she will marry him. Still not connecting the beautiful woman with the servant-girl he met earlier, Ramiro determines to find her and marry her (**5**). He searches from house to house and when he enters Magnifico's house he at once recognizes Cinderella as the lady he loves – and she is wearing the bracelet. At her wedding, Cinderella forgives Magnifico, Clorinda, and Tisbe for their treatment of her (**6**).

> **MUSIC** (**1**) Cenerentola: *Una volta c'era un re – Once there was a king*; (**2**) Don Magnifico: *Miei rampolli femminini – My female offspring*; (**3**) Don Ramiro/Cenerentola duet: *Un soave non so che – A sweet something*; (**4**) Alidoro: *Là del ciel nell'arcano profondo – In the secret depths of Heaven*; (**5**) Ramiro: *Si, ritrovarla io giuro – Yes, I swear to find her again*; (**6**) Cenerentola: *Non più mesta accanto al fuoco – No longer sad beside the fire.*

Other operas of note

Among Rossini's other operas are several that are produced irregularly but are worth hearing. They are never less than well constructed and dramatic or amusing, but the invention may be at a slightly lower level than in his two most popular works. The comedies include *L'italiana in Algeri* (*The Italian Girl in Algiers*, 1813), which from the start was very popular throughout Italy and was the first of his operas to be seen in Germany and Paris. It has regained some ground since the Second World War; *La gazza ladra* (*The Thieving Magpie*, 1817) concerns a servant-girl accused of stealing silver from her employer, saved from a death sentence when the true culprit is discovered to be a magpie. It is a long work, over 3½ hours of music – and

this may detract from its popularity – with less opportunity for florid vocal displays; and his penultimate opera, *Le Comte Ory*, set in France at the time of the Crusades, and with a French libretto. It was a huge success at its Paris première in 1828, and was performed in Europe and the USA over the next 20 years. It was revived in Florence in 1952 and has since received occasional productions. The more dramatic works include *Tancredi*, written for La Fenice, Venice. It had a favourable, rather than enthusiastic, reception but it was soon being performed in other Italian theatres. By the end of the century, in common with other *bel canto* works, it faded from the repertory, but since its revival in 1952, again in Florence, it has gained ground in Europe and the USA. *Otello* (1816) had a successful first performance and was staged in Italy and abroad until Verdi's opera appeared in 1887 (see pp.85–6) and wiped it off the map. Rossini wrote his last opera, *Guillaume Tell,* in 1829 when he was only 37. Based on Schiller's 1804 play *Wilhelm Tell*, it suffered from a poor, rambling libretto and its political subject. It is very long (about four hours) and slow-moving. The critics were quite enthusiastic when it was new but the public were not excited by it, despite the scene where Tell shoots the apple from his son's head.

ABOVE LEFT *La Cenerentola* is a modern production at the annual Rossini Opera Festival in Pesaro

Donizetti

Gaetano Donizetti
(1797–1848)

WHERE TO START
L'elisir d'amore
Lucia di Lammermoor
Don Pasquale

WHERE TO GO NEXT
Maria Stuarda
Anna Bolena

Gaetano Donizetti composed a large body of orchestral, chamber, choral, and vocal music, but little of any importance apart from his 65 operas. He was born in Bergamo where, just over 50 years later, he died. His parents were poor and not musical, but his talent was recognized early and he studied in his home town and in Bologna with some of the best teachers in Italy.

Donizetti's first opera was produced in Venice when he was 21 and brought him to the attention of the same impresario, Domenico Barbaia, who had brought Rossini to Naples, where Donizetti now moved. Over the next 12 years he wrote another 30 operas which were produced throughout Italy. In 1830 he had his first international success with *Anna Bolena*, which received its première

in Milan. As a result, he received commissions from all over Italy. In 1832 he composed the comedy *L'elisir d'amore* for Milan and in 1834–5 the dramas *Maria Stuarda* and *Lucia di Lammermoor*, both for Naples. From 1835 to 1837 he was professor of counterpoint at Naples Conservatory and became its director in 1837. In 1838 he settled in Paris and from 1842 to 1845 also was employed by the Habsburg court in Vienna, travelling between the two capital cities. In 1843, for Paris, he wrote what was to be his last major success, the comedy *Don Pasquale*.

Like his compatriot Rossini (see pp.66–8) Donizetti was able to write for a whole generation of superb singers. He composed quickly and in some ways this has been held against him and his works have been under-valued until quite recent times. (There has always been a tendency to consider this sort of "facility" something to sneer at and, nearer to our own time, the same accusation was hurled at Benjamin Britten's music.) Some of his comedies rival Rossini's and Verdi was to acknowledge his dramatic powers and to borrow from him melodically and rhythmically. It is not fanciful to regard Donizetti as the true precursor of Verdi.

Donizetti's personal life was punctuated by tragedy. In 1828 he had married Virginia Vasselli, whom he adored. Donizetti's parents died within a few weeks of each other in 1835–6 and in 1837 his wife died of cholera, aged 29, after giving birth to a stillborn child. She had had a previous stillbirth and also an abnormal baby who lived only 10 days. It is probable

that the deaths of his children were related to the syphilis that was to render Donizetti paralysed and mentally incapable by 1846. He was nursed by friends in his home town of Bergamo and died two years later, aged 51.

Several of Donizetti's lesser-known operas were revived in the late 20th century with varying degrees of success. But the five described below are his masterworks, all regularly in the international repertoire.

ANNA BOLENA
(*Anne Boleyn*), 1830

This was Donizetti's 30th opera and his first major success, no doubt because he had a librettist far superior to any with whom he had previously worked. Felice Romani (1788–1865) was an outstanding writer of words for music and the most sought-after librettist of his day.

Anna Bolena is an inaccurate but touching drama portraying the life of King Henry VIII's second wife, Anne Boleyn. Most of it was composed while Donizetti was staying at the villa on Lake Como of his friend the soprano Giuditta Pasta, who was to sing the title-role. It had a triumphant première in Milan, and was staged throughout Italy, in London and Paris the following year. It was successfully revived with Maria Callas in the title-role at La Scala in April 1957.

SYNOPSIS The opera opens in England in 1536, by which time the King (Enrico, bass) is losing interest in Anna (sop) in favour of her lady-in-waiting Jane Seymour (Giovanna, mez). Anna's servant and musician Smeton (mez, a

ABOVE **Gaetano Donizetti (1797-1848).**

ABOVE **Engraving of the gardens at Windsor Castle for a set design for Donizetti's *Anna Bolena*.**

travesti role), who is himself in love with her, reminds her of her first love, Riccardo (Lord Richard Percy, ten) **(1)**. Riccardo, recently returned from exile, has heard rumours of Anna's unhappiness and he questions her brother Rochefort (bass) **(2)**. At her brother's request, Anna agrees to see her former lover for a brief interview, not knowing that Smeton is hiding nearby and watching her. When she admits that the King no longer loves her, Riccardo declares his own love **(3)**. Frightened of the consequences, Anna tells him she will not see him again. He draws his sword and Smeton reveals himself, ready to defend Anna. The King enters and angrily accuses her of being unfaithful. Smeton offers to die to prove the Queen's innocence. Enrico insists she will defend herself in court and Anna realizes what fate awaits her **(4)**.

Giovanna tells her the King will spare her life if she admits her guilt and begs her to do so in the name of the King and also in the name of the next queen. Furious, Anna calls on heaven to punish her rival, at which the remorseful Giovanna falls at her feet begging forgiveness **(5)**. Anna, now realizing who her rival is, orders her to leave. Smeton, meanwhile, has

confessed to adultery with Anna, hoping this will save her life and Riccardo offers to die in her place. Anna reminds Enrico of his own infidelity and even Giovanna begs him to show mercy. In the Tower of London, Anna sings of her home and first love **(6)**. As she walks to the scaffold praying **(7)**, she hears the firing of cannons announcing the marriage of Enrico and Giovanna. Before her execution she calls for heaven to show mercy for her husband and his new wife **(8)**.

MUSIC (1) Smeton: *Come, innocente giovane – Unwitting youth*; **(2)** Riccardo: *Da quel di che, lei perduta – Since that day, having lost her*; **(3)** Riccardo: *S'ei t'abborre, lo t'amo ancora – If he loathes you, I still love you*; **(4)** Anna: *Giudici! Ad Anna! – Judges! For Anna!*; **(5)** Giovanna: *Dal mio cor punita io sono – By my heart I am punished*; **(6)** Anna: *Al dolce guidami castel natio – Lead me to the dear castle where I was born*; **(7)** Anna: *Cielo, a' miei lunghi spasimi – Heaven grant an end to my long agonies*; **(8)** Anna: *Coppia iniqua, l'estrema vendetta – Wicked couple, the final vengeance*.

L'ELISIR D'AMORE
(*The Elixir of Love*), 1832

During the composer's lifetime, this was his opera which had the most frequent performances and it has remained a firm international favourite. The comic libretto is again by Romani, who produced it within a week of the request, and Donizetti composed the music in two weeks in order to fulfil a commission for a Milan theatre that had been let down by another composer. It was an instant success, despite the composer's misgivings. He is said to have commented to his librettist: "…we have a German prima donna, a tenor who stammers, a *buffo* with a voice like a goat, and a French bass not up to much". He need not have worried.

SYNOPSIS In a 19th-century Italian village, the impoverished young farmer Nemorino (ten) is madly in love with a wealthy land-owner, Adina (sop), but too shy to confess his feelings to her. When he does eventually pluck up the courage, Adina declares that she can never love any one man **(1)**. The confident and conceited Sergeant Belcore (bar) has earlier proposed to Adina who asks for time to think about her answer.

ABOVE *L'elisir d'amore:* Nemorino (Luciano Pavarotti) surrounded by admiring girls, ROH, London, 1990

When the visiting quack Dr Dulcamara (bass) arrives to sell his wares for all ailments (2), Nemorino asks for help. Dulcamara sells him a bottle of "love-potion", which is really strong wine and he soon becomes inebriated. To Nemorino's dismay (3) Adina now accepts Belcore's proposal. At her wedding feast, Adina and Dulcamara sing a duet (4). She keeps delaying signing the marriage contract, waiting for Nemorino to arrive to witness the act. To earn money to buy more elixir, Nemorino has enlisted in the army, signing a contract produced by Belcore. The local girls learn that his rich uncle has died and left him money and this new-found wealth makes him attractive to them. Seeing him surrounded by beautiful young ladies, Adina realizes that she loves him. He, having noticed a tear in her eye (5), now has renewed hope for the future. Adina declares her love and buys him out of the army. Dulcamara take his leave of the village, convinced of the effectiveness of his elixir (6).

MUSIC (1) Adina: *Chiedi all'aura – Ask of the welcoming breeze*; (2) Dulcamara: *Udite, udite, o rustici – Listen, listen, o villagers*; (3) Nemorino: *Adina, credimi – Believe me, Adina*; (4) Dulcamara/Adina duet: *Io son ricco, tu sei bella – I am rich and you are lovely*; (5) Nemorino: *Una furtiva lagrima – One furtive tear*; (6) Dulcamara: *El corregge ogni difetto – It corrects every human failing.*

MARIA STUARDA
(*Mary Stuart*), 1834

This was based on Friedrich von Schiller's tragedy of 1800. Because of its Catholic content, it was banned in Naples while in rehearsal. Donizetti altered its title to *Buondelmonte* and changed the names of all the characters, and under this name it received its first performance at the San Carlo theatre in 1834. It was not well received and he withdrew it. The following year it had its La Scala première in its original version but again

ran into trouble from the censor. The soprano Maria Malibran (not in good voice) refused to alter the words from the original, however offensive the censors found them. As a result it had very few productions in the 19th century, but has gained ground since its revival at Bergamo in 1958 and can now be considered standard repertoire. It is historically inaccurate – the two women never met – but nevertheless dramatically enthralling.

SYNOPSIS The opera is set in England in 1567. At the Palace of Whitehall, Elisabetta (Queen Elizabeth I of England, sop) is approached by the Earl of Leicester (ten), whom she secretly loves. He asks her to grant an interview to her cousin Maria Stuarda (Mary Stuart, mez) who is imprisoned at Fotheringay Castle, accused of treason. She agrees, despite the jealousy that she feels because she fears Leicester loves Maria. At Fotheringay Maria sings of her envy of the clouds which can move freely (1). Leicester visits her to prepare her for the Queen's visit,

begging her to be humble if she hopes for mercy. When they meet, however, Elisabetta is openly hostile and insulting. Maria counters by describing the Queen as a "vile bastard" and the conversation turns into a slanging-match until the Queen orders her rival to be seized by guards and returned to custody. Some time later in Westminster, Elisabetta, encouraged by Lord Cecil (bar), signs Maria's death warrant. Leicester asks her to be merciful but, stung by his preference for her cousin, Elisabetta tells him that he must witness the execution. Back in Fotheringay, Maria is told her fate. She confesses her sins, her friends sing a chorus worthy of Verdi (2), and she asks them to join her in praying for those who have misjudged her (3). As the despairing Leicester looks on, she is escorted to the scaffold by her loyal companion Anna Kennedy (mez). Her aria before her execution is followed by her dignified final words as she mounts the scaffold: "Ah! Se un giorno da queste ritorte" ("Ah! Though one day from this prison").

BELOW Jonathan Miller's production of *Don Pasquale* at the ROH, London, 2004, with designs by Isabella Bywater showing all the rooms in the house

> **MUSIC** (1) Maria: *Oh, nube che lieve – O cloud that wanders*; (2) Chorus: *O truce apparato – Oh cruel display*; (3) Maria/Chorus: *Deh! tu di un' umile preghiera – Oh deign to hear our humble prayer.*

LUCIA DI LAMMERMOOR

(*Lucy of Lammermoor*), 1835

Donizetti wrote this work for the San Carlo, Naples, and based it on Sir Walter Scott's *The Bride of Lammermoor* of 1819. It was the first libretto provided for him by Salvatore Cammarano (1801–52), the Italian poet, painter, and dramatist who provided another seven for Donizetti before writing four librettos for Verdi, including that of *Il trovatore*. *Lucia di Lammermoor* was an immediate success and within 10 years it had been heard throughout Europe and the United States and has never been out of the repertoire, no matter how fashion and taste have changed. It contains one of opera's most famous mad scenes and a sextet rivalled in skill and popularity only by the quartet in Verdi's *Rigoletto* (see p.80).

SYNOPSIS The scene is Scotland, about 1700. Lucia (Lucy Ashton, sop) is in love with Edgardo (Edgar Ravenswood, ten). He and her brother Enrico (Lord Henry Ashton, bar) of Lammermoor are political enemies and her brother is furious and rages at her for entering into a relationship with his rival (1). Lucia and Edgardo meet secretly, her faithful nurse Alisa (Alice, mez) keeping watch. Enrico wants her to marry Arturo (Sir Arthur Bucklaw, ten) in order to save the family fortune, most of which he has lost, and enlists the help of Normanno (Norman, ten) in convincing Lucia that Edgardo has been unfaithful. Whilst Edgardo is in France defending the cause of the Stuarts, Enrico pleads with her to help him and the family (2). Believing that Edgardo has been disloyal to her, Lucia agrees to marry Arturo. The contracts are signed, but during the wedding feast Edgardo returns and curses Lucia and the Lammermoor family for their betrayal. Enrico swears vengeance. At this point we hear the justly famous sextet (3).

Raimondo (Raymond Bidebent, bass), Lucia's tutor and confidant, tells the wedding guests that she has just murdered her new husband. She appears, deathly pale, dagger in hand, covered in blood and raving insanely, believing that she is about to marry Edgardo. This is a long scene with a difficult coloratura aria for Lucia accompanied by solo flute **(4)**, at the end of which she collapses and dies. When he learns of her death, Edgardo looks forward to their reunion in heaven **(5)** and kills himself with his dagger.

> **MUSIC (1)** Enrico: *Cruda, funesta smania – A cruel, deadly torment*; **(2)** Lucia: *Il pallore, funesto, orrendo – The deadly, awful, pallor*; **(3)** Sextet: *Chi mi frena in tal momento – Who restrains me at such a moment?*; **(4)** Lucia: *Il dolce suono mi colpì di sua voce – I heard the sweet sound of his voice*; **(5)** Edgardo: *Tu che a Dio spiegasti l'ali – You who have spread your wings to heaven.*

DON PASQUALE, 1843

This was Donizetti's last major success and is the last of the comic operas of the first half of the 19th century to remain in the regular repertoire. It was composed for Paris in 1843 and was an immediate success. It was seen in London the same year and in New Orleans in 1845, by which time its composer was already showing signs of the syphilis that would incapacitate him both physically and mentally within the year.

SYNOPSIS Pasquale (bass) is awaiting the arrival of Dr Malatesta (bar) who he wants to consult about the chances of his siring an heir – he wants to disinherit his current heir, his nephew Ernesto (ten), as he disapproves of the young widow Norina (sop), who Ernesto wants to marry. To bring Pasquale to his senses, Malatesta enlists the help of Ernesto and Norina. He suggests to Pasquale that his "sister Sofronia", who is in a convent, would be a perfect bride **(1)**. Sofronia is Norina in disguise. Ernesto, threatened with disinheritance, sees his hopes of marrying Norina dwindling and looks ahead to a bleak and lonely future **(2)**. Sofronia is brought into Pasquale's presence, veiled and demure, and a wedding contract is prepared, giving the bride half of Pasquale's worldly goods. Once they are married (by Malatesta's cousin disguised as a notary), Sofronia changes overnight, becoming a real harridan and spending Pasquale's money at a fast rate. After she has deliberately dropped hints about having an assignation with another man, Pasquale consults Malatesta who encourages him to catch her with her lover **(3)**. In the garden. Ernesto sings a serenade **(4)** as he waits for Norina and they sing a romantic duet **(5)**. The outraged "husband" catches them together and is persuaded by Malatesta to have his "marriage" annulled, which Pasquale is only too glad to do. When all is revealed he is so relieved to be free again that he forgives them all for the deception and gives Norina and Ernesto his blessing.

> **MUSIC (1)** Malatesta: *Bella siccome un' angelo – Beautiful as an angel*; **(2)** Ernesto: *Cercherò lontana terra – Looking for a distant land*; **(3)** Malatesta/Pasquale duet: *Cheti, cheti, immantinente nel giardino – Ever so quietly we'll go down into the garden*; **(4)** Ernesto: *Com'è gentil – How calm is the night*; **(5)** Ernesto/Norina duet: *Tornami a dir che m'ami – Say the words I long to hear.*

Other operas of note

There are several other of Donizetti's operas that receive regular if infrequent airings. They include *Lucrezia Borgia*, an *opera seria* of 1833 (La Scala, Milan); *Roberto Devereux,* written for Naples in 1837; *Poliuto,* written in 1838 but first performed a decade later in Naples (revived in 1955 at the Baths of Caracalla, Rome, later the scene of the Three Tenors' first triumphant concert in 1990, and at La Scala in 1960 for Franco Corelli and Maria Callas); the comic opera *La fille du régiment* for Paris in 1840; *La favorite* in the same year, also for Paris; *Linda di Chamounix*, the first of his operas to have its première in Vienna in 1842, but with a cast that was all-Italian apart from the great French bass Prosper Dérivis; and *Maria di Rohan*, also for Vienna a year later. We can therefore regard a dozen of the almost 70 operas that he wrote over a period of around 30 years as undoubted successes – a record for which many composers would settle.

ABOVE **A ROH** *Don Pasquale*, with Gabriel Bacquier as Dr Malatesta and Geraint Evans in the title-role, 1973

Bellini

Vincenzo Bellini
(1801–35)

WHERE TO START
La sonnambula
Norma

WHERE TO GO NEXT
I Capuleti e i Montecchi
I puritani

Bellini was the last born of the three major *bel canto* composers, and the shortest lived – he died in Paris when he was only 33 years old. He produced in the last five years of his life a number of works that are absolutely fundamental to the repertoire of all major opera companies, among them masterpieces of the art of *bel canto*.

Vincenzo Bellini was born in Catania, in Sicily, the eldest of seven children. He had his earliest musical education from his father and his grandfather, both of whom were musicians. At 18 Bellini entered the San Sebastiano Conservatory in Naples, where he came under the influence of its director Niccolò Zingarelli, the elderly composer and violinist, who introduced him to the music of the old Neapolitan composers and also of Haydn and Mozart. He encouraged Bellini to write music as he felt it – from the heart, with melody the most important aspect. This was to result in such arias as Norma's "Casta diva", with its long, elegant lines and florid decoration that requires a voice of great agility and dramatic ability. Although Rossini's music dominated Naples at this time, Bellini did not hear a Rossini opera until 1824, his teacher feeling it important that he develop his own skills without being influenced by the older composer. His first commission was from the Teatro San Carlo, whose impresario, Barbaia, was also involved in running La Scala, Milan, and offered the young composer a contract for this theatre. He thus composed his third opera, *Il pirata*, for which he was fortunate in having, for the first time, Felice Romani (see p.69) as his librettist. The opera was a triumph and Romani remained his librettist for the other six operas he composed in Italy, four of which were hugely successful and have remained so to the present day. These are *I Capuleti e i Montecchi, La sonnambula, Norma,* and *I puritani*, all being both Romantic and tragic. Like Rossini and Donizetti, Bellini had top-class singers for whom he could write. Before he was 30 his reputation was well established throughout Europe and had reached the USA. He was a slow worker but was earning enough money from opera commissions not to have to take on teaching or administrative posts.

Bellini's personal life was complicated by a long-standing and passionate affair with the wife of a friend, which lasted from 1828 until her husband discovered it in 1833. In order to avoid the embarrassment that resulted, Bellini was relieved to accept an invitation and escape to England. In London he helped with successful productions of four of his operas at the King's Theatre and Drury Lane and when he left England he went to Paris en route to Italy. He wrote his last opera, *I puritani*, for the Italian Theatre in Paris, where he spent time with Rossini. The two men became firm friends and through this friendship he met other musicians such as Chopin as well as the German poet Heinrich Heine. He heard performances of Beethoven's orchestral music, which strongly impressed him. In 1835, before he was able to make plans to return to Italy, Bellini contracted acute gastroenteritis and died in September in isolation at a friend's house in a Paris suburb, as he was suspected of having cholera. He was buried in Paris, but in 1876 was re-interred in the cathedral of his native town, Catania.

Vincenzo Bellini became one of Italy's most influential composers, his rise to maturity more or less coinciding with Rossini's decision to abandon writing operas. Crucial to his style is the close relationship between the words and the music, a feature remarked upon in 1880 by no less a figure than Richard Wagner. The text and its clear representation in the music was important to him (in contrast, one might say, to Rossini's more cavalier attitude to the words). He also concentrated in his music on expressing emotions rather than delineating characters – the true defining of operatic characters had to wait for Verdi.

I CAPULETI E I MONTECCHI
(The Capulets and Montagues), 1830
This story of Romeo and Juliet is not based on Shakespeare but on *Giulietta e Romeo*, by Matteo Bandello and a play of the same name by Luigi Scevola written in 1818. Bandello (c.1480–1562) was the novelist whose stories supplied material for some of Shakespeare's plays, including *Romeo and Juliet*. Bellini agreed to write this opera quickly to come to the rescue of La Fenice, Venice, which had been let down by another composer. It was only possible for him to do this because Romani reworked a libretto he had written five years earlier for another composer, and Bellini used much of the music from an unsuccessful opera he had written for Parma the previous year. The first performance was in 1830.

ABOVE LEFT **Vincenzo Bellini, who died at the early age of 33 years**

SYNOPSIS In 13th-century Verona Capellio (Capulet, bass) refuses to allow his daughter Giulietta (Juliet, sop) to marry Romeo (mez), a member of the Montagues, even to bring about peace between the rival families. He wants her to marry Tebaldo (Tybalt, ten), a Capulet partisan. Giulietta awaits the arrival of Romeo (1), singing to a harp accompaniment. He tries unsuccessfully to persuade her to elope, but she cannot disobey her father. As her wedding to Tebaldo is arranged, the Capulet doctor Lorenzo (ten or bass) tells her that she can avoid the marriage by taking a sleeping-draught that will render her unconscious and give the impression that she is dead. She will be taken to the family burial vault and when she recovers consciousness, he and Romeo will be there with her. She agrees to this plan with some trepidation (2), but unfortunately Lorenzo is arrested. When Romeo arrives at

the tomb (3) he thinks she really is dead and himself takes poison. Giulietta recovers consciousness to find that Romeo is dying. Capellio and Lorenzo find her lying lifeless across the body of Romeo.

> **MUSIC** (1) Giulietta: *O! quante volte – O! How many times*; (2) Giulietta: *Morte io non temo il sai – Death I do not fear*; (3) Romeo: *Ecco la tomba – Here is the tomb*.

LA SONNAMBULA
(*The Sleepwalker*), 1831
Bellini was commissioned to write an opera for the Carcano Theatre, Milan. He settled on this subject and Romani based his libretto on that written by Eugène Scribe for *La sonnambule, ou L'arrivée d'un nouveau seigneur*, a ballet-pantomime by Jean-Pierre Aumer. It was an overwhelming success at its first performance.

SYNOPSIS The opera is set in a Swiss village in the early 19th century. The orphan Amina (sop) is grateful to the mill-owner, Teresa (mez) who has been like a mother to her (1). The hostess of the local inn, Lisa (sop), is jealous of Amina (2) who is to marry Elvino (ten), a wealthy farmer with whom Lisa is also in love. During the civil wedding, while Elvino is giving Amina a ring (3), Count Rodolfo (bass) returns to the village to claim his land after his father's death. Warned of the village ghost, he stays the night in the inn and is attracted to Lisa with whom he flirts. While they are together in his room, Amina enters through a window and Lisa, assuming she has come for a secret assignation with Rodolfo, rushes to tell this to Elvino. But Amina was sleepwalking and Rodolfo, realizing he has uncovered the mysterious ghost, leaves her in his room asleep on the sofa. Despite Amina's protestations of innocence (4), Elvino cancels

ABOVE **Design by Alexandre Benois (1870–1960) for a 1954 production of *La sonnambula***

BELOW *La sonnambula:* Linda Richardson as Amina, the sleepwalker of the title, Holland Park Opera, London, 2005

BELOW *La sonnambula:* Linda Richardson as Amina, the sleepwalker of the title, Holland Park Opera, London, 2005

the wedding, takes back his ring, and declares that he will marry Lisa instead. The villagers seek Rodolfo to ask him to explain what has happened. As they gather, they see Amina walking in her sleep across the roof of the mill, praying for Elvino **(5)** – the famous coloratura sleepwalking aria. Realizing that she was telling the truth, Elvino puts his ring back on her finger and she awakens to find him beside her. They are escorted to their wedding by the joyful villagers, Amina happy at last **(6)**.

> **MUSIC (1)** Amina: *A te, diletta, tenera madre – Dear and tender mother;*
> **(2)** Lisa: *Tutto è gioia, tutto è festa – All is gaiety and celebration;* **(3)** Elvino: *Prendi l'anel ti dono – Accept this ring I give you;*
> **(4)** Amina: *D'un pensiero e d'un accento – Neither by a thought nor a word;*
> **(5)** Amina: *Ah! Non credea mirarti – Scarcely could I believe it;* **(6)** Amina/ Elvino duet: *Ah! non giunge uman pensiero – Ah! beyond all human thought.*

NORMA, 1831

Included always in the list of *bel canto* operas, Norma demands a dramatic soprano for the title-role, albeit one capable of beautiful singing. Unusually for Bellini, it had a rather icy reception at its première at La Scala, Milan, which distressed the composer greatly. But for the rest of its 34 performances and at all subsequent productions it was greeted warmly and is probably his most popular opera. Its librettist, Romani, regarded it as Bellini's best opera, a view shared by Wagner.

SYNOPSIS The opera is set in Gaul about 50 BC (at the time of the Roman occupation). Norma (sop), a Druid priestess, is the daughter of the Archdruid Oroveso (bass). She is secretly in love with Pollione (ten), the Roman Pro-consul, by whom she has had two children, but knows he has lost interest in her. Pollione tells his friend Flavio (ten) of his love for another priestess, Adalgisa (mez), and how he fears Norma's reaction **(1)**. As the Gauls

gather to await the signal for a revolt against the Romans, Norma sings her invocation to the moon **(2)**. Adalgisa confides in Norma that she is in love with a Roman, and when Norma realizes that this is Pollione, she is distraught **(3)**. She contemplates killing her children rather than have them taken as slaves to Rome, knowing that she must die to atone for her actions. But she cannot bring herself to kill them and suggests that Adalgisa should leave with Pollione for Rome and take the children with her. Adalgisa had not previously known that the man she loves is the father of Norma's children and tells Norma she will leave Pollione **(4)**. She now begs him to stay with Norma. He refuses, and on hearing this Norma decides it is time to drive the Romans from Gaul. Pollione is taken prisoner while breaking into the virgins' temple. Norma offers to save his life if he gives up Adalgisa, an offer that he refuses. Norma confesses her guilty love to Oroveso and the other Druids and is

ABOVE Maria Callas in one of her most famous roles, Bellini's *Norma,* Paris, 1964

BELOW The American coloratura soprano Beverly
Sills as Elvira in *I puritani*, San Francisco, 1977

condemned to death. She asks her father to
care for her children (**5**). Pollione is so moved
by her courage that he mounts the funeral
pyre with her.

> **MUSIC** (**1**) Pollione: *Meco all'altar
> di Venere – At the altar of Venus*;
> (**2**) Norma: *Casta diva – Chaste
> goddess*; (**3**) Norma/ Adalgisa duet:
> *Mira, O Norma – See, O Norma*;
> (**4**) Norma/Adalgisa/ Pollione trio: *Vanne,
> sì, mi lascia, indegno – Leave me, yes,
> worthless man!*; (**5**) Norma: *Deh! Non
> volerli vittime – Do not let them be victims.*

I PURITANI (*The Puritans*), 1834–5

Bellini's final opera was premièred in Paris
eight months before his untimely death. Most
of it was written in a Paris suburb, Puteaux, at
the home of his English friend Samuel Levys,
the house where he later died. The libretto
was by Count Pepoli, an Italian poet (who
later became professor of Italian literature at
London University) who had no experience of
writing for the stage and took his time. It was
based on a French historical drama that was
derived from Sir Walter Scott's *Old Mortality*
(1816). The opera was an immense success.
Rossini wrote to a friend that it was "…the
most accomplished score [Bellini] has yet
composed". It was soon being performed
worldwide and has never totally disappeared
from the repertoire, most leading coloratura
sopranos having sung the part of Elvira.

SYNOPSIS The action takes place in
Plymouth, England, in the mid-17th century at
the time of the English Civil War. Elvira (sop) is
the daughter of Gualtiero (Lord Walton, bass)
the Puritan governor-general. She is to marry
the Puritan Riccardo (Sir Richard Forth, bar),
but she loves a Cavalier, Arturo (Lord Arthur
Talbot, ten). Her uncle Giorgio (Sir George
Walton, bass) tells her he has persuaded his
brother to allow her to marry the man she
loves (**1**). Arturo expresses his love for her
and his happiness (**2**), leading into a classical

Bellini ensemble. But he has vowed to save the
life of Enrichetta (Henrietta, widow of King
Charles I, sop) who is being tried as a spy.
Riccardo allows them to escape and Elvira's
wedding has to be postponed. In yet another
famous mad scene and in another wonderful
ensemble, Elvira imagines she is married to
Arturo (**3**). On his return, Arturo is sentenced
to death for his part in Enrichetta's escape. As
the mad Elvira talks to the imagined Arturo
(**4**), her uncle begs Riccardo to save Arturo's
life in order to save Elvira's sanity. He agrees,
but only on condition that Arturo, if he is
found to be fighting for the Royalists, must die.
Arturo returns and explains to Elvira where
he has been, but she imagines he is again
leaving her. Riccardo announces Arturo's death
sentence and this shocks Elvira back to sanity.
In another ensemble, led by Arturo, they all
express their feelings (**5**). A messenger brings
news that the war has ended and Elvira and
Arturo can be married.

> **MUSIC** (**1**) Giorgio: *Sorgea la notte
> folta – The dark night was approaching*;
> (**2**) Arturo: *A te, o cara – To you, beloved*;
> (**3**) Elvira: *Oh! vieni al tempio, fedele
> Arturo – Oh! Come to the church, faithful
> Arturo*; (**4**) Elvira: *Vien, diletto, è in ciel la
> luna! – Come, beloved, the moon is in the
> sky!*; (**5**) Arturo and ensemble: *Credeasi,
> misera! da me tradita – Unhappy girl, she
> believed I had betrayed her.*

Other operas of note

Bellini wrote 10 operas. Of the others, *Il pirata*
(1827), his third opera and earliest success
and his first with Romani as his librettist, is
occasionally performed. *Beatrice di Tenda*
(1833) is less often heard. This opera caused
a rift between the composer and his librettist,
Romani, who disliked the subject. Bellini
thought it as good as any of his operas and it
was the only one that was published in full
score during his lifetime.

Verdi

Giuseppe Verdi
(1813–1901)

BELOW Giuseppina Strepponi, the soprano with whom Verdi lived from 1846; she became his second wife in 1859

WHERE TO START

La traviata
Aida
Rigoletto

WHERE TO GO NEXT

Otello
Falstaff
Nabucco

ABOVE LEFT **Verdi, warmly attired for the Russian winter, in St Petersburg for the first performance of *La forza del destino*, 1862**

With Rossini, Donizetti, and Bellini, Verdi is one of the four major figures in Italian opera of the Romantic era, several of whose works have never been out of the repertoire of Western international opera houses. Of the 28 operas he wrote – some in more than one version – at least 10 are in the core repertory of most companies.

Giuseppe Verdi was born in 1813 in the village of Roncole, near Bussetto. His father Carlo was the local innkeeper and his mother Luigia the daughter of an innkeeper from Piacenza. Giuseppe was their first child. A daughter, Giuseppa, was born 3 years later but died when she was only 17 years old. Verdi was sent to school in Bussetto when he was 10, and had his early music education from the church organist. A local merchant, Antonio Barezzi, was so impressed by him that he offered to pay for his music education at Milan Conservatoire, but Verdi failed the entrance exam. By the time he was 17, Verdi was living with the Barezzi family and seems to have been closer to this "adopted father" than he was to Carlo Verdi.

In 1836 he married Barezzi's daughter Margherita. The same year he composed his first opera (now lost) and in 1839 completed *Oberto,* which was produced at La Scala, Milan, with some success. But it was a devastating period for Verdi: a few weeks before the first performance, his 15-month-old son died. His first child, a daughter, had died soon after the son was born. And in June 1840 Margherita died from meningitis or rheumatic fever.

He vowed to give up composition but was persuaded to compose *Nabucco*, and its triumph in 1841 put him in the forefront of Italian composers. He was able to buy a farm in nearby Sant' Agata and from then onward every opera he wrote was eagerly awaited. Sometimes there were problems with the censors, especially when his operas dealt with historical subjects that could be considered to be mirroring contemporary politics. (Why do opera directors in the 21st century think that their mania for making operas "relevant" to modern times is something new?)

Verdi's next success was *Ernani* of 1843–4, his first collaboration with the librettist Francesco Maria Piave (1810–76), who was to be his librettist for a further 10 operas. By the time *Ernani* reached the stage of La Fenice, Venice, in 1844, Rossini had more or less retired, Donizetti had given up composing due to deteriorating health, and Bellini was dead. This left the field of Italian opera wide open for Verdi, and he was a genius capable of grasping the opportunity.

In 1846 Verdi started to live with the soprano Giuseppina Strepponi (1815–97), who had created Abigaille in *Nabucco* (in "execrable voice" according to Donizetti). It is not clear why she and Verdi did not marry for so long – by 1853 she was known as Signora Verdi and he referred to her as his "wife", but they did not make the relationship legal until 1859. They had no children together, but adopted (Filomena) Maria, the eight-year-old daughter of a Verdi cousin.

The death of Strepponi in 1897 marked the end of Verdi's composing career. Four years later he died in the Hotel Milano, quite

LEFT Crowds following the cortège through the streets of Milan for Verdi's funeral

> **MUSIC** (1) Zaccharia and ens.: *Tremin gl'insani – Let the mad man tremble*; (2) Zaccaria and chor.: *Mio furor, non più costretto … Dalla genti sii reietto – My fury no longer constrained … Be rejected of men*; (3) Abigaille: *Anch'io dischiuso un giorno … Salgo già del trono aurato … I, too, once opened my heart … I now ascend the blood-stained seat*; (4) Chorus: *Va, pensiero, sull'ali dorate – Go, thought, on wings of gold*; (5) Nabucco: *Dio di Giuda! – Judah's God!*; (6) Nabucco: *O prodi miei, seguitemi – Follow me, my valiant men*; (7) Abigaille: *Su me … morente … esanime – To me … dying … faint.*

near to La Scala. Verdi dominated Italian opera for 50 years. He became a symbol of Italian life and art, greeted affectionately whenever he appeared in public. It is estimated that 300,000 people lined the streets of Milan for his funeral, at which Toscanini conducted a choir of 820 voices in the chorus "Va, pensiero", from *Nabucco*.

NABUCCO

(Nebuchadnezzar), 1841, rev. 1842

Nabucco had its first performance at La Scala on 9 March 1842 and within two years it was being produced all over Italy as well as in Vienna, Barcelona, and Lisbon. The audience in Milan, governed as they were by Austria, immediately identified with the Hebrew slaves whose Act 3 chorus, "Va, pensiero", quickly became something of a national anthem.

SYNOPSIS As Nabucco's Assyrian army presses into Jerusalem in 586 BC, the Hebrews shelter in the Temple. The high priest Zaccaria (bass) has taken Fenena (sop), daughter of Nabucco (bar), as a hostage. Fenena is in love with the Hebrew Ismaele (ten). Nabucco's elder daughter, Abigaille (sop), also loves Ismaele and promises to free him and his people if he gives up Fenena in favour of herself, an offer he refuses. Zaccaria threatens to kill Fenena (1) but Ismaele intervenes and the Hebrews curse him (2). In the Babylonian palace, Abigaille's secret has been discovered – she is not Nabucco's daughter, but the illegitimate child of a slave (3). The High Priest of Baal (bass) tells everyone, falsely, that Nabucco has been killed and Abigaille must be declared Queen. Zaccaria reveals that Fenena has converted to the Jewish religion. Abigaille and her priests dispute Fenena's right to inherit the crown but are interrupted when Nabucco appears. He orders everyone to treat him as God and for this blasphemy is struck by a thunderbolt and rendered insane. Abigaille takes his crown, declares herself the ruler, and tricks her father into signing Fenena's death warrant. On the banks of the river Euphrates, the Hebrews dream of their homeland (4). Nabucco prays to Jehovah (5), and his reason is restored. He summons his soldiers (6) and joins the Hebrews in prayer, telling them they will be free. Abigaille, realizing that her father has been restored to sanity, takes poison. As she dies, she begs Fenena's forgiveness (7).

RIGOLETTO, 1851

Rigoletto is based on a play by Victor Hugo, adapted by Piave, and has been a huge success since its first performance. It contains a quartet which ranks with the sextet from Donizetti's *Lucia di Lammermoor* (see pp.72–3) as one of the great ensembles in opera.

SYNOPSIS The scene is 16th–century Mantua. At a ball the Duke of Mantua (ten) expounds his theory that all women are the same to him (1). He flirts with Countess Ceprano (mez) whilst her annoyed husband (bass) looks on. Watching them is the hunchback court jester Rigoletto (bar). Count Monterone (bar), father of one of the Duke's previous conquests, curses both the Duke and his jester, which frightens Rigoletto. The jester later meets Sparafucile (bass), a professional assassin, who offers his services when needed (2). Since the death of his wife, Rigoletto has kept his daughter Gilda (sop) hidden, looked after by her nurse Giovanna (mez). The Duke has seen Gilda in church and followed her home. The Duke poses as a poor student, Gualtier Maldè, and persuades Giovanna to let him into the house. He tells Gilda of his feelings, which she reciprocates (3). Ceprano and the courtiers, still furious at the jester's gibes, decide to kidnap Gilda (4), assuming her to be

Rigoletto's mistress. They take her to the palace where the Duke seduces her. When Rigoletto finds out he swears to murder the Duke **(5)** and enlists the help of Sparafucile and his sister Maddalena (mez). Maddalena falls in love with the Duke. Gilda wants to forgive the Duke but her father takes her to watch at a tavern where the Duke is drinking and flirting with Maddalena **(6)**. In one of opera's great quartets, they each express their feelings **(7)**. Sparafucile agrees to Maddalena's plea to spare the Duke's life, but only on condition that they kill the next person to arrive at the tavern so that he has a body to deliver to Rigoletto. Gilda overhears their discussion and vows to sacrifice herself for the man she loves. She enters the inn and is stabbed by Sparafucile. Dying, she is put into a sack and handed over to Rigoletto. He believes this to be Mantua's body, until he suddenly hears the Duke's voice coming from the inn. He opens the sack and finds his daughter **(8)**, who dies in his arms to one of Verdi's many touching soprano/baritone, daughter/father duets. Monterone's curse has been fulfilled.

MUSIC (1) Duke of Mantua: *Questa o quella… – This woman or that…*;
(2) Rigoletto: *Pari siamo! – We are alike!*;
(3) Gilda: *Gualtier Maldè … Caro nome… – Gualtier Maldè … Dearest name…*;
(4) Chorus: *Zitti, zitti, moviamo a vendetta – Softly, softly, let's pursue our vengeance*;
(5) Rigoletto: *Cortigiani, vil razza dannata – You courtiers, vile accursed race*; **(6)** Duke: *La donna è mobile – Woman is fickle*;
(7) Duke/Maddalena/Gilda/Rigoletto: *Bella figlia dell'amore – Lovely daughter of pleasure*; **(8)** Gilda/Rigoletto duet: *V'ho ingannato… – I deceived you….*

IL TROVATORE
(*The Troubadour*), 1853

The first performance of *Il trovatore* took place in Rome in January 1853. The librettist was Salvatore Cammarano (1801–52), who died before the libretto was finished and it was completed by Leone Emanuele Bardare, a young teacher and librettist from Naples about whom little is known. *Il trovatore* was another hugely successful Verdi first night.

SYNOPSIS In 15th-century Spain Ferrando (bass), a captain in the army of Count di Luna (bar), recounts a summary of events **(1)** that took place before the opera begins (and is important in order to make sense of what is a complicated plot). The late Count di Luna had two baby sons. An old gypsy put a curse on the younger son and she was burnt as a witch. Her daughter Azucena (mez) swore to avenge her. Azucena also had a baby son. At her mother's funeral pyre, Azucena snatched the younger di Luna baby and threw him into the fire. Afterwards she could not be sure if she threw the di Luna baby or her own son. She raised the surviving baby as her son. He is now an adult, the troubadour Manrico (ten), and Azucena is an old lady. The older di Luna child has inherited his father's title.

Manrico and the Count are both in love with Leonora (sop), a lady-in-waiting at court, who loves the troubadour **(2)**. The two men fight a duel which Manrico wins, but something stops him making the final thrust. In a later battle, di Luna injures Manrico and he is nursed at the gypsy camp by Azucena **(3)** who confesses the story of the two babies. She is arrested and di Luna plans to burn her to avenge his brother. Leonora, believing that Manrico is dead, vows to enter a convent. Di Luna, distressed by this **(4)**, decides to kidnap her from the convent **(5)**. Manrico reappears and he and Leonora plan to marry. At their wedding ceremony Manrico is told of Azucena's imprisonment and leaves to rescue her **(6)** but is captured and imprisoned with her.

Leonora begs di Luna for mercy and offers herself to him in exchange for Manrico's release. Then, to avoid having to give herself to the Count, she takes poison. She enters the prison to see Manrico **(7)** and **(8)** dies at his feet. Di Luna finds Leonora dead in his rival's arms and orders the execution to go ahead. As

LEFT *Il trovatore*: Roberto Alagna as Manrico, the troubadour of the title, with Sondra Radvenosky as Leonora, Opéra Bastille, Paris, 2003

Manrico dies, Azucena tells di Luna that it was, in fact, *her* child that she threw on her mother's pyre – di Luna has just killed his own brother.

> **MUSIC (1)** Ferrando: *Di due figlia vivea padre beato – There lived a happy father of two sons*; **(2)** Leonora: *Ascolta! Tacea la notte placida – Listen! The serene night was silent*; **(3)** Azucena: *Stride la vampa! – The flame crackles!* (following the famous "Anvil Chorus"); **(4)** di Luna: *Il balen del suo sorriso – The flashing of her smile*; **(5)** di Luna: *Per me ora fatale – Hour, fatal for me*; **(6)** Manrico: *Di quella pira, l'orrendo foco – The horrible blaze of that pyre*; **(7)** Leonora: *D'amor sull'ali rosee – On the rosy wings of love*; **(8)** Leonora/Manrico/Chorus: *Miserere – Have mercy.*

LA TRAVIATA (*The Courtesan*), 1853

This is probably the most popular of Verdi's operas. "The Lady Gone Astray" would be a more accurate translation of its title. The text, again by Piave, is taken from *La Dame aux camélias* by Alexandre Dumas *fils*. Its première at La Fenice took place only six weeks after *Il trovatore* opened in Rome. Reviews after the first night were mixed, not least because the three lead singers were well below the standard the roles demanded. In May 1854 a smaller theatre in Venice engaged a first-rate cast and Piave as director, and this time Venice had an overwhelming success.

SYNOPSIS The scene is Paris and nearby, about 1850. Violetta Valéry (sop), a famed courtesan, is giving a party escorted by Baron Douphol (bar). Among her guests are her friend Flora (mez) with the Marchese d'Obigny (bass), Dr Grenvil (bass), and the handsome young Alfredo Germont (ten), who sings of the pleasure of wine (1). Alfredo is in love with her, not knowing that she has consumption (tuberculosis), and begs her to give up her life as a courtesan and go away with him. After her guests have left, she thinks over these events (2).

It is three months later: Alfredo and Violetta are living together in the country outside Paris. Alfredo learns from her maid Annina (sop) that Violetta has been selling her possessions in order to support them. He leaves for Paris to sort out his affairs. While he is away Violetta is visited by Giorgio Germont (bar), Alfredo's father. He begs Violetta to give up his son, as their relationship is threatening his daughter's chances of a suitable marriage (3) and eventually she reluctantly agrees to do so (4). Alfredo returns and they greet each other passionately (5). After she goes out, Annina brings him a letter informing him that Violetta is returning to her old life and admirer, Baron Douphol. He is distraught and his father's appearance from the garden cannot console him (6) – he is set on revenge.

Violetta is escorted by Douphol at Flora's party. Alfredo arrives, drinks too much, and gambles at the tables. In front of all the guests, he throws his winnings at Violetta in payment for her earlier services (7). The following year Violetta is dying. She has received a letter from Germont *père* which she reads for the umpteenth time (8). He has told his son of Violetta's sacrifice on behalf of their family and Alfredo is on his way to visit her. "Too late" (*È tardi!*), she cries. Alfredo arrives, and there is an emotional reunion as they dream of the future (9). His father also comes to visit her. But it *is* all too late – Violetta dies.

> **MUSIC (1)** Alfredo: *Libiamo ne' lieti calici – Let us drink from the joyous chalice* (the "Brindisi", the toast to drink to one's health); **(2)** Violetta: *È strano! … Ah, fors' è lui … Sempre libera – How strange! … Was this the man … Always free*; **(3)** Germont: *Pura siccome un angelo – God gave me a daughter*; **(4)** Violetta: *Ah! Dite alla giovine – Say to your daughter*; **(5)** Alfredo/Violetta duet: *Di lagrime avea d'uopo/Ah, vive sol quel core all'amor mio – I felt like crying/Her love for me is her whole life!*; **(6)** Germont: *Di Provenza il mar, il suol – The dear sea and soil of Provence*; **(7)** Alfredo: *Ogni suo aver tal femmina – For me this woman lost all she possessed*; **(8)** Violetta (reading a letter): *"Teneste la promessa…" – "You kept your promise…"*; **(9)** Alfredo/Violetta duet: *Parigi, o cara, noi lasceremo – We'll leave Paris, my dearest.*

SIMON BOCCANEGRA, 1857, 1881

Simon Boccanegra has a complicated genesis. The original libretto is by Piave. It was produced first at La Fenice, Venice, in 1857, but was not a success. In 1880 the poet and composer Arrigo Boito (1842–1918) was engaged to rewrite the libretto. He added a new scene to Act 1, known as the Council Chamber scene. It was produced at La Scala in 1881 with an excellent cast and was a triumph. This is the version described.

SYNOPSIS In and around 14th-century Genoa. In a prologue, two warring factions rule Genoa, the plebeians and the patricians. Jacopo Fiesco (bass), a patrician, does not approve of his daughter Maria's love for Simon Boccanegra (bar), a plebeian (**1**). The couple have had an illegitimate daughter. Maria dies. Fiesco can only forgive Boccanegra for her death if he hands over the child, called after her mother. But the young Maria has disappeared. The plebeians, led by Paolo Albiani (bar), have Boccanegra elected Doge, much to the fury of Fiesco.

The action moves on 25 years. Fiesco, living under the name of "Andrea", is the guardian of Amelia Grimaldi (sop), a foundling who was brought up as Count Grimaldi's daughter. She is in love with the Genoese patrician Gabriele Adorno (ten), whose father was killed by Boccanegra. She awaits Adorno's arrival (**2**) and they speak of their love (**3**). She and Gabriele receive the blessing of "Andrea" for their union. Boccanegra arrives and when Amelia shows him the portrait of her mother, he realizes that she is his long-lost daughter and they are reunited (**4**). In the Council Chamber scene, one of the finest and most dramatic scenes in any Verdi opera, the Doge intervenes to stop the fighting between the two factions. He is later told that Amelia has been kidnapped (by Paolo), but she has escaped. Adorno, dragged into the chamber by the crowd, suspects the Doge of being behind the abduction and is about to stab him when Amelia rushes in and stops him. Paolo is planning to poison Boccanegra. He suggests to Gabriele that Amelia and Boccanegra are lovers and enlists Gabriele's help in murdering the Doge in order to ensure his own guilt is not uncovered. Amelia dare not explain to Gabriele her true relationship to the Doge, and Gabriele prays for her to be restored to him (**5**). The Doge drinks the water that Paolo has poisoned and falls asleep. Gabriele approaches to kill him, but is interrupted by Amelia. Boccanegra wakes up and Gabriele learns the truth (**6**). The dying Boccanegra confesses to Fiesco that Amelia is his granddaughter Maria. Boccanegra and Fiesco are reconciled (**7**) and Amelia and Gabriele are married (**8**). Before he dies, Boccanegra names Gabriele Adorno as his successor.

> **MUSIC** (**1**) Fiesco: *Il lacerato spirito – The tormented spirit*; (**2**) Amelia: *Come in quest'ora bruna – In this dark hour, see how the stars and the sea are smiling*; (**3**) Amelia/Gabriele duet: *Vieni a mirar la cerula marina tremolante – Come and look at the shimmering blue sea*; (**4**) Boccanegra/Amelia duet: *Figlia! … a tal nome io palpito – Daughter! … I tremble at that name*; (**5**) Gabriele: *Cielo pietoso, rendila – Merciful heaven, restore her*; (**6**) Gabriele/Boccanegra/Amelia trio: *Perdono, Amelia… – Forgive me, Amelia…*; (**7**) Fiesco/Boccanegra duet: *Piango, perché mi parla… – I weep because through you…*; (**8**) Boccanegra/Amelia/Gabriele/ Fiesco quartet: *Gran Dio, ti benedici – Almighty God, in thy mercy bless them.*

ABOVE *Simon Boccanegra* at the Metropolitan Opera, NY, 2007, with Angela Gheorghiu (Amelia), Thomas Hampson (Boccanegra), and Marcello Giordani (Adorno)

UN BALLO IN MASCHERA
(*A masked ball*), 1859

Verdi asked the Venetian playwright Antonio Somma (1809–64) to adapt a libretto written by Eugène Scribe (1791–1861) on the true incident of the assassination in 1792 of King Gustav III of Sweden. The Naples censor refused permission for the staging of an opera about regicide. It was accepted by Rome, but the papal censor insisted it be set in a non-European country. Verdi and Somma settled on Boston before the American War of Independence. The première, in February 1859, was a resounding success. In this synopsis the characters' names are those of the Swedish version, with the Boston names in brackets.

SYNOPSIS Early 18th-century Sweden (Boston, 1700). Count Ribbing (Samuel, bass) and Count Horn (Tom, bass) are plotting to overthrow King Gustavus III (Riccardo, Count of Warwick, ten). The King's secretary Anckarstroem (Renato, bar) is married to Amelia (Amelia, sop), with whom the King is in love (1). Anckarstroem warns the King of the plot on his life (2). A negro fortune-teller, Mme Arvidson (Ulrica, cont) is being exiled for sorcery and the page Oscar (Oscar, sop *travesti* role) begs the King to be merciful (3). The King, in disguise, goes to visit the fortune-teller (4) and she warns him of death at the hands of the first person to shake his hand (5). This turns out to be Anckarstroem. The King and Amelia (6) meet secretly and she tells him they must sacrifice their love and remain loyal to her husband, his friend (7). Anckarstroem arrives at that moment and warns the King of a conspiracy and advises him to return home, offering to escort the veiled lady himself (8). Her veil slips and her identity is revealed. Anckarstroem swears vengeance. Amelia and Anckarstroem are invited to attend a masked ball at the palace (9). Oscar warns the King that there will be an attempt on his life, but keen to see Amelia one last time, he ignores the warning. Inadvertently, Oscar identifies the king by letting slip which costume he is wearing

RIGHT **King Gustavus III (Luciano Pavarotti) with his loyal page Oscar (Lillian Watson) in *Un ballo in maschera*, ROH, London, 1995**

(10). Anckarstroem kills Gustavus. As he is dying the King tells his friend that Amelia had never been unfaithful (11). He dies in Oscar's arms.

MUSIC (1) Gustavus: *La rivedrà nell' estasi – When I see her, pale and radiant*; (2) Anckarstroem: *Alla vita che t'arride – Your life, so rich in joy*; (3) Oscar: *Volta la terrea fronte alle stelle – When she turns her dusky brow to the stars*; (4) Mme Arvidson: *Re dell'abisso affrettati – King of the depths, make haste*; (5) Mme Arvidson/Gustavus/Oscar, Ensemble: *È scherzo od è follia – A joke or madness*; (6) Amelia: *Ma dall'arido stelo divulsa – When I have plucked the herb from its arid stem*; (7) Amelia/Gustavus duet: *Oh, qual soave brivida – Oh how sweet the thrill*; (8) Gustavus/Anckarstroem/Amelia trio: *Odi tu come fremono cupi – Do you hear the sombre tones*; (9) Oscar/Amelia/Anckarstroem: *Ah! Di che fulgor, che musiche – Ah! what brilliance, what music*; (10) Oscar: *Saper vorreste – You want to know*; (11) Gustavus: *Ella è pura – She is pure.*

DON CARLOS,
1867 (in French), 1884 (in Italian, as *Don Carlo*)

In 1865 Verdi agreed to write a new opera for performance during the Paris Exposition of 1867. He chose Schiller's verse-play *Don Carlos*. The libretto was begun by the elderly French playwright Joseph Méry (1797–1865), who died before it was finished, and it was completed by Camille du Locle (1832–1903), a librettist and theatre manager. Verdi wrote some new music and reduced it to four acts. For a long time this version was the more popular. The tendency nowadays is to restore the original first act to the 1884 four-act version, making five acts, and to sing the opera in its original French. This is the version that is described below.

SYNOPSIS The action is in France and Spain about 1560. In Fontainebleau Don Carlos (ten), the Spanish Infante, has secretly come to meet for the first time Elisabeth de Valois (sop), daughter of King Henry II of France, the bride chosen for him in the hope of bringing about peace between Spain and France (1). They declare their love for each

other (2). Her page Thibault (sop) enters and hails her as Queen of Spain – her father has agreed that she shall marry not the Infante but his father, King Philip II (bass). For the sake of her country she agrees to this union and she and Carlos unhappily part. In Spain, at the monastery of San Yuste, Carlos is greeted by his great friend Rodrigue, Marquis of Posa (bar), to whom he confesses his love for Elisabeth, now married to his father. Posa advises him to go to Flanders to help the people there oppressed by Philip's enforced Catholic rule. Carlos and Posa swear eternal friendship (3). Outside the monastery, Elisabeth's entourage is awaiting her return. Princess Eboli (mez) sings about a king who made love to a veiled lady only to find it was his own wife (4). Eboli hopes Carlos is in love with her. Carlos asks Elisabeth to persuade his father to send him

to Flanders. He also tells her that he still loves her (5). In a great confrontation, Posa begs the King to relax the measures against the people of Flanders, who are dying of starvation. The King resists his appeals, warns him to beware of the Inquisition, and at the same time asks him to keep a watch on the relationship between Carlos and Elisabeth.

Carlos receives an anonymous letter from a lady asking him to meet her. He believes it to be from Elisabeth and when she arrives, veiled, he declares his love for her (6) and is mortified to discover that it is Eboli. Eboli guesses he loves the Queen and threatens to tell Philip. The next scene is the *auto-da-fé*, the burning of the heretics in front of the large crowd outside the cathedral. Carlos begs the King to show mercy to his people in Flanders, and asks to be sent to govern them (7). The King refuses and Carlos draws his sword. He is led away by the guards.

After a sleepless night, the King realizes Elisabeth does not love him (8) and, urged on by the 90-year-old blind Grand Inquisitor (bass) (9), reluctantly agrees to Carlos's death for daring to plead for the Flemish heretics. The old man also denounces Posa as a heretic, making Philip very angry. Philip bemoans the fact that the throne must always bow to the church. An upset Elisabeth arrives – her jewel casket has been stolen (10). Philip produces it from his desk, forces it open, and discovers a portrait of his son. He accuses her of adultery. Eboli, full of guilt at what her jealousy has caused, later admits that it was she that stole the casket and also confesses to Elisabeth that she has been the King's mistress. Eboli curses her own beauty for getting her into this position and vows to enter a nunnery (11). But first she will save Carlos. In the dungeon where Carlos is confined, Posa visits him, prepared to die in his friend's place (12). While they are talking, men enter and Posa is shot. Before he dies, he tells Carlos that the Queen will be waiting for him at the monastery the next day (13). Carlos weeps

over his dead friend as Philip, the Grand Inquisitor, and Eboli (in disguise) enter the dungeon. At the sight of the dead Posa, Philip is full of remorse and presents his son to the people. Urged by Eboli, Carlos leaves. In the cloisters of San Yuste monastery, Elisabeth kneels before the tomb of Charles V (14). Carlos arrives and, as they say their farewells forever (15), Philip enters and asks the Grand Inquisitor to arrest her and Carlos, who draws his sword and moves towards his grandfather's tomb. The opera ends rather unsatisfactorily as a Friar appears looking like the late Charles V and drags Carlos into the cloisters.

MUSIC (1) Carlos: *Je l'ai vue, et dans son sourire… – I have seen her, and in her smile…*; (2) Elisabeth/Carlos duet: *De quels transports… – What rapture…*; (3) Carlos/Posa duet: *Dieu, tu semas dans nos âmes – God, you have instilled love in our hearts*; (4) Eboli: *Au palais des fées – In the fairy palace (Song of the Veil)*; (5) Carlos/Elisabeth duet: *O bien perdu …Trésor sans prix! – O lost blessing … Priceless treasure!*; (6) Carlos: *C'est vous! Ma bien-aimée – It is you, my beloved*; (7) Carlos: *Sire, il est temps que je vive! – Sire, it is time for me to start to live*; (8) Philip: *Elle ne m'aime pas! – She does not love me!*; (9) Grand Inquisitor: *Dans ce beau pays – In this beautiful country*; (10) Elisabeth: *Justice, Sire! J'ai foi – Justice, Sire! I have faith*; (11) Eboli: *Oh don fatal et détesté – O fatal and detested beauty*; (12) Posa: *Oui, Carlos! C'est mon jour suprême – Yes, Carlos! This is for me the supreme day*; (13) Posa: *Carlos, écoute … Ah! Je meurs l'âme joyeuse – Carlos, listen … Ah! I die with a happy soul*; (14) Elisabeth: *Toi qui sus le néant des grandeurs de ce monde – You who knew the emptiness of the pomp of this world*; (15) Elisabeth/Carlos duet: *Au revoir dans un monde où la vie est meilleure – Farewell till we meet in a world where life is better.*

ABOVE LEFT **Boris Christoff as King Philip in Verdi's** *Don Carlos*, ROH, London, 1979

ABOVE Franco Zeffirelli's authentic-looking *Aida*
for La Scala, Milan, 2006

AIDA, 1870–1

This opera was not, as is often said, composed for the opening of the Suez Canal, nor for the opening of the Cairo Opera House. It was commissioned by the Khedive of Egypt for performance in the new opera house and its première was on Christmas Eve 1871. Camille du Locle's French libretto was translated into Italian by Antonio Ghislanzoni (1824–93), a baritone, writer, and librettist. *Aida* is the archetypal "grand opera".

SYNOPSIS In Egypt at the time of the Pharaohs, Aida (sop), the daughter of King Amonasro (bar) of Ethiopia, was captured when the Egyptians defeated Ethiopia and is a slave to Amneris (mez), daughter of the King of Egypt (bass). Her father plans to rescue her. Aida is torn between her love for the Egyptian captain Radamès (ten), who loves her (1), and loyalty to her country (2). Amneris tricks Aida into admitting her love for Radamès (3) and insists on Aida accompanying her to the feast at which Radamès will be honoured (4). The King offers Radamès the hand of Amneris together with anything he desires. He asks for freedom for the prisoners, but is disappointed when told that both Aida and Amonasro must remain in captivity. The night before Amneris's wedding, she is accompanied to the temple by

Ramfis (bass), the High Priest. Radamès has arranged a last meeting with Aida by the Nile. Distressed at the thought that she might never again see her homeland (5), she is intercepted by Amonasro who begs her to extract from Radamès the plans of the Egyptian army. As Amneris and Ramfis emerge from the temple, Radamès tells Amonasro and Aida to flee and offers himself as a prisoner in their place. The Ethiopians are defeated, Amonasro is killed, and Aida disappears. Radamès is sentenced to be buried alive under the temple altar. After he has been entombed, he finds that Aida has hidden herself in the tomb – they will die together (6) as Amneris prays for Radamès in the temple above them (7).

MUSIC (1) Radamès: *Celeste Aida, forma divina – Heavenly Aida, divine form*; (2) Aida: *Ritorna vincitor! – Return victorious!*; (3) Amneris: *Ebben, qual nuovo fremito t'assal, gentile Aida? – What new anguish disturbs you, sweet Aida?*; (4) Orchestra: opening the second scene of Act 2, the Triumphal March takes place; (5) Aida: *O patria mia – O fatherland*; (6) Radamès/Aida duet: *O terra addio – O earth, farewell*; (7) Amneris: *Pace t'imploro – For peace, I pray*.

OTELLO, 1884–6, rev. 1887

The libretto, based on Shakespeare, was by the poet and composer Arrigo Boito (1842–1918). Verdi composed the music between March 1884 and December 1886 – a long period by his standards. The première at La Scala in 1887 was another Verdi triumph. The demanding title-role is one of the peaks of the Italian repertory. Wise tenors do not attempt it early in their career (but see p.19); others, equally wise, do not attempt it at all.

SYNOPSIS In 15th-century Cyprus the Venetians celebrate victory over the Turks. Otello (ten), Moor of Venice, arrives with his wife Desdemona (sop) to succeed Montano (bass) as Governor of Cyprus (1). Iago (bar), Otello's ensign, is jealous of Otello and of his Lieutenant Cassio (ten). Desdemona and Otello are left alone outside the castle (2).

Iago plots with the Venetian Roderigo (ten) to turn Otello against Cassio. When they succeed, Otello appoints Iago in Cassio's place. Iago suggests to Cassio that he ask for Desdemona's help to clear his name, knowing this will make Otello suspicious about the relationship between Desdemona and Cassio. Left alone, Iago expounds his evil creed (3). When Desdemona later pleads with Otello on Cassio's behalf, Otello's suspicions increase

FALSTAFF, 1893

Boito based his text on Shakespeare's *The Merry Wives of Windsor*. Although nearly 80, Verdi enjoyed writing the opera. The première at La Scala in 1893 aroused worldwide interest, and connoisseurs recognized it as a masterpiece.

SYNOPSIS In Windsor during the reign of King Henry IV, Sir John Falstaff (bar) is drinking with his cronies Pistol (bass) and Bardolph (ten) when they are interrupted by Dr Caius (ten). Falstaff is planning to seduce the wives of Ford (bar) and Page to gain access to their husbands' money. When his companions refuse to help him, he reads them a lesson on the subject of honour (1). Alice Ford (sop) and Meg Page (mez) receive letters from Falstaff and decide to teach him a lesson. Ford is told of Falstaff's plans and is determined to catch him red-handed. The Fords' daughter Nannetta (sop) is in love with Fenton (ten) (2) but her father wants her to marry the elderly Dr Caius. Alice and Meg ask Mistress Quickly to help them deceive Falstaff. She delivers their replies (3), making an assignation – Alice will meet Falstaff at the Ford house when her husband is out "between two and three". Falstaff is pleased and makes his plans (4). Ford comes to Falstaff disguised as "Signor Fontana", asking for help to woo Alice, only to be told that Falstaff already has a date with her. Left alone, Ford gives vent to his jealousy (5). At the Ford house Falstaff woos Alice romantically (6), but Meg Page warns them that Ford is on his way to catch them. The ladies bundle Falstaff into a laundry basket. Ford searches for Falstaff but finds only his own daughter and her lover. The contents of the laundry basket are tipped into the river below. Falstaff climbs out and arrives at the Garter Inn soaked and shivering (7). Mistress Quickly brings him another letter from Alice arranging a meeting at midnight in Windsor Park. She instructs him to come as the Black Huntsman who haunts the forest. Everyone else hides in the forest wearing a mask and as Falstaff attempts to woo Alice they emerge and he is terrified of

---

and she defends herself (4). Iago snatches Desdemona's handerkerchief from the hand of her maid Emilia (mez), who is his wife. It will later be found in Cassio's possession. Otello faces up to his wife's possible infidelity (5). Iago recounts, falsely, Cassio's words muttered in his sleep (6). Otello joins Iago in an oath of vengeance (7). Desdemona again pleads with Otello on Cassio's behalf. He demands that she confess her sinfulness (8). Alone with her maid, Desdemona tells Emilia the story of another young girl abandoned by her lover (9). She prays (10) before retiring to bed and feigning sleep. Otello enters the chamber and kisses his wife. He accuses her of being unfaithful and, despite her denials, smothers her with a pillow. Emilia enters announcing that Cassio has killed Roderigo. Seeing her mistress dying, she exposes Iago as a liar. Iago makes his escape. Otello, overcome by remorse, stabs himself and dies next to his wife (11).

> **MUSIC** (1) Otello: *Esultate! – Rejoice!*;
> (2) Otello/Desdemona duet: *Già nella notte… – Now in the silent night…*;
> (3) Iago: *Credo in un Dio crudel – I believe in a cruel God*; (4) Desdemona/Otello duet: *Se inconscia, contro te, sposo, ho peccato – If I in ignorance, my lord, have you offended*; (5) Otello: *Ora e per sempre, addio – Now and forever, farewell*;
> (6) Iago: *Era la notte, Cassio dormia – In the dark night, Cassio slept*; (7) Otello/Iago duet (the swearing of their oath): *Sì, pel ciel marmoreo giuro! – Heavens above, see me swear!*; (8) Otello: *Dio, mi potevi scagliar… – God, it has pleased you to heap on me…*; (9) Desdemona: *Piangea cantando …Salce! Salce! – The poor girl sat sighing …Willow! Willow!*;
> (10) Desdemona: *Ave Maria – Hail, Mary*; (11) Otello: *Niun mi tema – Let no one fear me.*

these "spirits of the forest". Falstaff realizes he has been made to look a fool but takes it all in good part and blesses the union of Nannetta and Fenton **(8)**.

MUSIC (1) Falstaff: *L'Onore! Ladri! — Your Honour! Scoundrels!*; **(2)** Nannetta/Fenton duet: *Labra di foco! — Lips that are burning!*; **(3)** Quickly/Falstaff: *Reverenza! — Your worship*; **(4)** Falstaff: *Va, vecchio John — Go, old John*; **(5)** Ford: *È sogno? O realtà … Due rami enormi crescon… — Am I dreaming? Or is it true…? I feel two enormous horns…* (known as Ford's Jealousy Aria); **(6)** Falstaff: *Quand'ero paggio del Duca di Norfolk — When I was a page to the Duke of Norfolk*; **(7)** Falstaff: *Mondo ladro. Mondo rubaldo — Wicked world. Vile world*; **(8)** Falstaff/Ford/Ensemble: *Tutto nel mondo é burla — All in the world's but folly* (the astonishing fugue in which everyone joins in the final scene of the opera).

Other operas of note

Two other Verdi operas receive fairly regular productions. *Macbeth* (1847) had its first performance in Florence and a revised version was premièred in Paris almost 20 years later. Verdi rehearsed the first Lady Macbeth in great detail, determined that the sleepwalking scene would look authentic. In 1859 Verdi agreed to write an opera for the Imperial Theatre in St Petersburg and settled on a Spanish play, *Don Alvaro*, or *The Force of Destiny*, from which Piave provided a libretto. The composer and his wife went to Russia for rehearsals and the work was a success when it made its first appearance in November 1862.

Many of Verdi's other operas appear occasionally somewhere in the world, from the early *Il giorno di regno* onward — *Ernani*, *I due Foscari*, *Attila*, *I masnadieri*, *Luisa Miller*, *Stiffelio*, and the French *Les vêpres siciliennes* certainly, the remainder maybe less often. They are always worth at least one hearing — by Verdi, how could they not be?

ABOVE **The Welshman Bryn Terfel in the title-role** of Verdi's *Falstaff*, ROH, London, 2002

Weber

Carl Maria von Weber
(1786–1826)

BELOW **Title-page of piano music for Weber's** *Der Freischütz* **(and other compositions)**

WHERE TO START
Der Freischütz

Whilst Weber can be regarded as the keeper of the gateway into German Romantic opera, it is pertinent to remember that he died a year before Beethoven. Weber's father was a musician and theatre impresario and his mother an actress and singer. He had lessons in Salzburg from Michael Haydn and in 1803 went to Vienna to study with Joseph Haydn, and came under the influence of the Abbé Georg Joseph Vogler, a much respected and stimulating teacher. His first employment was as *Kapellmeister* at the Breslau municipal theatre (1804–6) and he held various posts for the next eight years.

In 1813 he accepted the post of director of Prague Opera, which enabled him to encourage performances of the operas of Mozart in Prague. In 1817 he became Court *Kapellmeister* in Dresden, where he was expected to establish German opera on an equal footing

with Italian. He had little time for composition but in 1810, while he was working in Darmstadt, he met the writer (Johann) Friedrich Kind (1768–1843), who fashioned a libretto for him and by spring 1820 he had completed *Der Freischütz*. It was a triumph at its Berlin première in June 1821, and made his name throughout Europe.

Weber had already started writing *Die drei Pintos*, but he laid it aside (and never did finish it) when the success of *Der Freischütz* led to a commission for a new opera for Vienna for the 1822–3 season. For them he wrote *Euryanthe*, which was not a success. In 1824 he was commissioned to write an opera for London. By now he had contracted tuberculosis. He finished the new work, *Oberon*, and against medical advice he travelled to London for its première in February 1826. He stayed with the composer-conductor Sir George Smart (1776–1867). After the première of his opera, Weber became increasingly ill and died, in Smart's house, seven weeks later. He was buried in London. In 1844 Richard Wagner arranged for the coffin to be brought back to Germany for burial in Dresden, with Wagner giving the oration and providing the music for the funeral service. Aside from his undoubted masterpiece, *Der Freischütz*, Weber's operas were handicapped by poor librettos and they have struggled, usually unsuccessfully, to reach audiences. But he is now regarded as the man who set German opera free from Italian influence. His impact on those who followed him is more important than his own compositions. And nowhere is that more clearly seen than in the operas of Richard Wagner.

DER FREISCHÜTZ
(*The Freeshooter*), 1817–21
Weber first thought of writing an opera based on this legend in 1811. Six years later he took up the idea again. The opera, with its strong German folk influences, was an immediate success. It is a seminal work in the history of German Romantic opera.

ABOVE LEFT **Carl Maria von Weber in 1825, aged 39, in the year before his death in London from tuberculosis**

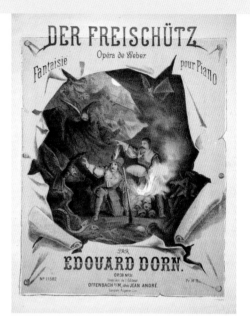

SYNOPSIS In a forest in 17th-century Bohemia, a peasant, Kilian (bar), has beaten a forester, Max (ten), in a shooting match and Max muses on his failure (**1**). The next contest is to take place before Prince Ottokar (bar) and Max must win in order to be allowed to marry Agathe (sop), daughter of the head forester Cuno (bass). Caspar (bass), another forester, has sold himself to Samiel (spoken role), the wild Black Huntsman (a manifestation of the devil). Caspar offers Max some magic bullets that can be forged in the Wolf's Glen where Samiel lives, hoping to sacrifice Max in his place (**2**). Agathe and her cousin Ännchen (sop) await the arrival of Max (**3**). They try unsuccessfully to stop him going to the Wolf's Glen. Once there, he and Caspar forge seven magic bullets. Six of the bullets will obey Max, the seventh will obey only Samiel. Max and Caspar share the bullets when hunting, each shooting three and Max keeping the seventh for the contest. Meanwhile Agathe has had a dream in which she is a dove and Max shoots her (**4**). She arrives on the scene, accompanied by the Hermit (bass), just as Max aims at a dove and she begs him not to shoot. But it is too late – and Caspar has been fatally wounded. This satisfies Samiel, who sets Max free.

> **MUSIC** (1) Max: *Durch die Wälder –
> Through the forests*; (2) Caspar: *Schweig,
> schweig, damit dich niemand warnt –
> Hush, hush, let no-one warn you*;
> (3) Agathe: *Leise, leise, fromme Weise –
> Softly, softly, my pure song*; (4) Agathe:
> *Und ob die Wolke sie verhülle – Even
> when clouds hide it.*

Other operas of note

Euryanthe (1822–3) has never been a popular
opera. It is too long, the plot is confusing,
and the characters uninteresting. *Oberon*
(1825–6) has delightful music, including the
famous "Ocean! thou mighty monster", but is
undramatic with little characterization in the
music. The comic opera *Die drei Pintos* was
begun in 1820 but left unfinished. It was
completed by Gustav Mahler (1860–1911)
in 1888 and produced that year in Leipzig.
Occasional productions have shown it to be
amusing and melodic and it was recorded in
1976, but its hybrid nature makes it a curiosity,
unlikely to become standard repertoire.

OTHER COMPOSERS OF THE GERMAN ROMANTIC ERA

Before considering the giant figure of Richard
Wagner, there are other German composers
of opera of that period who deserve mention:
HEINRICH MARSCHNER (1795–1861) was
considered the most important German opera
composer between Weber and Wagner – the
"missing link", so to speak. He was good at
depicting an atmosphere of horror and the
supernatural, but his librettos were weak
and few of his works are ever performed.
ALBERT LORTZING (1801–51) was a leading
composer of comic operas. He was mainly
self-taught, had a good sense of melody and
harmony, but lacked the genius necessary to
ensure his works would last. **FRIEDRICH VON
FLOTOW** (1812–83) wrote 30 operas, only
two of which are remembered today, *Alessandro
Stradella* of 1844 and *Martha* of 1847. Act 2 of
Martha contains "The Last Rose of Summer".

Alessandro Stradella is freely based on the life
of the Italian composer (1639–82), who led a
somewhat shady existence, often being pursued
by the law. His numerous affairs left a trail of
irate husbands keen to end his adventures.

German-born though they were, both
GIACOMO MEYERBEER (1791–1864) and
JACQUES OFFENBACH (1819–80) died in
Paris where they spent most of their lives and
they will be discussed with the French Romantic
composers. The Viennese-born **JOHANN
STRAUSS II** (1825–99), master of operetta,
cannot be ignored. From his "Blue Danube"
waltz to his "Thunder and Lightning" polka, his
light orchestral masterpieces in these genres
have not been equalled. In 1873–4 he wrote
for Vienna what is arguably the greatest of all

operettas, *Die Fledermaus* (*The Bat*). Of his
other operettas, only *Der Zigeunerbaron*
(*The Gypsy Baron*) has held the stage. The
work that can be considered stiff competition
for the title of "best operetta" is *Die lustige
Witwe* (*The Merry Widow*) by **FRANZ LEHÁR**
(1870–1948), premièred in 1905 and
therefore not strictly in the Romantic period.

Three of the greatest composers in the
German Romantic tradition – the Austrian
FRANZ SCHUBERT (1797–1828) and the
Germans **ROBERT SCHUMANN** (1810–56)
and **FELIX MENDELSSOHN** (1808–47) – all
wrote operas, but it is not through these that
their reputations have survived. Their lasting
achievements were in other genres. Which
leaves us with **RICHARD WAGNER**.

ABOVE **The soprano Alwyn Mellor as Agathe in
David Pountney's production of** *Der Freischütz*
for ENO, London, 1999

Wagner

Richard Wagner
(1813–83)

WHERE TO START
Lohengrin

WHERE TO GO NEXT
Die Meistersinger von Nürnberg

Richard Wagner is one of the most charismatic figures in the world of music, especially the world of opera, and one of the most controversial figures of the 19th century. He is one of a small number of composers who changed the course of music (others being Monteverdi, Beethoven, and Schoenberg).

Wagner was born in Leipzig in 1813, the same year as Verdi. His supposed father, Friedrich Wagner, died of typhus that year and his mother Johanna married the poet and painter Ludwig Geyer, whose mistress she was. Geyer brought Richard up as his own son and it is possible that he was. The Geyers moved to Dresden where his love of music was stimulated by Weber, who from 1817 was Court *Kapellmeister* in Dresden. At school young Wagner was more interested in theatre

ABOVE LEFT **Richard Wagner in Munich in 1864**

and music than anything else and in 1830 he entered Leipzig University to study music.

The first opera he completed was *Die Feen* (*The Fairies*), in which the mixture of history, myth, and fairy-tale was a pointer to the future. From 1833 Wagner spent a year in Würzberg as chorus master, becoming familiar with the operas of Marschner, Cherubini, and Meyerbeer. He moved to Magdeburg in 1834, conducting the German composers but also Rossini and Bellini, the latter being an influence on his next opera, *Das Liebesverbot* (*Forbidden Love*), based on Shakespeare's *Measure for Measure*. While working as music director of a small theatre, Wagner met the actress Christine Wilhelmine Planer, known as Minna, and married her in 1836. It was never a peaceful relationship and she left him for other men on more than one occasion. There were no children of the marriage.

From 1839 they lived in relative poverty in Paris. Here Wagner wrote most of *Rienzi* (1838–40) and *Der fliegende Holländer*, and earned a living writing articles, making piano arrangements, and preparing vocal scores for other composers such as Donizetti. It is sometimes said that it is from these days that his anti-Semitism stemmed: he felt that Jewish composers such as Meyerbeer and Halévy did not help him and that all the money-lenders to whom he was obliged to turn were Jewish.

LEFT Villa Wahnfried ("Peace from madness"), the home of Cosima and Richard Wagner from 1874, now a fascinating Wagner museum and archive. In front stands a bust of Wagner's patron, Ludwig II

With no hope of having his works staged in Paris, Wagner returned to Germany in 1842. Dresden staged his two latest operas (*Rienzi* and *Der fliegende Holländer*) with considerable success. As a result, he was appointed court opera conductor and in 1845 *Tannhäuser* was first produced in Dresden.

By now he had begun to write the words for a series of operas based on German and Scandinavian myths and the saga of the Nibelungs. He completed the libretto for the first of three operas, which he called *Siegfrieds Tod* (*Siegfried's Death*), in 1848. He had become politically involved and in the 1849 uprising sided with the Revolutionaries. When they were defeated by the Prussians he fled to avoid arrest. He went first to Weimar, visiting Lizst and his children (including the 16-year-old Cosima, whom he later married), and then settled in Zurich. Here he wrote a series of essays, including *The Art-Work of the Future* (1849) in which he visualized opera as a total artwork, and *Oper und Drama* (1851), in which he expounded his theory that the combination of music and drama was more important than anything else, including the needs of the singers. He also wrote *Judaism in Music* (1850), his infamous anti-Semitic pamphlet, which reflected not only his own feelings, but also the feelings of many people in 19th-century Europe.

Wagner continued writing his Nibelung librettos and composed the music for the first two operas, *Das Rheingold* and *Die Walküre*. He was, as usual, in dire financial straits and among his patrons was Otto Wesendonck, a wealthy Flemish merchant, with whose wife, Mathilde, Wagner had a passionate affair. The result was two important works, the *Five Wesendonck Songs*, which Wagner composed to words by Mathilde, and the opera *Tristan und Isolde*, both written between 1857 and 1859. He had started composing the music for the third Nibelung opera, *Siegfried*, but broke off at the end of Act 2 to write *Tristan und Isolde* (and did not return to the Nibelung legend until 1864). After the Wesendonck

BELOW **Cosima and Richard (top right) with
all their family on the garden steps at Wahnfried
in 1881**

affair it was time to leave Zurich and he and Minna took an apartment in Venice where he continued the second act of *Tristan*, finishing it in Lucerne, where the long-suffering Otto Wesendonck was still his patron.

Wagner hoped for a production of *Tristan* in Vienna, but it was cancelled as being "unperformable". In 1862 he moved to Mainz, where Minna joined him until they agreed to separate. There he began to write the words for *Die Meistersinger von Nürnberg*, his only comedy. In 1864 he left Vienna to avoid crippling debts. Fortunately for him, this was the year that the 19-year-old Ludwig became King Ludwig II of Bavaria. He was a great admirer of Wagner's music, paid off his debts, gave him a salary, a house in Munich, a piano, and a carriage. It was under the young King's patronage that *Tristan* was produced in Munich in 1865. It was conducted by the already-famous and cuckolded Hans von Bülow – for the previous two years Wagner had been in love with Bülow's wife Cosima, daughter of Liszt, and she had joined him in Munich in 1864 (bringing along her two Bülow children). Their first child, Isolde, was born in 1865, Eva in 1867, and a son, Siegfried, in 1869. Minna died in 1866. Cosima and Wagner bought a villa in Lucerne, called "Tribschen", where they lived from 1868. Cosima and Bülow divorced the year Siegfried was born and Wagner and Cosima were married in 1870. Two years later they moved to Bayreuth and planned the first Wagner festival. It took place in 1876 in a theatre built on land given by the local authority. In 1874 they moved into their house "Wahnfried", and there he completed the final Nibelung opera, *Götterdämmerung* (which started life as *Siegfrieds Tod*).

He was in London in 1877 to raise funds by conducting concerts at the Royal Albert Hall. He then composed *Parsifal*, which he completed in 1882. From 1878 he had a series of heart attacks, and he died from one in Venice in 1883. He was buried at Wahnfried

where his grave is a place of pilgrimage for visitors from all over the world who annually flock to Bayreuth for the festival of his operas at his *Festspielhaus*.

Together with that of Verdi, Wagner's music dominated the 19th century. He wrote his own librettos, researching his chosen subjects meticulously. He learned much from Cosima's father, Liszt, and from Berlioz, and was inspired by the German Romantic spirit of Weber and even by Meyerbeer's grandiose ideas. But he surpassed them all as he fulfilled his dream of music and drama, hand in hand

his *Zukunftsmusik*, music of the future. All the operas he wrote from *Der fliegende Holländer* onward are repertory works and are discussed below.

With the opening chords of *Tristan und Isolde* he moved music from the 19th to the 20th century. His use of chromaticism opened the door for the revolution of the Second Viennese School of Schoenberg, Berg, and Webern. He brought the use of leitmotiv (a term first mentioned when discussing the operas of Monteverdi, see pp.28–30) to its zenith, using them to depict not only people but also feelings and events. The orchestra was treated as part of the cast and singers had to develop a new way of singing that demanded of them the intelligence to convey the feelings he composed in the music. His influence on composers who followed him, be it good or bad, lives on to this day.

DER FLIEGENDE HOLLÄNDER

(*The Flying Dutchman*), 1840–1,
rev. several times

Wagner started writing the text of this work in Paris in 1840. He completed the libretto and composed the music, and it was accepted in Berlin. Various delays resulted in him withdrawing it from Berlin and it had its first performance in Dresden in 1843.

SYNOPSIS In 18th-century Norway, bad weather has forced Daland (bass) to anchor off the coast. Another ship appears out of the gloom, carrying the Dutchman (bar) who explains his situation (**1**): many years ago he tried to sail round the Cape of Good Hope in a violent storm, and he swore he would succeed, even if he had to sail for ever. The devil overheard this oath and condemned him to do just that. The only way he can be released is if he finds a woman who will be faithful to him for life. Once every seven years he is allowed to go ashore to search for such a woman. The Dutchman asks Daland for the hand of his daughter Senta (sop) in marriage, promising in return great wealth. Daland agrees. At their home, Senta is fascinated by the portrait of a man on the wall. She is teased about her obsession by her old governess Mary (cont) and the other women who are all spinning. She sings a ballad about the legendary Dutchman (**2**) which tells his story and she announces that she will be the woman who saves him. A hunter, Erik (ten), is in love with Senta and wants to marry her. He tells her of his dream (**3**) of a dark stranger and her reaction to him. Daland arrives home accompanied by the Dutchman, and asks Senta to welcome the stranger (**4**). She recognizes him as the man in the portrait. They are attracted to each other and she swears to be true to him for life. The Dutchman overhears Erik speaking to Senta of his love for her (**5**) and assumes she has been unfaithful to him, dooming him to a further seven years at sea. Senta tries to stop him but he leaves, telling her it is all hopeless (**6**), and she leaps into the sea in an attempt to follow him. Slowly his ship sinks and the Dutchman and Senta are seen together, rising above the vessel.

> **MUSIC** (**1**) Dutchman: *Die Frist is um…* *– The time is up…*; (**2**) Senta: *Traft ihr das Schiff im Meere an – Have you seen the ship upon the ocean?*; (**3**) Erik: *Auf hohem Felsen lag ich träumend – I lay dreaming on the high cliff*; (**4**) Daland: *Mögst du, mein Kind, den fremden Mann willkommen heissen? – Will you, my child, bid this stranger welcome?*; (**5**) Erik: *Willst jenes Tag du nicht dich mehr entsinnen – Do you no longer remember that day*; (**6**) Dutchman: *Du kennst mich nicht – You know me not.*

TANNHÄUSER UND DER SÄNGERKRIEG AUF WARTBURG

(*Tannhäuser and the Song Contest on the Wartburg*), 1843–5, rev. 1859–61

The genesis of *Tannhäuser* is very complicated. Wagner started to write the libretto in 1842 and the music in 1843, and the première was given in Dresden in 1845. Public reaction was not very enthusiastic and there were many revisions before the score was engraved, and many more for the Paris performances in 1861 (now known as the "Paris version"), the scene of a famous riot by members of the Jockey Club, with catcalls and whistles at all performances. Albert Einstein, in *Music in the Romantic Era* (London, J M Dent, 1947, p.347) appropriately described *Tannhäuser* as Wagner's "first fusion of lust and piety".

ABOVE *Der fliegende Holländer*, Bayreuth, 2003

LEFT **Model of a set for** *Tannhäuser* **showing the Venusberg grotto**

LOHENGRIN, 1845–8

Lohengrin was intended for Dresden, but Wagner's involvement with the Revolutionaries put paid to that plan, and it had its première in Weimar in 1850. Wagner was not present – as a result of his political activities, he had been exiled to Switzerland. The opera's best-known music is the Bridal March. Musically, *Lohengrin* is the most Italianate of Wagner's operas, with easily recognizable tunes.

SYNOPSIS In the first half of the 10th century, near Antwerp, King Heinrich of Saxony (bass) is in Brabant recruiting men to fight the invading Hungarians. Heinrich hears that Friedrich von Telramund (bar), the guardian of Elsa (sop) and Gottfried (silent role), children of the late Duke of Brabant, wanted to marry Elsa. The young Gottfried has disappeared. Elsa has refused to marry Telramund and he has instead married Ortrud (mez). Telramund suspects that Elsa murdered Gottfried so that she can inherit her father's land. Telramund considers himself the rightful heir to Brabant. Heinrich agrees to hear the facts and pass judgement. Elsa is summoned before him and tells how she has dreamed of a knight who will defend and protect her (1). The Herald (bass) summons the knight, Lohengrin (ten), to appear and he arrives on a boat drawn by a swan (2). He promises Elsa he will fight on her behalf and then marry her, but only on condition that she never asks him his name or whence he came (3). He wins the fight, but spares Telramund's life.

Telramund accuses Ortrud of lying about the death of Gottfried. Ortrud, thwarted in her plan to rule Brabant with Telramund, begs the pagan gods to help her regain power and tries to destroy Elsa's faith in her nameless knight (4). The Herald announces that Lohengrin will now rule Brabant and Telramund is banished. Lohengrin will marry Elsa and then lead the men of Brabant into battle.

After their wedding, Elsa and Lohengrin are in the bridal chamber (5). They express their love for each other, but Elsa, filled with the

SYNOPSIS In Thuringia, near Eisenach, in the 13th century, Tannhäuser (ten) begs Venus (sop) to release him from the grotto in the Venusberg – with all its drawbacks, he prefers a human existence to the Bacchantine orgy going on in the mountain. Venus curses him and warns him that one day he will ask her to take him back (1). He breaks away from the Venusberg and finds himself at the foot of the Wartburg. Hermann the Landgrave (bass) appears with his knights, and they recognize Tannhäuser, who deserted them years ago to be with Venus. He hears from Wolfram von Eschenbach (bar) that his former lover Elisabeth (sop) is missing him (2) and he leaves with them.

In the hall of the Wartburg Castle, Elisabeth greets the scene of Tannhäuser's earlier triumphs (3) and Wolfram leads Tannhäuser to her (4). The Landgrave announces a song contest in which the candidates must state the essence of love and promises that whoever wins the contest can marry Elisabeth. The first three contestants see love as a virtuous, moral condition. When Tannhäuser sings, he describes it as a sensual experience and tells them all to visit the Venusberg for lessons. Shocked, the other knights try to kill him, but Elisabeth intervenes. The Landgrave orders

Tannhäuser to make a pilgrimage to Rome to beg forgiveness from the Pope for his sinful thoughts and ways.

Elisabeth prays as she awaits his return – she is dying (5). Wolfram confesses his love for Elisabeth as he sings to the Evening Star (6). Tannhäuser returns, the Pope having refused to forgive him and so sentenced him to eternal damnation. He may as well return to Venus (7). Wolfram prays to Elisabeth's soul in heaven and as her coffin is carried by Tannhäuser dies, with the pilgrims granting him forgiveness.

MUSIC (1) Venus: *Zieh hin, Wahnbetörter – Begone, madman!*; **(2)** Wolfram: *War's Zauber, war es reine Macht? – Was it magic, or a divine power?*; **(3)** Elisabeth: *Dich, teure Halle, grüss ich wieder – You, dear hall, I greet again*; **(4)** Tannhäuser/ Elisabeth duet: *Gepriesen sei die Stunde – Blessed hour of meeting*; **(5)** Elisabeth: *Allmächt'ge Jungfrau, hör' mein Flehen! – Almighty Virgin, hear my pleading*; **(6)** Wolfram: *Oh du, mein holder Abendstern – Oh star of eve, so pure and fair*; **(7)** Tannhäuser: *Inbrunst im Herzen – The heat within my heart* (known as Tannhäuser's Narration).

BELOW *Lohengrin,* with Peter Hofmann in the title-role and Karen Armstrong as Elsa, Bayreuth, 1982

DER RING DES NIBELUNGEN
première as a cycle, 1876

Before describing the four operas of *Der Ring*, a short overview is helpful in perceiving the magnitude of what follows. Wagner described this work as *Ein Bühnenfestspiel für drei Tage und einen Vorabend* (A stage festival play for three days and a preliminary evening). It took him 28 years to complete and is on a larger scale than any other work in Western music. He wrote the librettos and the music. In these works he deliberately set out to write continuous dramatic works that are "through-composed" as opposed to the conventional recitatives, arias, and ensembles. The use of the leitmotiv is more obvious in the *Ring* than in any of Wagner's other operas, and listeners soon recognize the short musical phrases that represent various characters or events – there are over 100 of them! The first performance of *Der Ring des Nibelungen* was given in Bayreuth in 1876, conducted by Hans Richter. Wagner supervised every detail of the productions.

In the legends from which the story is taken, the Nibelung of the title is Alberich, one of a race of dwarfs who live in the bowels of the earth and mine for precious metals. A golden ring is stolen from him and this is the start of all the trouble that ensues over four evenings and 15 hours of music. The *Ring* is a mixture of poetry, politics, philosophy, revolutions, riddles, marital strife, and emotional conflict. It is comparable to a television series – each of the four operas is self-contained but they do follow on from one to the other and the listener is drawn in and wants to know "what happens next". To see a complete *Ring* in one week is an experience never forgotten. It is a week in which time turns upside-down and "normality" begins as the curtain goes up, the rest of the days having to be got through whilst awaiting the next episode. It is also four evenings of fascinating words, music, emotion – and wonderment. Wonderment that one human being could visualize, write, and compose this pinnacle of Romantic opera.

uncertainties planted by Ortrud, can resist no longer and asks her husband his name. Before he can answer, Telramund bursts into the bed chamber to attack Lohengrin and Lohengrin kills him. He then sadly asks Elsa to follow him to the King, to whom he will reveal all. He tells King Heinrich about Montsalvat and the Holy Grail in a distant land. His father is Parsifal, the Defender of the Grail, and his own name is Lohengrin **(6)**. The people see the swan returning. Lohengrin greets the swan **(7)**, hands his sword and ring to Elsa, and prepares to leave. Ortrud, thinking she is now the winner, boasts that she used sorcery to turn Gottfried into a swan. Lohengrin kneels in prayer and the swan changes into Gottfried, the rightful heir to Brabant. Lohengrin

proclaims Gottfried leader and leaves on his boat. Ortrud collapses as Elsa, calling for her lost husband, falls into her brother's arms.

MUSIC (1) Elsa: *In lichter Waffen Scheine – In splendid shining armour;* **(2)** Lohengrin: *Nun sei bedankt, mein lieber Schwann! – Now I thank you, my dearest swan!;* **(3)** Lohengrin/Elsa duet: *Wenn ich im Kampfe für dich siege – If I win this fight for you;* **(4)** Elsa/Ortrud duet: *Ortrud, wo bist du? – Ortrud, where are you?;* **(5)** Chorus (the Bridal March): *Treulich geführt, ziehet dahin – Faithfully guided, draw near;* **(6)** Lohengrin: *In fernem Land… – In a distant land…;* **(7)** *Mein lieber Schwann! – My dear swan.*

DAS RHEINGOLD (*The Rhinegold*), 1851–2 (libretto), 1853–4 (music)

Das Rheingold can be seen as the Prologue of the *Ring* cycle. Its first complete performance was in Munich in 1869. It is in one act, lasting 2 hours and 30 minutes. In *Das Rheingold* we meet the main character in the *Ring*, Wotan the ruler of the gods. He lost an eye breaking off a branch of the World Ash-tree from which he made the shaft of his spear. His ambition to rule the world leads, ultimately, to the downfall of the gods.

SYNOPSIS At the bottom of the Rhine the Rhinemaidens mock the dwarf Alberich (bar). He eyes the Rhine gold and they tell him that whoever can make a ring from it will rule the world. But only if they renounce love. Alberich forswears love and grabs the gold (1). High in the mountains lives Wotan (bass-bar),

husband of Fricka (mez) (2) (and later father of the Valkyries, the warrior-maidens, by the earth-goddess Erda (cont) and of two mortal children, all of whom we meet in the next opera). Wotan has asked the giants Fasolt (bar) and Fafner (bass) to build a castle (Valhalla) from where he can reign supreme. In payment, he has promised them his sister-in-law Freia (sop), who is being protected by her brothers Froh (ten) and Donner (bar). Freia is the keeper of the golden apples of eternal youth, without which the gods would wither and die, so Wotan is hoping that the wily Loge (ten), god of fire, will come up with a way of avoiding this payment. But Loge tells Wotan that Alberich has stolen the gold and made from it a magic helmet (the Tarnhelm) and a Ring, which gives him the power to rule the world (3). If the gods could gain the Ring, they could use it to pay the giants. Loge and Wotan descend underground to Nibelheim, home of the dwarfs. They watch as Alberich, who has forced his brother Mime (ten) to make the Ring and Tarnhelm, uses the power of the Ring to make everyone work for him. They capture Alberich and take the Ring, the Tarnhelm, and remaining gold. As Wotan puts the Ring on his finger, Alberich puts a terrible curse on it – it will bring unhappiness and death to those who wear it (4). Back on the mountain, the giants agree to accept the gold instead of Freia. The gods stack the gold in front of Freia to hide her, but the giants can see her through a small chink. Only the Ring will fill the space. Erda rises from the earth and warns Wotan to give up the Ring – if he keeps it, it will end in his own destruction (5). With great reluctance he hands it over and Freia is freed. The giants fight for possession of the Ring. Fafner kills Fasolt – the curse of the Ring is already working. Fricka and Wotan lead the gods across the rainbow bridge into Valhalla (6). Only Loge does not join them – he realizes (7) that in their efforts to rule the world, the gods will surely bring about their own downfall.

MUSIC (1) Alberich: *Der Welt Erbe gewänn' ich zu eigen durch dich? – The World's wealth I could win for myself through you?*; (2) Fricka/Wotan: *Wotan! Gemahl! erwache! – Wotan, husband, awake!*; (3) Loge: *Immer ist Undank Loges Lohn! – Ingratitude is always Loge's lot!*; (4) Alberich: *Bin ich nun frei? – Am I now free?*; (5) Erda: *Weiche, Wotan, weiche! – Yield, Wotan, yield!*; (6) Wotan: *Abendlich strahlt der Sonne Auge – The sun's eye sheds its evening beams*; (7) Loge: *Ihrem Ende eilen sie zu – They hasten to their end.*

DIE WALKÜRE (*The Valkyrie*), 1851–2 (libretto), 1854–6 (music)

The first complete performance of *Die Walküre* was in Munich in 1870. As well as the gods, in this three-act opera we meet Wotan's children by an unnamed human woman. As their father, he calls himself Wälse and his children are the Wälsung twins, Siegmund and Sieglinde. Their mother was killed by thugs who abducted Sieglinde. Siegmund was raised by Wälse but one day Wälse disappeared. He left behind a wolf-skin and Siegmund refers to his father as Wolfe.

SYNOPSIS In a house with an ash-tree growing through it, Sieglinde (sop) is alone while her husband Hunding (bass) is out hunting. A stranger, Siegmund (ten), collapses exhausted on her hearth. When Hunding returns he is very suspicious of the stranger, who tells them of his origins and how he killed a man and is being hunted by the dead man's friends. Hunding admits to being one of those friends. The laws of hospitality oblige him to offer the stranger shelter for the night – but tomorrow they fight. Sieglinde puts a sleeping-draught into her husband's drink. After he has retired, Siegmund recalls how his father promised him that if he was ever in trouble, there would be a sword for him (1). Sieglinde shows him a sword high in the ash tree (2).

ABOVE **The most famous Wotan of the 20th century, Hans Hotter, in *Das Rheingold*, ROH, London, 1957**

It was put there by a stranger (the disguised Wotan) on her loveless wedding day and nobody has had the strength to remove it. Siegmund does so and calls his sword "*Nothung*" (Old High German, Not = plight or need). As they talk and fall in love, they realize they are the twins, separated when their mother was killed and that their father is Wälse (Wotan) **(3)**. In the morning they run away into the forest with Hunding in pursuit.

Wotan gives an order to Brünnhilde (sop), his favourite Valkyrie daughter, telling her to ensure Siegmund wins his fight with Hunding. Brünnhilde tells him Fricka, the goddess of marriage, is angry that he encourages the twins' incestuous relationship **(4)** and after Fricka warns him his action will mean the end of the gods **(5)**, Wotan changes his mind, telling Brünnhilde that she must not save Siegmund **(6)**. Brünnhilde realizes he is prepared to betray his mortal son to pacify Fricka. She meets the fleeing twins. Siegmund refuses to leave Sieglinde at the mercy of Hunding, even though Brünnhilde explains to him that he is in danger of being killed and she cannot save him. Brünnhilde defies Wotan and saves the twins. As Siegmund and Hunding fight, Wotan arrives, furious at Brünnhilde's disobedience. His spear shatters Siegmund's sword and Hunding kills Siegmund (and Wotan then kills Hunding). Brünnhilde rides off with Sieglinde, to meet her eight sisters **(7)**. They are all too scared of Wotan to protect Sieglinde or Brünnhilde. Brünnhilde orders Sieglinde to escape to the forest, telling her she is going to give birth to the greatest hero. She gives her the pieces of Siegmund's shattered sword. Brünnhilde then faces up to

Wotan's anger. He orders her to be put to sleep on a rock and she will belong to the first man who wakes her. Left alone with her father, Brünnhilde asks him what she did that was so wrong **(8)** – she only did what he, in his heart, really wanted. He insists she must be punished. Accepting his verdict, Brünnhilde asks that she be surrounded by fire so that only a brave hero can reach her. This wish he grants her, and bids her a long and tender farewell **(9)**. Wotan places her on the rock in her armour and summons Loge to encircle her with fire **(10)**.

MUSIC (1) Siegmund: *Ein Schwert verhiess mir der Vater – My father promised me a sword*; **(2)** Sieglinde: *Eine Waffe lass mich dir weisen – Let me show you a sword*; **(3)** Siegmund/Sieglinde duet: *Winterstürme wichen dem Wonnemond – Wintry storms have vanished before Maytime*; **(4)** Brünnhilde: *Hojotoho! Hojotoho! Heiaha! … Dir rat ich, Vater – Hojotoho! Hojotoho! Heiaha! … Let me warn you, father*; **(5)** Fricka: *So ist es denn aus mit den ewigen Göttern – It is the end, then, for the everlasting gods*; **(6)** Wotan: *Ein andres ist's; achte es wohl – It is something else; listen carefully*; **(7)** Valkyries: *Hojotoho! Hojotoho! Heiaha! Heiaha! – The Ride of the Valkyries*; **(8)** Brünnhilde: *War es so schmählich, was ich verbrach…? – Was it so shameful, what I did…?*; **(9)** Wotan: *Leb' wohl, du kühnes, herrliches Kind! – Farewell, you bold, wonderful child!*; **(10)** Wotan: *Loge, hör! Lausche hieher! – Loge listen! Harken here!*

SIEGFRIED

1851–2 (libretto), 1856–7 and 1869–71 (music)

The hero of the *Ring* is Siegfried, the mortal son of Sieglinde and Siegmund. Wagner stopped writing the music to this opera in 1857 after completing the draft of Act 2. He then composed *Tristan und Isolde* and *Die Meistersinger von Nürnberg*. He returned to and finally finished *Siegfried* between 1869 and 1871, ie 12 years after he started it. Its first complete performance was as part of the first cycle in Bayreuth in 1876.

SYNOPSIS In his cave, Mime (ten) is trying to forge a sword that Siegfried (ten) cannot break. Siegfried enters leading a bear and is amused at Mime's obvious terror. Siegfried tells Mime how much he dislikes him, picks up the latest sword and breaks it. He questions the dwarf about his background and Mime tells him about his mother **(1)** and shows him the fragments of the sword, Nothung. Mime was given these by a dying woman (Sieglinde) who asked him to look after her son, Siegfried. Siegfried insists Mime must forge a sword from the fragments, and when he has it he will leave the cave and never wants to see Mime again – Siegfried is actually quite cruel to this dwarf who has raised him since he was a baby **(2)**. Siegfried leaves and the Wanderer enters – he is the disguised Wotan – and as they talk he insists that he and Mime ask each other three riddles, the stake being their lives. The Wanderer answers Mime's three questions, and Mime answers the first two that the man asks him. The third question – who will repair Nothung? – Mime is unable to answer. The Wanderer explains that it will be repaired only by someone who has never known fear. After the Wanderer has left, Siegfried returns and as Mime questions him it becomes clear that Siegfried does not know the meaning of fear. Siegfried snatches the pieces of metal from Mime and forges a sword which is so strong that he uses it to split the anvil in half **(3)**. Mime takes Siegfried to the cave where Fafner the giant, now metamorphosed by the Tarnhelm into a dragon, is guarding the gold, hoping to use Siegfried to gain the gold for himself. As Mime prepares food, Fafner rears up and Siegfried, fearless, plunges his sword into the dragon's heart and kills him. He licks some of the dragon's blood from his fingers and finds, to his amazement, that he can understand what the birds above are saying. The Woodbird (sop) tells him that the Ring and the Tarnhelm are now his and that he should not trust Mime (**4**). When the dwarf brings him a drink, Siegfried realizes it is poisoned and kills Mime. The Woodbird tells Siegfried of the sleeping Brünnhilde and leads him to her rock.

On the mountain where Brünnhilde is still asleep, surrounded by protective fire, Wotan has asked Erda how he can prevent the downfall of the gods (**5**). She cannot help him (**6**) and he resigns himself to passing on his power to his grandson Siegfried. He watches as Siegfried begins his ascent. Wotan tries to bar Siegfried's way, but the young man uses his sword to shatter Wotan's spear, the symbol of

ABOVE **Patrice Chéreau's ground-breaking production of** *Siegfried*, **Bayreuth, 1976, with Manfred Jung as Siegfried and Heinz Zednik as Mime**

his power, and Wotan retreats. Fearless, Siegfried walks through the fire. Seeing Brünnhilde, covered with shield and helmet, Siegfried assumes it is a man, but as he removes the armour he realizes it is a woman (**7**), the first he has ever seen, and for the first time he feels fear. He kisses her, and slowly she awakens and greets the sun and the daylight (**8**). She recognizes that Siegfried is the hero who has rescued her and they vow eternal love (**9**).

> **MUSIC** (**1**) Mime: *Als zullendes Kind zog ich dich auf* – I brought you up, a puling babe; (**2**) Siegfried: *Und diese Stücken sollst du mir schmieden* – And these fragments you must forge for me; (**3**) Siegfried: *Nothung! Nothung! Neidliches Schwert!* – Nothung! Nothung! Trusty sword!; (**4**) Woodbird: *Hei! Siegfried gehört nun der Niblungen Hort!* – Hey! The Nibelung's treasure now belongs to Siegfried!; (**5**) Wanderer: *Wache, Wala! Wala! Erwach!* – Waken! Wala! Wala, awake!; (**6**) Erda: *Männertaten umdämmern mir den Mut* – My mind grows misty with the deeds of men; (**7**) Siegfried: *Dass ist kein Mann!* – That is no man!; (**8**) *Heil dir, Sonne! Heil dir, Licht!* – Hail to thee, sun! Hail to thee, light!; (**9**) Brünnhilde/Siegfried duet: *O kindischer Held!* … – O childlike hero! …

GÖTTERDÄMMERUNG
(*Twilight of the Gods*), 1848–52 (libretto), 1869–74 (music)

As with Siegfried, the première of *Götterdämmerung* was as part of the first Bayreuth cycle in 1876. This final episode in the saga is the opera that started life as *Siegfrieds Tod* back in 1848, but it – and we – have come a long way since then. Wotan's actions in *Das Rheingold* now lead to their disastrous conclusion.

SYNOPSIS On the Valkyrie rock, the three Norns (cont, mez, sop), daughters of Erda, are spinning the rope that links the past with the

present and the future. The rope snaps – the link is broken. Brünnhilde and Siegfried come down from her rock. He takes the Ring from his finger and gives it to her as a symbol of his faithfulness and sets out, riding on her horse, Grane, in search of new heroic adventures (**1**). At the hall of the Gibichungs on the banks of the Rhine live the siblings Gunther (bar) and Gutrune (sop) and their half-brother Hagen (bass), illegitimate son of Alberich and the evil one of the family. Hagen is determined to gain back the gold that his father stole from the Rhinemaidens. He advises his brother and sister to marry and suggests Brünnhilde for Gunther and Siegfried for Gutrune, as this will give him access to the gold. Siegfried sails in and is made welcome. Gutrune gives Siegfried a potion (**2**) which will make him forget his love of Brünnhilde, so Gunther can then use Siegfried to gain Brünnhilde as his own bride. Siegfried drinks the potion and falls in love with Gutrune. He offers to use the Tarnhelm to disguise himself as Gunther and woo Brünnhilde. Gunther and Siegfried set off for Brünnhilde's rock, leaving Hagen on watch (**3**). Brünnhilde has been visited by one of her Valkyrie sisters, Waltraute (mez), who tells her how Wotan is sitting in Valhalla awaiting the end of the world. If Brünnhilde will return the Ring to the Rhinemaidens, this will free the gods of Alberich's curse (**4**). Brünnhilde will not part with the Ring, the symbol of Siegfried's love. Hearing Siegfried's horn, she rushes to meet him, to be confronted by "Gunther" (Siegfried in disguise), who drags the Ring from her finger and forces her to go with him to meet the real Gunther.

At the Gibichungs' hall Hagen is visited in his sleep by his father Alberich (**5**), who makes sure he understands they must continue with their plans to take the Ring. Siegfried returns and hands Brünnhilde over to Gunther (**6**). Brünnhilde sees the Ring on Siegfried's finger and claims him as her husband. He, with no memory of her, denies this, swearing his innocence on Hagen's sword (**7**). The distraught

Brünnhilde will wreak vengeance on the unfaithful Siegfried. She reveals to Hagen that Siegfried's back is vulnerable to attack. Siegfried and Gutrune enter, ready for their wedding, and Hagen makes Gunther and Brünnhilde join them for a double ceremony, calling his vassals to the marriage feast. Hagen arranges a hunting-party and encourages Siegfried to join them. On a river bank Siegfried meets the Rhinemaidens, who warn him of impending death if he keeps the Ring. As he is telling his hunting companions the story of his life (8), Wotan's two ravens fly over and Siegfried turns to look up at them. Hagen stabs him in the back. As he dies, he remembers Brünnhilde and swears he will return to her (9). His body is carried by the men back to the Gibichungs' hall (10). Gunther and Hagen fight over the Ring and Hagen kills Gunther. As he makes to take the Ring from Siegfried's finger, the dead man raises his arm and Hagen retreats, frightened. Brünnhilde has learned from the Rhinemaidens how she and Siegfried have been duped by Hagen. She orders that Siegfried's body be placed on a funeral pyre (11). She takes the Ring from Siegfried and places it on her own finger. The fire is started and Brünnhilde mounts her horse Grane and rides into the flames to die with Siegfried (12). The flames spread and destroy the Gibichungs' hall. The Rhine overflows

and Hagen and the Rhinemaidens are seen in the water. The Rhinemaidens triumphantly recover the Ring from Brünnhilde, dragging Hagen down in the depths of the river. At last the Ring is back where it belongs. Through the smoke and the flames, Valhalla can be seen burning – it is the twilight of the gods.

MUSIC (1) Orchestral interlude: *Siegfried's Journey down the Rhine*; (2) Gutrune: *Willkommen, Gast, in Gibichs Haus – Welcome, Guest, to the Gibich house*; (3) Hagen: *Hier sitz' ich zur Wacht – Here I sit on watch*; (4) Waltraute: *Höre mit Sinn, was ich dir sage! – Listen carefully to what I tell you* (known as Waltraute's Narration); (5) Alberich: *Schläfst du. Hagen mein Sohn? – Are you asleep, Hagen, my son?*; (6) Gunther: *Gegrüsst sei, teurer Held – Greetings, dear hero*; (7) Siegfried: *Helle Wehr! Heilige Waffe! – Shining spear, hallowed weapon!*; (8) Siegfried: *Mime hiess ein mürrischer Zwerg – Mime was the name of a surly dwarf*; (9) Siegfried: *Brünnhilde, heilige Braut – Brünnhilde, holy bride*; (10) Orchestra: *Siegfried's funeral march*; (11) Brünnhilde: *Starke Scheite schichtet mir dort – Stack stout logs for me in piles there*; (12) Brünnhilde: *Grane, mein Ross, sei mir gegrüsst! – Grane, my steed, greetings!*

TRISTAN UND ISOLDE

(*Tristan and Isolde*), 1857 (libretto), 1856–9 (music)

This is one of the works owed to Wagner's affair with Mathilde Wesendonck (see p.90). He was also inspired by reading the philosophy of Schopenhauer and by various other literary works. The hoped-for première in Vienna was cancelled after 77 rehearsals, the work being considered "unperformable". The first performance was given in Munich in 1865. The opening chords of this opera almost single-handedly changed the face of Western music.

SYNOPSIS An Irish princess, Isolde (sop), accompanied by her maid Brangäne (mez), is being escorted by sea from Ireland to Cornwall to marry King Mark (bass). Her escort is the Cornish knight, Tristan (ten), nephew of the King, accompanied by his friend Kurwenal (bar). Between them, Isolde and Kurwenal tell the story that led up to this point: Isolde was engaged to Morold, who was killed by Tristan, who was also injured. Isolde, knowing him only as "Tantris", had nursed Tristan back to health. When she recognized him, she resisted the temptation to kill him and found herself falling in love with him. Although he loves her, Tristan is now taking her to marry his uncle, the King. This is the point at which the opera begins. Isolde believes that Tristan does not love her and she plans to drink poison rather than marry the King who she does not love. Tristan, summoned by Isolde (1), agrees to share the drink with her. Unknown to either of them, Brangäne has substituted a love-potion. They drink it and fall passionately into each other's arms (2). They arrive at the King's castle and Isolde is escorted to her rooms. She arranges a signal with Tristan – she will extinguish the torch near her door when the coast is clear for him to come to her. Brangäne, suspicious of the intentions of Melot (ten), a supposed friend of Tristan, is reluctant to put out the torch (3), so Isolde does so herself. Tristan arrives and they spend the night together in the garden (4), with Brangäne keeping watch from the nearby tower. They ignore her warning that it is almost daylight and they should part (5) and reflect on the idea of

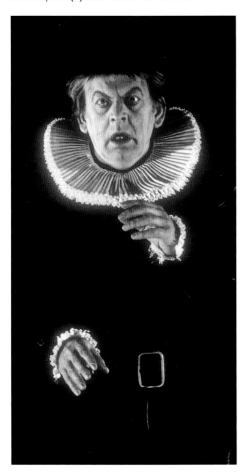

dying together – the love-death (*Liebestod*) principle (6). Kurwenal comes to tell them that King Mark is on his way. He arrives with the treacherous Melot and accuses Tristan of betraying his trust (7). As Tristan kisses Isolde, Melot draws his sword and Tristan deliberately falls on it. He is taken back to his estate in Brittany and nursed by the loyal Kurwenal (8), who has sent for Isolde, the only person able to heal his master's wound. As she arrives, Tristan tears off his bandages and rushes to meet her. The effort is too much, and he collapses and dies. King Mark, having heard about the love-potion, arrives too late to forgive Tristan. Melot and Kurwenal fight; Melot is killed and Kurwenal mortally wounded. Isolde sings of Tristan (9) and collapses over his body.

> **MUSIC** (1) Isolde: *Herrn Tristan bringe meinen Gruss – Convey to Lord Tristan my greetings*; (2) Tristan/Isolde duet: *Tristan! …Treuloser Holder/Isolde! … Seligste Frau! – Tristan! Faithless darling!/Isolde! Blessed lady!*; (3) Brangäne: *…O hör mein Warnen! – …O, listen to my warning!*; (4) Tristan/Isolde duet: *O sink hernieder, Nacht der Liebe – Descend, O night of love*; (5) Brangäne: *Einsam wachend in der Nacht – You upon whom love's dream smiles*; (6) Tristan/Isolde duet: *So stürben wir… – So might we die (Liebestod)*; (7) Mark: *Tatest du's wirklich? – Have you indeed?*; (8) Kurwenal: *Wo bist du? – Where are you?*; (9) Isolde: *Mild und leise wie er lächelt – How softly and sweetly he smiles.*

DIE MEISTERSINGER VON NÜRNBERG

(*The Mastersingers of Nuremberg*), 1845, 1861–2, 1866–7 (libretto), 1862–4, 1866–7 (music)

This is Wagner's only comedy but, as with all good comedy, there is a serious side. The première was in Munich in 1868, although many excerpts had already been performed, some of them before Wagner had finished the composition. The text is primarily Wagner's invention, but the main character is based on a real person, the 16th-century poet–shoemaker Hans Sachs, who lived most of his life in Nuremberg, and belonged to the Guild of Mastersingers.

SYNOPSIS In 16th-century Nuremberg, a knight, Walther von Stolzing (ten), has fallen in love with Eva (sop), daughter of the goldsmith Veit Pogner (bass). A singing competition is to be held on Midsummer's Day (tomorrow), but only members of the Mastersingers' Guild may enter. Walther is not a member, so he must join. For his initiation he has to sing a song that must follow certain rules. Eva's companion Magdalene (mez) suggests her boyfriend David (ten), who is Sachs's apprentice, can teach him these rules (1). Pogner announces that the prize for the winner will be Eva's hand in marriage (2). The town clerk Sixtus Beckmesser (bass-bar) marks Walther as he sings (3) and fails him. Only the widowed cobbler Hans Sachs (bass), who also loves Eva, but acknowledges that he is too old for her, recognizes that Walther's singing has great artistry – he just needs to know the rules. Sachs sends David home and sits outside his shop, under an elder tree, reflecting on the situation (4). Eva consults Sachs about the best way to ensure that the man she loves is the winner.

Having failed his initiation into the guild, Walther and Eva decide to elope but their plan is foiled by Sachs. As Beckmesser serenades beneath Eva's window (not knowing that Eva's place at the window has been taken by Magdalene), Sachs, repairing shoes, "marks" him by striking his hammer on the shoe-last (5). Beckmesser's singing and Sachs's marking get louder and louder, until the entire neighbourhood is awakened. David, finding Beckmesser serenading Magdalene, starts a fight in which everyone joins. The chaos is brought to an end by the arrival of the Nightwatchman (bass) to extinguish the street lights (6).

The next day Sachs sits thinking about the night before (7). He takes Walther into his workroom and together they shape and write down the song that Walther will sing, which is based upon a dream that Walther had the night before. They leave the room, and Beckmesser peers through the window, sees the song and assumes that Sachs is also a competitor. Sachs finds him there, assures him he is not a rival and even allows him to take the song. Eva comes to Sachs's workroom, where Walther is dressing for the contest, and Magdalene and David are also there. Sachs acknowledges the inevitability of the relationship between Eva and Walther and they all voice their feelings and thoughts (8).

Sachs announces that a new master-song has been born and needs to be baptized. The Mastersingers gather in the meadow on the banks of the river ready for the song-contest (9). Beckmesser sings his own distorted version of the song he got from Sachs, causing such hilarity and ridicule that he slinks away. Sachs announces the true writer of the song and Walther performs it (10). He is clearly the winner. Eva places the victor's wreath on his head. Pogner attempts to put the Masters' chain of office round Walther's neck, but the young knight refuses it – he does not want to join the guild that made things so difficult for him. Sachs tells him he should not mock the Guild or German art (11). Walther agrees to accept the honour. Eva removes the wreath from Walther's head and places it on Hans Sachs. He, in his turn, gives Walther the chain of office as the crowd sing in praise of Holy German Art (12).

MUSIC (1) David: *Mein Herr! Der Singer Meisterschlag gewinnt sich nicht in einem Tag* – Sir, the touch which makes a Mastersinger is not to be gained in a day; (2) Pogner: *Nun hört und versteht mich recht!* – Listen! And understand me aright!; (3) Walther: *"Fanget an!" So rief der Lenz in den Wald* – "Begin!" So the spring cried to the forest; (4) Sachs: *Was duftet doch der Flieder, so mild, so stark und voll* – So mild, so strong and full of scent of the elder (*Fliedermonolog*); (5) Beckmesser: *Den Tag seh' ich erscheinen…* – The day I see appear…; (6) Nightwatchman: *Hört, ihr Leut', und lasst euch sagen* – Hear, people, what I say; (7) Sachs: *Wahn! Wahn! Überall Wahn!* – Madness! Madness! Everywhere madness! (*Wahnmonolog*); (8) Sachs/Eva/Walther/Magdalene/David quintet: *Selig wie die Sonne* – As blissfully as the sun; (9) Chorus: *Wach auf, es nahet gen den Tag* – Awake! The dawn is drawing near; (10) Walther: *"Morgenlich leuchtend im rosigen Schein…"* – "Shining in the rosy light of morning…"; (11) Sachs: *Verachtet mir die Meister nicht* – Scorn not the Masters, I bid you; (12) Chorus: *Ehrt eure deutschen Meister* – Honour your German Masters.

PARSIFAL

1865, 1877 (libretto), 1877–82 (music)

Wagner's last opera is a work that divides writers. It is based on the concept of compassion, and the main literary source was an early 13th-century epic poem *Parzifal*. Wagner called *Parsifal* a *Bühnenweihfestspiel*, a stage dedication play, in three acts, and wanted it to be performed only at the Bayreuth Festival, who had the copyright on it until the end of 1913 (although this was infringed by performances in American and European cities). Views differ as to its allegorical meaning: some consider it a totally religious work, others a story of religious eroticism, but whichever view one takes there is no denying

ABOVE **The magician Klingsor's Enchanted Garden** in *Parsifal*, 1914

the beauty of the score and the fascination of the story. Its first performance was at Bayreuth in 1882.

SYNOPSIS In the Middle Ages, Amfortas (bar) is in charge of the Spear that pierced Christ's side and the Grail, the chalice in which the blood of Christ on the cross was caught. Amfortas's father Titurel (bass) built Monsalvat, the Castle of the Knights, to house these relics. On the other side of the mountain live the magician Klingsor (bass), who wants to destroy the Knights of the Grail, and Kundry (sop). She has been condemned to roam the world seeking redemption because she laughed at Christ on the Cross. Under the influence of Klingsor she seduced Amfortas. Klingsor stole the Spear and wounded Amfortas with it. Amfortas was brought back to Monsalvat by a senior knight, Gurnemanz (bass), and it is from him that we learn the background described above (1). Amfortas's wound will not heal and he is becoming weaker and unable to carry out the ritual unveiling of the Grail. In a dream he learns that "only an innocent fool, wise through compassion" will be able to help him. A young man wanders into Monsalvat, having just killed a swan. He is unaware that he has done anything wrong and does not even know his own name. Gurnemanz, hoping this is the youth who can help cure Amfortas, takes him into the castle. Only Kundry knows that he was kept innocent of worldly affairs by his mother, who is now dead (2). He does not understand the significance of the Grail and is distressed as Amfortas describes his agony when he attempts to uncover the Grail (3).

That night he wanders towards Klingsor's castle, reaching the magic garden inhabited by the Flower Maidens. Klingsor orders Kundry to seduce the youth. He cannot resist her and she calls him Parsifal (ten), a name he has heard in a dream about his mother (and a name familiar from the opera *Lohengrin*, whose eponymous hero declared himself the son of Parsifal, see p.94). Kundry kisses him, but Parsifal is suddenly reminded of Amfortas's

agony, and refuses to submit to her (4) and she calls on Klingsor for help (5). Klingsor throws the Spear at Parsifal. It hovers in mid-air above Parsifal, who takes it and instinctively crosses himself, whereupon Klingsor's castle disappears. As Parsifal leaves he tells Kundry that she knows where she can find him again.

Many years have passed. Amfortas is still suffering and unable to unveil the Grail. In the forest Parsifal meets Gurnemanz, now an old man, and explains how he has travelled far in his effort to find Amfortas and return the Spear to where it belongs (6). Gurnemanz has found the half-dead Kundry in the forest. She washes Parsifal's feet and dries them with her hair. Parsifal is anointed by Gurnemanz as the new King of the Grail, and Parsifal then baptizes Kundry, redeeming her from Klingsor's spell. Gurnemanz leads them to Amfortas in the castle (7), where the funeral of Titurel is taking place. Amfortas begs his fellow-knights to end his suffering by killing him (8). Parsifal touches Amfortas's wound with the Spear and it immediately heals (9). Parsifal uncovers the Grail and as he kneels in prayer, Kundry dies at his feet. Parsifal, from being the "innocent fool", has become the compassionate saint.

MUSIC (1) Gurnemanz: *Titurel, der fromme Held, der kannt' ihn wohl – Titurel, the godly hero, knew him well*; **(2)** Kundry: *Den Vaterlosen gebar die Mutter – His mother bore him fatherless*; **(3)** Amfortas: *Nein! Lasst ihn unenthüllt! – Oh! No, leave it covered! Oh!*; **(4)** Parsifal: *Auf Ewigkeit wärst du verdammt mit mir – For evermore would you be damned with me*; **(5)** Kundry: *Hilfe! Hilfe! Herbei! – Help! Help! Hither!*; **(6)** Parsifal: *Zu ihm, des tiefe Klagen – To him, whose deep lamenting*; **(7)** Gurnemanz: *Gewisslich, unsrer harrt die hehre Burg – Assuredly, the great castle awaits us*; **(8)** Amfortas: *Ja, Wehe! Wehe! Weh' über mich! – Alas indeed! Alas! Woe be on me!*; **(9)** Parsifal: *Nur eine Waffe taugt – Only one weapon serves.*

Meyerbeer

Giacomo Meyerbeer
(1791–1864)

WHERE TO START
Les Huguenots

WHERE TO GO NEXT
Le prophète

It may seem perverse to begin discussion of French Romantic opera with the name of a German, but Meyerbeer was a French composer in everything except name and nationality. Large-style French opera had developed at the end of the 18th century because of the desire to glorify the Revolution and the Empire and also because the audiences for opera had increased during and after the Revolution (as they did in Britain during the Second World War) as people turned to the arts as a contrast to the tragedy around them. Added to traditional opera form were huge choruses and spectacular scenes, similar to those used earlier by Rameau and Gluck. Many of these developments rubbed off on German opera composers, but never travelled to Italy. So this form of opera was well established in Paris, the term "grand opera" (with accompanied recitatives) being used in contrast to "*opéra-comique*" (with spoken

dialogue). By the 1830s there were also large doses of passionate romance or violence in the stories and in the music composed, and the subject for an opera was more likely to come from medieval or modern history, often with contemporary political or religious overtones.

Jakob Liebmann Beer was born near Berlin, of wealthy Jewish parentage, and he prefixed the "Meyer" in 1810 after receiving a legacy from a relative of that name. He visited Italy for the first time in 1816 and stayed for nine years, collecting folk-songs and starting to compose operas. As his interest in opera developed he came to admire Rossini and wrote six Italian operas between 1817 and 1824, all well received. *Il crociato in Egitto (The Crusader in Egypt)* of 1824 (one of the last works written for a castrato) was a success in Venice and in Paris two years later and he then went to work in Paris. His first French opera, *Robert le diable,* with Eugène Scribe as the librettist, was commissioned for the Paris Opéra in 1831. It was on a large scale and in it he combined Italian melody and German harmony with the grand French declamatory style. It was a huge success. His

next two operas were *Les Huguenots* (1836) and *Le prophète* (1836–49), both with Scribe, the latter being the first opera staged at the Paris opera house using electric lighting effects. He returned to Berlin in 1842 for seven years as General Music Director, but went back to Paris in 1863 to supervise rehearsals of his longest opera, *L'africaine,* on which he had worked for over 20 years.

Together with his librettist, Eugène Scribe, Meyerbeer is considered the composer of quintessential French grand opera of the mid-19th century. His operas were usually in five acts and lasted over four hours. They had spectacular sets, historical plots with a touch of the supernatural, and the obligatory ballet. His orchestral effects were bold and brilliant and he provided opportunities for his singers to show off their voices. One of the things that has militated against the production of his works in the middle to late 20th century and beyond – apart from a change in tastes – is the difficulty of finding satisfactory casts. His works were written for soloists of a high calibre and a vocal technique very difficult to find today. They are also expensive to stage and have a limited appeal.

ABOVE LEFT **Giacomo Meyerbeer in 1843, aged 51**

ABOVE **A dramatic scene of the crusaders' arrival in the first act of Meyerbeer's *Il crociato in Egitto*, La Scala, Milan, 1826**

Offenbach

Jacques Offenbach
(1819–80)

WHERE TO START
Les contes d'Hoffmann

WHERE TO GO NEXT
La belle Hélène

Jacques (originally Jacob) Offenbach was born in Cologne, the second son of a Jewish cantor. He showed such musical promise that in 1833 his father sent him to the Paris Conservatoire. Offenbach spent most of the rest of his life in France and can be regarded as the creator of French operetta. His first success was *Orphée aux enfers* (*Orpheus in the Underworld*) of 1858 with its famous can-can, and he also composed *La belle Hélène*, *La vie parisienne*, *La Périchole*, and *La Grande-Duchesse de Gérolstein*. In 1877 Offenbach started his only grand opera, *Les contes d'Hoffmann* (*The Tales of Hoffmann*), but died before completing it. Ernest Guiraud (1837–92), the American-born French composer and teacher, completed the work for its Paris première in 1881. He dropped the Giulietta act, set in Venice, and moved the Antonia act (set in Munich) to Venice in order not to lose the famous Barcarolle in the dropped act. The Giulietta act is usually now included.

ABOVE Jacques Offenbach, the founder of French operetta, photographed c.1865, aged 46

LES CONTES D'HOFFMANN
(*The Tales of Hoffmann*), 1877–80

Jules Barbier's libretto is based on tales by the German writer-composer ET A Hoffmann (1776–1822). The opera begins and ends in a tavern. The three central acts tell the story of Hoffmann's loves, Olympia, Antonia, and Giulietta. In all acts are characters who link the work together: Hoffmann himself, his muse Nicklausse (a *travesti* role), four baritone/bass roles (Lindorf/Coppélius/Dr Miracle/Dapertutto), and four tenor roles (Andrès/Cochenille/Pittichinaccio/Frantz). There are various editions of this opera, so the action may vary from that described below.

SYNOPSIS Hoffmann (ten) and Nicklausse (mez) are drinking in a Nuremberg tavern (1). Hoffmann loves the opera singer Stella (sop), who is also loved by Lindorf (bass), for whom she finally leaves Hoffmann. Hoffmann blames Lindorf for thwarting all his love affairs and describes the incidents to students in the tavern.

The inventor Spalanzani (ten) shows his singing doll Olympia (sop) to the public. He repeatedly winds up her mechanism while she sings (2). Hoffmann falls in love with her (3), believing her to be human. Spalanzani's rival,, Coppélius (bar), destroys Olympia.

In Munich Hoffmann falls in love with Antonia (sop). She is seriously ill and her father Crespel (bar/bass) forbids her to exert herself by singing. She nevertheless does so (4) and Hoffmann finds her and they declare their love (5). Dr Miracle (bar), who was responsible for her mother's death, forces Antonia to sing and she dies.

In Venice the beautiful courtesan Giulietta sings the Barcarolle (6). Dapertutto (bar/bass), a sorcerer, gives Giulietta a diamond to tempt her to obtain Hoffmann's soul (7). Hoffmann and Giulietta fall in love. During their duet (8) she gets the reflection of him that Dapertutto is demanding. Hoffmann obtains the key to Giulietta's room. He goes to rescue her, and sees her disappearing in a gondola with the hunchback servant Pittichinaccio (ten).

Back in the tavern, Nicklausse points out that all Hoffmann's loves have been manifestations of Stella. Stella arrives, but leaves with Lindorf – whose other manifestations have appeared in the other episodes. Nicklausse consoles Hoffmann with the observation that his poetry will be all the better for his sad experiences in love.

> **MUSIC** (1) Hoffmann: *Il était une fois à la cour d'Eisenach – There was once at the court of Eisenach*; (2) Olympia: *Les oiseaux dans la charmille – Birds in the arbour*; (3) Hoffmann: *Ah, vivre deux – Ah, to live together*; (4) Antonia: *Elle a fui, la touterelle! – The turtle-dove has flown*; (5) Hoffmann/Antonia duet: *C'est un chanson d'amour qui s'envole – It is a love-song that soars aloft*; (6) Giulietta/Nicklausse duet: *Belle nuit, ô nuit d'amour – Beautiful night, o night of love* (Barcarolle); (7) Dapertutto: *Scintille, diamant! – Sparkle, diamond!*; (8) Giulietta/Hoffmann duet: *Si ta presence m'est ravie/Extase, ivresse inassouvie – If I am deprived of your presence/Ecstasy, unsatiated rapture*.

ABOVE RIGHT **Natalie Dessay as Olympia, the mechanical doll brought to life by her maker Spalanzani (Sergio Bertocchi) in *Les contes d'Hoffmann*, Opéra Bastille, Paris, 1999**

Berlioz

Hector Berlioz
(1803–69)

LEFT Hector Berlioz in Paris in 1863, aged 60

WHERE TO START
Béatrice et Bénédict

WHERE TO GO NEXT
Les troyens

The earliest-born of the native French Romantic composers was Hector Berlioz. The son of a doctor, at the age of 18 he was sent to medical school in Paris. He showed an early aptitude for music, started having lessons in 1822, and was soon composing choral and orchestral pieces. Two years later, he formally abandoned his medical studies to concentrate on music. In 1826 he entered the Paris Conservatoire and composed his first opera, *Les Francs Juges*, a medieval drama. A year later he saw *Hamlet* given by J P Kemble's English company and fell in love with Shakespeare and with the actress who played Ophelia, Harriet Smithson. They met in 1832 and were married 10 months later. For the next 10 years he produced some of his greatest works, including his second opera *Benvenuto Cellini*, about a Florentine metal-worker. Berlioz was an excellent writer and supplemented his income by writing music criticism. His *Mémoires* read more like a novel. His marriage to Harriet broke up in 1841 and he formed a relationship with a singer, Marie Recio. He visited London on four occasions and went to Russia. In 1856 he started his masterpiece, the opera *Les troyens*, for which he wrote the words (based on Virgil's *Aeneid*) and the music. It took him two years to complete but he could not persuade the Paris Opéra to stage it. Berlioz's last work, written in 1860–2, was the comic opera *Béatrice et Bénédict*, based on Shakespeare's *Much Ado About Nothing*. It received its première in Baden-Baden in 1862; it was not performed in Paris until 1890.

The greatest influences on Berlioz's music were Gluck, whom he greatly admired, as well as Spontini, Cherubini, and others of this period. He heard as much of their music as he could once he arrived in Paris, much preferring their grand operas to those of Rossini. Later he was very impressed by Weber's *Der Freischütz* (see pp.88–9). For the last 25 years of his life he acted as a consultant for productions of other people's operas – Gluck's *Alceste*, for instance, or Weber's *Der Freischütz*, for a production of which in 1841 he composed recitatives, as spoken dialogue was not allowed at the Opéra, and he orchestrated Weber's piano piece *Invitation to the Dance* for use as the ballet which was then *de rigueur* in French opera.

He wrote only five operas. *Benvenuto Cellini* is an amalgam of the comic and of grand opera, an original work that had a bad start, surviving only four performances. More recently it has been staged but it has not become standard repertory. His other two mature operas, which do receive regular stagings, are *Les troyens* and *Béatrice et Bénédict*.

LES TROYENS

(The Trojans), 1856–8, revised in two parts 1859–60

Having failed to persuade the Paris Opéra to stage *Les troyens*, Berlioz divided it into two parts: the first two acts became *The Capture of Troy* and Acts 3–5 became *The Trojans at Carthage*. He saw the second half, in an inadequate production by the Théâtre-Lyrique, Paris, in 1863, and was greatly distressed by its failure. The first part of the opera was not staged until 1890, in Karlsruhe, as part of the first complete performance of the work, more than 20 years after the composer's death.

SYNOPSIS Part I, *La Prise de Troie*, takes place in Troy in the 12th–13th century BC. The Trojans have, after 10 years, driven out the Greeks, who have left behind a large wooden horse as an offering to Pallas Athene. Cassandre (mez), daughter of King Priam (bass), foretells the destruction of Troy and tries to persuade her fiancé **(1)**, the Asian Prince Chorèbe (bar), to flee but he refuses to leave her **(2)**. The people try to destroy the wooden horse, but their leader is devoured by serpents. King Priam's son Hector has been killed in battle. Priam orders the horse to be brought within the city walls and placed in

ABOVE *The Capture of Troy*, the second part of *Les troyens*, Paris, 1899

LEFT Ann Murray and Philip Langridge quarrelling in the title-roles of Berlioz's *Béatrice et Bénédict*, ENO, London, 1990

front of Athene's Temple. Hector's Ghost (bass) tells the Trojan hero Énée (Aeneas, ten) to leave and found a new Troy in Italy (**3**). Chorèbe is killed and Cassandre informs the Trojan women that she will die rather than fall into the hands of the Greeks. Some of the women fear death and leave, but others vow to die with her (**4**). Cassandre stabs herself and the remaining women follow her to their death to the horror of the Greek soldiers.

Part 2, *Les troyens à Carthage* opens in the palace of Queen Didon (mez) as her people celebrate their success over the past seven years, and promise to defend her from the Numidians (**5**). Didon's husband has been killed by her brother, and her sister Anna (alto) urges her to remarry. The Trojans, en route to Italy, are driven ashore by a storm and Didon, remembering her own wanderings (**6**), gives them shelter in her palace. While they are sheltering, the Numidians attack Carthage and Énée leads his followers, together with the Carthaginians, into battle. During the well-known *Royal Hunt and Storm* scene, Didon and Énée admit they have fallen in love (**7**). The gods send endless ghostly messages to Énée to continue on to Italy, and eventually, when the storm has subsided, he and the Trojans reluctantly set sail to build a new Troy there. Feeling deserted, Didon says farewell to her friends and country (**8**) and stabs herself with her lover's sword. She then ascends a pyre she has built to burn all memories of her lover. Her final vision is of an Eternal Rome.

MUSIC (**1**) Cassandre: *Malheureux roi – Ill-fated King*; (**2**) Cassandre/Chorèbe duet: *Quitte-nous dès ce soir – Leave us tonight*; (**3**) Hector's Ghost: *Ah! fuis, fils de Vénus – Ah! Fly, son of Venus*; (**4**) Cassandre/Women's Chorus: *Complice de sa gloire – Partaking in her glory*; (**5**) Chorus: *Gloire à Didon – Glory to Dido*; (**6**) Didon: *Errante sur les mers – Wandering on the seas*; (**7**) Didon/Énée duet: *Nuit d'ivresse et d'extase infinie – Night of boundless ecstasy and rapture*; (**8**) Didon: *Adieu, fière cité – Farewell, proud city.*

BÉATRICE ET BÉNÉDICT

(*Beatrice and Benedict*), 1860–2, rev. 1863

Berlioz wrote this libretto himself, adapting it from *Much Ado About Nothing*. It was to prove his last major work. It is not a very long opera and the numbers are separated by spoken dialogue in the manner of *opéra-comique*. The opera centres on a short episode from the play, in which the stormy love-match between Beatrice and Benedick is contrasted with the romantic love between Hero and Claudio. Berlioz invented the comic character Somarone, the fussy and old-fashioned court musician, to replace Shakespeare's Balthazar. It is an enchanting piece, beautifully scored, which needs singers who can also act and deliver the spoken text convincingly. At Buxton Festival in 1980 it was produced by Ronald Eyre and the title-roles were played by the not-yet-married Ann Murray and Philip Langridge, throwing off the Shakespearean lines as if they'd been trained in Stratford-upon Avon. It was a memorable operatic evening.

SYNOPSIS In Messina, Hero (sop), the daughter of the governor Léonato (spoken role), is to marry the victorious Claudio (bar) and she is overjoyed at the thought of his return from the Moorish Wars (**1**). Béatrice (mez), the governor's niece, is in love with a young army officer, Bénédict, but will not admit it. They are constantly at war and mock each other (**2**). Bénédict declares he will happily remain a bachelor (**3**). Don Pedro (bass), an army general, plots with Claudio to trick them into admitting their love for each other. It is arranged for Bénédict to overhear a conversation in which it is said that Béatrice is in love with him and he is astonished but pleased (**4**). Hero and her companion Ursula (mez) play a similar trick on Béatrice, who now learns that Bénédict loves her. They laugh and comment on the beautiful night (**5**). Somarone (bass) rehearses the bridal music he has written for Claudio and Hero's wedding. Béatrice remembers how she dreamed of Bénédict when he was away (**6**) and admits her feelings. Together with Hero and Ursula she sings of the joy of marrying the man one loves (**7**). After Claudio's and Hero's wedding ceremony, the registrar offers a second contract and Béatrice and Bénédict reluctantly admit their feelings for each other and acknowledge the power of true love (**8**).

MUSIC (**1**) Hero: *Je vais le voir – I shall see him*; (**2**) Béatrice/Bénédict duet: *Comment le dédain pourrait-il mourir? – Is it possible disdain should die?*; (**3**) Bénédict: *Me marier? – I marry?*; (**4**) Bénédict: *Ah! je vais l'aimer… – Ah! I will love her…*; (**5**) Hero/Ursula duet: *Nuit paisible et sereine – Serene and peaceful night*; (**6**) Béatrice: *Il m'en souvient… – It comes back to me…*; (**7**) Béatrice/Hero/Ursula trio: *Je vais d'un coeur aimant – I am to be a loving heart's [chief joy]*; (**8**) Béatrice/Bénédict duet: *L'amour est un flambeau – Love is a torch.*

Gounod

Charles Gounod
(1818–93)

WHERE TO START
Faust

WHERE TO GO NEXT
Roméo et Juliette

Gounod was a gifted painter and used the opportunity when studying in Rome to soak up all the art he could find. He also studied the religious music of the 16th century, particularly that of Palestrina (1525/6–94). Gounod visited Germany and Austria and met Mendelssohn, whose musical influence can be detected in some of his music. He looked back to the Classical period as a model for his works, admiring the balance of Classical culture generally.

He seriously thought about becoming a priest but he abandoned the idea to concentrate on composition. Opera was not his first enthusiasm, his early compositions being sacred choral works and short instrumental pieces for religious services. Living in Paris, he met the singer Pauline Viardot and her husband Louis Viardot, a critic

and impresario. It was they who secured for him a commission from the Opéra, and suggested a Classical subject, *Sapho*. It was not a success with the public, although some more perceptive critics, including Hector Berlioz, were very supportive. In 1851 Gounod married Anna Zimmermann, daughter of his piano teacher at the Conservatoire. He taught some of his father-in-law's students and thus met Bizet, whose works show the influence of Gounod (see pp.109–10). Similarly, he encouraged the young Saint-Saëns and the two men became firm friends.

Gounod's attempts at two more operas were failures but his two symphonies and a Mass all proved popular. Then in 1856 he received a commission to write an historical opera *Ivan le terrible*. He started this, but gave it up (and the libretto, much altered, was used by Bizet to compose an opera on the same subject). The same year Gounod was introduced to the writers and librettists Michel Carré and Jules Barbier and with them he had his first real operatic success in the shape of *Faust*. He began composition in 1856 but laid it aside the following year and composed another opera, *Le médecin malgré lui*, also with Carré and Barbier. Although not much of a success, the composer considered this his best opera to date. In 1858 he resumed work on *Faust*, which had its première in March 1859. Its reception was mixed, the more progressive critics being supportive (again including Berlioz) and within the next five years it achieved its place in Parisian musical life.

In the eight years following the *Faust* première, Gounod wrote five more operas, all with the same librettists. The most popular of these was *Roméo et Juliette,* which had its first performance in Paris during the International Exposition of 1867. It proved the high point of his career, soon achieving international success.

Throughout the rest of his life Gounod had periods when he composed very little. He suffered from what he called "mental fatigue", which on occasions required him to undergo

medical treatment. He had several close relationships with women in his arts circle, both in Paris and in London where he lived for three years. Gounod's religious faith sustained him through many difficult periods in his life, both personal and professional. He died in 1893 after a year of illnesses and received a state funeral in Paris.

Of his 15 operas, *Faust* and *Roméo et Juliette* can be considered repertory works. Few of his other operas are performed, only *La Colombe* (1860) and *Mireille* (1862–4) receiving rare airings.

FAUST
1856–9 (ballet added 1868–9 for a Paris revival)

Gounod's opera was based partly on Goethe's *Faust* and partly on *Faust et Marguerite* by Michel Carré, who was joint librettist with Jules Barbier. It was composed with spoken dialogue but Gounod soon replaced this with accompanied recitative.

SYNOPSIS Faust (ten) yearns for sensual pleasures and the devil, Méphistophélès (bass), promises to provide them in return for his services in the underworld. Faust agrees and is transformed into a young nobleman (1). Valentin (bar) is going off to battle and asks his

ABOVE LEFT **A French portrait of Charles Gounod** (1818–93)

ABOVE **Nicolai Ghiaurov as Méphistophélès in** Gounod's *Faust*, **his début at the Metropolitan Opera, NY, 1965**

RIGHT Angela Gheorghiu and Roberto Alagna as the lovers in Gounod's *Roméo et Juliette*, ROH, London, 2000

friends Wagner (bar) and Siébel (sop, *travesti* role) to look after his sister Marguerite (sop). They are joined by Méphistophélès who sings a blasphemous song (2). Faust approaches Marguerite, who rejects him. Later he sings in her garden (3). Siébel leaves flowers for Marguerite and Méphistophélès adds a jewel-case. When Marguerite sees the jewels she is ecstatic (4). Her guardian Marthe (mez) is attracted to Méphistophélès. Faust and Marguerite sing a duet (5) and despite her protests Faust, encouraged by Méphistophélès, seduces her. She bears him a child and is ostracized by her friends. Siébel tries to cheer her up as she sits spinning (6). Valentin and the army return (7) and Faust admits to Valentin that he is responsible for Marguerite's downfall. They fight and Valentin is killed. As he dies, he damns his sister for eternity. On Walpurgis Night (the eve of 1 May) in the mountains, Faust sees a vision of Marguerite, who has been imprisoned for killing her child. Méphistophélès gives him the key to her cell and he begs her to run (8). Méphistophélès tries to persuade them to follow him, but Marguerite calls for divine protection (9) and as Faust looks on helplessly she rises to heaven.

MUSIC (1) Faust/Méphistophélès duet: *A moi les plaisirs – Bring me the bliss*; (2) Méphistophélès: *Le veau d'or – The golden calf*; (3) Faust: *Salut! demeure chaste et pure – Pure and chaste abode*; (4) Marguerite: *Ah! je ris de me voir – Ah! I see beauty laughing* (the Jewel Song); (5) Faust/Marguerite duet: *Laisse moi, laisse moi contempler ton visage – Let me look at your face*; (6) Marguerite: *Il ne revient pas – He is not returning*; (7) Chorus: *Gloire immortelle de nos aïeux – Immortal glory of our ancestors* (Soldiers' Chorus); (8) Faust/Marguerite duet: *Oui, c'est toi je t'aime – Yes, it is you I love*; (9) Marguerite: *Anges pure, anges radieux – Pure and radiant angels*.

ROMÉO ET JULIETTE, 1865–7

For this opera after Shakespeare, the librettists were the same as for *Faust*. Much of the play was cut and altered to suit the drama of the opera, with its focus on the two title-roles. Again Gounod provided a ballet in Act 4 for a later production. There are several editions of this work, so the action may vary from one production to another.

SYNOPSIS At a ball in Verona, Juliette (sop) is led in by her father Capulet (bass). Roméo (ten), a Montaigu, emerges from hiding with his friends Benvolio (ten) and Mercutio (bar). Mercutio sings of the fairy queen (1). Juliette discusses with her nurse Gertrude (mez) her lack of interest in marriage (2). She then meets Roméo and her attitude changes. Capulet's nephew Tybalt (ten) is angry with the Montaigus for gate-crashing the party.

In the Capulets' garden, Roméo sings of Juliette (3), she comes out and they agree to marry. Frère Laurent (bass) marries Roméo and Juliette. The Montaigu page Stéphano (sop, *travesti* role) taunts the Capulets (4) and in the resultant fight Roméo kills Tybalt and is sent into exile. The lovers spend the night together (5) and then agree they must part. Capulet tells his daughter she must marry the elderly Paris (bar). Frère Laurent helps them

to avoid this by supplying Juliette with a potion that will send her into a deep sleep and make her appear dead. She summons up her courage, drinks it, collapses, and is taken to the family crypt. But Roméo has not received the letter explaining all this to him, and when he sees her he assumes she is really dead and he takes poison. Juliette awakens as he is dying. They sing of their love (6) and she stabs herself and dies next to Roméo.

MUSIC (1) Mercutio: *Mab, la reine des mensonges – Mab, queen of illusions*; (2) Juliette: *Ah! je veux vivre – Ah! I want to live*; (3) Roméo: *Ah! lève-toi soleil – Ah! arise o sun*; (4) Stéphano: *Que fais-tu, blanche tourterelle – What are you doing, white turtledove*; (5) Juliette/Roméo duet: *Nuit d'hyménée, O douce nuit d'amour – Bridal night, sweet night of love*; (6) Roméo: *Console-toi, pauvre âme – Console yourself, poor soul*.

Saint-Saëns

(Charles) Camille Saint-Saëns
(1835–1921)

WHERE TO START
Samson et Dalila

Born in Paris, Camille Saint-Saëns was one of the most gifted children of his generation. He entered the Paris Conservatoire in 1848, when he was 13. From 1853 to 1877 he played the organ in various Paris churches and was considered one of the great French organists of the 19th century. In 1852 he became a friend of Ferencz (Franz) Liszt (1811–86) and was much influenced by him.

Saint-Saëns's private life, even after all these years, remains just that – private. Rumours of homosexuality are all conjecture. In 1875 he married 19-year-old Marie-Laure-Émile Truffot but the marriage was a disaster. They had two sons, André and Jean-François, both of whom died tragically in 1878: André, aged two-and-a-half years, fell to his death from a fourth-floor window and six weeks later six-month-old Jean-François died from pneumonia. The marriage was already fragile and they separated legally in 1881, although they never divorced. Marie died in 1950 aged 95. She never discussed their relationship.

ABOVE LEFT A signed photograph of Camille Saint-Saëns, dedicated to the composer Reynaldo Hahn (1874–1947) in 1921

Saint-Saëns's life spanned a vast arc of musical development: when he was born, Meyerbeer was composing *Les Huguenots* (see p.102); by the time he died 86 years later, Alban Berg (see pp.160–1) had almost finished writing *Wozzeck*. He was an active composer in every genre throughout his long life. He wrote 13 operas, but only *Samson et Dalila*, on which he began work in 1868, has survived in performance to the present time.

Saint-Saëns travelled widely. His first visit to Algiers was in 1873, Algiers being at that time like a French provincial city, and it was there that he died in a hotel in 1921. His funeral service was conducted by the Archbishop of Algiers, after which his coffin was transported by sea to France for burial after a state funeral service in the Madeleine where he had once been organist.

SAMSON ET DALILA, 1868–77
Saint-Saëns's first idea was to use the biblical story of Samson for an oratorio and it was his librettist, Ferdinand Lemaire (fl.1860–70), who recognized the theatrical possibilities and suggested it would be better as an opera. It was not performed in France until 1890 when it had a production in Rouen. Two years later it had its first Paris production.

SYNOPSIS In Gaza in 1150 BC, Samson (ten) encourages the Hebrews to revolt against the Philistine oppressors (1). As they pray, they are taunted by the Satrap, Abimélech (bass). He attacks Samson, who kills him. Dalila (mez), a Philistine who is mortified at having been rejected by Samson, determines revenge. She uses her charms and begs him to visit her again, dancing to entice him to her quarters (2). The High Priest of Dagon (bar) tells Dalila she must find out from Samson the secret of his enormous strength (3). This time Samson admits that he loves her and she tells him he must trust her fully with the secret of his strength (4). Eventually he tells her it lies in his hair. While he is sleeping Dalila cuts it off and the

Philistines are able to overcome Samson and blind him. The Hebrews feel betrayed by their leader. As he turns the treadmill to which he is bound (5), Samson prays to God that, just once, his strength will return. His prayers are answered and he pulls down the pillars supporting the temple, killing himself and his enemies within.

> **MUSIC** (1) Samson: *Arrêtez, ô mes frères!* – *Enough, my brethren*; (2) Dalila: *Printemps qui commence* – *Spring that returns*; (3) High Priest: *Notre sort t'est connu* – *Our lot is known to you*; (4) Dalila: *Mon coeur s'ouvre á ta voix* – *My heart opens to your voice* (usually translated as "Softly awakes my heart"); (5) Samson: *Vois ma misère, hélas, vois ma détresse!* – *See my misery, alas, see my affliction*.

Bizet

Georges Bizet
(1838–75)

WHERE TO START
Carmen

WHERE TO GO NEXT
Les pêcheurs des perles

Born in Paris of musical parents, Bizet started to study at the Conservatoire there just before he was 10 years old. His composition teacher was the composer Fromental Halévy (whose daughter he later married) and outside the Conservatoire he came into contact with Gounod, the single greatest influence on him. Bizet was a brilliant pianist and his piano compositions and songs are of high calibre. Much of his short composing career was devoted to opera, culminating in 1875 with *Carmen*, one of today's best-loved and most often performed operas.

Bizet's early operas are mainly comic, more Italianate than French, and the models for them are clearly Rossini and Donizetti. His later works show the influence of Meyerbeer, Verdi, Weber, and especially Gounod. His first opera, *Le maison du docteur* (*The Doctor's House*) of c.1855 was written while he was a student for performance at the Conservatoire. *Le Docteur Miracle*, which followed in 1857, won a competition run by Offenbach to promote *opéra-comique* and was given a performance at the Bouffes-Parisiens theatre. Shortly after this, Bizet won the prestigious Prix de Rome, which paid for him to live and work in Rome for nearly three years from the beginning of 1858. Whilst there he composed another opera, *Don Procopio*, a comedy that was never produced in his lifetime and has rarely been seen since. His next effort was a grand opera, *Ivan IV*, to a libretto that Gounod had tried to set but had abandoned. It was thought that Bizet burnt the score, but according to Winton Dean (*Fanfare for Ernest Newman*, ed. Herbert van Thal, London, 1955) the autograph score has been in the Paris Conservatoire library since 1929.

From the mid-1940s performances have been given by various (mainly amateur) companies and in 1975 it was broadcast by BBC Radio 3.

Bizet now turned his attention to *Les pêcheurs des perles* (*The Pearlfishers*), which he composed and revised in 1863. It had its first performance at the Théâtre-Lyrique but was slaughtered by the critics (except for Berlioz) and was not popular with the public. Bizet described it as an "honourable, brilliant failure". *Le jolie fille de Perth* (1866–7) had a better reception, but *The Pearlfishers* has proved more enduring, the duet sung by the two leading men ("Au fond du temple saint – In the grounds of the holy temple") being a popular party-piece.

In 1869 Bizet married Geneviève Halévy, the daughter of his teacher. She was severely neurotic and her mother had episodes of insanity – a combination that put a great emotional strain upon the composer. Shortly after his marriage he composed a one-act comic opera, *Djamileh*, but it had little success. Despite this, the director of the Paris Opéra-Comique had great faith in Bizet, and suggested that he should co-operate with the writers Henri Meilhac and Ludovic Halévy (a nephew of his father-in-law, the composer Fromental Halévy with whom Bizet had studied) who had provided the libretto for Offenbach's *La belle Hélène*. As a subject Bizet suggested the 1845 novella *Carmen* by Prosper

ABOVE RIGHT **Célestine Galli-Marié (1840–1905) who created the title-role in *Carmen* in 1875**

Mérimée. The opera was composed between 1873 and 1875 and was not an immediate success. Bizet became ill with infections and then had two heart attacks, dying in 1875 without seeing *Carmen* become one of the most popular of all operas. Bizet's music generally is an amalgam of unforgettable melodies and colourful orchestration and in *Carmen* he wrote an opera that packs a dramatic punch to compete with both Verdi and Wagner.

CARMEN, 1873–5

In his most popular opera, Bizet introduced elements that had never been seen on the stage before. The chorus is used as characters in the story, entering in small groups, the girls smoking, arguing, and fighting. It was not a typical *opéra-comique*, it had an immoral leading lady, and the first audience response was cool. But it survived 35 performances and by the time it was revived in Paris in 1883 it had been successfully received in many countries, including the UK and the USA. After its première the spoken dialogue was replaced

with recitatives composed by Ernest Guiraud (see p.103), but it is usually performed now with spoken dialogue.

SYNOPSIS In Seville soldiers are sitting around talking, imitated by the local children (1). Micaëla (sop) comes looking for a soldier, Don José (ten). The women emerge from the cigarette factory, smoking and arguing. Among them is the gypsy Carmen (mez) who attracts everyone's attention (2). She flirts with Don José and throws him a flower. When the girls return to work, Micaëla brings him a message and a letter from his mother (3). The women again emerge and in a fight Carmen cuts another girl's face. The Captain Zuniga (bass) orders José to escort Carmen to prison. She continues to flirt with him (4) and he allows her to escape for which he is sent to jail. Carmen joins her friends Frasquita (sop) and Mercédès (mez) in the inn run by Lillas Pastia (spoken role) and they entertain the officers (5). Carmen learns from Zuniga that José has been released. The bullfighter Escamillo (bar)

arrives at the inn (6). Remendado (ten) and Dancaïre (ten/bar) announce the evening's plans to smuggle goods over the mountains. When José arrives, Carmen dances for him (7) but he is determined to return to his barracks. He shows her the flower he has kept (8) and when Zuniga tries to commandeer Carmen, José hits him. Now he has to leave the army or be arrested. He joins Carmen and the other gypsies in the mountains. The three girls read fortunes in the cards and Carmen sees her own and José's death. Micaëla joins them (9) and then Escamillo arrives (10). He tells José that he is infatuated with Carmen, and José is ready to fight him. Escamillo invites Carmen to his bullfight. Micaëla leaves with José to visit his dying mother. Outside the bullring, Escamillo parades with Carmen on his arm. Her friends warn her that José is in the crowd. She waits outside knowing he will come to her. When she tells him that she no longer loves him, he stabs her. As the crowd inside cheer Escamillo, José throws himself on Carmen's body.

MUSIC (1) Children's chorus: *Avec la garde montante – With the changing of the guard*; (2) Carmen: *L'amour est un oiseau rebelle – Love is like a rebellious bird* (the Habanera); (3) Micaëla/José duet: *Parle-moi de ma mère – Tell me about my mother*; (4) Carmen: *Près des remparts de Séville – By the city walls of Seville* ("Seguedilla"); (5) Girls' trio: *Les tringles des sistres tintaient – The sistrum bars jangled*; (6) Escamillo: *Votre toast … je peux vous le rendre – Your toast … I can return it*; (7) Carmen: *Je vais danser en votre honneur – I'm going to dance in your honour*; (8) José: *La fleur que tu m'avais jetée – The flower which you threw me* (the "Flower Song"); (9) Micaëla: *Je dis que rien ne m'épouvante – I say that nothing daunts me*; (10) Escamillo: *Je suis Escamillo, toréro de Grenade – I am Escamillo, the toreador of Grenade*.

ABOVE **Set design by Émile Bertin for a production of** *Carmen* **at L'Opéra Garnier, Paris, in the 1950s**

Massenet

Jules Massenet
(1842–1912)

WHERE TO START
Manon

WHERE TO GO NEXT
Werther

Massenet was the son of a businessman and
a musical mother who was a good pianist. He
studied at the Paris Conservatoire from the
age of 10. He spent three years in Rome from
the age of 21. He returned to Paris in 1866,
married Constance (Ninon) de Sainte-Marie,
and spent the rest of his life there. Their only
child was born in 1868. Massenet played the
timpani in the Opéra orchestra, learning
much about orchestration and developing an
instinct for theatre that was to stand him in
good stead all his composing life.

Massenet did not begin his first opera until
1867. His first success came with *Le roi de
Lahore* in 1877, a traditional grand opera. It
received a spectacular production at the Opéra
and made his name among young French
composers and internationally. The following
year he became professor of composition at the
Paris Conservatoire and most of his composing
was done in the summer away from Paris.

Many of Massenet's compositions combine
human drama with a religious background, the
first of these being *Hérodiade*, a version of the

biblical story of Salome, which had its successful
première in Brussels in 1881. But he also
composed operas with more intimate personal
stories and in 1882 he started writing *Manon*,
based on Prévost's novel *Manon Lescaut* (later
set by Puccini, see p.129). Its première at the
Opéra-Comique in 1884 confirmed Massenet's
position as a leading French opera composer
and it quickly became an international success.
His next success was with another intimate
story, *Werther*, based on Goethe. Its first
performance was in Vienna in 1894.

Massenet composed quickly and seldom
did much revision once he completed an
opera. His characters were richly drawn and
he liked to include children in his casts. He had
a rare understanding of the human voice and
wrote roles for singers he admired, especially
the soprano Sibyl Sanderson. For her he wrote
Esclarmonde (1889), the most Wagnerian of
his operas, and *Thaïs* (1892).

Between 1865 and his death in 1912
Massenet provided the lyric theatre with a

series of important and fruitful works. He had
an instinct for what would work in the theatre
comparable with Verdi, Wagner, Puccini, and
Strauss. *Manon* and *Werther* are in the repertory
of most companies and are described below.
Whilst *Manon* is possibly the best-known,
many consider *Werther* his masterpiece.

MANON, 1882–3

The subject of Manon Lescaut, from the novel
(1731) by the Abbé Prévost, was suggested
to Massenet by the librettist Henri Meilhac
(1831–97), who worked with the journalist
and dramatist Philippe Gille (1831–1901) to
produce the text. It was a success from the start
and has proved to be one of the most enduring
operas of the entire French repertoire.

SYNOPSIS In Amiens about 1720, De
Brétigny (bar) and Guillot de Morfontaine (ten)
are drinking in an inn. The stagecoach arrives
bearing Lescaut (bar), due to meet his cousin
Manon (sop) who is on her way to a convent.
This is her first experience of travel (1). Guillot

ABOVE Jules Massenet, aged 60, photographed in
Paris in 1902

LEFT Poster for a production of *Werther* at the Opéra-Comique, Paris, 1893, a year after its Vienna première

makes advances to her and Lescaut warns Manon to be wary of strangers (2). Des Grieux (ten) introduces himself and Manon leaves to live with him in Paris. He writes to his father of his lovely Manon (3). Lescaut and De Brétigny arrive and De Brétigny tempts Manon to go with him and live in luxury. While Des Grieux is out, she bids farewell to their life together (4).

Near the Seine, Manon is with De Brétigny and Lescaut. Des Grieux's father, Le Comte Des Grieux (bass), tells De Brétigny that his son is to take holy orders. Des Grieux is haunted by memories of Manon (5) and when she appears in his church they run off together. Lescaut and Guillot are playing the tables in an illegal gambling room. Manon and Des Grieux arrive and she persuades him to join in. Des Grieux wins, but Guillot sends for the police and they arrest him and Manon, accusing them of cheating. Des Grieux is freed but Manon is to be deported. Lescaut bribes the guards to let her stay behind, but it is too late – she is weak and ill, and dies in Des Grieux's arms.

> **MUSIC** (1) Manon: *Je suis encor' tout étourdie – I'm still completely dizzy*; (2) Lescaut: *Regardez-moi, bien dans les yeux! – Look me straight in the eyes!*; (3) Des Grieux: *On l'appelle Manon – Her name is Manon*; (4) Manon: *Adieu, notre petite table – Farewell, our little table*; (5) Des Grieux: *Ah! fuyez, douce image – Ah! vanish, sweet memory.*

WERTHER, 1885–7

Based on Goethe, the libretto was written by three men including Massenet's publisher, who first had the idea for this opera. When it was finished it was turned down by the Opéra-Comique as being too depressing. Its première took place in Vienna in 1892, where *Manon* had been such a great success two years earlier. *Werther* soon entered the repertoire of many companies.

SYNOPSIS Near Frankfurt in the 1770s lives the widowed Bailli (bass), a magistrate, and his six children. The two elder girls, Sophie (sop) and Charlotte (mez), look after the family. The young and melancholy Werther (ten) enters and listens to the children singing. The Bailli introduces him to Charlotte and they go to a ball together, leaving the 15-year-old Sophie to look after the other children. Albert (bar), Charlotte's fiancé, unexpectedly arrives at the house looking for her (1). Charlotte tells Werther that she promised her dying mother that she would marry Albert. Werther, though clearly in love with her, accepts her decision.

Three months later Charlotte and Albert, now married, arrive at church for a blessing. Werther watches Albert and Charlotte together (2). Charlotte bids Werther farewell – he must go away, but she suggests they might meet again at Christmas. Left alone, Werther thinks of suicide. He leaves, telling Sophie he will never come back. The following Christmas Werther does arrive at their home. Alone, Charlotte admits that Werther's letters move her (3) and prays for help (4). Werther enters (5) and they embrace. Full of guilt, Charlotte flees the room and Werther leaves. Albert receives a message from him – he is going on an extended trip and would like to borrow Albert's pistols. That evening, Charlotte rushes to Werther's house and finds him in his study, dying from gunshot wounds. She tries to revive him and confesses her love for him. They kiss for the first and last time as Werther dies.

> **MUSIC** (1) Albert: *Quelle prière de reconnaisance – What a prayer of thankfulness and love*; (2) Werther: *Un autre son épou – Another man is her husband*; (3) Charlotte: *Werther… Werther…* ; (4) Charlotte: *Va, laisse couler mes larmes – Yes, let my tears flow*; (5) Werther: *Oui, c'est moi! Je reviens… – Yes, it is I! I have come back…*

Other operas of note

Of Massenet's other operas, some receive less frequent airings. *Cendrillon* has music that is charming and witty with romantic love music for Cinderella and her Prince Charming (a *travesti* soprano role). *Chérubin* is older than in Mozart's *Figaro* – all of 17 – but still attracted to lovely ladies. *Thaïs* is the story of an Egyptian harlot converted to Christianity by a monk who then falls in love with her. The last of his successes was *Don Quichotte*, based on Cervantes. It was popular at the time of composition and has been revived occasionally in recent years.

ABOVE The German mezzo-soprano Brigitte Fassbaender as Charlotte in *Werther*, Bavarian State Opera, Munich, 1977

Glinka

Mikhail Glinka
(1804-57)

WHERE TO START
A Life for the Tsar

WHERE TO GO NEXT
Ruslan and Lyudmila

Russian composers did exist before the 19th century, but their names do not trip off the tongue. In the early to mid-18th century, music in Russia was incidental to plays or court pageants. Then in the time of Catherine the Great (1762–96), St Petersburg became a centre for opera, but this was imported Italian opera, French *opéra-comique*, and German *Singspiel*. In the last quarter of the century, original Russian operas began to appear, often incorporating folk-song. None of these has survived other than in archives. By the time of Alexander I (1801–25) Russia was affected like the rest of Europe by an upsurge of nationalism and music started to reflect this. On the whole, national operas do not travel well and it was not until the appearance of Glinka's *A Life for the Tsar* in 1836 in St Petersburg that Russian opera can be said to have become truly international by being acceptable outside Russia.

Mikhail Glinka was from a family of landowners and in his youth had no formal music education, although he learned to play the piano and violin and was a gifted amateur singer. It should be remembered that St Petersburg Conservatory was not founded until 1862 and Moscow Conservatory did not open its doors until 1866. Music was usually learned through church choirs and the sound of Russian orthodox church music can be heard in many Russian operas of the Romantic era and earlier. Glinka's enthusiasm for opera was aroused when he heard the French operas being performed in St Petersburg and by the time he was 20 he had also developed an interest in Italian opera. In 1830 he went to live in Italy and when he returned to Russia three years later he had absorbed the Italian operatic tradition but decided that he wanted

to write his own operas in a Russian idiom. In 1834 he started to compose what is in effect the first Russian nationalist opera, *A Life for the Tsar* (originally known as *Ivan Susanin*). It had an enthusiastic reception at its première at the St Petersburg Bolshoi Opera in 1836. It is based on an incident in 1613 when a peasant, Ivan Susanin, saved the life of the Romanov

Tsar and was captured and executed by Polish troops. Until the Revolution of 1917 it was the most-performed opera in Russia, and although originally slow to travel, it can still sometimes be seen outside Russia.

Glinka next set the romantic story *Ruslan and Lyudmila*, based on the 1820 poem of the same name by Pushkin. He hoped the author would provide the libretto, but Pushkin was killed in a duel. A series of not-very-good writers concocted an amateurish libretto and Glinka took five years to compose the music. It was a failure at its St Petersburg première in 1842. Nevertheless it can be regarded as a seminal Russian work. Uneven it may be, not well constructed, and with characters not well defined, but it is very, very Russian. Glinka had the skill to combine drama and Western melodic lines with music that could only have come out of Russia and later Russian composers found much in it to admire and even to imitate. Glinka can therefore be regarded as the father of Russian opera.

ABOVE **Stage design for a production of *Ruslan and Lyudmila*, Moscow 1842**

Musorgsky

Modest Musorgsky
(1839–81)

BELOW The great Russian bass Fyodor Chaliapin
as Boris Godunov, a role with which he became
inseparably associated

WHERE TO START
Boris Godunov

WHERE TO GO NEXT
Khovanshchina

Musorgsky is one of the two masters of
19th-century Russian opera, the other being
Tchaikovsky (see pp.116–18). He was one
of five Russian composers known as the
"Mighty Handful", a name given to them by
the critic Vladimir Stasov. Their leader was
Mily Balakirev (1837–1910), who did not
write any operas. The others were César Cui
(1835–1918), who wrote 15, none of which
is still heard; Aleksandr Borodin (1833–87),
whose only opera is *Prince Igor*; and Rimsky-
Korsakov (see p.119). They were all largely
self-taught, only Rimsky-Korsakov, when
already a teacher himself, having any serious
music education.

Modest Musorgsky was born outside St
Petersburg, the son of a landowner and a
musical mother who taught him piano from

the age of six. He also learned folk-songs from
his nurse. At 12 he attended a training school
for military officers, and soon after that
published (at his father's expense) his first
composition, a polka. He sang in the school
choir, and studied the music of contemporary
and earlier composers. In 1856 he graduated
from the cadet school and was commissioned
in the Russian Imperial Guard. Later that year
he was invited to concerts in the home of the
composer Aleksandr Dargomizhsky (1813–69)
and through him met Stasov, Borodin, Cui, and
Balakirev. He was by now having bouts of
"mental crisis" that were to dog him for the
rest of his life and may, even then, have been
related to excess alcohol. In 1858 he resigned
his commission and returned to St Petersburg
for lessons with Balakirev, studying the scores
of Gluck, Mozart, and Beethoven. In 1859 he
was invited to Moscow to help to prepare a
production of Glinka's *A Life for the Tsar* (see
p.113) and this gave him his first experience
of practical theatre.

By 1863 Musorgsky had held various minor
government posts and was living in a commune
where he learned much by discussing not just
the arts, but religion, politics, and philosophy.
He was inspired by the idea that music, as well
as entertaining, must educate and uplift its
listeners. He went with Stasov to see a new
Russian opera and a few months later started
to compose his own first opera, *Salammbô*,
based on a novel by Flaubert about ancient
Carthage. After the death of his mother in
1865 he suffered a bout of severe alcoholism
and this may have contributed to his loss
of interest in the opera, which was never
completed, but some of the music found its
way into *Boris Godunov*, which he began to
compose in 1868.

Musorgsky's output was limited – he was
only 42 when he died – his major works being
his 65 songs, the piano piece *Pictures at an
Exhibition* (later orchestrated by Ravel and
others), the orchestral *St John's Night on a Bare
Mountain*, and three operas. The last of these,

ABOVE LEFT **Modest Musorgsky shortly before his
death in 1881, painted by Ilya Repin**

Sorochintsy Fair, was begun in 1876 and was
unfinished when he died. It is a light-hearted
comedy based on Gogol. The version that is
occasionally seen today was completed by
Vissarion Shebalin (1902–63) in the 1930s.
Musorgsky's other two operas are nationalist
works, *Boris Godunov* and *Khovanshchina*. For
the latter, also unfinished at his death, he
started to write the libretto as soon as he
finished revising *Boris Godunov* in 1872. It is
based on Russian history during the rule of
Peter the Great (1682–98), when there was
a massive change from the old to the new
Russia, involving many social changes, and
there were religious objections to the new
order. The opera contains good character
studies and some fine music, but it is neither
as original nor as well constructed as *Boris
Godunov*. Nevertheless, well produced and
sung, it makes for an impressive evening in
the opera house.

BELOW "Grand opera" personified: the
Coronation scene in *Boris Godunov*, 1947

By the time Musorgsky finished *Boris Godunov* and saw it successfully produced, he had descended into chronic alcoholism and on occasions there was trouble with the police. His friends did their best to support him, but his condition degenerated until he was sleeping rough and wearing rags. Eventually even his closest allies gave up on him. In February 1881 he had his first epileptic fits, brought on by excess alcohol, and was taken to a military hospital. There was an initial improvement but a month later he died on his 42nd birthday. Glinka's sister, an old friend of Musorgsky, said that his death was "an irreplaceable loss for art and for his friends. But for his own future, there was nothing better in view".

BORIS GODUNOV,
1868–9, rev. 1871–2

This is Musorgsky's masterpiece. It is difficult to think of a work by any composer with which to compare it. It is the Russian nationalist opera *par excellence*. It is based on Pushkin and the composer devised the libretto. Composition took from October 1868 to July 1869 and by December that year he had orchestrated it. It was rejected by the Mariinsky Theatre in St Petersburg for various political and musical reasons – for instance, there was no role for a leading lady. Musorgsky revised it in 1871–2, adding a new act set in Poland, in which there is a leading female role, and changing much else. It was staged in St Petersburg in 1874. The première was very successful. The English conductor and authority on Russian music David Lloyd-Jones has asserted that "…no other first opera which has subsequently been acknowledged as a masterpiece has ever been created with such meagre compositional experience and against such a negative cultural and political background" (*Viking Opera Guide*, 1993, p.718). It is an episodic work, really a series of tableaux, with the chorus – some would say the chief character – holding the whole picture together.

SYNOPSIS Tsar Fyodor (the elder son of Ivan the Terrible) has died and Boris Godunov (bass), his regent, has accepted the throne. The plot moves forward six years: the old monk Pimen (bass) recalls **(1)** the murder of the younger son, Dimitri, the rumour being that Boris killed him. A young novice monk, Grigori (ten), who is the age Dimitri would have now been, flees to Poland to raise an army to defeat Boris so that he can become Tsar. In the Kremlin the late Tsar's betrothed, Xenia (sop), Boris's daughter, sits with her brother (also Fyodor) and mourns the loss of the Tsar **(2)**. Boris thinks of the suffering of the people and of his own crime **(3)**. Prince Shuisky (ten), Boris's rival, announces the appearance of somebody calling himself Dimitri (Grigori in disguise). In Poland, Princess Marina (mez) has fallen in love with Dimitri **(4)** and is reminded by her Jesuit confessor Rangoni (bar) that, if she inherits the throne with Dimitri, it will be her duty to convert Russia to Catholicism. In Moscow a Simpleton (ten) accuses Boris of murder **(5)**. When Pimen tells him of a miracle at Dimitri's tomb, Boris collapses and dies **(6)**. The crowd follows the false Dimitri.

MUSIC (1) Pimen: *Yeshchó odnó – Just one more tale*; **(2)** Xenia: *Gdye ty, zhewnikh moy – Where are you, my beloved*; **(3)** Boris: *Dostig ya výshey vlásti – I have won supreme power*; **(4)** Marina/Dimitri (Grigori) duet: *Tebyá, tebyá odnú, Marina – It is you, you alone, Marina*; **(5)** Simpleton: *Lyéytes, lyéytes slyózy górkiye – Flow, flow, O bitter tears*; **(6)** Boris: *Proshcháy, moi syn, umiráyu – Farewell, my son, I am dying.*

Tchaikovsky

Pyotr Tchaikovsky
(1840–93)

BELOW Pyotr Tchaikovsky painted in 1893, the year of his death

WHERE TO START
Eugene Onegin

WHERE TO GO NEXT
The Queen of Spades

The son of a mining engineer, Tchaikovsky moved with his family to St Petersburg when he was eight years old. He was very close to his mother, and her death when he was 14 resulted in psychological and emotional trauma that made his relationships with women difficult for the rest of his life.

Tchaikovsky was one of the earliest Russian composers to receive a formal music education. He studied at St Petersburg Conservatory from 1862 to 1865. From 1866 he was professor of harmony at the newly opened Conservatory in Moscow. His early attempts at opera were not a great success – there was little Russian opera for him to study (he was a year younger than Musorgsky) – but he had a good sense of theatre. Inevitably he was influenced by Balakirev and his group (his fantasy-overture *Romeo and Juliet* is dedicated to Balakirev) and by the time he composed his fourth opera, *Vakula the Smith* of 1874, he incorporated both nationalism and folk music into his work. After that his works, both orchestral and operatic, show less of the nationalist side and more of his individual style of composition. He had a lifelong love of Mozart and admired much French music, especially that of Bizet and Saint-Saëns. Tchaikovsky is one of the most popular composers with the general public, his music being tuneful, richly and colourfully scored, and outright emotional.

His personal life was traumatic in the extreme. Whilst writing the libretto for *Eugene Onegin* he had received a letter from a young lady unknown to him, Antonina Milyukova, who had been a pupil at the Conservatory, saying she was in love with him. He met her and in 1877 they married. It was a disaster and

psychologically catastrophic for Tchaikovsky, a homosexual. They separated after less than three months and he attempted suicide. The whole experience had such an effect on him that for some time he was unable to compose any new music. Shortly after this he developed his only other close relationship with a woman. She was Nadezhda von Meck, a wealthy widow who admired his work so much that she gave him an annual allowance that enabled him to abandon teaching and concentrate wholly on composition. They never met, but carried on a vast correspondence. The manner of Tchaikovsky's death has for many years been the source of much speculation. There have been several theories posited, including that of suicide. But there is still much controversy and no conclusive proof.

Only two of Tchaikovsky's operas, *Eugene Onegin* and *The Queen of Spades,* are regularly performed outside Russia and he is more famous in the Western world for his orchestral and ballet music, the latter considered by many, and with good reason, to be the greatest ballet music ever composed. But he spent more of his working life composing operas than music in any other genre.

EUGENE ONEGIN, 1877–8

The composition of this opera was inextricably bound up with the emotional disaster of his marriage, much of the story reflecting episodes in his own life. He wrote the libretto himself, based closely on Pushkin. The first performance was given in 1879 by students at the Moscow Conservatory. After its première there were several productions in Russia, but only after it was produced in St Petersburg, in 1884, did it rapidly gain ground and it has become the most performed Russian opera outside Russia.

SYNOPSIS In the 18th century on the Larin family estate, Madame Larina (mez) sits with the old family nurse Filipyevna (mez) and listens to her daughters Tatyana (sop) and Olga (mez) talking (**1**). Their neighbour Lensky (ten) visits, accompanied by his friend Onegin (bar). Lensky admits he is in love with Olga (**2**). Onegin and Tatyana are attracted to each other and after the men leave and she goes to bed, she writes him a letter telling him of her feelings (**3**). He calls at the house a few days later and brutally rejects her love (**4**), leaving her humiliated. The two men attend her birthday party, at which she is serenaded (**5**) by the elderly Frenchman Triquet (ten). Onegin is bored and sorry he came and humours himself by flirting with Olga and making Lensky jealous. This leads to a quarrel and despite all Madame Larina's efforts to prevent it, Lensky (**6**) challenges Onegin to a duel. At dawn the next day Lensky sings of his love for Olga (**7**) while awaiting the arrival of his friend. Both men wish they had never got into this situation, but honour demands they see it through. Lensky is killed and a horrified Onegin leaves the area. He returns years later, still full of remorse, and at a ball meets his friend Prince Gremin (bass). He is disturbed to find that Gremin's wife is Tatyana. Gremin tells Onegin of his love for her (**8**). Onegin realizes he loves Tatyana. They meet at her home the following day and she reminds him of his rejection and of how close to real happiness they came (**9**). She admits she still loves him, but she will not leave her husband and she sends Onegin away.

MUSIC (**1**) Olga: *Ya ne sposobna k grusti tomnoy – I'm not the sort to sit in silence*; (**2**) Lensky: *Ya lyub lyu vas – How I love you*; (**3**) Tatyana: *Puskay pogibnu ya – "Ya k vam pishu – chevo zhe bole?" – Even if it means I die … "I write to you – and then?"*; (**4**) Onegin: *Kogda bi zhizn domashnim krugom… – Were I wanting to pass my life…*; (**5**) Triquet: *A cette fête convivé – What a cordial celebration*; (**6**) Lensky: *V vashim dome! – Here in your house!*; (**7**) Lensky: *Kuda, kuda vi udalilis – Where, where have you gone*; (**8**) Gremin: *Lyubvi vsye vozrastï pokornï – Love is no respecter of age*; (**9**) Tatyana: *Onegin! Ya togda molozhe – Onegin, I was younger then.*

THE QUEEN OF SPADES, 1890

Based on a short story of the same name by Pushkin, the libretto for *The Queen of Spades* was written by the composer and his brother Modest, who had already worked on it as a libretto for another composer who didn't use it. It was given an elaborate first production with excellent singers at the Mariinsky Theatre in St Petersburg on 19 December 1890, and was highly successful with the audience, less so with the critics. The singers playing Hermann and Liza were a married couple and she was pregnant, so after two months the performances had to be suspended. Critical opinion soon became more favourable and the opera quickly travelled to Moscow and other Russian towns and to Prague.

SYNOPSIS In 18th-century St Petersburg Hermann (ten), a German-born officer, watches his fellow-officers gambling without risking anything himself. He tells Tomsky (bar) that he is in love with a lady he has seen but has not discovered her name (**1**). Prince Yeletsky (bar) announces his engagement to Liza (sop). She appears with her grandmother the old Countess (mez), and Hermann recognizes her as the lady he loves. Tomsky recounts the story (**2**) of the old Countess who, in her youth in Paris, was a gambler known as the Queen of Spades. She lost heavily at cards and a count gave her the secret of three cards that would always win. She revealed the secret to her husband and also to one of her lovers. A ghost visited her

ABOVE **Onegin and Lensky argue at Madame Larina's party in the première production of** *Eugene Onegin*, **given by students of the Moscow Conservatoire at the Maly Theatre, Moscow, 1879**

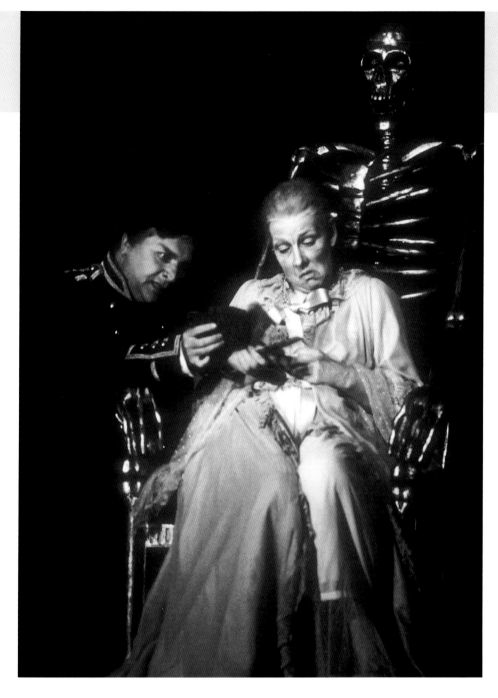

LEFT **Yuri Masurin as Hermann and Felicity Palmer as the terrified Countess in *The Queen of Spades*, Glyndebourne, 1995**

gamble. Liza is so upset when he leaves her that she drowns herself in the river. Hermann plays cards with Yeletsky and the stakes are very high. Hermann wins with the "three", then again with the "seven". He then stakes all his winnings on the "ace" and turns the card over. It is not the ace but the Queen of Spades – the Countess has fooled him and he has lost everything. He stabs himself.

> **MUSIC** (1) Hermann: *Ya imeni yeyo ne znayu – I don't even know her name*; (2) Tomsky: *Odnazhdy v Versalye – Once at Versailles*; (3) Hermann: *Prosti, prelestnoe sozdanye – Forgive me, loveliest of creatures*; (4) Yeletsky: *Ya vas lyublyu bezmermo – I love you beyond measure*; (5) Countess: *Je crains de lui parler la nuit – I fear to speak for him in the night –* (an aria from Grétry's opera *Richard, Coeur de Lion*).

Other operas of note

None of Tchaikovsky's other operas is in the regular repertoire. *The Maid of Orleans* (1878–9) is the story of Joan of Arc. It is probably the weakest of his operas, written after the trauma of his marriage and suffering from his attempts to produce a French grand opera, with a large chorus and spectacular scenes. It was never successful and is rarely performed. *Mazepa* (1881–3) had premières in Moscow and St Petersburg within three days, both in lavish productions. Many consider this one of his best operas, but it has never secured a regular place in the repertoire. It has some beautiful love music, the characters (especially the two lovers, Mazepa and Mariya) are well defined, and it is very dramatic. Its time may yet come. *Cherevichki* (*The Slippers*) of 1885–6 finds its way into some opera festival programmes. It started life as *Vakula the Smith* in 1874 and is based on Gogol's *Christmas Eve*. It is an amusing tale set in the Ukraine and blends village life with the supernatural. Tchaikovsky valued it highly among his works but it remains neglected.

and told her she would die if she told the secret to anyone else.

Liza is alone in her room when Hermann enters and she responds to his amorous overtures (3). At a ball Yeletsky tells Liza of his love for her (4). Later she meets Hermann and slips him the key to her room, which he can only approach through the Countess's quarters. Hermann realizes that if he can find out the secret of the three cards, he can make his fortune, and win Liza. He hides in the Countess's room. Her maids prepare her for

bed and leave her sitting in a chair recalling her past (5). Hermann emerges from hiding and asks her the secret of the three cards. She refuses to reply and he threatens her with a gun. She is so frightened that she dies of shock. Later, her ghost visits Hermann and tells him that the cards are "three, seven, ace". Hermann leaves Liza to go and play cards and she realizes he has used her to get at the secret of the cards. She still loves him and they meet beside the canal at midnight and sing of their love. But he refuses to go away with her, wanting only to

Rimsky-Korsakov

Nikolay Rimsky-Korsakov
(1844–1908)

WHERE TO START
The Golden Cockerel

WHERE TO GO NEXT
The Snow Maiden

Born near Novgorod, Rimsky-Korsakov was the youngest of a group of five Russian composers known as the "Mighty Handful" (see p.114). The others were Balakirev, Cui, Borodin, and Musorgsky.

Rimsky-Korsakov was born into an aristocratic family and followed his much older brother into a naval career. He developed an interest in opera as a young naval cadet in St Petersburg, where there was plenty of opportunity to attend the theatre. When he was 17 he met Balakirev, who taught him the rudiments of composition. He did not have any serious music education until he was about 28 when he was appointed as a professor at the St Petersburg Conservatory and was able to take advantage of his position to study as well. In 1872 he married Nadezhda Purgol'd and they had six children.

ABOVE Nikolay Rimsky-Korsakov, aged 54, painted in 1898

His wife was a good pianist and an astute critic of his compositions.

He composed his first opera, *The Maid of Pskov*, between 1868 and 1872 and it was accepted by the Mariinsky Theatre. From 1877 to 1878 Rimsky-Korsakov helped Balakirev edit Glinka's operas for publication and this gave him valuable experience. His next opera, *May Night* (1878–9), is a comedy based on Gogol and there is lots of folk-music for the chorus. It pops up now and then, but more successful was *The Snow Maiden* of 1880–1, given a splendid production by the Mariinsky Theatre and very popular with the public.

After the death of Musorgsky in 1881, Rimsky-Korsakov prepared his friend's works for publication, completing and orchestrating Musorgsky's last (unfinished) opera *Khovanshchina*. He did a similar favour for Borodin's *Prince Igor*.

In 1889 Rimsky-Korsakov heard Wagner's *Ring*, produced for the first time in St Petersburg, and this was the musical stimulus he needed to start him again on the road to creativity. He was soon composing *Mlada*, a work demanding very large forces and complicated stage effects and showing the influence of Wagner in its orchestration. It was not a success, but it was a turning point for him and for the rest of his life he concentrated on writing works for the theatre. However, it

was not a good time in his personal life: in two years from 1890 his mother died, two of his children died, his wife was seriously ill, his own health deteriorated, and his friendship with Balakirev came to an end. But he produced another 10 operas in the 10 years before his last opera, *The Golden Cockerel*.

The most often performed of Rimsky-Korsakov operas, although hardly core repertory, *The Golden Cockerel* of 1906–7, is based on Pushkin. It contains considerable political satire on the poor showing of Russia in the Russo-Japanese war and this did not go down well with the powers that be. The composer never heard his opera, as he died from a heart attack before its première, which took place in Moscow in 1909. Rimsky-Korsakov was buried in the grounds of the Alexander-Nevsky monastery, near the graves of Borodin, Musorgsky, and Glinka.

Rimsky-Korsakov's most characteristic operas all have an element of fairy-tale or fantasy. His early works were influenced by Glinka, his late ones by Wagner, and he often incorporated folk-tunes. The music was always more important than the drama and his orchestral effects are masterly. But maybe even more important than his own works are the works of other composers, and especially of Musorgsky, that we owe to Rimsky-Korsakov's diligence and his generosity of spirit.

ABOVE Elena Kelessidi as the Queen of Shemakha in Rimsky-Korsakov's *The Golden Cockerel,* ROH at Sadler's Wells, London, 1998

Smetana

Bedřich Smetana
(1824–84)

WHERE TO START
The Bartered Bride

WHERE TO GO NEXT
The Two Widows

This Bohemian composer was the 11th child of a German-speaking family and the first son to survive infancy. His father was a reasonably prosperous brewer and a competent violinist who gave his son music lessons. Smetana was an early starter, playing in a string quartet when he was five, giving a piano recital aged six, and starting to compose at eight. When he was 19 he went to study in Prague, despite his father's initial misgivings. Prague was a growing city – it had electricity, early hackney carriages and buses, and a developing railway system. The premières of Mozart's *Don Giovanni* (1787) and *La clemenza di Tito* (1791) had been staged there. The Prague Conservatoire had opened in 1811. The main "Estates Theatre" (Theatre of the Nobility) was where *Don Giovanni* had taken place and Weber had been music director from 1813 to 1816. Musical life was thriving when Smetana arrived and he took full advantage of the opportunities offered, and when he finished his studies in 1847 he started giving recitals. Two years later he married Kateřina Kolářová. They had four daughters, only one of whom survived.

In 1856 he went to Sweden as a piano teacher and recitalist. Kateřina died later that year and the following year he remarried and with his wife, Bettina, returned to Prague. At about this time he started to learn Czech, having spoken only German – Bohemia was still under Austrian rule. With the rise of nationalism throughout Europe in the 19th century, speaking the Czech language became a symbol of support for nationalism in Bohemia. Smetana became conductor of the newly formed Czech Choral Society and head of the music section of the Artists' Club also

formed that year. For the laying of the foundation stone of the National Theatre in 1868, Smetana composed his opera *Dalibor*, and he wrote the ceremonial opera *Libuše* for the coronation of Franz Joseph, but the government refused to allow the coronation to be seen as a nationalist occasion and the opera was withdrawn.

Smetana had already won a prize with *The Brandenburgers in Bohemia*, a patriotic opera written in 1862 that had some success. In 1866 he composed *The Bartered Bride*, about village life in Bohemia, but its première was overshadowed by the Austro-Prussian war. Smetana's music was not always popular, some considering him too modern and too much in thrall to Wagner. There was also a general desire for Czech opera to align itself with the Italian rather than German tradition. Smetana's comic opera *The Two Widows* of 1873–4 does appear occasionally but, whilst quite amusing, it is not in the same class as *The Bartered Bride*.

By 1874 Smetana was starting to have serious health problems. He complained of a sore throat, dizziness, and of "buzzing and tingling in the ears like a waterfall", so he was

ABOVE Bedřich Smetana, aged 39, in 1863

unable to hear the pitch of notes accurately. Despite this, he continued to compose and many of his best orchestral and chamber works come from this period, as well as two operas, *The Kiss* and *The Secret*. But he was already showing signs of syphilis and he died in a Prague lunatic asylum in 1884.

Smetana is considered the founder of Czech music and the outstanding Czech opera composer of the 19th century. His orchestral tone-poem *Má vlast* and his two string quartets are familiar in concert halls, and of his operas *The Bartered Bride* alone is enough to keep his name at the forefront of the Romantic tradition. Like many opera composers, he was guided in his compositions by the voices available to sing them. Much as he inclined towards Wagnerian idioms, his operas are Italianate rather than German in sound and he made good use of the chorus. *The Bartered Bride* embodies the Czech tradition and it was one of very few Czech opera to achieve international success before the advent of Janáček (see pp.146–51).

THE BARTERED BRIDE

(*Prodaná nevěsta*), 1863–6, rev. 1869–70
This opera was composed to a libretto by Karel Sabina, who had earlier written *The Brandenburgers in Bohemia*. When it was revised a few years later, its spoken dialogue was replaced by accompanied recitatives. It was not outstandingly popular at first, but it steadily gained ground and by the late 1870s was recognized as the quintessential Czech opera, and thus it has remained. It was written for the voices available, Esmeralda being created by a well-known soubrette and the spoken role of the Circus Master by a Czech actor. Much of the music makes use of dance rhythms, the chorus has less to do than was usual at the time, and it contains a succession of brilliant duets.

SYNOPSIS At a village fair in Bohemia, Mařenka (sop) tells her lover Jeník (ten) that her father wants her to marry Vašek (ten), the

son of Micha (bass) and Hata (mez), to settle a debt between the families. She knows little of Jeník's past, other than that he left home and she asks him about this **(1)**. He explains that when his mother died his father remarried and his stepmother sent him away. They swear eternal love **(2)**. Mařenka's parents, Krušina (bar) and Ludmila (sop) talk with the village marriage-broker Kecal **(3)** about their choice of husband for their daughter. Mařenka tells Kecal that she loves Jeník and the broker tries to bribe Jeník into giving her up. Mařenka and Vašek meet, but Vašek, who has a pronounced stammer, does not realize this is the girl his parents have chosen for him and he tells her how he must obey his mother **(4)**. She tells him that the girl "Mařenka" is in love with somebody else and if forced to marry Vašek she will make sure he quickly dies! She makes him swear he will not marry Mařenka **(5)**. Meantime, Jeník has given in to Kecal's plea not to marry Mařenka, but on condition that Mařenka will marry only "Micha's son" and that Krušina's debt to Micha will be cleared.

The circus arrives in town. The Circus Master (spoken role) and the dancer Esmeralda (sop) persuade Vašek to replace their star turn who is drunk and unable to perform **(6)**. Thinking that Jeník has rejected her, Mařenka contemplates marriage to Vašek **(7)** and refuses to listen to Jeník's explanations. His parents are amazed to hear him now claiming his right to marry Mařenka as "Micha's son". He is indeed Micha's son, who left home when his father married Hata. As Vašek enters in a bear costume to perform in the circus, Micha gives Jeník and Mařenka his blessing.

MUSIC **(1)** Mařenka: *Kdybych se cos takového – Should I ever happen to learn*; **(2)** Jeník/Mařenka duet: *Věrné milování – Faithful love*; **(3)** Kecal: *Jak vám pravím, pane kmotře – As I'm saying, my dear fellow*; **(4)** Vašek: *Má ma-ma-matička povidala – My m-m-other said to me*; **(5)** Mařenka/ Vašek duet: *Známt' já jednu dívčinu – I know a maiden fair*; **(6)** Esmeralda/Ringmaster duet: *Milostné zvířátko vděláme z vás – We'll make a graceful little bear of you*; **(7)** Mařenka: *Ten lásky sen – That dream of love*.

ABOVE Solveig Kringelborn as Mařenka and Julian Gavin as Jeník in *The Bartered Bride*, Glyndebourne, 2005.

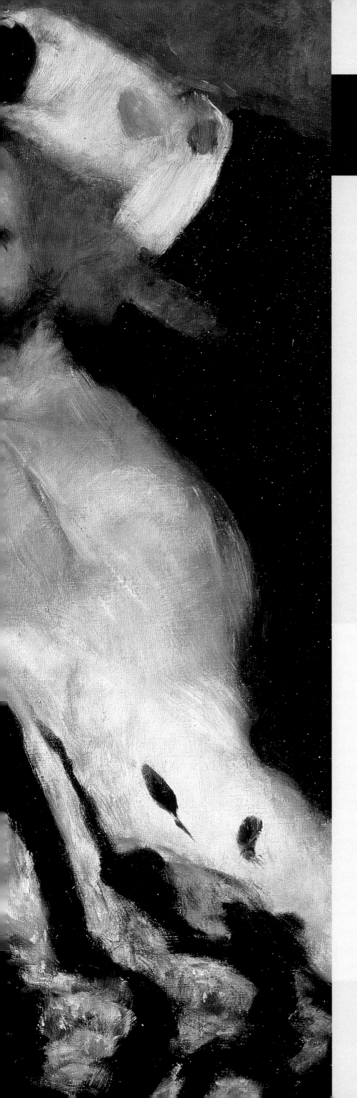

The Late Romantics

late 19th and early 20th century

While it is convenient and a good *aide-mémoire* to divide history – of any topic – into categories, in the case of opera this period is not so very different from the one that preceded it. The next major change in idiom did not take place until the advent of the Second Viennese School of Schoenberg, Berg, and Webern, and the Neoclassical world of Stravinsky.

The late 19th century saw great advances in the sciences, including medicine: the discovery of X-rays, Louis Pasteur's research into the cause of infection, early atomic physics, the invention of the motor car and the aeroplane, the microphone, gramophone record, and radio, the first electric light bulb, and many more.

FEATURED OPERAS

MASCAGNI
Cavalleria rusticana *1888–9*

LEONCAVALLO
Pagliacci *1892*

PUCCINI
Manon Lescaut *1889–92, 1893, 1922*
La bohème *1893–5, 1896*
Tosca *1896–9*
Madama Butterfly *1901–3, 1904, 1905, 1906*
Turandot *1920–4, 1925–6*

HUMPERDINCK
Hänsel und Gretel *1890–3*

STRAUSS
Salome *1904–5*
Elektra *1906–8*
Der Rosenkavalier *1909–10*
Ariadne auf Naxos *1912, 1916*
Arabella *1930–2*
Capriccio *1940–1*

DEBUSSY
Pelléas et Mélisande *1893–5, 1901–2*

JANÁČEK
Jenůfa *1894–1903*
Katya Kabanová *1919–21*
The Cunning Little Vixen *1922–3*
The Makropulos Affair *1923–5*

LEFT Detail from Renoir's *La Loge* of 1874 (*loge* is French for "box" in the theatre)

The Late Romantic Period and the Early 20th Century

At the same time, education generally and music education in particular had vastly improved and audiences had become more discerning and more demanding. The first exhibition by the Impressionist painters took place in Paris in 1874. It should be no surprise that the influence of the Impressionists on music was first felt by French composers, and is heard most obviously in the music of Debussy and Ravel. Contemporaneously there developed a vogue for all things oriental: Chinese poems were set by Gustav Mahler (1860–1911), the action of Puccini's *Madama Butterfly* is in Japan, and the gamelan music of Java, heard in Paris at the Universal Exhibition of 1889, certainly had its effect on Debussy's compositions.

Whilst nationalism still influenced some composers, realism was starting to impinge on pure Romanticism. "Realism" is more easily understood in literature and the visual arts, but is rather a vague term in music. In opera it applies more to the words than the music, referring to the story and the way in which the characters relate to each other. It is most clearly seen in the Italian *verismo* operas, ie works true to life, portraying situations that would be familiar to the audience. An early work in this category was Bizet's *Carmen*, which has already been discussed (see pp.109–10), concentrating as it did on the seedier aspects of life. This theme was taken up by several Italian composers, most prominently by Puccini; by the German Richard Strauss in his earlier operas (all of these are discussed below); and by the Frenchman Gustave Charpentier (1860–1956) in his opera *Louise* (1889–96), which owed much to the sort of squalid realism found in the novels of Émile Zola (1840–1902).

Some composers born in the second half of the 19th century were still composing at their peak up to the middle of the 20th century and it is arguable in which category they should be included. Some will be discussed in the next chapter. For the purposes of this book, the cut-off point is about 1925–30, by which time Debussy and Puccini were dead; Janáček was at the end of his life but his music had not yet travelled outside his native Czechoslovakia; Strauss already had a major reputation and was still producing masterpieces; in England, the "land without music", Vaughan Williams still had another 30 years to live and compose; the first native American opera composers (Gershwin and Barber) were just emerging; Shostakovich's first opera had already been termed "decadent" by the Soviet authorities; the composers of the Second Viennese School were beginning to shock; and, in 1913, Stravinsky had already shocked with *The Rite of Spring*.

Notwithstanding the English, American, Russian, Czech, Austrian, and French composers just mentioned, at the turn of the century Italy and Germany were still the bedrock of opera composition. As Verdi and Wagner led the field in the Romantic era, so in this later period did Puccini and Richard Strauss inherit their mantles. Puccini is known today almost entirely for his operas, Strauss for his operas and equally for his masterly tone-poems and *Lieder*.

ABOVE **The Universal Exhibition, Paris, 1889: the Central Dome as painted by Louis Béroud (1852–1930)**

Italian composers had never been influenced by their German counterparts – they were not interested in the works of Gluck in the 18th century (see pp.46–9) and were similarly resistant to Wagnerism in the 19th. Even *Lohengrin*, which may be regarded as Wagner's most Italianate opera (see pp.93–4), was not accepted at Italian opera houses until the 1880s, after the composer's death. Italian opera, firmly rooted as it was in its traditions and its national life, saw no point in changing the status quo and in few Italian operas of this period can a Wagnerian Romanticism be detected. Apart from which, in the late 19th century, other Italian composers such as Mascagni and Leoncavallo were beginning to make their mark in the *verismo* mode, the complete antithesis to the Wagnerian world. The *verismo* movement did not last long – it arose in the 1890s and had all but disappeared by the turn of the century. These operas were written deliberately to shock, to cause a sensation, to display great passion. They usually succeeded in their aims, but most of the works written in this style were short, often one-act, intense, and concentrated, but soon exhausted the material. Only the best of them survive.

Some composers are justifiably famous for only one regularly performed opera and little else, such as Leoncavallo (*Pagliacci*), Mascagni (*Cavalleria rusticana*), and Humperdinck (*Hänsel und Gretel*); some for one opera but also for music in other genres, such as Debussy (*Pelléas et Mélisande*); and others are better known as composers of music in many genres, whose operas are regularly but infrequently performed, such as Ravel, Busoni, Dvořák, Nielsen, Wolf, and Vaughan Williams.

In the first quarter of the 20th century three main factors continued to influence opera composition: Impressionism, post-Wagnerian Romanticism, and nationalism, and new names emerged in almost all major nations. Impressionism could be found especially in French music, not only in Debussy, but also in Dukas's *Ariane et Barbe-Bleue* (based, like *Pelléas et Mélisande*, on Maeterlinck), in Ravel's two one-act operas, and in Fauré's *Pénélope*. All three influences were heard in Germany in, for instance, Schreker's *Der ferne Klang*, Wolf-Ferrari's operas, d'Albert's *Tiefland*, Pfitzner's *Palestrina*, and the operas of Zemlinsky and his pupil Korngold; in Hungary in Bartók's *Duke Bluebeard's Castle* and Kodály's *Háry János*, in Poland in Szymanowski's *Król Roger*; in Italy in the operas of Giordano, Respighi, and Montemezzi; and in England in Delius (really an honorary Frenchman), Holst, Vaughan Williams, and Ethel Smyth. What we will never know is what we lost from the world of music with the deaths in the First World War of several promising young composers of all nationalities.

And then, to remove any feelings of tradition, romance, Impressionism, or even complacency, and to upset the apple-cart with a vengeance, along came the Second Viennese School and Neoclassicism, both of which will be discussed in the next chapter.

Mascagni

Pietro Mascagni
(1863–1945)

LEFT Pietro Mascagni in 1901, aged 38

WHERE TO START
Cavalleria rusticana

WHERE TO GO NEXT
L'amico Fritz

Mascagni was born in Livorno, the son of a baker. In 1883 he entered Milan Conservatory as a pupil of Amilcare Ponchielli (1834–86), composer of the opera *La Gioconda*. After two years Mascagni was forced to leave for failing to complete assigned work, and he earned his living by playing the double-bass in a theatre and conducting a touring operetta company. In 1886 he and his wife Lina, who was pregnant, settled in Cerignola in Puglia where Mascagni gave music lessons.

Mascagni was the first of the Italian *verismo* composers to triumph when, in 1888–9, he wrote a one-act opera, *Cavalleria rusticana* for a competition held by the publisher Sonzogno. It won and was produced in Rome in 1890, achieving for its composer overnight fame and success. His next opera, *L'amico Fritz* (1891), a rustic comedy set in Alsace, was a much more innocent and gentle work, disappointing those expecting the passion of *Cavalleria rusticana*. Other relative successes were *Iris* in 1898, set in Japan, and *Il piccolo Marat* of 1921, set against the background of the French Revolution. Apart from his operas, Mascagni wrote little music of note – some sacred and some secular choral works, songs, and a few orchestral and chamber works, much of it unpublished. None of his other operas did much for his reputation, which rests entirely on *Cavalleria rusticana*.

In 1929 Mascagni succeeded Toscanini as music director of La Scala, Milan, and his last opera, *Nerone*, was premièred there in 1935 but after its initial performances has rarely been seen since. In 1940, on the 50th anniversary of its first performance in Rome, Mascagni conducted *Cavalleria rusticana* at La Scala. He had associated himself with Mussolini's Fascist regime and, soon after its fall in 1945, he died in an obscure hotel in Rome.

CAVALLERIA RUSTICANA
(*Rustic Chivalry*), 1888–9

The speed with which *Cavalleria rusticana* gained popularity has been unequalled. It was a resounding success from its first performance and has remained so. Together with Leoncavallo's *Pagliacci* (see p.127), which it inspired, it is a standard double bill in opera houses worldwide. It is the *verismo* opera *par excellence*, a story of passions that can be seen as true to life.

SYNOPSIS Easter Day in a Sicilian village. Before Turiddu (ten) left with the army, he had an affair with Lola (mez), but when he returned he found she had married Alfio (bar). Turiddu seduced a village girl Santuzza (sop/mez) who became pregnant and was excommunicated by the church. Turiddu resumes his relationship with Lola. Everyone is in church for the Easter service except Santuzza and Turiddu's mother, Mama Lucia (cont/mez). They join in the singing of the Easter Hymn (1) and then Santuzza tells Lucia the whole sad story (2). When Turiddu appears, Santuzza tells him of her love and begs him to return to her. He rejects her. In an act of jealous revenge, she tells Alfio of Lola's unfaithfulness and he vows vengeance (3). Everyone emerges from the church (4). Alfio challenges Turiddu to a duel. Turiddu bids his mother farewell and asks her to look after Santuzza (5). The women gather in the square and off-stage a girl screams the news that Turiddu has been killed.

> **MUSIC** (1) Santuzza/Lucia/Chorus: *Ineggiamo, il Signor non è morto – Let us rejoice that our Lord is not dead – "Easter Hymn"*; (2) Santuzza: *Voi lo sapete, o mamma – O mother, you know*; (3) Alfio/Santuzza duet: *Infami loro – It is they who are vile*; (4) Orchestral Intermezzo; (5) Turiddu: *Mamma, quel vino è generoso – Mamma, that wine is strong.*

ABOVE **The Easter Sunday procession in** *Cavalleria rusticana*, Sarasota Opera, 2005

Leoncavallo

Ruggero Leoncavallo
(1857–1919)

WHERE TO START
Pagliacci

WHERE TO GO NEXT
La bohème

Born in Naples, the son of a well-to-do family, Leoncavallo entered the Conservatory of his home city at the age of nine and studied there for ten years. He then moved to Bologna University where he planned to write a trilogy on the Italian Renaissance, the Italian answer to Wagner's *Ring*, but could not interest a publisher. He moved to Paris and in 1888 he became friendly with the baritone Victor Maurel, who created Verdi's Iago and Falstaff, and Maurel persuaded Ricordi to publish Leoncavallo's work. Leoncavallo married the singer Berthe Rambaud and returned to Milan.

Mascagni's success with *Cavalleria rusticana* in 1890 (see p.126) attracted Leoncavallo to the *verismo* style of opera. Anxious to establish himself as a composer, he quickly wrote *Pagliacci* to his own libretto, which was

ABOVE **Ruggero Leoncavallo in 1894, aged 37**

published by Ricordi's rival Sonzogno. It was a huge success at its first performance in Milan in 1892. In 1893 the Metropolitan Opera, New York, staged *Pagliacci* in a double bill with Mascagni's *Cavalleria rusticana* and the two operas became stage companions, affectionately known as "Cav and Pag".

After this triumph, Leoncavallo abandoned the proposed trilogy. When he learned that Puccini was working on *La bohème* (see pp.129–30), he set about composing the same work himself. Although his version contains some lovely music and realistic Parisian scenes, it has never been a serious rival to Puccini's opera. He visited the USA in 1906 and started to write operettas and he also wrote many fine songs, the best-known being "Mattinata". His last attempt at a comic opera was interrupted by the First World War and abandoned. At the time of his death he left several works unfinished. His reputation rests entirely on *Pagliacci* which is likely to keep his name before the public.

PAGLIACCI (Clowns), 1892

Leoncavallo wrote this opera with prologue and two acts after the success of Mascagni's one-act *Cavalleria rusticana*. Following its 1892 Milan première, Leoncavallo became famous overnight.

ABOVE **Rafael Dávila as Canio in *Pagliacci*, Sarasota Opera, 2005**

SYNOPSIS About 1870 in a Calbrian village: the hunchback Tonio (bar) tells the audience that they are about to see a real-life drama (1). A troupe of strolling players is setting up its stage. The head of the troupe, Canio (ten), is married to Nedda (sop), with whom Tonio is in love. Nedda is having a secret affair with one of the villagers, Silvio (bar), and rejects Tonio's overtures (2). In revenge Tonio tells Canio of his wife's plan to meet her lover. Canio accuses her of being unfaithful. She refuses to name her lover and another player, Beppe (ten), prevents Canio thrashing Nedda. As the villagers gather for the performance, Canio applies his clown make-up (3). During their play, Columbine (Nedda) is serenaded by Harlequin (Beppe) and then by the clown Taddeo (Tonio). The other clown, Pagliaccio (Canio), overhears Harlequin arranging to meet Columbine, and assumes that he is her lover. Canio stabs Nedda. Silvio tries to save her, and Canio stabs him also, before addressing the audience (4).

MUSIC (1) Tonio: *Si può? Signore, Signori* – By your leave, ladies and gentlemen; **(2)** Nedda/Tonio duet: *Sei là? – It's you?;* **(3)** Canio: *Recitar! … Vesti la giubba – A performance! … On with the motley;* **(4)** Canio: *La commedia è finita – The comedy is ended.*

Puccini

Giacomo Puccini
(1858–1924)

RIGHT **Adina Nitescu in the title-role of** *Manon Lescaut*, Glyndebourne, 1997

WHERE TO START
La bohème

WHERE TO GO NEXT
Madama Butterfly
Tosca

Puccini is regarded as the greatest Italian opera composer after Verdi. Apart from his two earliest works, all his operas are in the standard repertoire, some of them being among the most frequently performed, and most loved by audiences. They are quite likely to be the first operas heard by many people. Puccini was the greatest of the *verismo* composers (see Mascagni and Leoncavallo) and was Verdi's natural successor. He is the last Italian composer to have written operas that remain part of the international standard repertory.

Giacomo Antonio Domenico Michele Secondo Maria Puccini was born in 1858 in Lucca, about 12 miles from Pisa. His great-grandfather was a member of the Accademia Filarmonica of Bologna (to which Mozart was admitted in 1772) and his grandfather,

Domenico, had written an opera that had been highly commended by Paisiello. They had both been organist and choirmaster at Lucca's cathedral. Giacomo was one of seven children, and when his father died in 1863 his mother Albina, who was also musical, was determined that Giacomo would follow the family's musical tradition and become the cathedral organist. He had early lessons in singing and playing the organ from an uncle, and was then enrolled in the city's music school (the Istituto Musicale Pacini, of which his father had been director) and graduated in 1880, having written a mass – the *Messa di Gloria*. He then went to the Milan Conservatory and studied with, among others, Ponchielli, sharing a room with Mascagni.

Puccini wrote his first opera, *Le villi*, in 1883 and entered it for Sonzogno's competition, which five years later would be won by Mascagni's *Cavalleria rusticana* (see p.126). *Le villi* was turned down because it was illegible, but a number of his friends arranged for a performance to be given in Milan in 1884 and this brought the young composer to the attention of Giulio Ricordi, who had published many of Verdi's works. Ricordi paid him a retainer that enabled him to concentrate on composition. His next opera, *Edgar* (1889), was a failure, but late in 1893 his *Manon Lescaut* had a triumphant première in Turin and from then Puccini never looked back. He was able to build a villa at Torre del Lago and there he wrote the rest of his output. Ricordi had recommended to him as librettists Luigi Illica and Giuseppe Giacosa and they wrote the librettos for his next three operas, *La bohème*, *Tosca*, and *Madama Butterfly*. All three operas soon became, and have remained, worldwide favourites, and established him as Italy's leading composer.

From 1886 Puccini lived with a married woman, Elvira Gemignani, and they had a son. Shortly after her husband died she and Puccini married. It was not a very happy marriage – he was frequently unfaithful and she was very

jealous. The most notorious episode of this period was the suicide of a former maidservant of the Puccini household. Elvira was convinced her husband was having an affair with the girl and that she was pregnant by him, but the post-mortem examination proved this to be untrue. The scandal and court case took a considerable amount of his time and Puccini's next opera, *La fanciulla del West* (*The Girl of the Golden West*) did not appear until 1910. During the First World War Puccini wrote *La rondine* (*The Swallow*) and the three one-act operas that formed *Il trittico*. These were *Il tabarro*, *Suor Angelica*, and the comedy *Gianni Schicchi*, all first performed in New York after the war. Puccini's final opera, *Turandot*, was begun in 1920. By now the composer had developed throat cancer. While being treated in a Brussels hospital in 1924 he died, leaving *Turandot* unfinished.

Puccini was a lover of blood sports and motor cars but he was also a sensitive man, often lonely and melancholy, and much of his own temperament can be found in his operas. He was a supreme master of melody, producing memorable and beautiful arias, duets, and ensembles one after another in all his operas, assimilating into his own style the influences of the French masters such as Massenet, and the German idiom personified by Wagner. As with all the best opera composers, he had a natural theatrical instinct and knew what would and would not work on the stage. He was the greatest of the *verismo* composers simply because he was the most talented. He has always been the most popular composer with the public, but less so with the critics, who have been reluctant to give him credit for being a serious composer and have condemned him for manipulating audiences' emotions. Times change, and increasingly Puccini is being seen as a composer and dramatist of the highest calibre. And if, at the same time, he is popular with the public, this is not in itself a reason to sneer at him or his operas.

ABOVE LEFT **Giacomo Puccini in 1906, aged 48, painted by Arturo Rietti**

MANON LESCAUT,
1889–92, rev. 1893 and 1922

This, Puccini's first success, was a triumph at its Turin première and established the composer's reputation. It is the work of a young man, clearly showing the influences on him, especially of Verdi and of Wagner. Sir John Barbirolli once remarked that *Manon Lescaut* had enough tunes in it to set up any other opera composer for life! Like Massenet's *Manon* (see pp.111–12), it is based on the novel by the Abbé Prévost.

SYNOPSIS The action is in France and America in the 18th century. Count des Grieux (ten) drinks with his friend in Amiens. A coach arrives in the square bearing Lescaut (bar), his sister Manon (sop), and the elderly Geronte (bass) who is in love with her. Her brother is escorting her to a convent to complete her education. Des Grieux falls in love with her and after she leaves he pours out his feelings (1). Manon returns (2) and they commandeer Geronte's carriage to transport them to Paris where they set up a simple home. Des Grieux's money runs out and Manon, wanting luxury, returns to Geronte as his mistress. But she is bored and tells her brother how she hankers after the life she had with Des Grieux (3). The Count comes to her and there is a passionate

reunion (4). They plan to leave together, but Manon is so anxious to collect up the expensive jewellery Geronte has bought her that she delays their departure and Geronte returns. Furious, he brings the police to arrest Manon as a prostitute and thief and she is put on a ship to be deported. Des Grieux persuades the ship's captain to allow him to come on board to see Manon and he and Lescaut attempt to rescue her (5). They manage to escape, but as they wander through the desert, lost, Manon becomes ill. While Des Grieux searches for water, Manon muses on her past (6). He returns, Manon bids him farewell, and dies in his arms.

MUSIC (1) Des Grieux: *Donna non vidi mai – I never before beheld such a lady*; (2) Manon: *Vedete? Io son fedele all parola mia – You see? I am faithful to my word*; (3) Manon: *In quelle trine morbide – In those soft hangings*; (4) Manon/Des Grieux duet: *Tu, tu, amore?/Ah Manon! – You, you, beloved/Ah, Manon!*; (5) Manon/Des Grieux: *Des Grieux, fra poco lungi sarò …/Ah! guardami e vedi – Des Grieux, I shall soon be far away … / Oh, look at me*; (6) Manon: *Sola, perduta, abbandonata – Alone, lost, forsaken*.

LA BOHÈME
(*Bohemian Life*), 1893–5, rev. 1896

The opera in four acts is based on short stories by the French novelist Henri Murger (1822–61). Puccini and Leoncavallo both set it, but Puccini's opera, despite its initial muted reception, soon wiped Leoncavallo's off the map. It is one of the most often performed works in the repertoire of European and American opera houses.

SYNOPSIS Christmas Eve, 1830, in Paris. A poet Rodolfo (ten) and a painter Marcello (bar) are working in their cold attic. The philosopher Colline (bass) and musician Schaunard (bar) arrive, bringing wine and meagre rations. They all celebrate Christmas, interrupted by a knock on the door. Their landlord, Benoit (bass), demands the rent. They ply him with wine and throw him out when he is sufficiently drunk to forget what he came for. Rodolfo decides to finish writing his article, whilst the others set off for the Café Momus. There is a knock at the door. It is their neighbour Mimì (sop). Her candle has gone out and she asks for a light. She is exhausted and coughing and Rodolfo insists she rests. She drops her key and they search for it in the dark. Rodolfo finds it and pockets it. Their

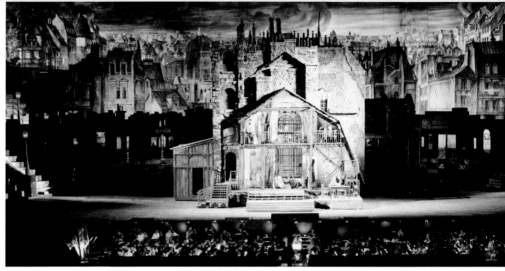

hands touch **(1)**. They tell each other of their lives **(2)**, fall in love, and then leave together to join the others **(3)**.

In the Café Momus the toy-seller Parpignol (ten), followed by a crowd of children, adds to the jollity. After Rodolfo buys Mimì a bonnet, she and the four Bohemians find a table. Marcello's old love, Musetta (sop), enters with the wealthy, foppish, elderly Alcindoro (bass). She ensures Marcello notices her **(4)** and he becomes very agitated – they are clearly still in love. She sends Alcindoro on an errand; she and Marcello declare their love and join the others. They all depart, leaving the bill for Alcindoro to settle on his return.

Two months later a frail Mimì, wracked by coughing, is looking for Marcello who comes out from a tavern. She tells him that she and Rodolfo must part, as his jealousy is making their lives impossible. Rodolfo also comes out of the inn and Mimì hides. She overhears him telling Marcello that she is dying and he cannot provide for her. Mimì emerges and they take passionate leave of each other, but then agree to stay together until the spring. At the same time, Musetta and Marcello embark on one of their furious rows **(5)**.

Back in the garret, Rodolfo is missing Mimì and Marcello yearns for Musetta **(6)**. The four men cheer themselves up by acting the fool,

and in the midst of all the hilarity Musetta arrives with Mimì, who is dying of consumption (tuberculosis). Colline decides to pawn his much-loved overcoat **(7)** to raise money to help Mimì, and Musetta gives her earrings to Marcello to pay for medicine. Colline and Schaunard set off to buy medicine, Marcello and Musetta to buy a muff to warm Mimì's hands. Alone at last, Rodolfo and Mimì reminisce about their first meeting and re-affirm their love **(8)**. The friends return with the medicine and muff but they are too late. Rodolfo, the last to realize that Mimì is dead, collapses sobbing over her body.

MUSIC **(1)** Rodolfo: *Che gelida manina!* – How cold your little hand is ("Your tiny hand is frozen"); **(2)** Mimì: *Mi chiamano Mimì* – They call me Mimì; **(3)** Rodolfo/Mimì duet: *O soave fanciulla* – Oh, lovely girl; **(4)** Musetta: *Quando men' vo soletto per la via* – As I walk alone through the street (Musetta's Waltz Song); **(5)** Rodolfo/Mimì/Marcello/Musetta double duet: *Dunque è proprio finità?* – So it's really over?; **(6)** Rodolfo/Marcello: *O Mimì, tu più non torni* – Oh Mimì, you won't return; **(7)** Colline: *Vecchia zimarra, senti* – Listen, my venerable coat; **(8)** Mimì: *Sono andati?* – Have they gone?

ABOVE LEFT **Mirella Freni (Mimì) and Luciano Pavarotti (Rodolfo) in *La bohème*, Salzburg Easter Festival, 1975**

BELOW One of opera's most famous confrontations: Maria Callas (Tosca) and Tito Gobbi (Scarpia) in Zeffirelli's production, ROH, London, 1964

TOSCA, 1896–9

Victorien Sardou's play *La Tosca* was first suggested to Puccini as a subject for an opera in about 1889 by his earliest librettist and was then given to another composer, Alberto Franchetti. When Puccini showed interest in it in 1895, Ricordi persuaded Franchetti to cede it. Puccini was meticulous in his research, consulting a priest about the religious aspects and travelling to Rome to visit the places where the action would take place. As with *La bohème*, *Tosca* had a muted reception at its first performance in Rome in 1900, but soon established itself in the standard repertoire, being seen in London and New York within a year or so of its première.

SYNOPSIS In the church of Sant' Andrea della Valle in Rome in June 1800, an escaped political prisoner, Angelotti (bass), hides in a side chapel, unseen by the Sacristan (bar). The painter Mario Cavaradossi (ten) enters the church to finish his painting of the Madonna, whose face reminds him of the woman he loves, the diva Floria Tosca (sop) (1). When the Sacristan has left, Angelotti shows himself to his old friend, a known Republican sympathizer. Cavaradossi gives him food and tells him where to hide from Baron Scarpia (bar), the sadistic Chief of Police. Tosca, arriving at the church to visit Cavaradossi, overhears him in conversation and accuses him of talking to another woman. He reassures her and they proclaim their feelings for each other (2). To mark the supposed defeat of Napoleon, Scarpia attends a *Te Deum* in the church (3). He lusts after Tosca, who is going to sing that evening in celebration of the victory. Angelotti's escape is discovered and Scarpia, believing that Cavaradossi is somehow involved, tries to trick Tosca into revealing the fugitive's whereabouts.

In his room in the Farnese Palace, Scarpia has sent for Tosca. He is told by one of his soldiers that Cavaradossi has been arrested on suspicion of helping the prisoner escape. Cavaradossi denies his involvement. As he is

BELOW **An invitation card to the world première** of *Tosca*, Rome, 14 January 1900

led into the next room to be tortured, Tosca enters. Hearing Cavaradossi's screams of pain, she reveals Angelotti's hiding-place. The painter is brought out, and denounces Tosca for her betrayal. Cavaradossi is delighted when it is revealed that Napoleon was in fact victorious in battle, and Scarpia has him imprisoned. Now Tosca and Scarpia are alone and he offers her a choice: she can submit to him or be the cause of Cavaradossi's execution. She despairingly sings of her art and her love **(4)**, and finally agrees to submit to Scarpia. He summons his henchmen and pretends to arrange a "mock" execution. As he writes a safe-conduct, which will allow Tosca and Cavaradossi to leave Rome, she notices a sharp knife on his dining-table. He reaches for her and she stabs him. As he dies, she spits out the words: "And before him, all Rome trembled!" ("*È avanti a lui tremava tutta Roma!*"). She takes the safe-conduct from his hand and, to comply with her religious feelings, places candlesticks each side of him and a crucifix on his chest, before she flees from the room.

At dawn, as church bells ring out over the battlements of the Castello Sant'Angelo, Cavaradossi awaits execution. He thinks of

Tosca and his own approaching death **(5)**. Tosca appears, shows him the safe-conduct and instructs him how to act in the "mock execution", and they speak of their future together **(6)**. The firing squad arrives. They shoot, and Cavaradossi falls. Tosca waits until the soldiers have left and then urges him to get up. But Scarpia has double-crossed her – the execution was not faked and Cavaradossi is dead. The soldiers, having found Scarpia's body, rush in to arrest Tosca. But she defies them by jumping from the parapet and falling to her death.

MUSIC (1) Cavaradossi: *Recondita armonia – Oh hidden harmony*; **(2)** Cavaradossi/Tosca duet: *Quale occhio al mondo puo star di paro – What eyes in the world can compare*; **(3)** Scarpia/ Chorus: *Va, Tosca! … Te Deum laudamus – Go, Tosca! … Te Deum laudamus*; **(4)** Tosca: *Vissi d'arte, vissi d'amore – I lived for art, I lived for love*; **(5)** Cavaradossi: *E lucevan le stelle – And the stars shone*; **(6)** Cavaradossi/Tosca duet: *O dolci mane/Senti, l'ora è vicina – O sweet hands/Listen, the hour is near.*

MADAMA BUTTERFLY,
1901–3, rev. 1904, 1905, 1906

This was the third and last Puccini opera with Illica and Giacosa as librettists. They based it on a play by the American David Belasco (1853–1931) Puccini had seen in London. The première at La Scala in 1904 was a complete failure and over the next few years Puccini made various revisions. It is now as popular as his two previous operas and some would say it is his greatest. Butterfly is certainly the only Puccini heroine whose character develops from act to act: she begins as an innocent young girl and ends as a mature, self-sacrificing mother.

SYNOPSIS Early 20th century, near Nagasaki, Japan. An American naval officer, Lieut. B F Pinkerton (ten) has made arrangements through the marriage-broker Goro (ten), for a Japanese wedding to a 15-year-old bride, Cio-Cio-San (sop), known as Madam Butterfly. Pinkerton does not take the wedding too seriously – he is taking pleasure where he can find it **(1)**. Sharpless (bar), the American Consul, tries to explain to him that Butterfly regards it as a binding contract and has even converted to Christianity for the wedding. For this she has been cursed by her uncle the Bonze (bar) and her family is rejecting her. The commissioner performs the wedding ceremony. Butterfly's maidservant Suzuki (mez) prepares her for her wedding-night and she and Pinkerton are left alone **(2)**. He obviously enjoys her flattery as they walk in the garden, whilst she declares her abiding love for him **(3)**.

Three years have passed. Pinkerton left for America soon after their marriage and Butterfly has heard nothing from him. She is sure he will return **(4)** and has turned down an offer of marriage from Prince Yamadori (ten). Sharpless comes to visit Butterfly, with a letter from Pinkerton, to tell her that Pinkerton's ship is docking in Nagasaki. He tries to warn her that Pinkerton's American wife, Kate (mez), will be with him, but she is

BELOW Frontispiece for the score of Puccini's *Madama Butterfly*

so excited that she will not let him finish his sentences (5). He is horrified to learn that Butterfly has a child, Pinkerton's son, called Trouble (silent). He hasn't the heart to tell her about Kate. After he leaves, Butterfly and Suzuki excitedly prepare the room for Pinkerton's return, strewing flowers all round. Donning her wedding gown, Butterfly, her son, and Suzuki keep an all-night vigil, waiting for Pinkerton's arrival (6). When he does arrive, Sharpless is with him, and Kate waits outside. Pinkerton asks Suzuki to talk to Kate. Seeing her distress, he realizes what his thoughtlessness has cost Butterfly (7) and rushes from the house, leaving Sharpless with the cruel task of telling Butterfly that Pinkerton and Kate want to take the child back to America with them. Butterfly agrees, but on one condition: Pinkerton must come himself to collect his son. Kate and Sharpless leave and Butterfly dismisses Suzuki and prepares to kill herself with her father's dagger (8). Suzuki sends the child in to her in the hope of deterring her. Butterfly blindfolds her child so that he is unaware of what is happening, and kills herself with her father's ceremonial sword, just as Pinkerton hurries in, calling her name.

ABOVE Geraldine Farrar as Cio-Cio-San at the American première of *Madama Butterfly*, attended by the composer, Metropolitan Opera, NY, 1907

> **MUSIC** (1) Pinkerton: *Dovunque al mondo – Everywhere in the world*; (2) Pinkerton/Butterfly: *Viene la sera – Night is falling*; (3) Pinkerton/Butterfly duet: *Vogliatemi bene, un bene piccolino/Dammi ch'io baci le tue mani care – Love me with a little love/Give me your dear hands and let me kiss them*; (4) Butterfly: *Un bel di vedremo – One fine day we'll see*; (5) Sharpless/Butterfly: *Ora a noi. Sedete qui – Our turn now. Sit down here*; (6) Humming Chorus (offstage); (7) Pinkerton: *Addio, fiorito asil – Farewell flowery refuge*; (8) Butterfly: *Con onor muore – He died with honour*.

TURANDOT, 1920–4, completed by Franco Alfano 1925–6

After *Madama Butterfly*, Puccini composed three more operas (see below) before returning to the Far East for the setting of this, his last opera. As with all his works, it underwent numerous quite drastic revisions. By the end of March 1924 only the final scene of the third act remained to be composed, including an extended duet for Turandot and Calaf. Before he could begin work on it, Puccini died. Some sketches remained, and from these a young composer, Franco Alfano (1875–1954), who had written several operas himself, completed the last act and he is better known for his completion of *Turandot* than for

his own works. It is not an altogether satisfactory completion and there is no doubt that the temperature drops considerably when Alfano's music takes over. Many people believe it would be better to give the work exactly as Puccini left it, as indeed did Toscanini when he conducted the first performance at La Scala in 1926 without the Alfano ending.

SYNOPSIS In ancient Peking, China, the beautiful but heartless Princess Turandot (sop) has been promised in marriage to anyone who can solve three riddles. Those who try and fail must die – many have already done so. Among the crowds in the street awaiting the execution of the latest failed contestant, is the blind old King Timur (bass), who has lost his throne and is penniless. He is being guided by a beautiful young slave girl, Liù (sop). He is joined by Ping (bar), Pang (ten), and Pong (ten), three ministers of Turandot's father, the Emperor Altoum (ten). They all attempt to stop an Unknown Prince (ten), who is actually Timur's son Calaf, from attempting to solve the riddles. He asks Liù to look after his father (1) and strikes the gong to indicate the arrival of a new suitor.

The ministers and Altoum, tired of all the executions, beg Calaf to withdraw from the contest, but he will not change his mind. Turandot first explains that, having been inspired by an ancient story, she has vowed to keep herself chaste (2). She then announces

her riddles. Much to everyone's amazement, the Prince answers them all correctly. So now Turandot is committed to marry him and begs her father to release her from this promise. Calaf offers her one last chance of freedom – if she can tell him his name before daybreak, he is willing to release her and to die himself. Otherwise, she must marry him. Turandot agrees to the bargain, and decrees that all her ministers will die if they do not discover the Unknown Prince's name.

Calaf contemplates his inevitable victory (3). Timur is seen talking to the Prince and is brought in by the guards together with Liù. Turandot tries to force Timur into revealing the name, but Liù tells her that she alone knows the answer. She resists all attempts to make her tell the name, telling the Princess that, through her sacrifice, Turandot will learn about love (4). Liù then kills herself with a soldier's dagger. Timur, heartbroken, follows the procession carrying her body (this funeral music is the last that Puccini wrote). Calaf and Turandot are left alone. She responds to his kiss and he tells her his name. Now his life is in her hands. Turandot summons the people and tells them: "His name is Love!" They all celebrate with her.

> **MUSIC** (1) Calaf: *Non piangere, Liù – Do not cry, Liù*; (2) Turandot: *In questa reggia – In this palace*; (3) Calaf: *Nessun dorma questa notte in Pekino – None shall sleep tonight in Peking*; (4) Liù: *Tu che di gel sei cinta – You who are girded with ice*.

Other operas of note

There are seven Puccini operas (including a triptych of one-act works) that have not been described in detail. His first two operas, *La villi* and *Edgar*, rarely achieve performances, his fame beginning with *Manon Lescaut*. The others all deserve some discussion. In 1907 Puccini went to New York for the first time to supervise the American premières of *Manon Lescaut* and *Madama Butterfly*. While there he saw David Belasco's play *The Girl of the Golden West* and decided to set it. There were delays for various reasons (including the suicide of the maidservant and subsequent scandal described on p.128), but eventually the opera had its first performance, appropriately in the USA, in 1910 at the Metropolitan Opera, New York. It was an immediate success. It is set in California in the 1849–50 goldrush and Puccini's representation of American frontier life is historically realistic. It is an harmonically advanced score, more daring than any of his others. It is also a complicated plot with complex stage action and it requires very good singing actors. These may be some of the reasons that the opera has never been a repertory piece, but it deserves to be seen more often.

After writing *La fanciulla del West*, it was some time before Puccini settled on another subject. It was suggested to him in 1913 that he write an operetta for Vienna and from this eventually emerged *La rondine* (*The Swallow*). It was based on a German libretto, translated

into Italian, and tells how Magda, the mistress of the elderly Rambaldo, falls in love with the latter's friend, Ruggero. Puccini finished the score in 1915 but the First World War caused more delays and it did not have its first performance until 1917 in the neutral territory of Monte Carlo. It has never been among the most-performed of Puccini's operas, possibly because the main characters are not too well-defined and there is an extensive but weak sub-plot. But in the last few years it has been gaining ground with productions in Europe and the USA and Magda's Act 1 aria, "Chi il bel sogno Doretta poté indovinar?" ("Who can interpret Doretta's beautiful dream?") has become well known in recitals.

After *La rondine* and before *Turandot*, Puccini produced three one-act operas known collectively as *Il trittico*. They are *Il tabarro* (*The Cloak*), *Suor Angelica* (*Sister Angelica*), and *Gianni Schicchi*. They are at their best when seen in one evening (each lasts about an hour), as the composer intended, but this happens only occasionally. More often two

of them will be performed or one of them will be paired with another one-act opera by a different composer as a double bill, the one most often seen this way being the comic *Gianni Schicchi*. *Il tabarro* is a dramatic tale of adultery and passion, set on a barge beside the Seine. The characters are all well-defined and the orchestration highly innovative, with some exotic sounds. *Suor Angelica* is set in a convent in 17th-century Italy. Angelica has been put in the convent as punishment for having an illegitimate child. Her aunt visits and tells her the child is dead and she drinks poison, damning herself to purgatory. But the Madonna brings her dead child to lead her to heaven. The comedy *Gianni Schicchi* is the best-known of the three, making one wish that Puccini had composed more comedies. It opens in the bedroom of the rich Buoso Donati who has just died. His large family is gathered round his bed, pretending to be distressed and hoping that he has left them his money. Rumour has it that he has left it all to a monastery. A frantic search for the will ensues and when found it shows that he has indeed left everything to the church. Help is asked of the cunning Gianni Schicchi, whose daughter Lauretta needs the money in order to marry Rinuccio, and her pleas for his help form one of the best-known arias in all Puccini, "O mio babbino caro" ("O my beloved Daddy"). He suggests concealing the death long enough for him to pose as Buoso and draw up a new will. They send for an attorney and each of them bribes Schicchi to leave them the most. The notary arrives and when he reads the "new will" they find that "Buoso" has left most of his fortune to "my good friend Gianni Schicchi". They can do nothing about it without revealing their own part in the illegal plot! Lauretta is able to marry the man she loves and Schicchi is well satisfied with the outcome. The work has a large cast of well-drawn characters, and its musical invention shows how much Puccini owed to Verdi and particularly to Verdi's last masterpiece, *Falstaff*.

ABOVE **Set design for** *Turandot*, La Scala, Milan

Humperdinck

Engelbert Humperdinck
(1854–1921)

WHERE TO START
Hänsel und Gretel

WHERE TO GO NEXT
Königskinder

Engelbert Humperdinck was born near Bonn, the son of a school-master. He started to write works for piano from the age of seven. He entered Cologne University in 1871 to study architecture but after a year he switched to music. He won many prizes which enabled him to travel. In Naples in 1880 he met Richard Wagner, who engaged him as his assistant for the first production of *Parsifal* at Bayreuth in 1882 (see p.100). From 1882 onwards Humperdinck was a teacher at conservatoires in Barcelona and Cologne and also an editor for Schott's music publishers. He married Hedwig Taxer in 1892 and their first child was born a year later. From 1890 to 1896 he was a professor at the Hoch Conservatory in Frankfurt and from 1900 he was director of a music academy in Berlin. He was also a music critic.

Humperdinck wrote relatively few orchestral or chamber works, but a great deal of choral music, songs, and incidental music for plays. In 1890 his sister asked him to set some songs for the Grimm fairy-tale *Hänsel und Gretel* for her children to perform and thus began his most successful opera which, within a year of its première, had over 50 productions worldwide. His only other opera to achieve any success was *Königskinder* (*Royal Children*). It is an interesting work containing what can be described as early *Sprechgesang* ("speech-song"), anticipating by several years a method which would be developed by Schoenberg (see pp.158–9). Although popular with early audiences, it has not held its place in the repertoire.

In 1912 Humperdinck suffered a massive stroke and, although he recovered, his left hand remained paralysed. His wife died in 1916 and he had another stroke in March 1921. In the autumn he attended performances of Weber's *Der Freischütz* (see pp.88–9), his son's début as a director, during which he had a heart attack and died shortly afterwards. He was buried in Berlin. Humperdinck's reputation virtually rests on one work, but it rests very securely with *Hänsel und Gretel*.

HÄNSEL UND GRETEL
(*Hansel and Gretel*), 1890–3
In 1890 Humperdinck's sister, Adelheid Wette, wrote her own, less scary, version of *Hänsel und Gretel* for her children to perform. She asked her brother to provide music for songs in the play, and they later made it into a full-scale opera. The first performance was in Weimar in 1893, conducted by Richard Strauss. It was an immediate success and has remained so.

ABOVE LEFT Engelbert Humperdinck, *c.*1885, aged about 30

SYNOPSIS In medieval Germany, Hänsel (mez, *travesti* role) and Gretel (sop) are the children of Peter (bar), a broom-maker, and his wife Gertrud (mez). The family is very poor and Gretel tries to take her brother's mind off his hunger by dancing with him (1). Gertrud sends them out to pick strawberries. Peter is upset to hear the children are in the Ilsenstein forest. A Witch (mez) lives there who tempts children into her house and then bakes them alive, turning them into gingerbread.

Hänsel and Gretel are lost and frightened. The Sandman (sop, *travesti* role) throws sand in their eyes (2). They say their prayers and fall asleep (3). Next morning they are woken by the Dew Fairy (sop) (4). They see a house and fence made of gingerbread and they take little bites. The Witch uses magic to catch them, puts Hänsel in a cage to fatten him up, and sets Gretel to work (5). Gretel frees Hänsel and together they push the Witch into her oven. As the oven explodes, the garden fence changes into a row of children who had been baked by the Witch. The Witch is turned into gingerbread and they all rejoice (6).

> **MUSIC** (1) Gretel: *Brüderchen, komm tanz' mit mir – Little brother, come and dance with me*; (2) Sandman: *Der kleine Sandmann bin ich, st! – The little Sandman am I, sh!*; (3) Hänsel/Gretel duet: *Abends will ich schlafen gehn – When I lay me down to sleep*; (4) Dew Fairy: *Der kleine Taumann heiss' ich – I am the little Dewman*; (5) Witch: *Hokus pokus, Hexenschuss! – Hocus pocus freeze the blood!*; (6) Hänsel/Gretel/Gertrud/Peter/Children: *Wenn die Not aufs höchste steigt – When need is more than we can stand.*

ABOVE Hänsel (Ethna Robinson) and Gretel (Cathryn Pope), sitting outside the gingerbread house, ENO, London, 1989

Strauss

Richard Strauss
(1864–1949)

WHERE TO START
Der Rosenkavalier

WHERE TO GO NEXT
Salome

LEFT **A portrait of Richard Strauss painted by Max Liebermann in 1918**

Richard Strauss is one of a few major composers who have succeeded in several genres. His tone-poems are among the great works of the orchestral repertoire; his *Lieder* are indispensable to recitalists; and many of his operas are standard repertoire throughout the Western world. From an early age he was equally well-known as a conductor. He is included among the late Romantics, even though he produced six operas (and other major works) between 1925 and his death in 1949 because in style and sound he is as much a late Romantic composer as Puccini, the two men being the natural successors to Wagner and Verdi.

Strauss's father Franz was principal horn-player in the Bavarian (Munich) Court Opera for almost 50 years and his mother, Josephine, was a member of the Pschorr family of wealthy brewers. Richard was their only son, his sister Johanna being born three years later. He had no formal music education – his early lessons were given to him by one of his father's colleagues.

When he was 16 his First Symphony was played by the Court Orchestra conducted by Hermann Levi (who was to conduct the first performance of Wagner's *Parsifal* at Bayreuth two years later). In 1885 he became assistant to Hans von Bülow at Meiningen, the following year moved to Munich opera as third conductor, and in 1889 became conductor of Weimar Court Opera. At Weimar he conducted the première of Humperdinck's *Hänsel und Gretel* in 1893 (see p.136) and, in 1894, of his own first opera, *Guntram*, in which the leading soprano was Pauline de Ahna. They were married later that year. She was apparently a fine interpreter of his *Lieder*, and Strauss's ability to write so sympathetically for

the female voice owes much to her influence. Their only child, Franz, was born in 1897.

In 1894 Strauss returned to Munich Opera, becoming chief conductor there two years later. In 1895 he conducted *Guntram* in Munich where it was savaged by the critics. In 1898 he was appointed chief conductor of the Royal Opera in Berlin, and in 1919 became co-director at the Vienna State Opera. In 1920 he was a founder of the Salzburg Festival. He resigned from Vienna in 1924 for political reasons (as had many before him and as did many after him). During his years there he conducted legendary performances of Mozart and Wagner, as well as his own works.

It was some seven years before Strauss embarked on his next opera, the one-act *Feuersnot*. It had its première in Dresden in 1901 and Strauss was so pleased with the result that seven more of his operas had their first performances there. His next two operas were *Salome* and *Elektra*, both one-act emotional blockbusters. *Salome* fell foul of the censors in several cities, but both operas were successful with the public and *Elektra* was significant for being Strauss's first collaboration with the poet who would prove to be his greatest librettist, Hugo von Hofmannsthal (1874–1929). Together they produced five more operas, some of which rank among the greatest in the repertoire: *Der Rosenkavalier, Ariadne auf Naxos, Die Frau ohne Schatten, Die ägyptische Helena*, and *Arabella*. Hofmannsthal refused to be involved with the opera *Intermezzo*, which was based on an incident in the life of the Strauss family, and the composer wrote his own text. Hofmannsthal died suddenly during the composition of *Arabella* and Strauss was devastated.

Strauss was introduced to the Austrian playwright and novelist Stefan Zweig (1881–1942) and was delighted with the libretto Zweig wrote for the comedy *Die schweigsame Frau*. But it was 1935, Zweig was Jewish, and the Nazis were already in power. Zweig realized it would be impossible for them to collaborate further and recommended the historian Joseph Gregor (1888–1960), who wrote the librettos for the next three operas, although Strauss did not make life easy for the poor man and Zweig had an unofficial hand behind the scenes. The operas were *Friedenstag, Daphne*, and *Die Liebe der Danae*. For Strauss's last opera, *Capriccio*, he rejected two librettos by Gregor and eventually the composer and the conductor Clemens Krauss, devised it between them.

Strauss was 75 when the Second World War began. He had worked with the half-Jewish Hofmannsthal and the Jewish Zweig. He has been criticized for remaining in Germany where he had seen various Kaisers come and go, and he believed that Hitler would go the same way. He somewhat naively considered himself impervious to politics and politicians, but was slowly to learn that these people were different. When the Nazis first came to power, Strauss accepted the post of president of the *Reichsmusikkammer* (state music bureau). He has been accused of co-operating with the Nazis because he conducted at Bayreuth in 1933 when Toscanini withdrew for political reasons, and conducted a Berlin Philharmonic concert when Bruno Walter was ordered not to do so (he gave his fee to the orchestra, whom Walter was going to pay). It is very easy, with the benefit of hindsight, to be critical of him. But Germany was his home and his heritage. Apart from music, the most important thing to him was his family. His only son had married Alice, a part-Jewish girl, and his two grandsons were therefore partly Jewish. The children had been stoned in the street and their parents had been questioned by the Gestapo. In total

BELOW Birgit Nilsson as Salome, drooling over Jochanaan's severed head on a silver platter, Bavarian State Opera, Munich, 1955

32 members of Alice's family were to die in Theresienstadt concentration camp. To protect his family from what he called "these barbarians" was his major consideration.

After the war, the 81-year-old Strauss and his wife moved to Switzerland, where he continued to compose, mainly short orchestral works. In 1948 he was cleared by the de-Nazification Board and in the same year composed the *Vier letzte Lieder* (*Four Last Songs*). He returned to his home in Garmisch in May 1949 and died there four months later.

SALOME, 1904–5

Strauss was first sent Oscar Wilde's play in 1902 by the Austrian poet Anton Lindner, who offered to fashion a libretto, but after he saw the play in Hedwig Lachmann's German translation from the French, Strauss set about adapting his own libretto. The first performance nearly came to grief when some of the singers

returned their parts at the first rehearsal as being too difficult. Marie Wittich, the creator of Salome, refused to perform the Dance of the Seven Veils, with her famous remark "I'm a respectable woman!" A stand-in was used. Some theatres refused to stage it, and the Kaiser remarked that it would do Strauss a great deal of harm. Strauss commented that the harm it did him enabled him to build his villa in Garmisch. It was a wild success at its première in Dresden and within two years had been produced at 50 opera houses. It is in one act. The title-role is a wonderful study in obsession and Strauss said that the ideal Salome should look 16 and have the voice of Isolde – one is not often that fortunate. Despite the dissonances in the score, it is very firmly tonal, not atonal as is sometimes stated, and the large orchestra is used with great imagination and delicacy.

SYNOPSIS It is about AD 30 in Tiberias, on the Galilee. Narraboth (ten), a Syrian captain, is enchanted by Salome (sop) (**1**), daughter of Herodias (mez), the second wife of King Herod (ten). In a cistern below the terrace is imprisoned Jochanaan (John the Baptist) (bar), who has insulted Herodias. Salome is fascinated by Jochanaan's voice and orders the guards to allow him out. When she tells Jochanaan she is Herodias's daughter and she wants to touch him and kiss him, he rants against her and her mother (**2**), curses her, and returns to the cistern. Narraboth is so upset by her behaviour that he kills himself. A group of learned Jews argue with Herod that Jochanaan cannot be a holy man (**3**). Herod leers at Salome and asks her to dance for him (**4**). He offers her generous bribes – jewels and silver – but only when he offers her anything she chooses does she agree to dance. She performs the Dance of the Seven Veils, finishing naked before him. Then she claims her reward: the head of Jochanaan on a silver salver! Even Herod is revolted, but Herodias is proud of her daughter. All appeals to her to change her mind fail and ultimately

Herod sends an executioner down into the cistern. He emerges with Jochanaan's head on a silver platter. Salome drools over it – now he cannot stop her kissing him (**5**). Herod, horrified, orders his guards to kill her and they crush her to death with their shields.

> **MUSIC** (**1**) Narraboth: *Wie schön ist die Prinzessin Salome heute Nacht! – How beautiful is Princess Salome tonight!*; (**2**) Jochanaan: *Wo bist er, dessen Sündenbecher jetzt voll ist? – Where is he, whose cup of abomination is now full?*; (**3**) First Jew: *Wahrhaftig, Herr, er wäre besser – Truly, my lord, it would be better*; (**4**) Herod: *Tanz für mich, Salome – Dance for me, Salome*; (**5**) Salome: *Ah! Du wolltest mich nicht deinen Mund küssen lassen, Jochanaan! … Ah! Ich habe deinen Mund geküsst, Jochanaan; – Ah! Thou wouldst not suffer me to kiss thy mouth, Jochanaan … Ah! I have kissed your mouth, Jochanaan.*

ELEKTRA, 1906–8

Hofmannsthal's play *Elektra* was adapted from Sophocles in 1903. Strauss probably saw it in a production by Max Reinhardt revived in Berlin in 1905. He met the author and mentioned that he wanted to set it as an opera, but was reluctant to tackle such a similar subject so soon after *Salome*. Hofmannsthal was persuasive and Strauss began the music in the summer of 1906. Progress was slow because he was conducting 60 performances a season at the Berlin Court Opera. Although Hofmannsthal contributed a few extra lines as needed, the libretto is Strauss's very skilful reduction of the play. Again, it is in one continuous act. There are passages in the score that can be described as atonal or bitonal, but the whole score is in fact, like *Salome*, tonal. Its first performance was in Dresden in 1909. Strauss wrote three glorious roles for the female voice that have continued to attract many great dramatic singers.

DER ROSENKAVALIER, 1909–10

This is Strauss's most popular opera. It is usually given its original title even when performed in English – *The Knight of the Rose* doesn't have quite the same resonance. From an audience point of view it has everything: three glorious female roles, a mid-18th-century Viennese setting, a triangular love-story, comedy, and arias and ensembles to turn the heart over. It was Strauss's first complete collaboration with Hugo von Hofmannsthal and he was so delighted with the libretto that he wrote to his librettist: "…it'll set itself to music like oil and melted butter". The first performance, in Dresden, had an inadequate producer, but the eminent Max Reinhardt went to supervise (without any credit in the programme), and the sets and costumes were by the well-known artist Alfred Roller. It was a triumph and it has never lost its popularity.

SYNOPSIS The 32-year-old Marschallin (sop) has spent the night with her 17-year-old lover Octavian (sop/mez *travesti* role). Baron Ochs (bass), the Marschallin's somewhat boorish cousin, arrives and Octavian has to hide. Ochs asks the Marschallin to recommend a nobleman to take the traditional silver rose to his fiancée, Sophie von Faninal (sop). The Marschallin recommends Octavian, who reappears disguised as a maid called Mariandel, with whom Ochs flirts. The Marschallin's morning levée begins: various tradesmen arrive, including two intriguers, Annina (mez) and Valzacchi (ten), and an Italian Singer (ten) who serenades her (1). When they depart, she muses on the passing of time and how she soon will be the "old princess" and she knows that Octavian will leave her for a younger woman (2). She sends him to deliver the rose.

The excited Sophie, her duenna Marianne Leitmetzerin (sop), and her father, the *nouveau-riche* Herr von Faninal (bar) await the arrival of the Knight of the Rose. Octavian presents Sophie with the rose, their eyes meet, and there is a mutual attraction (3). When Ochs arrives Sophie is appalled to realize her father wants her to marry this lecherous man. Octavian vows

SYNOPSIS In ancient Mycenae, before the opera begins, Queen Klytemnästra (mez) and her lover Aegisth (ten) have murdered her husband Agamemnon. Klytemnästra has two daughters, Elektra (sop) and Chrysothemis (sop). Elektra lives in the grounds like a wild animal and the servants all mock her. Elektra is lonely (1) and is waiting for her brother Oreste (bar) to return from exile and she dreams of avenging her father's death. Chrysothemis is not interested in revenge, just in getting married, having a family, and leading a normal life (2). Klytemnästra, bedecked with jewels, talks to Elektra about the bad nightmares she is having (3). Her daughter tells her they will stop only when somebody has been sacrificed – and that sacrifice will be Klytemnästra herself. To her relief, Klytemnästra is told, falsely, that Oreste is dead. When Elektra hears this news, she realizes she will have to wreak revenge on her mother herself (4) and starts digging for the axe she has

hidden in the courtyard. Oreste enters and at first Elektra does not recognize him (5). Then she convinces him that their mother and her lover must die. He enters the palace and soon Klytemnästra's screams are heard. These attract Aegisth who rushes into the palace and meets the same fate. Elektra dances a frenetic dance of joy, at the end of which she collapses, dead (6).

> **MUSIC (1)** Elektra: *Allein! Weh, ganz allein – Alone! Alas, all alone*; **(2)** Chrysothemis: *Ich kann nicht sitzen und ins Dunkel starren wie du – I cannot sit and stare into the dark like you*; **(3)** Klytemnästra: *Ich habe keine guten Nächt – I have bad nights*; **(4)** Elektra: *Nun denn, allein! – Well then, alone!*; **(5)** Oreste/Elektra: *Die Hunde auf dem Hof erkennen mich/Oreste! Oreste! – The dogs in the yard recognize me/ Oreste! Oreste!*; **(6)** Elektra: *Schweig, und tanze! – Be silent, and dance!*

BELOW **Marlis Petersen (Zerbinetta)**, leader of the *commedia dell'arte* troupe, with Timothy Robinson, Jeremy White, and Barry Banks, *Ariadne auf Naxos*, ROH, London, 2004

to prevent the marriage and challenges Ochs to a duel. Ochs is slightly injured but behaves as if his wound is major. Annina and Valzacchi have arrived to support Ochs, but Octavian wins them over and Annina delivers to Ochs a message from "Mariandel" agreeing to an assignation. Ochs is thrilled at the prospect (4).

In an inn, Octavian rehearses Annina, Valzacchi, and others as apparitions to scare Ochs. He then dresses as "Mariandel" and returns for supper with Ochs. Supper is served by Ochs's bastard son Leopold (silent). Ochs plies Mariandel with wine and tries to seduce her (5). As he becomes more amorous and "she" more maudlin, apparitions appear, including children who claim him as their father. He sends for the police and introduces Mariandel/Octavian as his fiancée Sophie. But Valzacchi has sent for Sophie and her father, who refute Ochs's story. The Marschallin, summoned by Leopold, enters and assures everyone that the whole thing is "just a masquerade". She advises Ochs to leave, which he gladly does. In a sublime trio, the young lovers and the Marschallin sing of their feelings (6). She accepts the situation gracefully and leaves Octavian and Sophie to vow their love for each other (7) before they follow her.

MUSIC (1) Italian Tenor: *Di rigori armato il seno – My bosom armed with severity*; (2) Marschallin: *Die Zeit, ist ein sonderbar Ding – Time is a strange thing*; (3) Octavian/Sophie duet: *Mir ist die Ehre widerfahren – To me is given the honour*; (4) Ochs: *Mit mir, mit mir, keine Nacht dir zu lang – With me, with me, no night is too long for you*; (5) Octavian (as Mariandel): *Nein, nein, nein nein, I trink ka Wein – No, no. no. no, Oi'll not drink no woin*; (6) Octavian/Marschallin/Sophie trio: *Marie Theres!/Habs mir gelobt/Mir ist wie in der Kirchn – Marie Therese!/I vowed to myself/I feel as if I were in a church*; (7) Sophie/Octavian: *Ist ein Traum/Spür nur dich – It is a dream/I feel only you.*

ARIADNE AUF NAXOS, 1912, 1916

Ariadne auf Naxos began as a Molière play, *Le bourgeois gentilhomme*, for which Strauss wrote incidental music, followed by a spoken linking scene, then a short opera interwoven with elements of *commedia dell'arte*, all to be performed for the *bourgeois gentilhomme*, M. Jourdain. This made for a very long evening and required a drama company and an opera company. Realizing this was not very practical, Strauss and Hofmannsthal jettisoned the play, and replaced the linking scene by a sung Prologue set back-stage in the house of "the richest man in Vienna", for whom the *opera seria* would then be performed. This had its première in 1916 and is the version which has become standard repertoire.

SYNOPSIS In the rich man's house in Vienna, an opera company and a *commedia dell'arte* troupe are preparing entertainment. There is typical back-stage chaos: the Composer (mez, *travesti* role) wants more rehearsal, the Tenor who will play Bacchus in the opera does not like his wig, the soprano who is to sing Ariadne refuses to rehearse. Zerbinetta (sop), leader of the comedians, is attracted to the Composer, who has just thought of a new tune for his opera (1). The Music Master (bar) complains to the man's Major Domo (spoken) about the opera his pupil is writing being followed by such vulgar entertainment. The Major Domo now drops a bombshell: to make sure the entertainment is over in time for a firework display, the two companies must perform simultaneously. Zerbinetta teases the Composer about the opera's plot, declaring that nobody dies for love. The Composer is distraught – his music is a holy art (2).

In the opera proper, on the Island of Naxos, Ariadne (sop) has been deserted by Theseus. She sleeps, guarded by three nymphs, Echo (sop), Dryad (cont), and Naiad (sop), who describe her distress (3). When she wakes, she weeps, praying for death to end her misery (4). The comedians fail to cheer her up, despite all Zerbinetta's efforts to convince her to fall in love with somebody else – her motto is "off with the old, on with the new" (5). Ariadne retreats into her cave and the comedians perform their dance, the four men courting Zerbinetta. The young god Bacchus (ten) arrives, having escaped from the sorceress Circe (6). Ariadne mistakes him for Theseus and then for Hermes (The Messenger of Death). But she gradually abandons the idea of death, happy to go with Bacchus and find love (7) – as Zerbinetta predicted.

MUSIC (1) Composer: *Du, Venus' Sohn – You, Venus-Son*; (2) Composer: *Musik ist eine heilige Kunst – Music is a holy art*; (3) Echo/Dryad/Naiad trio: *Ach, wir sind es eingewöhnet – Oh, we are used to it now*; (4) Ariadne: *Es gibt ein Reich, wo alles rein ist – There is a realm, where all is pure*; (5) Zerbinetta: *Grossmächtige Prinzessin – Most gracious Princess*; (6) Bacchus: *Circe, kannst du mich hören? – Circe, can you hear me?*; (7) Ariadne/Bacchus duet: *Du Zauberer, du! – You magician, you!*

ARABELLA, 1930–2

Strauss had for years been asking his librettist Hofmannsthal for "a second *Rosenkavalier*". Hofmannsthal felt that *Arabella* would fit the bill. After alterations and additions to Act 1, Strauss sent a telegram of thanks and congratulations to Hofmannsthal. It was never opened. It arrived on the day of the funeral of Hofmannsthal's son, who had committed suicide. While dressing to attend the service, Hofmannsthal had a stroke and died. Strauss was inconsolable. He dedicated the opera to the conductor and intendant at Dresden State Opera, where the première would take place. When the Nazis dismissed both these men in 1933, Strauss withdrew the score, but Dresden held him to his contract. The critics received it coolly, and it took some time to become one of his best-loved operas.

SYNOPSIS Vienna 1860. Count Waldner (bass) and his wife Adelaide (mez) have two daughters, Arabella (sop) and Zdenka (sop). The family is hard-up and cannot afford to "bring out" two daughters, so Zdenka is kept dressed as a boy while a suitably wealthy husband is found for Arabella. Among her admirers are three Counts: Elemer (ten), Dominik (bar), and Lamoral (bass). There is also a young army officer Matteo (ten) who has received letters from Arabella and believes she loves him. He does not know they were written by Zdenka, who does love him and who he, of course, thinks is a boy. Zdenka chides her sister about her lack of interest in Matteo and Arabella says that when the right man comes along, she will know him (1). She has seen a stranger standing outside the hotel, who looks interesting. Tonight Arabella will be queen of the annual Cabbies' Ball and before it ends she must decide who to marry. Waldner has sent Arabella's photograph to an old army friend in Croatia. The friend has died and his nephew, the wealthy landowner Mandryka (bar), arrives at the hotel to court the lady in the picture and tells the Waldners how he came by it (2). After he leaves, Arabella enters, telling Zdenka that she knows that marriage to Elemer is not possible (3).

At the ball Mandryka is introduced to Arabella who recognizes him as the stranger outside. They immediately fall in love and Mandryka tells Arabella of an old Croatian custom: betrothed girls present a cup of clear water to their fiancé as a token of chastity and commitment (4). The Fiakermilli (sop), the Cabbies' mascot [*Fiaker* = hansom cab] hails Arabella as queen of the ball (5). Arabella agrees to have a final dance with each of her three suitors to bid them farewell. Zdenka gives Matteo a letter purporting to come from Arabella and containing the key to her room (in reality, to Zdenka's room). Mandryka overhears their conversation and thinks Arabella is being unfaithful. He gets drunk and flirts with the Fiakermilli.

Back at the hotel, Matteo emerges from a bedroom, believing he has been in bed with Arabella. So he is surprised to see her enter the hall still in her ballgown. He cannot understand why she is so cool with him and she has no idea what he is talking about. Her parents and Mandryka return from the ball and when Mandryka sees Matteo this confirms his suspicions about Arabella's unfaithfulness. Arabella denies his accusation. Suddenly Zdenka runs down in her nightdress, upset at the confusion she has caused. She confesses all to Arabella **(6)**, and Matteo is astounded to realize it is Zdenka to whom he has made love. They all retire, leaving Arabella and Mandryka alone. She says goodnight and ascends the stairs, asking a servant to bring her a glass of water to quench her thirst. Alone, Mandryka muses on events **(7)**. Then he sees Arabella descending the stairs with the glass of water, just as in the Croatian custom **(8)**. He takes it and breaks the glass so no one else can drink from it, and they declare their love **(9)**.

> **MUSIC (1)** Arabella: *Aber der Richtige – But the right one*; **(2)** Mandryka: *Der Onkel ist dahin – My uncle is no more*; **(3)** Arabella: *Mein Elemer! – My Elemer!*; **(4)** Arabella/Mandryka duet: *Und du wirst mein Gebieter sein – And you will be my lord*; **(5)** Fiakermilli: *Die Wiener Herrn verstehn sich auf die Astronomie – The gentlemen of Vienna are well versed in astronomy*; **(6)** Zdenka/Arabella duet: *Mama! Papa!/Was ist geschehen? … Ich bin bei dir – Mother! Father!/What's happened? … I'll stand by you*; **(7)** Mandryka: *Sie gibt mir keinen Blick – She doesn't look at me*; **(8)** Arabella: *Das war sehr gut, Mandryka, dass Sie noch nicht fortgegangen sind – It is good, Mandryka, that you haven't gone yet*; **(9)** Arabella/Mandryka duet: *Und so sind wir Verlobte – And so we are betrothed.*

CAPRICCIO, 1940–1

For his last opera, which is described as "a conversation piece", Strauss chose a subject that fascinated him: the relationship between words and music in opera. The subject had been suggested to him by Zweig, who together with Gregor devised a scenario. Unhappy with Gregor's text, Strauss wrote one himself with the help of the conductor Clemens Krauss. It had its première in Munich in 1942 during the air raids, which did not prevent the theatre being full every night. It was written in one act, but is often divided into two. When it was suggested to Strauss that he should write another opera, his reply was: "One can only leave one testament".

SYNOPSIS In her château in Paris in about 1775, the young widowed Countess Madeleine (sop), with her brother the Count (bar), listens to a string sextet **(1)** written for her birthday by the composer Flamand (ten). Another guest, the poet Olivier (bar), has written a celebration play and the Count is going to act in it together with the actress Clairon (mez) with whom he is infatuated. It will be produced by the theatrical director La Roche (bass). When Clairon arrives, she and the Count declaim from his manuscript a sonnet Olivier has written **(2)**. To the poet's annoyance, Flamand sets it to music and sings it. The two men now quarrel about whose work it is, and the Countess tells them it is now hers, their present to her. Flamand tells her he loves her and asks for her answer – does she love him **(3)**? She promises to tell him next morning in the library. Hot chocolate is served. La Roche introduces a ballerina and then an Italian tenor and soprano who sing for the Countess **(4)**. They all discuss the relative merits of words and music, leading to first a laughing octet and then a quarrelling octet. La Roche silences them all, describing his work as a director **(5)**. The Countess suggests Flamand and Olivier should write an opera for La Roche to direct for her birthday entertainment. The Count thinks the subject should be the events of their day. They all agree and leave for Paris. The servants tidy up, discussing the events so far, then prepare the Countess's supper. The Countess enters. She is alone and stands in the moonlight. Her Major Domo (bass) tells her Olivier will be in the library tomorrow morning to find out how the opera should end. She wonders – how should it end? Words or music? Olivier or Flamand **(6)**? Is there an ending that is not trivial (*"Gibt es einen, der nicht trivial ist"*)? She goes in to supper, humming the music of the sonnet…

> **MUSIC (1)** String sextet, often played in chamber concerts; **(2)** Count/Clairon: *Kein Andres, das mir so Herzen loht – Naught else there is that flames so in my heart*; **(3)** Flamand: *Sie sagen, dass ich Euch liebe! – They say that I love you!*; **(4)** Italian Tenor/Soprano: *Addio, mia vita, addio – Farewell, my life, farewell*; **(5)** La Roche: *Hola! Ihr Streiter in Apoll! – Hola! You champions of the Muses!*; **(6)** Countess: *Morgen mittag un elf! – Tomorrow morning at eleven!*

RIGHT Felicity Lott, an elegant and moving
Countess Madeleine in Strauss's *Capriccio*,
Glyndebourne, 1987

Other operas of note

There are two other Strauss operas that
must be discussed at some length. The
difficulties in staging and casting make
them relative rarities, but they do receive
productions somewhere in the opera world
most years. The first of these has another
Hofmannsthal libretto. It is *Die Frau ohne
Schatten* (*The Woman without a Shadow*),
composed 1914–17 and premièred in Vienna
in 1919. The "shadow" of the title is a fertility
symbol – a woman without a shadow is
infertile. The scenes veer between the spirit
world and the human world, with a third
plane for the Emperor and Empress of the
South Eastern Isles. It is full of symbolism and
has been described as incomprehensible,
but Strauss thought it was Hofmannsthal's
masterpiece. The main characters are the
Emperor (ten) and Empress (sop), Barak
the Dyer (bar) and his Wife (sop), and the
strange character of the Nurse (mez), who
guides the Empress down to the real world
of Barak's Wife. The story centres round
the Empress, the woman without a shadow.
Unless she can cast a shadow, ie become
pregnant, her husband will be turned to
stone. The Nurse takes the Empress to visit
Barak's Wife. She has no children but she
is fertile and the Nurse offers to buy her
shadow for the Empress. The Empress, in the
end, cannot achieve her own happiness, even
to save her husband, by depriving Barak's wife
of her shadow. She would rather die with her
husband. As soon as she makes this decision
she is given her own shadow and the
Emperor returns to life – she has learned
about humanity. When seen with five top-
class singers and a suitable production, it is
tempting to call it not just Hofmannsthal's
but Strauss's masterpiece.

The second opera is *Intermezzo*, which
took from 1919 to 1923 to compose and
Strauss also wrote the libretto. The story is
based on an incident in the life of the Strauss
family: whilst Strauss was away conducting,
Pauline opened a letter addressed to him
from a young lady asking for tickets for a
performance – it was really an innocent
letter, and was anyway intended for another
conductor with a similar name. But Pauline
jumped to all the wrong conclusions and filed
for divorce. This shook Strauss, who had to
rush home to sort it all out and they had a
grand reunion. He made the incident into the
opera. He and his wife became Robert and
Christine Storch and on the opening night the
two singers of these roles were made up to
look like Strauss and Pauline. *Intermezzo* is
called "a bourgeois comedy with symphonic
interludes" but it could, like *Capriccio*, be called
a conversation piece. In form it owes much
to the cinema and broke new ground with
tobogganing and telephone calls, probably the
first time a telephone had been used on stage.
There are many changes of scene, which
makes it expensive to stage, but it is a
delightful piece.

His other operas are all stage-worthy and
contain lovely *echt*-Strauss music, especially
Daphne, a one-act "bucolic tragedy". The
comedy *Die schweigsame Frau* (*The Silent
Woman*), based on Ben Jonson, has a story not
dissimilar to Donizetti's *Don Pasquale* (see p.73).

Debussy

(Achille-) Claude Debussy
(1862–1918)

RIGHT Angelika Kirchschlager and Simon Keenlyside in the title-roles of *Pelléas et Mélisande*, Salzburg Easter Festival, 2006

WHERE TO START
Pelléas et Mélisande

Debussy is rare among composers in that his music seems unrelated to anyone else's. He is a "one-off" composer, with an unmistakable aural sound, sometimes described as the aural equivalent of the Impressionist painters, a description he disliked.

He was born outside Paris, one of four children of non-musical parents who owned a shop selling crockery. His father fought in the Franco-Prussian War, being imprisoned for a year for his role in support of the Commune. During this time the family was helped by his father's sister, with whom Achille-Claude and his sister went to stay. From his aunt he had his earliest piano lessons, but soon began lessons with Madame Mauté, who was the mother-in-law of the poet Paul Verlaine (1844–96), some of whose poetry Debussy later set to music. When he was 10, Debussy entered the Paris Conservatoire. Even as a young student he was more interested in composition than piano-playing. In 1880 and 1881 he visited Russia as pianist to Tchaikovsky's patron,

Nadezhda von Meck. From 1884 he spent two years in Rome, meeting Liszt and Verdi and hearing his first Wagner (*Lohengrin*). This impressed him so much that he went to the Bayreuth Festivals of 1888 and 1889, but whilst he acknowledged Wagner's greatness, he did not wish to follow him, recognizing that Wagner's individualistic style could prove a dead end for other composers. At the Paris Universal Exhibition of 1889 he heard Javanese gamelan, which remained an influence on him. His friendships with painters, writers, and poets of the period all had an effect on his music, as did his interest in Musorgsky's *Boris Godunov* (see p.115). Despite all these influences he remained, all his life, a *musicien français*, as he liked to describe himself.

After Rome Debussy returned to Paris at a time when France was in a depression. Governments were elected and fell in rapid succession and there was rumour of impending war with Germany. By 1889 the economy was improving, and precipitated the *belle époque*, the public turning to entertainment, as so often happens in a country riven by war or depression. It was the time of the opening of the Eiffel Tower, the Moulin Rouge, and the Folies Bergères. About this time he became friendly with a wealthy fellow-composer, Ernest Chausson (1855–99), who helped him financially.

Debussy was not a composer of symphonies and concertos, his energies being directed into smaller orchestral pieces, chamber music, outstanding piano works, and beautiful songs. For the stage he wrote ballets and incidental music for plays (including *King Lear*). He completed only one opera. In May 1893 he saw a performance of *Pelléas et Mélisande* by Maurice Maeterlinck (1862–1949) and started to sketch an opera, which was not finished and staged until 1902. In 1901 he became a music critic of an important periodical, and a collection of his writing was published in Paris in 1921 and translated into English in 1962 (*Monsieur Croche antidilettante*).

Debussy had a series of stormy love affairs, some of which inspired his music. In 1899 he married a mannequin, Rosalie (Lilly) Texier. He left her after five years for a singer and banker's wife, Emma Bardac. She gave birth to his child in 1905 and they married in 1908. In 1910 Debussy developed cancer and was a semi-invalid until his death in 1918.

PELLÉAS ET MÉLISANDE, 1893–5, 1901–2

Debussy started to set Maeterlinck's play soon after seeing it. He devised the libretto himself. He found Maeterlinck's mixture of realism and symbolism a challenge, and told a friend that he would use "silence" as a means of expression. The opera was accepted in 1898 by the

ABOVE LEFT **Claude Debussy (1862–1918)**

ABOVE **Scottish-born American soprano Mary Garden**, chosen by Debussy to create Mélisande in the 1902 world première of *Pelléas et Mélisande* in Paris

Opéra-Comique, but was not performed until 1902 and in the intervening years Debussy made many revisions. During rehearsals he composed interludes to cover scene changes and these do show the influence of Wagner. Maeterlinck wanted his mistress to sing Mélisande, but Debussy was determined to have Mary Garden. As a result of this argument, Maeterlinck wrote to the papers saying he did not approve of his play being turned into an opera and hoped it would fail.

The opera takes place in a series of tableaux and the music is unusual – there are no arias or set-piece ensembles, the words being declaimed, a note for each syllable, halfway between singing and recitative. This gives the whole work an ethereal quality, very atmospheric, but there is full-blooded passion as well. The audience at the dress rehearsal was so puzzled by it that there was nearly a riot. Despite these unpromising beginnings and the vocal difficulties inherent in casting the leading roles, especially that of Pelléas, the first performance was a success and the work soon entered the repertoire.

SYNOPSIS The action takes place at an unspecified time in the Kingdom of Allemonde. The king, Arkel (bass), has a daughter Geneviève (mez). She has two sons by different marriages, Golaud (bar) and Pelléas (ten/high bar). Golaud has a young son Yniold (sop *travesti* role) from an earlier marriage. Out hunting, Golaud finds the fragile Mélisande (sop) lost in the forest (1). He marries her and takes her home to his castle where she meets the family. She and Pelléas enjoy each other's company. Whilst out together near a fountain, Mélisande plays with her wedding ring and it falls into the water and is lost (2). She arrives back at the castle to find that at the exact time she dropped the ring, Golaud was thrown from his horse and was injured. He notices the missing ring and she explains its loss. Pelléas watches as Mélisande combs her long hair by the window (3), catching her hair and winding it round himself. Golaud teases them about their childish games, but he is suspicious that she is being unfaithful to him. He lifts up Yniold so that he can see through the window of Mélisande's room and spy on her when she is talking to Pelléas, but the child can find nothing untoward to report to his father (4). Pelléas is leaving the castle to travel. He bids farewell to the now pregnant Mélisande and they admit their love for each other (5). The suspicious Golaud, who has been watching them, rushes in and kills Pelléas with his sword.

Mélisande dies whilst giving birth to a daughter. Despite all Golaud's entreaties and Mélisande's denials (6), he is left after she dies still unsure of the truth about her relationship with his half-brother.

MUSIC (There are no arias or ensembles as such. These are entry points to look out for as an aid to following the action): (1) Golaud/Mélisande: *D'où êtes vous? Où êtes-vous née?/Oh, oh! Loin d'ici, loin, loin – Where are you from? Where were you born?/Oh, oh! Far from here, a long way*; (2) Mélisande/Pelléas: *Il est tombé dans l'eau!/Où est-il? – It has fallen in the water/Where is it?*; (3) Mélisande: *Mes longs cheveux descendent – My long hair falls*; (4) Golaud/Yniold: *Que font-ils?/Ils ne font rien, petit père – What are they doing?/Nothing, Daddy*; (5) Pelléas/Mélisande: *Tu ne sais pas pourquoi il faut que je m'éloigne … je t'aime/Je t'aime aussi – You don't know why I must leave …I love you/I love you too*; (6) Golaud/Mélisande: *As-tu … avez-vous été coupables? Dis, dis, oui, oui, oui/Non, non, nous n'avons pas été coupables – Were you … were you both guilty? Say, tell me, yes, yes, yes/No, no, we weren't guilty.*

Janáček

Leoš Janáček
(1854-1928)

LEFT Leoš Janáček (1854–1928)

WHERE TO START
Jenůfa
The Cunning Little Vixen

WHERE TO GO NEXT
Katya Kabanová
The Makropulos Affair

Is Janáček a late-Romantic or a 20th-century composer? Many of his greatest works were composed in the last 10 years of his life, and *sound* like 20th-century music. But much of his output was composed before 1900 and he died in 1928. So he can be included in the period under discussion even though, like Richard Strauss, he overlaps both periods. As has been remarked earlier, it is often neither easy nor desirable to be too strict in categorizing composers.

Leo Eugen Janáček was born in a Moravian village now called Hukvaldy, near the Polish border but at that time nearer to Prussia. He was the tenth of 14 children, five of whom died in infancy. Like his father and grandfather, he was expected to become a teacher and when he was 11 he was sent to the Augustinian monastery in Brno, which was primarily a German-speaking town. The monastery had its own music school and he became a chorister. He later acted as choirmaster and his first compositions were for unaccompanied choirs. He qualified in 1872 to teach in Czech-speaking schools – pride in his national heritage influenced the change in his name from Leo to the Czech Leoš – and then studied at Prague Organ School for two years and later at the music conservatories in Leipzig and Vienna. Poverty in his student days precluded his taking full advantage of the music on offer in these cities and, although he managed to attend several concerts, he was unable to afford the opera.

He became engaged in 1880 to his 15-year-old piano pupil, Zdenka Schulzová, who came from a very Germanic background. They married in 1881, just before her 16th

birthday. Later that year he founded an Organ School in Brno, where he taught and of which he was director. The Provisional Czech Theatre opened in Brno in 1884 and for four years Janáček edited a journal to review its activities. His marriage was tense and unhappy. They had a daughter in 1882, then separated for two years. A son was born in 1888 but died from scarlet fever when he was two years old.

In 1887 he began to compose his first operaa, *Šárka*, based on Czech mythology, the text having originally been intended for Dvořák. Disappointed at the lack of interest in his opera (it was not performed until 1925), he spent the next few years editing Moravian folk-songs and composing dances, but in 1891 he wrote a one-act opera, *Počátek románu* (*The Beginning of a Romance*), which consisted mainly of folk-dances with voices added. But, significantly, the text was adapted from a short story by Gabriela Preissová, who also wrote a play called *Její pastorkyňa* (*Her Stepdaughter*) and he next set to work to turn that into an opera, now known as *Jenůfa*. Janáček was 40 when he began work on it, and it took him nine years to complete. During composition his only surviving child, 21-year-old Olga, became ill and died. From about 1897 he became interested in "speech-melody", and this, together with folk-song, influenced his vocal compositions from then onward. The première of *Jenůfa* took place in Brno in 1904, Prague having turned it down. It was his first real success, and he was almost 50.

Janáček resigned from his teaching posts in 1904 to concentrate on composing and running his Organ School. His next opera,

Osud (*Fate*), reflected contemporary life but was not produced in his lifetime and has never achieved regular performances. He had written, with Fedora Bartošová, the libretto for *Osud*, and he wrote the libretto for his next opera, begun in 1908, the comedy *Mr Brouček's Excursion to the Moon*, which took him almost 10 years to compose. He wrote a sequel called *Mr Brouček's Excursion to the 15th Century*, dedicating it to the first president of Czechoslovakia, T G Masaryk. At the same time he was writing orchestral and chamber music and major choral works.

By the time Janáček was 60 he was acknowledged as a composer in Brno and was making a good living as director of the main teaching institute in Moravia. Outside Moravia he was virtually unknown. Then in 1916, with help and persuasion from his friends, Prague National Theatre at last agreed to produce *Jenůfa*. It was a triumph and was soon translated into German and performed in Cologne and Vienna. The spur to his creativity brought about by this success was astonishing. In the last decade of his life he wrote another five operas as well as major works in other genres. Nevertheless, it was not until after the Second World War that his operas were regularly seen abroad. None of his operas were produced in Britain until well after the war and they did not establish a foothold until the 1960s.

Apart from the success of the Prague *Jenůfa*, Janáček's other inspiration was his friendship with Kamila Stösslová. She was the wife of an antique dealer in Bohemia, and was 38 years younger than the composer. After he met her on holiday in 1917, he wrote to her almost daily (there are 700 letters) and kept a diary about his feelings for her. In 1925 he considered deserting his wife for Kamila, but did not do so, probably because Kamila did not reciprocate his passionate feelings. In the six years from 1919 to 1925 he wrote three of his best operas – *Katya Kabanová*, *The Cunning Little Vixen*, and *The Makropulos Affair* –

as well as his First String Quartet, instrumental and orchestral works. These three operas were all premièred in Brno, followed by Prague, which could no longer ignore him. By now his fame was spreading and *Jenůfa* was being performed in translation all over Germany and *Katya Kabanová* was performed in Cologne and Berlin. *Jenůfa* was staged in New York in 1924, but was not a success.

In 1928 Janáček went back to his home in the village of his birth, taking with him work to revise and orchestrate away from the hustle of his now public life in Brno. For the first time he was joined there by Kamila, her husband, and their 11-year-old son. The child got lost and Janáček went searching for him. He caught a cold and quickly developed pneumonia. He was rushed to hospital, where he died. His funeral in Brno was a large public occasion and the last scene of *The Cunning Little Vixen* was played. In 1930 Janáček's last opera, *From the House of the Dead*, was performed. Zdenka lived for 10 years after Leoš and when she

died in 1938 her estate was left to Masaryk University to form the basis of the Janáček Archive. Kamila died in 1935.

Leoš Janáček is now acknowledged as Czechoslovakia's greatest opera composer and one of the most important composers of the late 19th and early 20th centuries. Four of his operas are in the repertory of most big companies, and the others receive infrequent but regular performances. They are dramatic and absorbing and those described below all have outstanding roles for dramatic sopranos.

JENŮFA
(*Její pastorkyňa = Her Stepdaughter*), 1894–1903

Janáček first became aware of the playwright Gabriela Preissová's *Její pastorkyňa* (*Her Stepdaughter*) in 1891, the year after its first performance in Prague. He adapted the libretto himself and began composition in about 1894 but did not finish it until 1903. He offered the première to the National Theatre

in Prague, but it was turned down by the conductor, who had taken offence at Janáček's review in 1887 of one of his own operas. So Brno gave the first performance of *Jenůfa* in 1904 and it was another 12 years before the hugely successful Prague première. It was given in Vienna in a German translation two years later and by the time of Janáček's death in 1928 it was considered a repertoire piece in Czechoslovakia and Germany. It took many years to reach the rest of Europe and the USA, but it is probably now his most popular opera.

SYNOPSIS After Jenůfa's mother died, her father, son of Grandmother Burya (cont), married again. He is now dead and Jenůfa (sop) lives with his widow, Petrona Burya, the Kostelnička (sacristan of the village church) (sop). The girl is loved by her cousins, Števa Burya (ten) and his younger half-brother Laca Klemeň (ten). Jenůfa wants to marry the wayward Števa. The Kostelnička's marriage had not been happy, as her husband squandered their money on drink. She is anxious that Jenůfa does not meet a similar fate, and forbids their wedding – they must wait until Števa stops drinking (1). In a fit of jealousy over her love for Števa, Laca slashes Jenůfa's face with his knife.

When the Kostelnička learned that Jenůfa was pregnant by Števa, she kept her hidden in their cottage where, months later she has produced a son. The Kostelnička hopes Števa will marry her, but he no longer desires her now her beauty has gone and refuses (2). Her hopes now rest with Laca, who is distressed when he hears about the baby. The Kostelnička tells him, untruthfully, that the baby died, and she then has to make this statement come true. She gives Jenůfa a sleeping-draught, takes the baby and drowns him in the icy river. Jenůfa awakens and presumes her mother has taken the baby to show to the mill workers (3). She prays to the Virgin (4). The Kostelnička returns and tells Jenůfa that, whilst she was sleeping, her baby became ill and died.

ABOVE **Gabriela Beňačková as Jenůfa, Leonie Rysanek as the Kostelnička, and Wieslaw Ochman as Laca**, San Francisco Opera, 1986

RIGHT Jonathan Miller rehearsing *The Cunning Little Vixen*, Glyndebourne, 1975

Preparations are made for the wedding of Jenůfa and Laca. The Kostelnička, full of guilt and remorse, has become withdrawn. The Mayor and Mayoress arrive for the wedding with their daughter Karolka (mez), who is engaged to Števa. As Grandmother Burya blesses the kneeling couple, a farmhand rushes in and announces that a baby's body has been found under the melting ice. Suspicion falls on Jenůfa until the Kostelnička confesses that she committed the crime **(5)** and the townfolk condemn her. Jenůfa, who realizes that her stepmother acted in what she saw as Jenůfa's

ABOVE LEFT **Elena Prokina, a vulnerable and touching Katya Kabanová, ROH, London, 1994**

best interest, forgives her **(6)**. The Kostelnička is led away for trial. Jenůfa imagines that Laca will now no longer want her, but he assures her that he still feels the same and they declare their love for each other **(7)**.

MUSIC (1) Kostelnička: *A tak bychom šli celým životem – We could spend our whole lives like that*; **(2)** Števa: *Proto, že se jí bojím – Because I am scared of her*; **(3)** Jenůfa: *Mamličko, mám těžkou hlavu – Mother, my head is so heavy*; **(4)** Jenůfa: *Zdrávas královno – Hail Mary* (Jenůfa's Prayer); **(5)** Kostelnička: *To můj skutek – That was my deed*; **(6)** Jenůfa: *Vstaňte, pěstounko moja! – Stand up, my step-mother*; **(7)** Jenůfa/Laca duet: *Odešli. Jdi také!/Ty odejdeš do světa … – They have left. You should go too!/Will you go out into the world …*

KATYA KABANOVÁ
(*Kát'a Kabanová*), 1919–21

This is the first opera of Janáček's great creative period in the last 10 years of his life. By the time of the successful Prague première of *Jenůfa* in 1916 he was 62. In the next 10 years he wrote four more successful operas as well as many works in other genres. Janáček again wrote his own libretto, basing it on the play *The Thunderstorm* by the Russian Alexander Ostrovsky (1823–86). *Katya Kabanová* was dedicated to Kamila Stösslová, the young woman who was the object of his unrequited love and who provided the inspiration for his late works. Janáček began work on the opera in 1919 and finished it, quickly for him, in 1920, but he continued to make revisions to it up to the première in Brno in 1921. The Prague première followed, and then there were productions in Cologne and Berlin. But again the work was slow to travel and did not reach England until 1951 (it was Janáček's first opera to be heard in Britain) and the USA in 1957. It is now in the repertoire of all self-respecting opera companies.

SYNOPSIS In mid-19th century Russia, Katya (sop) is married to Tichon (ten), son of Marfa Kabanová, known as Kabanicha (sop), who also has a foster-daughter Varvara (mez). Kabanicha is sour-natured and resents her son's marriage and his wife, accusing the couple of showing her no respect **(1)**. Katya is not very happy – Tichon is weak and under his mother's thumb. Katya tells Varvara of her unhappiness and how, as a child, she liked to be as free as a bird, but now has no freedom **(2)**. Kabanicha's friend Dikoj (bass) has a nephew Boris (ten) who has fallen in love with Katya. Katya admits to Varvara her feelings for Boris. Boris confesses his feelings to his friend Váňa, who is in love with Varvara. Tichon is sent away on business by his mother, who insists that he tells his wife exactly how to behave in his absence **(3)**.

One night, while Kabanicha is entertaining Dikoj, Katya and Varvara slip out into the garden to meet Boris and Váňa. Váňa sings an old song while waiting for the girls **(4)**. Varvara and Váňa send the other couple for a walk and they admit their love for each other **(5)**.

Two weeks later there is a violent storm and Váňa, an engineer, gives Dikoj a lecture on the electric nature of storms. Dikoj insists that storms signify God's punishment. As they shelter from the rain, Varvara tells Boris about her concern for Katya, who is so full of guilt that she is almost unhinged and is dreading Tichon's return **(6)**. When he does come home, she confesses to him, and Kabanicha, that she has been unfaithful with Boris **(7)**. She then runs from the house. She meets Boris and learns that his uncle is sending him to Siberia. They console each other and then say their farewells **(8)**. She hears Tichon searching for her as she drowns herself in the Volga, unable to face the future with her tyrannical mother-in-law. Her body is carried onto the river bank by Dikoj and placed in front of the Kabanicha. As Tichon flings himself down, sobbing, the Kabanicha hypocritically thanks all the villagers for their concern **(9)**.

THE CUNNING LITTLE VIXEN

(*Příhody Lišky Bystroušky = The Adventures of the Vixen Bystrouška [Bystrouška = sharp-ears]*), 1922–3

This delightful, though sad, nature-opera was based on a series of illustrated stories, published in the Brno newspaper in 1920, about a vixen who is caught by a gamekeeper but escapes back to the woods to meet her mate and raise a litter. In 1921 the story and illustrations were published as a book which remains popular to this day. Janáček again wrote his own libretto, based on the book by Rudolf Těsnohlídek. The opera had its Brno première in 1924, just after the composer's 70th birthday. It received a now famous production by Walter Felsenstein in Berlin in 1956, which set the opera on the road to worldwide success.

SYNOPSIS In summer in a forest the Gamekeeper (or Forester) (bar) lies down to have a rest (1). While he sleeps, surrounded by various birds and insects, a Frog (child sop), trying to catch a Mosquito (ten), lands on his nose. The Vixen Bystrouška (sop), attracted by the Frog, comes near and the Gamekeeper catches her and takes her home and ties her up in his farmyard. She kills the Cock (sop) and all the Hens (all sop), then bites through her leash and escapes into the forest, where she takes over the home of the Badger (bass).

In an inn, the Gamekeeper, a Schoolmaster (ten), and a Priest (bass) drink and play cards together. The Gamekeeper teases the Schoolmaster about his lack of success in love (2) and the Schoolmaster teases him about the Vixen's escape. They split up and all wander home through the forest. The Gamekeeper shoots at the Vixen, but misses her. The Vixen meets the Fox (mez) and they fall in love (3). They are married and all the animals join in their celebrations (4).

149

In the autumn, the poultry-dealer Harašta (bass) **(5)** is accused by the Gamekeeper of poaching. He tells the Gamekeeper he is going to marry the gypsy Terynka, who the Schoolmaster also fancies. The Gamekeeper sets a trap for the Vixen, but she and the Fox and their litter laughingly avoid it **(6)**. Harašta sees the Vixen and chases after her, but falls over and she and her family kill all his chickens. Harašta is so angry that he shoots and kills the Vixen. The Gamekeeper realizes that the Schoolmaster is upset about Terynka's marriage to Harašta. On his way home through the forest, the Gamekeeper has his usual nap. He dreams of all the forest creatures, including a little vixen, who looks just like her mother did. When he tries to catch her, he catches only a frog – the grandson of the one which landed on his nose in the summer **(7)**. No matter what the humans do, Nature renews itself each season.

> **MUSIC (1)** Gamekeeper: *Dostaneme bouřku spolehnu si na chviličičku – Going to be a storm soon; I'll sit here and rest;* **(2)** Gamekeeper: *Bývalo, bývalo … – Once long since, long ago … ;* **(3)** Vixen/Fox: *Jsemli opravdu tak krásná/ Hezounká je, hezounká – Am I really so beautiful?/She is lovely, so lovely;* **(4)** All animals: Wordless chorus; **(5)** Harašta: *Déž sem vandroval – When I went a- wandering;* **(6)** Little Foxes: *Beěží liška k Táboru – Vixen runs to Tabor town;* **(7)** Gamekeeper: *Hoj! Ale neni tu Bystroušky! – Hey! But I can't see the Vixen there.*

THE MAKROPULOS AFFAIR
(Věc Makropulos), 1923–5

Although he had only just started composing *The Cunning Little Vixen*, when Janáček saw Karel Čapek's new play *The Makropulos Affair* in 1922, he immediately thought of it in terms of an opera libretto which he started writing before he finished the score for *Vixen*. The première was in Brno in 1926 and in Prague two years later. It was to be the last time the composer attended one of his premières – he died five months later. Čapek's play treated the subject of somebody living for 300 years as a comedy; Janáček saw it much more seriously, especially the agonies the heroine suffered in her very long extended life.

SYNOPSIS Before the opera begins: Elina Makropulos, given an elixir of life invented by her father, has lived for over 300 years. She has become a great opera singer, moving round the world and changing her name so no-one will become suspicious, but she has always used the same initials, E M . It is now 1922 and she is in Prague and known as Emilia Marty. A 100-year-old lawsuit is nearing its end in Prague: Albert Gregor is claiming that he is a descendant of Ferdinand Gregor who should have inherited the estate of Baron Prus who died in 1827. The Prus family deny any legacy and are counter-claiming.

The opera opens in the office of Dr Kolenatý (bass-bar), the lawyer acting for Albert Gregor (ten). The lawyer's clerk Vítek (ten) is consulted by Gregor who wants to know how things now stand. Vítek's daughter Kristina (sop/mez) returns from the opera, where she has watched Emilia Marty rehearsing. She is besotted by the diva and wants to concentrate on nothing but music. She is in love with Janek (ten), the son of Jaroslav Prus (bar), the counter-contender of the will. She leaves the office with her father, as Dr Kolenatý enters with Emilia Marty **(1)**. Marty is surprisingly knowledgeable about the lawsuit he is handling. For instance, she knows that Ferdinand Gregor was Baron Prus's illegitimate son, and that somewhere in the Prus house there is a will which would settle the case in favour of Gregor. Kolenatý must go and find it. She then tells Gregor about his ancestor Ferdinand's mother, who was the singer Ellian MacGregor. Kolenatý returns with Prus and the will. But there is still some evidence missing, and Marty promises she will provide it.

At the theatre where Marty is performing, Kristina meets Janek and tells him they must forgo their relationship for the sake of her career **(2)**. In her dressing-room, Marty receives the old and decrepit Hauk-Šendorf (ten), who recognizes her as the gypsy-girl he once loved, Eugenia Montez, who apparently died many years ago **(3)**. Jaroslav Prus also comes to see Marty, and tells her that Ferdinand Gregor's mother was Elina Makropulos, not Ellian MacGregor as she had stated, so he has no claim on the Prus estate. He also tells her that with the will was found a sealed envelope – if she will sleep with him, he will give her the envelope.

Marty and Prus spend the night in a hotel. In the morning, despite complaining that she was like a corpse, Prus hands over the envelope. Just then he learns that his son Janek has killed himself **(4)**. Marty is unmoved and Prus rushes out, passing Gregor, Kolenatý, Kristina, and others coming in to the room to interrogate her, believing her guilty of fraud. While Marty goes to get dressed, the others search through her luggage and find various legal papers in all her other names. She admits that she is Elina Makropulos, 337 years old. In the envelope Prus gave her is the formula of the life elixir. Everyone is incredulous, but as she begins to age and starts reciting the Lord's Prayer in Greek, her mother tongue, they believe her. She is too tired to want to take anymore or live any longer – death will be a blessing **(5)**. She gives the formula to Kristina, who burns it as Elina Makropulos dies.

> **MUSIC** (1) Kolenatý/Marty: *Tady prosim, jenom račte/Tedy vy jste advokát – This way, do come in/So you are the lawyer;* (2) Kristina: *Janku! Mezi námi konec je – Janek! It's all over between us;* (3) Hauk-Šendorf: *Ona byla cigánka – She was a gypsy;* (4) Prus: *Oh, proto tedy, proto – Oh, so that's why he did it, that's why;* (5) Marty: *Ach, nemá se tak dlouho žit! – Oh, life should not last so long.*

Other operas of note

Two more of Janáček's works should be discussed. The only one of his operas to receive its first performance outside Brno was *The Excursions of Mr Brouček (Výlety pán Broučka)*, which had its première in Prague in 1920. The two acts were originally written as two separate works, the one-act (four scenes) *Mr Brouček's Excursion to the Moon* (1908–17) and *Mr Brouček's Excursion to the 15th Century* (1917), added after he decided he didn't like the final scene of the first opera. Mr Brouček is a heavy-drinking Prague landlord who dreams of a life free of lodgers and money worries. He falls into a drunken sleep and is transported

to the moon. Everyone he meets there is somebody he knew on earth and he soon realizes that life there is not all honey and nectar and decides to return to earth. When he arrives there, Prague has returned to the 15th century at the time of the Hussite Wars. Again, all the people resemble those he knew at home. For refusing to fight he is sentenced to be burned in a barrel. He wakes up to find himself in a barrel, the one into which he fell when he collapsed, drunk! This is Janáček's only comedy and it must be admitted that there are boring periods in it and that the second act falls away musically. But it can be quite charming and entertaining, though difficult to stage.

Janáček's last opera, *From the House of the Dead (Z mrtvého domu)*, composed 1927–8, did not receive its first performance, in Brno, until 1930, two years after the composer's death. The music of the overture grew out of a proposed but never written violin concerto. Janáček's wrote his own libretto, based on Dostoevsky's novel of 1862 describing his harrowing experiences in a Siberian prison. There is very little plot, the opera consisting of a chorus of prisoners, some of whom recount the story of how they come to be there. The cast is all-male (apart from one very small role), the action is episodic, there are no recognizable arias, the music is sparingly scored, and there is no apotheosis or climax. For these reasons it was assumed the work was incomplete at the time of his death, and before the première some of Janáček's pupils re-orchestrated it and made the ending more optimistic. It took years before the composer's original intentions were recognized and restored. It is hard to imagine such a depressing subject providing a satisfactory evening in the opera house. But by the end one is uplifted by the human spirit's ability to rise above and survive such deprivation and degradation and even to find humour in it. It is Janáček's most unusual work and musically way ahead of its time. It deserves to be produced more often.

The Rest of the Late Romantics

Many composers, some better known for their works in other genres, wrote at least one opera during the late 19th and early 20th centuries. Many have faded into oblivion, but some that survive as almost standard repertory works are discussed here.

ITALY AMILCARE PONCHIELLI (1834–86) was a teacher of Mascagni and Puccini. One of his operas dating from 1876 is still performed, *La Gioconda* (*The Joyful Girl* or *The Ballad Singer*), another opera known by its untranslated title. Based loosely on Victor Hugo, it is a story of greed, lust, and revenge, and is almost a *verismo* work. It is a powerful story, but its best-known music is a ballet divertissement, "The Dance of the Hours".

FRANCESCO CILEA (1866–1950) is remembered for little other than his opera *Adriana Lecouvreur* (1901–2). Some of the characters in the opera did exist, including Adriana (1692–1730) who in life, as in the opera, was an actress in Paris. The dramatic soprano title-role is probably why it remains a regular, if infrequent, repertory piece.

UMBERTO GIORDANO (1867–1948) became

involved in the *verismo* movement after the success of Mascagni's *Cavalleria rusticana* (see p.126). His talent, like many *verismo* composers, was limited. *Andrea Chénier* (1896), based on the life of a poet, André Chénier, during the French Revolution, was his first success. There is some fine music, including Revolutionary songs and the French National Anthem, and the chorus plays a big part. The opera has remained in the repertory since its first performance. Giordano's next opera, *Fedora*, set in Russia, is very dramatic, has good arias, and is occasionally revived.

ERMANNO WOLF-FERRARI (1876–1948) had success with the première in 1906 of *I quatro rusteghi* (*The Four Curmudgeons*, usually translated as *School for Fathers*), then considered the best comedy after Verdi's *Falstaff*. His most popular opera, composed about 1909, is *Il segreto di Susanna* (*Susanna's Secret*), its small cast of two singers making it cheap to produce. Susanna's secret is that she smokes, the smell of tobacco making her husband suspect she has a lover. It is light, the music is appealing, and the story easy to understand. After that his *verismo* opera *I gioielli della Madonna* (*The Jewels of the Madonna*) came as something of a shock with its tale of jealousy and revenge. It was more successful in English-speaking countries than in Italy.

GERMANY The Austrian-born **HUGO WOLF (1860–1903)** is remembered as a *Lieder* composer. His opera *Der Corregidor* of 1894 contains some songs he wrote earlier. His knowledge of theatre was scant and the music is Wagner influenced. Its success was limited.

The Italian-born **FERRUCCIO BUSONI (1866–1924)** lived most of his life in Germany, writing and playing piano music, but he composed some operas, writing the librettos himself. He was interested in modern trends, but remained his own man. His most important opera, *Doktor Faust* (1916–24), was incomplete when he died. It is based on the Faust story; the music is tonal and symphonic.

ABOVE LEFT The 1876 world première at La Scala, Milan, of Ponchielli's *La Gioconda*, with Senora Mariani-Mosi in the title-role

HANS PFITZNER (1869–1949) was born in Moscow where his father was working. The family soon returned to Germany. He wrote several operas, of which *Palestrina* (1917) is his most impressive. It is long, has a very large cast, there is no romantic interest, and it is based on the composer Palestrina's theory about the value of pure music in the Roman Catholic church. It is a "big" opera in every way and it is essential that the audience understand the words. Somehow it works, but I don't quite know why!

ALEXANDER ZEMLINSKY (1871–1942) was most influenced by Gustav Mahler (1860–1911) who staged Zemlinsky's first opera, *Es war einmal* (*Once upon a Time*), in Vienna. In modern times his most performed operas have been two one-act works, *Eine florentinische Tragödie* (*A Florentine Tragedy*) of 1915–16 and *Der Zwerg* (*The Dwarf*) of 1920–1, both based on stories by Oscar Wilde. The latter was his most successful opera in his lifetime.

FRANCE Born in England, **FREDERICK DELIUS (1862–1934)** can be considered an honorary Frenchman, having lived in France most of his adult life. He wrote six operas, three of which were staged in his lifetime. Some of his best music is heard in *A Village Romeo and Juliet* (1899–1901) and the story of the young lovers who prefer to die together than be separated was a favourite theme of his. It is in six scenes and the most familiar music from it is an entr'acte known as "Walk

LEFT Pencil sketch (1932) of Frederick Delius by the celebrated cartoonist Edmund Xavier Kapp

to the Paradise Garden" (a run-down riverside inn), often played as a concert piece.

A real Frenchman, **GUSTAVE CHARPENTIER** (1860–1956), began his only successful opera, *Louise*, in 1889 and its première was in 1900 in Paris. The action mimics poverty-stricken Bohemian life in Montmartre, the artistic Paris area where the composer had lived as a student. It portrays the attraction this life had for the primly brought up heroine, whose parents are horrified at her choice of partner and her clearly stated desire for sexual satisfaction, a daring subject to portray on the stage at the time. *Louise* held its place in the French repertoire for many years and will no doubt return, though at the present time it seems to be out of favour. The lovely aria "Depuis le jour" ("Since the day", often sung in English as "O day of joy") is the best-known music from it.

PAUL DUKAS (1865–1935) is known almost exclusively for his delightful orchestral work of 1897, *The Sorcerer's Apprentice*. Another major work was the opera based on the Bluebeard legend, *Ariane et Barbe-Bleue*. It was composed in 1899–1906, to a libretto by Maeterlinck. Dukas had heard Debussy play the unfinished score of *Pelléas et Mélisande* to friends on the piano and there are places where it is possible to recognize the influence of, and even short quotations from, Debussy's opera. But the music on the whole is as much Wagnerian as French. It requires several very good female voices and is not as popular as Bartók's on the same subject (see below).

EASTERN EUROPE The reputation of the Czechoslovakian **ANTONÍN DVOŘÁK** (1841–1904) does not depend on his operas. He was a major composer of orchestral and chamber music, including arguably the greatest Cello Concerto ever written. But at various periods of his life he did compose operas, of which only *Rusalka* (1900), his most popular and successful one during his lifetime, survives as a near-repertory piece. It is a fairy-tale based on the *Undine* legend with something of

Hans Christian Andersen's *The Little Mermaid* included, with good characterizations, touching nature scenes, and, as with all Dvořák's music, magical melodies warmly orchestrated. *Rusalka*'s soprano aria, "The Hymn to the Moon", was famous even before the opera was known outside Czechoslovakia.

The Hungarian **BÉLA BARTÓK** (1881–1945) wrote only one opera, *Duke Bluebeard's Castle* of 1911, which sounds like an *echt*-20th century work, and it and its composer will be discussed on p.172.

ENGLAND There were few composers of opera at this time in England. **ARTHUR SULLIVAN** (1842–1900) always remained disappointed that his serious opera, the 1891

Ivanhoe after Sir Walter Scott's novel, was a failure. He nevertheless achieved immortality with the series of operettas he wrote with the librettist W S Gilbert known as the Savoy operas, including *The Mikado*, *The Yeomen of the Guard*, and *Ruddigore*.

EDWARD ELGAR (1857–1934), the most famous British composer of this period, left only sketches of an opera, *The Spanish Lady*. **GUSTAV HOLST** (1874–1934) wrote several operas, of which the one-act *Savitri* (1908) occasionally sees the light of day. **RALPH VAUGHAN WILLIAMS** (1872–1958) will be discussed in the next chapter (see pp.174–5).

And, strange though it may seem, **AMERICA** had still not entered the field.

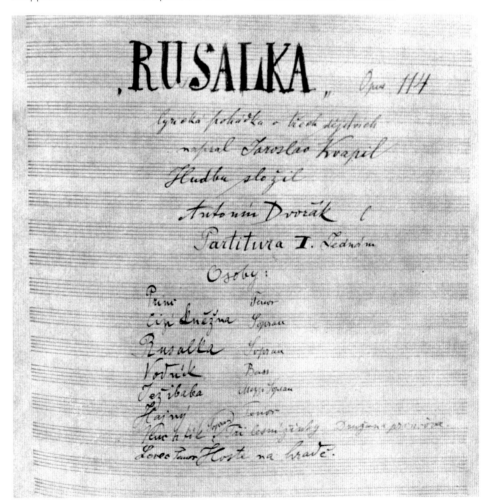

ABOVE **Title-page of the manuscript score of** Dvořák's *Rusalka*

New techniques made it possible to listen to recorded
music in the garden, c.1925

20th Century and Beyond

1900 to the present day

A number of promising composers died during the First and Second World Wars, and the music of those who survived was influenced either by their wartime experiences or by the dictatorships under which they now lived. In the visual arts, Cubism and Surrealism were new and controversial notions of art. A similar movement in music, the Second Viennese School of Arnold Schoenberg (1874–1951) and his pupils, overturned the traditional view of harmony and melody.

FEATURED OPERAS

SCHOENBERG
Moses und Aron 1930–2

BERG
Wozzeck 1914–22
Lulu 1928–35

WEILL
Die Dreigroschenoper 1928

HENZE
Boulevard Solitude 1951
Elegy For Young Lovers 1959–61

STRAVINSKY
The Rake's Progress 1947–51

PROKOFIEV
The Love For Three Oranges 1919

SHOSTAKOVICH
Lady Macbeth of the Mtsensk District 1930–2

BARTÓK
Duke Bluebeard's Castle 1911

RAVEL
L'heure espagnole 1907–9
L'enfant et les sortilèges 1920–5

VAUGHAN WILLIAMS
Riders to the Sea 1925–32

WALTON
Troilus and Cressida 1947–54, 1963, 1972–3
The Bear 1965–7

TIPPETT
The Midsummer Marriage 1946–52

BRITTEN
Peter Grimes 1944–5
The Rape of Lucretia 1945–6, 1947
Albert Herring 1946–7
Billy Budd 1950–1, 1960
Gloriana 1952–3
The Turn of the Screw 1954
A Midsummer Night's Dream 1959–60
Death In Venice 1971–3, 1973, 1974

MUSGRAVE
Mary, Queen of Scots 1976–7

BIRTWISTLE
Punch and Judy 1966–7

MAXWELL DAVIES
The Lighthouse 1979

WEIR
A Night at the Chinese Opera 1987

ADÈS
The Tempest 2004

GERSHWIN
Porgy and Bess 1934–5

BARBER
Vanessa 1956–7, 1964

ADAMS
Nixon in China 1987

20th Century and Beyond

Until the 20th century music was centred on a basic key scheme, the eight notes of the standard octave being related to each other in an accepted way. Now composers were abandoning tonality and writing "atonal music", ie music not based on any one key. Schoenberg – and his pupils Alban Berg (1885–1935) and Anton Webern (1883–1945) – introduced "12-note" music (the 12 notes being the seven white and five black keys of an octave on the standard keyboard). He preferred the term "pantonal" and postulated the theory that each note had an equal value. From this developed "serialism", in which a strict series of notes and intervals (the note-row) governed the development of a composition. For ears used to listening to the Romantics and their immediate successors, this new sound was strange, dissonant, and chaotic.

But, like Surrealism and Cubism, atonality "caught on", although not with everyone. Edward Elgar (1857–1934) and Ralph Vaughan Williams (1872–1958) achieved fame in England by traditional tonal means. And in the USA the first generation of native composers of real standing emerged: George Gershwin (1898–1937) and Samuel Barber (1910–81), with Charles Ives (1874–1954) best described as a maverick. In France Maurice Ravel (1875–1937) and Francis Poulenc (1899–1963) wrote tonal music, as did the Englishman Frederick Delius. Two German composers, Paul Hindemith (1895–1934) and Kurt Weill (1900–50), were showing signs of modernism, whilst one of the most interesting composers of this period was the Czech Leoš Janáček (1854–1928) (see pp.146–51). The Russians Sergei Rachmaninov (1873–1943) and Sergey Prokofiev (1891–1953) were still considered to be late-Romantics.

While Schoenberg was expounding his atonal theories, other composers were writing more sparsely orchestrated works, in the style of the 17th and 18th centuries, as a reaction against the lush music of the late 19th-century Romantics. This new Classicism had elements of strong rhythms and enough influence of serialism to make the harmonies sound very 20th century. One of the earliest works in this mode was Prokofiev's 1916 "Classical" Symphony; one could apply the term Neoclassical to Strauss's opera *Ariadne auf Naxos* of 1912; and some of Hindemith's compositions can be so described. But Igor Stravinsky (1882–1971) can justifiably claim to have promoted this Neoclassical movement in earnest in many of his works, culminating in his 1951 opera *The Rake's Progress* (see p.167).

During and after the Second World War, the arts were influenced in various ways by dictatorships. In Germany, Hitler banned any music that did not fit his ideological views of Aryan supremacy. Many Jewish composers fled Nazi Germany in the early 1930s. Of those who remained, many perished in concentration camps, including Viktor Ullmann (1898–1944). Anything adjudged too "modern", was labelled *Entartete Musik* ("degenerate music") and its performance was forbidden. It was not only Jewish composers who had problems in Nazi Germany. Richard Strauss was banned from working with the Jewish librettist Stefan Zweig (who committed suicide in a pact with his second wife in 1942 in Brazil).

In Stalin's Russia, Dmitri Shostakovich (1906–75) fell foul of the authorities in 1936 when his opera *Lady Macbeth of the Mtsensk District* was savagely attacked in *Pravda*, the

ABOVE **Pablo Picasso (1881–1973) in his Surrealism period:** *The Dream* (1932)

official Soviet newspaper, for the modernism of its score and was withdrawn. Shostakovich learned to survive by writing works that would not bring down Stalin's wrath on his head. After the dictator's death in 1953, there was a gradual but limited liberalization of artistic creativity.

The founding in 1946 of the International Summer School at Darmstadt was responsible for the introduction of much new music after the Second World War. Olivier Messiaen (1908–92), a radical from his early years, taught there, as did his pupils Pierre Boulez (b. 1925) and Karlheinz Stockhausen (1928–2007). Messiaen's music was heavily influenced by his deep Catholic faith. He wrote one opera, *Saint François d'Assise* (1975–83). There are no Boulez operas and Stockhausen's ventures in this field revolve round *Licht* (*Light*), a cycle of operas, one for each day of the week, composed 1977–2003. In Paris in 1948 Pierre Schaeffer (1910–95) began composing using pre-recorded sounds, for which he coined the term *musique concrète*, the forerunner of electronic music.

But not all post-war composers wanted to follow this path. Richard Strauss, who continued to create new works until the year before his death at the age of 85, remained a tonal composer, having verged towards atonality in *Salome* and *Elektra* (see p.138–9) and then having made the decision that that was as far as he wanted to go. In Britain there were composers happy to follow a more traditional line, albeit with harmonies and rhythms that place their works firmly in the 20th century. These included Ralph Vaughan Williams, William Walton (1902–83), Michael Tippett (1905–98), and especially Benjamin Britten (1913–76).

By the 1960s and 1970s classical music had begun to absorb some of the elements of rock music and the growing interest in African music with its repeated rhythmic patterns, parallelled in the West by minimalism – one pattern repeated over and over again, such as is heard in the music of the Americans Philip Glass (b. 1937) and John Adams (b. 1947), and the Englishman John Tavener (b. 1944). Others of a similar age, such as Peter Maxwell Davies, Harrison Birtwistle, both born in 1934, and Alexander Goehr (b. 1932), chose a more conventional path. Hans Werner Henze (b. 1926) is the most famous German composer of this period, producing works in all genres. Aribert Reimann (b. 1936) has been much influenced by Berg and Webern, as can be heard in his opera *Lear*.

As the 20th century drew to a close and the 21st century began, new names started to make their mark. These include Americans John Adams, John Harbison (b. 1938), John Corigliano (b. 1938), Tobias Picker (b. 1954), and Jake Heggie (b. 1961), who have all had operas premièred by major companies; and the same applies to the British composers Judith Weir (b. 1954), Mark-Anthony Turnage (b. 1960), and Thomas Adès (b. 1971). The Finn Kaija Saariaho (b. 1952) has had major opera premières in recent years; and the operas or theatre-pieces of the Dutchman Louis Andriessen (b. 1939) are beginning to be recognized. It is a brave writer prepared to forecast which of these composers and their operas will survive the test of time.

One of the most puzzling facets of 20th-century opera is the absence of any influential Italian composer after Puccini. Italy and Germany (to a lesser extent) seem to have passed the baton to Britain and America.

ABOVE **Soviet dictator Joseph Stalin (1879–1953):** he strongly criticized Shostakovich, Prokofiev, and others, considering their music too modern and discordant

Schoenberg

Arnold Schoenberg (Schönberg)
(1874–1951)

WHERE TO START
Moses und Aron

WHERE TO GO NEXT
Erwartung

Arnold Schoenberg was one of the most influential figures in the history of music and one of the few who changed the face of classical music. He was born in Vienna of Jewish parentage, the eldest of three children. He learned the violin from the age of eight and soon began to compose small pieces. The family was not well off and when his father died when Arnold was 16 he had to leave school and work in a bank to help support them. He was a largely self-taught musician, but he joined a small orchestra conducted by the composer Alexander von Zemlinsky, who gave him lessons. The two men became firm friends. In 1901 he married Zemlinsky's sister Mathilde and they had two children. They went to live in Berlin and Schoenberg worked on the music side of *Überbrettl*, a form of cabaret all the vogue in Berlin at that time.

Schoenberg's early works, such as the string sextet *Verklärte Nacht* (*Transfigured Night*) of 1899 and the choral *Gurrelieder* (*Songs of Gurre*), begun in 1900, were typical post-Wagnerian Romantic music. Richard Strauss was so impressed with the latter work that he recommended Schoenberg as a teacher at the Stern Conservatory in Berlin, thus relieving him of working in *Überbrettl*. He returned to Vienna in 1903, where he met Mahler who, although he did not always agree with the younger man's ideas, nevertheless became a supporter. By now Schoenberg had a reputation as a teacher and from 1904 his most important pupils and lifelong disciples were Alban Berg and Anton Webern. Schoenberg, Berg, and Webern formed the nucleus of what became known as the Second Viennese School.

From about 1903 Schoenberg started to experiment with sounds, stretching chromaticism to its limits and by 1908 he had abandoned harmony and tonality as we know it and developed a way of composing known as atonality, which did not rely on key structures. His first works in this idiom were either cheered or sneered at. As a result, he founded in Vienna a Society for the Private

Performance of Music, where applause was forbidden and critics were excluded. His *5 Piano Pieces* (1923) introduced his method of composing with 12 notes, these being the seven white keys and five black keys in one octave on a piano keyboard. He postulated the theory that all 12 notes and their intervals had equal value and importance and formed a "note-row" that governed the way in which music was written. This was the start of serialism. For the rest of his life his compositions followed this method, although he was prepared to vary his system according to the work he wanted to write. As if changing the face of music was not enough, Schoenberg was also a very gifted artist, and his friends included the great Expressionist painters of the day such as Egon Schiele, Gustav Klimt, and Vassily Kandinsky.

In 1923 Schoenberg's wife died and the following year he married Gertrud Kolisch, whose brother Rudolf was his pupil and leader of a string quartet that played his chamber music. They had three children (the eldest married the Italian avant-garde composer Luigi Nono). In 1925 he was appointed Director of a masterclass in composition at the Academy of the Arts

ABOVE LEFT **Arnold Schoenberg, not only a composer, but also a talented artist, as this self-portrait from 1910 confirms** in Berlin; he took up the position in January 1926 and stayed in the city for the next seven years. During this time he composed several important larger works, including the operas *Von Heute auf Morgen* and the first two acts of *Moses und Aron*. By 1933, with the rise of Adolf Hitler, blatant anti-Semitism was having its effect in the arts as elsewhere. Schoenberg was removed from his post at the Academy of the Arts and went with his family to France. Whilst there he returned to the Jewish faith, which he had rejected in 1898. At the end of October 1933 he arrived in Boston, USA, to take up a teaching post. The following year he moved to Los Angeles where the climate was better for his health and lived there the rest of his life, changing the spelling of his name from the original German "Schönberg". He died in Los Angeles in 1951.

Schoenberg wrote four operas: *Erwartung* (*Expectation*) of 1909, is a nightmarish monodrama (one solo singer) in which a woman finds the body of her lover, over which she sings a long monologue – a sort of 20th-century *Liebestod*. It may be relevant that in 1908 Schoenberg's first wife had an affair with an artist. She returned to her family, but the artist committed suicide. The work has become quite fashionable in recent years, providing as it does a great display piece for a soprano. His next two operas are rarely performed, but his last, the unfinished *Moses und Aron*, is growing in favour.

MOSES UND ARON
(*Moses and Aaron*), 1930–2

Schoenberg's fourth opera is on a big scale and employs a large chorus. He wrote the libretto himself, but the music was unfinished when he died. It was not staged until 1957 in Zurich. It is sometimes described as an opera–oratorio, but it is fully stageworthy and very dramatic. The spelling of the title is interesting: Schoenberg was superstitious and he dropped an "a" from Aaron because he didn't want 13 letters in the title! He completed the first two

acts by early 1932, then as his asthma was bad he went to Barcelona for the winter. The following year he left Nazi Germany, settling in the USA, where he revised the text but could not afford the time to work on the music. It has never become a repertory piece, but has had several productions in the past 50 years, with the last act spoken as the composer left it or omitted altogether.

SYNOPSIS The story is biblical. Moses (spoken) hears the Voice of God telling him to lead the Israelites to the Promised Land. Knowing he is no orator, he worries how he can convince them to follow him. God tells him to speak to them through his brother Aaron (ten) (**1**). Aaron interprets to the people Moses's words in a literal and simplified form. When he tells them of Moses's belief in "only one God", visible only to the righteous, they are sceptical. They need more concrete proof. Aaron performs miracles to try to convince them and promises that God also will perform miracles to feed them as they walk through the desert to a land flowing with milk and honey. Moses goes up the Mountain to receive the stone tablets containing the new laws of

God. He is away for 40 days and the Israelites grow restless (**2**). To calm them and restore their belief, Aaron builds a Golden Calf for them to worship (**3**). They dance around this image and a drunken orgy follows, during which Moses returns. He banishes the Golden Calf (**4**), and the people flee. Aaron defends his actions to his brother (**5**). Moses smashes the tablets, frustrated at his own inarticulacy. In the spoken third act, Aaron is seen in chains. Moses continues to chide him for needing a solid image to worship. Why can he not just accept that there is a God? Moses releases Aaron, but as soon as he is free he dies.

> **MUSIC** (**1**) Aaron/Moses duet (Moses spoken throughout): *Du Sohn meiner Väter – You, son of my father*; (**2**) Chorus/ Aaron: *Wo ist Moses? – Where is Moses?*; (**3**) Aaron: *Dieses Bild bezeugt – This gold image attests*; (**4**) Moses: *Vergeh, du Abbild des Unvermögens – Be gone, you image of powerlessness*; (**5**) Moses/ Aaron/Chorus: *Aaron, was hast du getan?/Nichts Neues – Aaron, O what have you done?/Nothing different.*

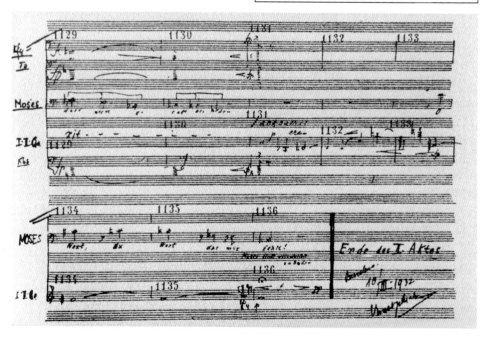

ABOVE **The final page of the manuscript of Act 1 of** Schoenberg's *Moses und Aron*, composed 1930–2

Berg

Alban Berg
(1885–1935)

WHERE TO START
Wozzeck

WHERE TO GO NEXT
Lulu

Berg was one of Schoenberg's most dedicated pupils and disciples (the other being Anton Webern, who did not write operas). Of these three leaders of the Second Viennese School (see pp.155–6), Berg was the one with the natural sense of theatre, and his two operas have become more or less repertory works.

Alban Berg was the third of four children born in Vienna into a well-to-do and cultivated family. He was widely read and loved to attend plays. His father died when Alban was 15, causing financial hardship for the family. When young Berg was 17 he fathered an illegitimate daughter with a kitchen-maid. His first job was in the Civil Service. Other than piano lessons,

he had little music education, but from the age of 15 composed romantic songs. He began his studies with Arnold Schoenberg in 1904. He was fortunate enough to witness first hand an important period in Schoenberg's own creative development of atonal composition. In 1906 Berg was able to give up his job and devote his time to music.

Follower of Schoenberg though he was, Berg's music, influenced in its early years by Claude Debussy and Gustav Mahler, retained tonal leanings. He adapted Schoenberg's serial technique to suit his own style and there is always an element of Romanticism in his compositions. This may be why his music is more generally approachable than that of his colleague or of his teacher.

Berg was living in Vienna during one of the most exciting periods in that city's cultural history. He had a lively interest in all things new in the arts, reading the latest literature, attending the opera (where Mahler was the conductor), seeing modern plays, and attending exhibitions in the company of artists such as Gustav Klimt. In 1906 he met Helene Nahowski and, despite the opposition of her family, they married in 1910. Berg dedicated two of his *Altenberglieder* of 1912 to her. These *Five Songs on Picture Postcard Texts by Peter Altenberg* were for soprano with orchestral accompaniment. When two of the songs were first performed in Vienna in 1913, conducted by Schoenberg, the evening was repeatedly interrupted by the angry audience and had to be abandoned, an experience that undermined Berg's confidence.

In 1914 Berg attended the Vienna première of the last play written by Georg Büchner (1813–37), the German doctor and playwright who died of typhus. As soon as he saw *Woyzeck*, the story of a simple soldier who killed himself and his wife because he could not cope with life's injustices, Berg knew he wanted to make it into an opera. Work on it was constantly interrupted, initially by the outbreak of the First World War, in which he

served in the Austrian army and later in the War Ministry, then demands made on him by Schoenberg, whose music he was helping to promote, and also by his duties in administering his family's estate. *Wozzeck* eventually had its first performance in Berlin in 1925. After its première Berg was keen to find a subject for a second opera. He settled on Frank Wedekind's two "Lulu" plays, adapting them himself for the libretto.

Like Schoenberg, Berg suffered from asthma and illness often prevented him working. And after the Nazis came to power his music was labelled decadent and banned in Germany and Austria. He had all but completed the full score of *Lulu* when he developed septicaemia from an abscess on his back and he died on Christmas Eve, 1935, at only 50 years of age. (Six years later penicillin could have saved his life.)

ABOVE LEFT **Alban Berg looks out of a window above a portrait of himself painted in 1935 by his teacher Arnold Schoenberg**

ABOVE **Berg's *Wozzeck*, with Håkan Hagegård in the title-role and Anne Schwanewilms as his wife, Marie, Santa Fe, 2001**

RIGHT Constance Hauman as Berg's Lulu, Danish
National Opera, Copenhagen, 1996

WOZZECK, 1914–22

The composition of this opera took Berg eight years, with various hold-ups for long periods. At its 1925 Berlin première it was a *succès de scandale*, with many disturbances in the theatre during the performance. As so often with works given a hostile press, this led to productions all over Austria and Germany until, in 1933, the Nazis banned Berg's music. The opera, like the play, has many short scenes and the language is brusque and brutal.

SYNOPSIS The soldier Wozzeck (bar) shaves his Captain (ten) who moralizes about Wozzeck having an illegitimate child by Marie (sop) (**1**). Wozzeck works in a field with another soldier, Andres (ten), and feels the place is haunted. Marie is teased by her friend Margret (cont) for showing too much interest in the Drum-Major (ten). Marie sings a lullaby (**2**) to her child (treble). The Doctor (bass) in the soldiers' camp uses Wozzeck for dietary experiments (**3**), paying him a small fee. Wozzeck takes the money to Marie, who has been given earrings by the Drum-Major (**4**). The Doctor and Captain taunt Wozzeck about Marie's affair. Wozzeck watches jealously as Marie dances with the Drum-Major (**5**). Later the two men fight. Wozzeck and Marie walk near a lake (**6**). Wozzeck kisses her then cuts her throat. Demented, he returns to the scene to find the knife (**7**) and throws it into the lake. He wades into the water and drowns. Marie's child learns that his mother is dead.

> **MUSIC** (**1**) Captain: *Er hat ein Kind ohne den Segen der Kirche – You have a child unblessed by the church*; (**2**) Marie: *Eia, popeia… – Hush-a-bye, baby…;* (**3**) Doctor: *Die Natur kommt! – Nature insists!*; (**4**) Marie: *Was die Steine glänzen! – Don't the jewels shine!*; (**5**) Wozzeck: *Er! Sie! Teufel! – Him! Her! Hell and damnation!*; (**6**) Wozzeck: *Fürch'st dich, Marie? – Are you afraid, Marie?*; (**7**) Wozzeck: *Das Messer? Wo ist das Messer? – The knife? Where is the knife?*

LULU, 1928–35

Having settled on Wedekind's two "Lulu" plays (*Erdgeist* of 1895 and *Die Büchse der Pandora* of 1903), Berg reduced the texts to a libretto. He composed the music and started to score it, first making an orchestral suite. He had just started scoring Act 3 when he fell ill and died. His widow asked Schoenberg and Webern to complete it but they refused and the work was performed with the last act mimed to music from the symphonic suite. A completion by Friedrich Cerha was first heard in 1979 in Paris and has been used ever since, although some productions still prefer the two-act version with the mimed third act. Many roles, eg Schön and Jack the Ripper, are doubled by the same singer.

SYNOPSIS In late 19th-century Germany, Dr Schön (bar) and his son Alwa (ten), a composer, watch Schön's lover, Lulu (sop), having her portrait painted (the portrait appears in all acts) (**1**). Alwa also loves her. After they leave, the Painter (ten) tries to seduce Lulu. Her husband arrives, sees them together, has a stroke, and dies. She marries the Painter, his portraits sell well, and they are rich. An old tramp, Schigolch (bass), her "father-figure", visits her (**2**). As he leaves, Schön arrives – he wants to end his affair with Lulu and marry his fiancée (**3**). He reveals their past to the Painter, who kills himself. Lulu threatens to marry an African Prince who admires her, and Schön realizes he cannot live without her. They marry, Alwa still protesting his love. Also attracted to Lulu is the lesbian Countess Geschwitz (mez) (**4**), of whom Schön disapproves. Jealous of these and all her other relationships, Schön gives Lulu a gun to kill herself, but instead she kills him (**5**). Lulu is imprisoned. Alwa, helped by Schigolch and Geschwitz, arranges her escape. Lulu and Alwa live together. The market collapses and they are very poor. Lulu works as a prostitute (**6**), and Schigolch and Alwa steal from her clients. One of her clients kills Alwa. Her last client is Jack the Ripper (bar). He murders both Lulu and the Countess who is staying with her.

> **MUSIC** (The following are not easily recognizable arias or ensembles, but indicators to the action at various points) (**1**) Alwa/Schön/Lulu: *Darf ich eintreten?/Mein Sohn!/Das ist ja Herr Alwa – Can I join you?/My son!/This must be Mr Alwa*; (**2**) Schigolch: *So hab' ich es für dich gedacht – Just what I had desired for you*; (**3**) Dr Schön: *Lass mir aus dem Spiel! – Leave me out of this*; (**4**) Geschwitz: *Sie glauben nicht, wie ich mich darauf freue – You won't believe how pleased I am*; (**5**) Lulu: *Ich habe ihn erschossen… – I shot him with his pistol*; (**6**) Lulu: *Werden sie mich wieder einmal besuchen? – May I expect you'll pay another visit?*

Weill

Kurt Weill
(1900–50)

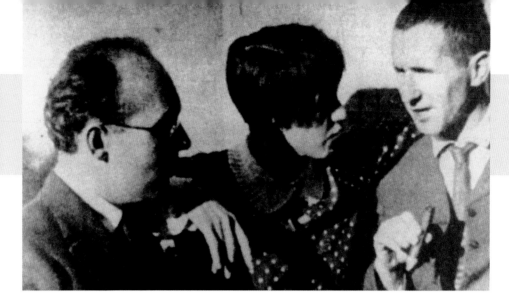

WHERE TO START
Die Dreigroschenoper

WHERE TO GO NEXT
Street Scene

Kurt Weill is one of the most important composers for the theatre – rather than of opera – in the 20th century. It is convenient, but not really helpful, to divide his works into two compartments: the operas he wrote in Germany and the "musicals" he wrote in America, and to consider the two as completely different. But are they?

Weill was the third of four children of the chief cantor of a synagogue in Dessau, himself a composer mainly of liturgical music. The children had music lessons from an early age and were regularly taken to the opera and to concerts. By the time Kurt was 15 he was showing sufficient signs of creative ability for his father to arrange for him to have lessons with Albert Bing, a conductor. At 18 he entered the Berlin Musikhochschule to study with Humperdinck (see p.136). He wanted to study with Schoenberg, but was unable to afford it and in 1919 he returned to Dessau and worked at the theatre under the conductor Hans Knappertsbusch. He took a job as conductor of a very small opera company and then went to Berlin to study at Busoni's masterclasses. Weill was soon having works published and played at concerts.

His first opera, *Der Protagonist*, was given in Dresden in 1926 and he was hailed as the best opera composer to emerge in Germany since the First World War. He next collaborated with the dramatist and theatre producer Bertolt Brecht (1898–1956), whose radical outlook greatly influenced theatre in Germany before and during the Nazi period. They produced a *Songspiel* using Brecht's verses and it was so successful at its Baden-Baden première that they developed from it (in 1927–9, after finishing other works) a full-length opera, *Aufstieg und Fall der Stadt Mahagonny* (*The Rise*

and Fall of the City of Mahagonny). The *Songspiel* was the start of a fruitful collaboration.

In 1926 Weill had married the mezzo-soprano Lotte Lenya (1898–1981), who created Jenny in the Weill–Brecht opera *Die Dreigroschenoper* (*The Threepenny Opera*). The financial success that followed meant that Weill could now devote himself to composition. But with his Jewish ancestry he was a prime target when the Nazis came to power and by 1932 his works were being pushed out of state theatres and he realized he was going to have to make his career outside Germany.

He fled to Paris in 1933 but it soon became apparent that even France would not be a safe base. He and his wife travelled to New York for a production of a work he had been writing in collaboration with the writer Franz Werfel and producer Max Reinhardt. The production was postponed but they decided to stay in the United States. His first works written there were not successful, but with nothing to tempt him back to Europe he applied for American citizenship. Starting with *Knickerbocker Holiday*, he then produced a string of successful musicals in collaboration with some of the finest writers of the day, including Ira Gershwin, Alan Jay Lerner, S J Perelman, and Ogden Nash. *Knickerbocker Holiday* contained "September Song", which quickly became his first "hit" and made Weill's name known to a wide audience. His other works of this period included two huge successes, *Lady in the Dark* (1940) and *One Touch of Venus* (1943).

After the Second World War his first "American opera" appeared on Broadway in 1946. This was *Street Scene* based on Elmer Rice's drama. It was not immediately a great success, but he considered it one of his best

works, an opinion with which I would not argue. He composed several more successful works in this genre and had started working on a musical version of *Huckleberry Finn* when his long-standing heart trouble worsened and he died at the early age of 50. It is probably still too early to judge his place in music history.

DIE DREIGROSCHENOPER
(*The Threepenny Opera*), 1928
Described in the score as a "play with music", this is a version of John Gay's *The Beggar's Opera* of 1728. The rehearsals were chaotic, and it was some time before the opera reached its final version. The theatre was not full on the night of the 1928 première in Berlin and the critics' notices were mixed. But it soon established itself and became one of the most popular works on the German stage and was quickly produced throughout Europe and in the USA.

SYNOPSIS In Soho, London, in 1900 a Street-Singer (bar) tells in a ballad of "Mack the Knife" (1). Macheath (ten) has eloped with Polly (sop), daughter of Jonathan Jeremiah Peachum (bar) and Mrs Peachum (mez), who are determined to hand him over to the police. After their wedding, Polly entertains their guests with a song (2). Macheath and Polly say a passionate farewell before he goes into hiding (3). He is given away by Jenny Diver (mez), a prostitute bribed by Mrs Peachum. Macheath used to be her pimp and they reminisce about those days (4) before Macheath is arrested by Commissioner Tiger Brown (bar), whose daughter Lucy (sop) was going to marry Macheath. At the courtroom Macheath sings of the good life. Lucy, pretending to be pregnant, first joins Polly in expressing their mutual jealousy (5) and then

LEFT **Kurt Weill with his wife Lotte Lenya and the dramatist Bertolt Brecht, Berlin, 1928**

helps him to escape. He is found with a whore and again arrested and this time he is sentenced to be hanged. He bids farewell to the world, begging everyone for forgiveness (6). Polly goes to visit him in prison. He is given a last-minute reprieve. In honour of the forthcoming Coronation, he is pardoned, made a peer, given a castle and a pension, and he and Polly are reunited.

> **MUSIC (1)** Street-Singer: *Und der Haifisch, der hat Zähne – And the shark's teeth*; **(2)** Polly: *Meine Herren, heut' sehen sie mich Gläser aufwaschen – Well, gentlemen, today you see me rinse out the glasses*; **(3)** Macheath/Polly duet: *Siehst du den Mond über Soho?/Ich sehe ihn, Liebe – You see that moon over Soho?/ I see it, my love*; **(4)** Macheath/Jenny: *In einer Zeit, die längst vergangen ist/ In jener Zeit, die jetzt vergangen ist – So many years have vanished / So many years since then, dead and gone*; **(5)** Lucy/Polly duet: *Komm heraus, du Schönheit von Soho – Come out here, you Soho beauty queen*; **(6)** Macheath: *Ihr Menschenbrüder, die ihr nach uns lebt – My fellow-men, who will live after me.*

Other opera of note

Of Weill's other works, *Street Scene* (1946) warrants discussion. He had seen Elmer Rice's play in Europe and he met the author in 1936, soon after he arrived in America. He was keen to make an opera of *Street Scene*, and although Rice had refused permission to other composers, he agreed to Weill's proposal. The result was remarkable. The black poet Langston Hughes supplied the lyrics and he and Weill toured the streets of New York taking note of street sounds and children's cries. Despite working in a foreign language, Weill seemed to have no difficulty coping with all the spoken dialogue. The action takes place in 24 hours in a tenement block and describes the life of the working-class tenants and their efforts to come to terms with their lot or claw their way out of their environment. They drink, they use drugs, they use sex – or they study in the hope of escaping the trap they are in. There is no happy ending. It did not have an unqualified success and its first production in Germany in the 1950s was a failure with the audience and the critics. It had its first performance in an opera house when New York City Opera revived it in 1959, nearly ten years after the composer's death. His faith in it was at last justified.

ABOVE **Final scene from *Die Dreigroschenoper's* première production, Berlin, 1928, with Erich Ponto (Peachum), Roma Bahn (Polly), Harold Paulsen (Macheath), and Kurt Gerron (Brown)**

Henze

Hans Werner Henze
(b. 1926)

WHERE TO START
Boulevard Solitude

WHERE TO GO NEXT
Elegy for Young Lovers

Henze is the most prolific German composer at the present time. He studied Schoenbergian serialism at Darmstadt, and his works also reflect his strong left-wing views. He was born in Westphalia, the eldest of six children. His father Franz was a schoolteacher and a good amateur musician and Hans had his first piano lessons as soon as he started school. With the advent of Nazism, Franz became a member of the party, and his older boys were obliged to wear the brown shirts of Hitler Youth. Because his father wanted to hear all the propaganda, a radio was available in the house and Hans listened to classical music. At school he formed an ensemble with other children, and attended chamber concerts with his piano teacher (in a partly Jewish home).

By 1942 his father accepted that Hans was destined to be a musician and sent him to Brunswick State Music School. He sang in the

cathedral choir, played timpani in the school orchestra, earned money as an accompanist for fellow students, and went to as many concerts and operas as he could, getting to know and love the operas of Mozart. In 1943 his father rejoined the army and never returned from the Eastern front. Hans came to hate the Nazis, fascism, and war generally. He was conscripted and sent to an armoured tank division in Magdeburg. He continued to compose, even without a piano. For a short time he was a British prisoner-of-war and took advantage of this to improve his English, to learn as much as possible about life outside the Third Reich, and to listen to BBC music broadcasts.

After the war he lived at the family's new home near Bielefeld and took a job as a transport worker to help support his mother and siblings. He also worked as a *répétiteur* for the local theatre. He became a composition student of Wolfgang Fortner (1907–87) in Heidelberg, where he had a solid grounding in all the disciplines and was introduced to music by composers such as Hindemith, Stravinsky, Berg, and Bartók. In 1946 he attended his first Darmstadt Summer School. He gradually moved away from Neoclassicism and started to explore 12-note music, becoming the first young German composer to embrace this form of composition. But slowly he started to question some of the tenets of the 12-note composers, preferring a more flexible tonality.

Although Henze's earliest compositions were choral and chamber, from the beginning he composed for the theatre, and he has said that all his music starts from and returns to the theatre. His output of operas, ballets, and music-theatre is prodigious. As his fame spread, he soon had more commissions than he could cope with. One of these was for a modern opera based on *Manon Lescaut*, and this became *Boulevard Solitude* of 1951, his first full-length opera. In 1953, stressed out, as we would say today, Henze left Germany and settled in Italy for the next 12 years, first on the island of Ischia in the Bay of Naples and later near

Rome. He learned the language, composed, and critically analyzed his own compositional methods. He dedicated his 1958 opera, *Der Prinz von Homburg*, based on a Kleist play, to Stravinsky. He then composed a chamber opera, *Elegy for Young Lovers*, to a libretto by W H Auden (1907–73) and Chester Kallman (1921–75), about the relationships among a group of people staying in an Alpine inn. The same poets adapted Euripides's *The Bacchae* for Henze's 1965 opera *The Bassarids*, which is generally accepted as his masterpiece, although as an introduction to his music some of his other operas are more easily approachable. Shortly after this he changed direction and his music took on a more political flavour, reflecting revolutionary ideas and dogmas. His *L'Upupa und der Triumph der Sohnesliebe* (*The Hoopoe and the Triumph of Filial Love*) (2000–3) was inspired by an Arab story about a father who wants to capture a legendary bird and in his efforts to do so puts his son's life at risk. It was performed at the 2003 Salzburg Festival. Henze is still composing – his latest opera, *Phaedra*, was premièred in Berlin in 2007 – and time will be the judge of the staying-power of his music.

ABOVE LEFT **Hans Werner Henze, aged 75, in London in 2001**

ABOVE *Boulevard Solitude*: **Alexandra von der Weth (Manon) and Pär Lindskog (Des Grieux) in Nikolaus Lehnhoff's award-winning production, ROH, London, 2001**

BOULEVARD SOLITUDE, 1951

The libretto is based on the Abbé Prévost's *Manon Lescaut*, which had already been set by Massenet (see pp.111–12) and Puccini (see p.129). Henze's version is set in Paris and updated to just after the Second World War. The music switches between tonal and atonal and incorporates jazz and the blues.

SYNOPSIS In a railway station, Manon (sop) meets Armand Des Grieux (ten). She is on her way to finishing school in Switzerland, he to continue his studies in Paris. They fall in love and she goes to live with him in his attic (1). They are very poor. Manon's brother Lescaut (bar) needs money and forces her to live first with Lilaque (ten), an old but rich admirer (2), and later with Lilaque's wealthy son (bar). The distraught Armand takes to drugs and confides his unhappiness to his friend Francis (bar) (3). Armand visits Manon in Lilaque *fils*'s apartment (4). Lescaut arrives and steals a painting. Lilaque *père* accuses him of the theft, and Lescaut kills him and transfers the gun to the innocent Manon's hand. Lilaque's son finds Manon and Armand with his father's body and Manon is arrested and thrown into prison. Armand desperately tries to see Manon (5), but they are unable to talk before she is taken away.

> **MUSIC** (1) Armand/Manon duet: *Ahnen Sie, Manon, was jetzt gescheh'n ist?/Leise, sinnenthoben schon schweben wir – Do you know, Manon, what has happened?/Softly, quietly we float away*; (2) Lescaut: *Er steht vor'm Haus, Er ist dick, alt, und reich! – He's waiting outside. He's fat, old and rich!*; (3) Armand: *Wie leer, ach wie leer – Such waste, oh such waste*; (4) Manon/Armand duet: *Aus dem goldnen Spiegel schaut dich der charmante Armand/Du gehst und gehst und trägst mein ganzen Leben – In the golden mirror I see my dear charming Armand/You travel on and drag behind your footsteps my whole life*; (5) Armand: *Zum letzten Mal in meinem Leben – Today again, and for the last time.*

ELEGY FOR YOUNG LOVERS, 1959–61

Henze and his librettists dedicated this work to the memory of Hugo von Hofmannsthal, who was Richard Strauss's librettist. It has a cast of six and centres on a poet who ruthlessly uses everyone around him to stimulate his creativity. The widow's coloratura hallucinations are based on Donizetti's mad scene in *Lucia di Lammermoor* (see pp.72–3). *Elegy for Young Lovers* was first performed at the Schwetzingen Festival in German in 1961, and was heard in its original English later that year at Glyndebourne.

SYNOPSIS The poet Mittenhofer (bar) has come to the Alpine inn "Der Schwarze Adler" to write his spring poem, accompanied by his wealthy patron-cum-secretary Carolina (cont), his young companion Elizabeth Zimmer (sop), his doctor Reischmann (bass), and Reischmann's son Toni (ten). At the inn is Hilda Mack (sop), who dresses in the style of 40 years ago when she first came here on her honeymoon with her bridegroom, who disappeared on the mountain. Demented, she still awaits his return (1). Mittenhofer makes notes of everyone's comments and Hilda's hallucinations. They are interrupted by the mountain guide Joseph Maurer (spoken), who announces that a body, thought to be Hilda's husband, has been found in a glacier. Elizabeth consoles Hilda (2). Toni and Elizabeth have fallen in love, much to Mittenhofer's fury (3). Hilda regains her sanity and bids them all farewell as she leaves (4). Toni and Elisabeth set off down the mountain but become trapped by bad weather and are resigned to death together on the slopes (5). Mittenhofer makes use of all these events to write his new poem, called "Elegy for Young Lovers", which he later recites to an audience in Vienna (6).

> **MUSIC** (1) Hilda: *Schnee fällt aufs Blütenmeer Felder und Wald – Snow falls on blossoming woodland and meadow*; (2) Elizabeth/Hilda duet: *Bitte, hören sie. Vierzig Jahre schon sind Sie hier/Vierzig Jahre? So sagt ihr; Doch bin ich erstest gestern hier – Please listen. You've been here forty years/Forty years? So you say. But I came only yesterday*; (3) Mittenhofer: *Wiederum erkenne ich, das ein Poet zu niemand gehört – Once again I'm made to learn that a poet must depend only on himself*; (4) Hilda: *Im Morgen wird die Welt, die ich versäumte erstehn – Tomorrow to a world that must be faster, I can't wait*; (5) Toni/Elizabeth duet: *Nicht zum Lieben wurden wir hergeführt … / Not just for love, were we brought here … ;* (6) Mittenhofer: *Eins, zwei, drei, vier, Wen bewundern wir? – One, two, three, four, Whom do we adore?*

Stravinsky

Igor Stravinsky
(1882–1971)

LEFT Igor Stravinsky enjoying a press conference – and a cigarette – in Boston, 1955

WHERE TO START
The Rake's Progress

WHERE TO GO NEXT
Oedipus Rex

Igor Stravinsky, the major advocate of Neoclassicism, was one of the most influential figures in 20th-century music. He was born near St Petersburg, his mother being an amateur musician, and his father, Fyodor (who died in 1902), principal bass-baritone at the Mariinsky Theatre. Igor entered St Petersburg University in 1901 to read law, but concentrated more on composing. From 1903 he had private lessons from Rimsky-Korsakov (1844–1908) at whose weekly musical soirées some of Stravinsky's earliest works were performed.

He married his cousin Katerina (Katya) in 1906 and they had four children. With Rimsky-Korsakov's help many of his works were performed and published. In 1908 he started to sketch an opera, *Le Rossignol*, based on Hans Christian Andersen's *The Emperor and the Nightingale* (not completed until 1914). Then in 1909 his two short pieces *Fireworks* and *Scherzo fantastique* were performed in St Petersburg. On the strength of these works Sergei Diaghilev (1872–1929), who had worked at the Mariinsky from 1899 to 1901 and later founded the Ballets Russes in Paris, asked him to orchestrate some of Chopin's music for Mikhail Fokine's ballet *Les Sylphides*. As a result, he received a telegram from Diaghilev which would change not only his life but ultimately the course of 20th-century music. He asked Stravinsky to compose a full-length ballet on a Russian fairy-tale, *The Firebird*. At rehearsals for the first performance in Paris in June 1910, the orchestral players had great difficulty understanding the music and the dancers had even more of a problem and often missed their entrances. But the ballet was a sensational success and Stravinsky became a household name. His next ballet,

Petrushka, received its first performance in 1911 with Vaslav Nijinsky in the title-role, and was another triumph. Back in Russia he began work on his third Diaghilev ballet, *The Rite of Spring*. Its Paris première in 1913 was a famous occasion, with riots in the theatre on a par with those at the first Paris performances of Wagner's *Tannhäuser* more than 50 years earlier (see p.92–3). Nevertheless, Diaghilev staged another six Stravinsky ballets.

In 1920 the family went to live in Paris and the following year settled in Biarritz, partly for the sake of Katya's fragile health. From the time they moved to Paris, Igor had various affairs, most significantly with Vera, wife of

Diaghilev's stage designer Sergey Sudeykin. By the summer of 1921 she had left her husband and Stravinsky was openly living a double life, Katya having little option but to go along with the situation rather than risk him leaving her altogether. At this time he began work on *Mavra*, a one-act opera based on Pushkin, in which he determined to abandon the lush orchestration of the Romantics and replace it with a more Classical style – a "numbers opera", with arias, ensembles, recitatives, and more sparsely orchestrated accompaniments. This was the start of Neoclassicism, which now pervaded his orchestral works, and was the antithesis of the atonality and serialism that was all the rage among the followers of Schoenberg. *Mavra* failed in Paris in 1922 and has rarely been performed since.

His next idea was for an opera in Latin on an ancient subject which would be known to everybody (his faith in education then being greater than it might be today). He settled on Sophocles's *Oedipus tyrannus* and the libretto was written (in French) by Jean Cocteau (1889–1963), who felt it essential to have a commentary the audience could understand. A speaker introduces each scene, which then proceeds in Latin. The cast is masked and immobile, moving only heads and hands. *Oedipus Rex* is one of Stravinsky's great works.

It is arguable whether it is an opera or an oratorio – its Paris première in 1927 was in concert form – but despite the lack of stage movement it can be very dramatic.

Katya Stravinsky died in 1939 having spent most of her last four years in a sanatorium being treated for tuberculosis. Four months earlier their elder daughter had died of the same disease, aged 29, and four months after Katya's death, Stravinsky's 84-year-old mother died. The composer and two of his other children were also treated for tuberculosis. In September 1939, three weeks after the outbreak of war, Stravinsky sailed to the USA to give six lectures at Harvard and to conduct. In January 1940 Vera joined him and in March they were married in Massachusetts. They moved to West Hollywood in 1941 and were granted citizenship four years later. Although he had been in the USA before (this was his fourth visit), settling was not easy – Igor and Vera spoke little English, had few friends, and life in California at that time was very different from the sophistication of Paris.

Stravinsky wrote little for the stage during the war years, but in 1947 he saw in Chicago an exhibition of works of William Hogarth (1697–1764) and this planted the idea for his last opera. Theatrically speaking, Stravinsky's masterpiece is *The Rake's Progress*, with a brilliant libretto by W H Auden and Chester

Kallman. It is the climax of his Neoclassical compositions. The score is complex, with the influence of Mozart obvious.

In 1969, with his health declining, Igor and Vera moved to New York, where he died in his Fifth Avenue apartment in 1971. His funeral was held in New York, but his body was flown to Venice and interred near to Diaghilev's grave on the cemetery island of San Michele.

THE RAKE'S PROGRESS, 1947–51
The first performance took place at the Teatro La Fenice, Venice, on 11 September 1951. Stravinsky conducted, but the production was not to his liking and the singing was variable. It has nevertheless achieved a permanent place in the operatic repertory.

SYNOPSIS In 18th-century England, Anne Trulove (sop) and Tom Rakewell (ten) are to marry. Her father, Trulove (bass), is concerned about the marriage **(1)**. Nick Shadow (bar) informs Tom that he has inherited a fortune **(2)** and Tom leaves with him for London to attend to his finances. In her brothel Mother Goose (mez) and Shadow try to teach Tom about vice, before she takes him to bed. Anne realizes she must go and rescue Tom **(3)**, who is bored with his wealthy life in London. Shadow suggests that he marry the bearded lady Baba the Turk (mez) and when Anne

arrives to visit him he begs her to go, introducing Baba as his wife. Tom dreams of abolishing all the misery in the world **(4)**. His life degenerates until he is bankrupt and everything he owns, including Baba, is sold by Sellem (ten) the auctioneer **(5)**. Baba advises Anne to go to Tom **(6)**. Shadow now claims Tom's soul in payment for his services. He suggests that Tom's fate be decided by a game of cards. Prompted by Anne's voice of love (offstage), Tom wins the game and Shadow, furious, condemns Tom to a life of insanity **(7)**. Trulove takes Anne to visit Tom in Bedlam. She sings him to sleep and leaves **(8)**. On waking and finding Anne has gone **(9)**, Tom dies of grief. In a sung Epilogue, the moral of the story is told by the cast **(10)**.

MUSIC (1) Anne/Rakewell/Trulove duet-trio: *The woods are green/O may a father...*; **(2)** Shadow: *Fair lady, gracious gentleman*; **(3)** Anne: *I go, I go to him*; **(4)** Rakewell: *Vary the song, O London, change!*; **(4)** Rakewell: *Thanks to this excellent device*; **(5)** Sellem: *Ladies both fair and gracious, gentlemen*; **(6)** Baba: *You love him, seek to set him right*; **(7)** Shadow: *I burn! I freeze!*; **(8)** Anne: *Gently, little boat*; **(9)** Rakewell: *Where art thou, Venus?*; **(10)** Leading cast: *Good people, just a moment.*

LEFT **American première of *The Rake's Progress*,** NY, 1953: Norman Scott (Trulove), Mark Harrell (Shadow), Hilde Gueden (Anne), Eugene Conley (Tom), Stravinsky, W H Auden, conductor Fritz Reiner, Chester Kallman

ABOVE **Megan Latham as the bearded Baba the Turk**, *The Rake's Progress*, Aldeburgh Festival, 2006, conducted by Martyn Brabbins

Prokofiev

Sergey Prokofiev
(1891–1953)

WHERE TO START
The Love for Three Oranges

WHERE TO GO NEXT
War and Peace

From childhood Prokofiev was a composer for the theatre, although that is not how he is seen at the present, his orchestral works being performed more than his operas. He was born in the Ukraine into an affluent family, the only one of three children to survive infancy. He began piano lessons with his mother when he was four and his earliest attempts at composition date from this time. His mother took him to the opera in Moscow and St Petersburg and by the time he was ten he had tried his hand at writing one. In 1904 he entered St Petersburg Conservatory. By the time he graduated in 1914 he had written five operas; he was to complete a further six and leave three unfinished. Like Stravinsky, he composed ballets for Diaghilev, *Cinderella* and *Romeo and Juliet* being standard fare to this day.

After the October Revolution of 1917, Prokofiev realized that he would be artistically stifled and decided to emigrate. In 1918 he settled in the United States. He tried at first to support himself as a pianist, playing his own works. Whilst making his Chicago début recital in 1919 he received a commission for an opera, *The Love for Three Oranges*. Various events delayed its première until 1921, but it became his most performed and successful opera in his lifetime. From 1920 he spent the summers in Europe and in 1922 went to live in Germany, where the following year he married the Spanish singer Lina Llubera. His next completed opera, *The Fiery Angel* (1919–27), was not performed in his lifetime. He and Lina soon moved to Paris where he wrote more ballets for Diaghilev. His earlier opera, *The Gambler* (1915–17), had its première in Brussels in 1929.

In 1927 Prokofiev toured the Soviet Union giving concerts. In private he was critical of the Soviet political system, but he was keen to return to his homeland. He made many visits over the next few years and in 1936 went to live there with his wife and their two sons. This was the year that Shostakovich was savaged in the Soviet press (see p.170) and it was made clear that art was to follow Soviet socialist principles. Prokofiev was allowed to travel to Europe and the USA until 1938 when his passport was withdrawn. He continued to compose, including notable film music and music for children. In 1939 he wrote a cantata for Stalin's 60th birthday and also in that year wrote his first opera for ten years, *Semyon Kotko*. Like much of his music at this time, it was politically motivated. It failed in the Soviet Union and has never been a success. Undaunted, he began his next opera to a libretto by Mira

Mendelson, for whom Prokofiev left his family in 1941 and whom he later married. This opera was *Betrothal in a Monastery*, after Sheridan's comic opera libretto *The Duenna*. It had its première in Prague after the Second World War and has appeared intermittently since then.

Prokofiev's major composition during the war years was the opera *War and Peace*, begun in 1941 and based on Tolstoy. Post-war, certain of Prokofiev's works, especially *War and Peace*, were banned by the Soviet authorities and he acknowledged his alleged "artistic errors" in an open letter of apology. Worse was to come, his first wife Lina being arrested and sentenced to 20 years in a labour camp for "spying". (She was set free in 1956 and died in London in 1989.) After the war, none of Prokofiev's works was very successful. Little of his music was published or performed and he suffered financial hardship. He was granted a very modest pension. His health suffered and he had several heart attacks. He continued to work on *War and Peace*, revising it extensively in the hope of a production, but the full version was not given in the Soviet Union until 1956. Prokofiev died on 5 March 1953, an event that went largely unreported: Stalin died the same day.

THE LOVE FOR THREE ORANGES
(*Lyubov' k tryom apel'sinam*), 1919
This was commissioned by Chicago Opera and was the first major work Prokofiev composed after settling in the USA the previous year. Following its 1921 première it became his most popular opera and since its European première in 1925 it has been his most often performed. The libretto, by the composer, is in Russian (translated into French for the première).

ABOVE LEFT **Sergey Prokofiev, pictured in the 1920s**

ABOVE *The Love for Three Oranges* at the Bolshoi Theatre, Moscow, 1999, with Marina Shutova and Yuri Vedeneyev

RIGHT The gigantic cook in Frank Corsaro's production of *The Love for Three Oranges*, imaginatively designed by Maurice Sendak, Glyndebourne, 1982

SYNOPSIS The action takes place before on-stage observers: the Prince (ten), son of the King of Clubs (bass), suffers from melancholia. If he cannot be made to laugh, he will die (1). This would suit the Prime Minister Leandro (bar), who wants to succeed to the throne with the King's niece Clarice (cont). Smeraldina (mez) announces that her mistress, the witch Fata Morgana (sop), will prevent the King's protective magician, Chelio (bass), from helping the situation. All attempts to make the Prince laugh fail (2). He laughs for the first time when the disguised Fata Morgana falls over, legs kicking in the air. Furious, she puts a spell on him (3): he will fall in love with three oranges and must travel the world seeking them. The Prince sets off, accompanied by the clown Truffaldino (ten) and blown on his way by the devil Farfarello (bass) using a large bellows. The oranges are in the kitchen in Creonte's castle. Chelio warns them to open the oranges only near water. He gives them a magic ribbon to distract the Gigantic Cook (bass) while they steal the oranges. This works

and they escape back to the desert. While the Prince is asleep, Truffaldino, needing a drink, opens two of the oranges, and out step two Princesses, Linetta (cont) and Nicoletta (mez), who both die of thirst. Truffaldino flees, so when the Prince awakens he is alone with two dead princesses. When he opens the third orange, Princess Ninetta (sop) emerges and they fall in love (4). Observers provide water and she is saved from death. Smeraldina sees Ninetta as a rival for the Prince's love and turns her into a rat, taking her place with the Prince. They return to the palace. On the throne sits a large rat, who Chelio turns back into the princess (5). Everyone toasts the Prince and his Princess as Fata Morgana and her conspirators make their escape.

Other opera of note

Prokofiev's longest opera (four hours), based on one of Russia's literary masterpieces, was in difficulties from the beginning. *War and Peace* (*Voina i mir*) is an episodic work of many short scenes concerning the private lives, loves, and sorrows of individuals. But the political climate was such that he was obliged to add heroic, patriotic, and political elements to the war sections to meet the official party demands of composition, putting the emphasis on state events rather than on the characters. The opera grew so long that it was divided into two parts to be performed on consecutive nights. Only the first part was heard in Prokofiev's lifetime, in concert performances in Moscow and a staged performance in Leningrad. He continued to revise it in the forlorn hope of a complete performance. The full opera (minus two scenes), given in one evening, had its première in Florence on 26 May 1953, two months after the composer's death. It is now acknowledged in and outside Russia as a masterpiece and performances have increased in number.

ABOVE The ball scene in *War and Peace*, produced by Tim Albery, ENO, London, 2001

Shostakovich

Dmitri Shostakovich
(1906–75)

WHERE TO START
Lady Macbeth of the Mtsensk District

WHERE TO GO NEXT
The Nose

With Shostakovich we come to one of the artistic giants of the 20th century. He was born in St Petersburg, the middle child of musical parents who were comfortably off. He began piano lessons with his mother when he was nine and advanced very quickly. He also started to compose small pieces. He saw his first opera in 1915, began private music lessons the same year, and entered St Petersburg Conservatory in 1919. With perfect pitch, a good memory, and an ability to sight-read with ease, he was soon tackling Beethoven piano sonatas and exploring works of composers such as Bartók and Hindemith. At the Conservatory he attended meetings with others keen to learn about new music developments in the West.

However, the years preceding Lenin's financial policies of 1921 were ones of famine. Artistic institutions were grossly under-funded. Shostakovich's family also felt the pinch. His father died in 1922 and his mother had to work as a typist. A small grant enabled Dmitri to continue his studies, which he completed in 1923. With the first performance in 1926 of his First Symphony, Shostakovich shot to fame, the symphony being taken up by top conductors in the West.

The need to earn money to help his mother led Dmitri to accept a succession of commissions for film music, ballets, and incidental music for theatres, which allowed little room for experimentation with new Western techniques. In 1927 he visited Berlin and later that year he met Prokofiev who was visiting the Soviet Union for the first time since he had emigrated to the USA in 1918. The same year he met 18-year-old Nina Varzar, a physics student, whom he married in 1932. Their marriage was always shaky and

only the arrival of their first child in 1936 prevented a separation. In June 1927 Berg's *Wozzeck* had its Leningrad (St Petersburg) première and stimulated Shostakovich's interest in the avant-garde. His first opera, based on Nikolai Gogol's short story *The Nose*, dates from this period and shows the influence of Expressionism as he experienced it in the Berg opera. *The Nose* had its first performance in 1930 and the critics were hostile. For the first time Shostakovich was accused of "formalism", a description that had long since lost its original meaning and was directed at anything in the arts that did not conform to Soviet ideology. Nevertheless it was the first Russian opera for 15 years to be accepted into the repertory, seldom though it is produced nowadays.

If Shostakovich's Expressionist tendencies were recognizable in *The Nose*, how much more was this so in his second opera, *Lady Macbeth of the Mtsensk District*, composed between 1930 and 1932. The first performance was in Leningrad in January 1934 and the Moscow première was two days later. It was highly praised by critics, other musicians, and the public. Over the next two years it had over 170 performances in Leningrad and Moscow, as well as numerous productions elsewhere in the Soviet Union and abroad. From 1934 Stalin's "Great Terror" purges threatened the careers of all artists, and many were imprisoned or killed. Shostakovich, the most prominent Soviet composer, was an easy target when the axe finally fell. Stalin and other high-ranking officials attended a performance of *Lady Macbeth* at the Bolshoi on 26 January 1936. Two days later the now notorious article headed "Muddle instead of music" appeared in the official Soviet newspaper, *Pravda*. It savaged Shostakovich, accusing him of "leftist distortion … petty-bourgeois sensationalism … and formalism". It has been said that this article was written by Stalin himself; it certainly expressed his views. It must have seemed that Shostakovich's career was over and indeed it

ABOVE **Dmitri Shostakovich at work on a score** in the 1930s

LEFT *Lady Macbeth of the Mtsensk District*, ROH, London, 2004, with Katarina Dalayman (Katerina Ismailova), and John Tomlinson (Boris)

standing affair, but she twice turned down his marriage proposal. In 1962 he married for the third time, to Irina Supinskaya, a young literary editor. Shostakovich visited England in 1958, 1960, and 1974, becoming a close friend of Benjamin Britten (see pp.179–187). In 1958 he had been diagnosed with a form of poliomyelitis, and after his first heart attack in 1966 his health was fragile. But his later works are powerful and demonstrate his anger and bitterness at the tragic turn of events in his homeland. When he died in 1975 *Pravda*'s obituary described him as "a true son of the Communist Party". Despite the publication in 1979 of memoirs attributed to him (*Testimony: the Memoirs of Dmitri Shostakovich as Related to and Edited by Solomon Volkov*) and about which controversy still rages, it is unlikely that we yet know the truth of his opinions or of his life under the suppressive Soviet regime. But we do know that his mastery was never dimmed, that he left a succession of great and life-enhancing works in many genres, and they are his testimony.

LADY MACBETH OF THE MTSENSK DISTRICT

(Ledi Makbet Mtsenskovo uyezda), 1930–2
Few operas can have given their composers as much extra-musical grief as this one. In 1956–63 Shostakovich revised it as *Katerina Ismailova* (the heroine), but since the composer's death the original has been favoured. The libretto is taken from a short story in which Katerina is cruel and selfish, but in his opera Shostakovich treats her sympathetically, seeing her as a victim of her surroundings.

SYNOPSIS Russia, 1865: Katerina (sop) is unhappily married to Zinovy Ismailov (ten). While her husband is working away, she interrupts their farmhand Sergei (ten) molesting Aksinya (sop), their cook (**1**), and fights with him. Zinovy's father Boris (bar), who lusts after Katerina, sends her to her room (**2**). Sergei follows her and they make love. The following week as he leaves her

room he is seen by Boris who whips him and sends for his son to come home. Katerina puts rat poison in Boris's mushrooms and he dies (**3**). When Zinovy returns he spots Sergei's belt in Katerina's room, and uses it to whip her. She and Sergei kill Zinovy and hide his body in the cellar. They plan to marry, but at the wedding festivities a Shabby Peasant (ten) (**4**), looking for more wine in the cellar, finds Zinovy's body. Katerina and Sergei confess their guilt and are arrested. On the road to Siberia, Sergei is attracted to a young convict, Sonyetka (cont) and rejects Katerina (**5**), who pushes the girl into the icy river and then jumps in to her death.

MUSIC (**1**) Aksinya: *Ay, besstýshy, oy, nye, shchipli – O you shameless creatures*; (**2**) Katerina: *Zherebyónok k kobýlke torópitsa – The foal runs after the filly*; (**3**) Boris: *Gribkí vkúsnyye – They're delicious mushrooms*; (**4**) Shabby Peasant: *U menyá bylá kumá – Once a lady friend of mine*; (**5**) Katerina: *V lesú, v sámoy, cháshche yest' ózero – In the wood, right in a grove, there is a lake.*

would be many years before he again felt secure as a composer. He now had to find the means to survive creatively, a way of placating the authorities by writing "acceptable" music whilst at the same time remaining true to himself. He avoided writing for the stage, and never wrote another opera, continuing instead to compose chamber and orchestral music. He settled in Moscow in 1943, teaching at the Conservatory, but was again attacked for "formalism" in 1948 and relieved of his teaching post. Many of his works of this date were not performed until after Stalin's death when there was a more liberal but limited cultural climate, which included also a limited freedom to travel.

In 1954 Shostakovich's wife died and the following year his mother died. He married again in 1956 but this ended in divorce after three years. He wanted to marry his former pupil, the composer Galina Ustvolskaya (1919–2006), with whom he had had a long-

ABOVE RIGHT **Poster advertising the world première of** *Lady Macbeth of the Mtsensk District*, **at the Maly Theatre, Leningrad, 1934**

Bartók
Béla Bartók
(1881–1945)

WHERE TO START
Duke Bluebeard's Castle

Bartók is often described as Hungary's greatest composer, but perhaps we should add "since Liszt" (1811–86), as he can hardly be ignored. Together with Zoltán Kodály (1882–1967) and Ernö Dohnányi (1877–1960), Bartók is a founder of 20th-century Hungarian music.

Béla Bartók was the elder of two children, his parents being teachers and good amateur musicians who encouraged their son's music education. He started piano lessons with his mother when he was five, at seven was found to have perfect pitch, and by ten had composed his first piece of music. His musical ability rapidly developed and in 1892 he gave his first public piano recital. Despite a lot of childhood illnesses he passed all his school exams and started at the Budapest Academy of Music in 1899. He was able to attend concerts by the Budapest Philharmonic Orchestra and go to the opera.

Bartók claimed that a turning point in his career came in 1902 when he first heard

Strauss's tone-poem *Also sprach Zarathustra* (which achieved popular fame a century later as music for the film *2001: A Space Odyssey*). His style of composition altered as a result of this hearing. Although he was still dissatisfied with his compositions, his prowess as a pianist was remarkable. From 1907 to 1934 he was on the staff of the Budapest (later known as the Liszt) Academy.

Meanwhile Bartók had started to collect folk-songs with the intention of adding piano accompaniments and making them into art-songs. This national music found its way into his work, giving it a more individual voice. In 1909 he married Márta Ziegler, and two years later he dedicated his only opera to her. *Duke Bluebeard's Castle*, with its libretto by Béla Balázs, relied on a declamation of the text based upon the rhythms and inflections of folk-song. Bartók entered it into a competition for one-act operas, but it failed to win and he could not get it staged until 1918. Even then the opera had a mixed reception and it was not produced again in Hungary until 1936. Its popularity has recently increased.

During the 1914–18 war Bartók composed songs and piano pieces and a successful ballet. After the war his compositions approached an atonal phase, but then he visited Italy and some Baroque elements entered his works. In 1939 he decided to emigrate to the USA, where he lived with his second wife, Ditta Pásztory, from 1940. He was unwell for much of the time, leukaemia being diagnosed in 1943. He died in New York in 1945, just before his works achieved popularity after the Second World War.

ABOVE LEFT **Béla Bartók**, photographed shortly before his death from leukaemia in 1945

DUKE BLUEBEARD'S CASTLE
(*A Kékszakállú herceg vára*), 1911
Legendary times: Judith (sop) has married Bluebeard (bar) and returned with him to his gloomy castle (**1**). Leading off the main hall are seven doors (**2**). Judith wants to open them to let in some light. Bluebeard gives her a key. She opens the first door to reveal a torture chamber, its walls covered with blood. Behind the second door is Bluebeard's armoury, also blood-stained. Door number three reveals a treasury of jewels and blood-stained gowns. The fourth door opens on to a garden of red-spotted flowers (**3**). Behind door five is Bluebeard's kingdom, the clouds above bright red. Despite her husband's obvious reluctance, Judith opens the sixth door to reveal a lake of tears. She questions him and realizes he has killed his former wives (**4**). The seventh door swings open of its own accord and the three wives appear (**5**). Bluebeard dresses Judith in a gown, jewels, and a crown (**6**). She follows the other wives through the last door, which shuts behind them. Once again Bluebeard is alone.

> **MUSIC** (**1**) Judith: *Ez a Kékszakállú vára? – Is this really Bluebeard's castle?*; (**2**) Judith: *Nagy csukott ajtókat látok – Ah, I see seven great shut doors*; (**3**) Bluebeard: *Judit, szeress, sohse kérdezz – Judith, love me, ask no questions*; (**4**) Judith: *Tudom, tudom, Kékszakállú – I have guessed your secret, Bluebeard*; (**5**) Bluebeard: *Lásd a régi asszonyokat – Hearts that I have loved and cherished*; (**6**) Bluebeard: *Szép vagy, szép vagy, százszor szép vagy – Thou art lovely, passing lovely.*

ABOVE *Duke Bluebeard's Castle*, Metropolitan Opera, NY, 1989, with Samuel Ramey as Bluebeard and Jessye Norman as Judith

Ravel

Maurice Ravel
(1875–1937)

WHERE TO START
L'heure espagnole
L'enfant et les sortilèges

Ravel was born in the Basque region of
France and had a lifelong affection for all
things Spanish which often invaded his music.
He entered the Paris Conservatoire in 1889.
Ravel's prime influence was his teacher
Gabriel Fauré (1845–1924), but his music
also owes something to early Debussy and
the Russian nationalist composers. He
completed only two operas, both in one act
(which are sometimes staged as a double
bill), and he helped Stravinsky prepare a new
edition of Musorgsky's opera *Khovanshchina*,
which was performed by Diaghilev's Ballets
Russes in 1913. Ravel was very depressed by
the First World War, and even more by the
death of his mother in 1917 – he had never
married and was very close to her. From
1920 his health declined but he managed to
tour Europe and America, the stimulus of the
visits boosting his morale. In 1932 a taxi in
which he was travelling was in a collision in
Paris and, although his injuries were minor, his
health worsened and he became increasingly
incapacitated. In 1937 he was admitted to
hospital for brain surgery but rapidly slipped
into a coma and died a few days later.

L'HEURE ESPAGNOLE
(*Spanish Time*), 1907–9
This "vaudeville set to music", premièred in
Paris in 1911, is a comedy with many *doubles
entendres*, but it never sinks to crudity.
SYNOPSIS 18th-century Toledo: while
the clockmaker Torquemada (ten) is out of
the shop regulating the town's clocks, his wife
Concepción (sop), who is awaiting her lover,
the poet Gonzalve (ten), has to serve the
mule-driver Ramiro (bar) (1). The banker Don
Inigo Gomez (bass) comes to court her (2). To
keep the men separated, she hides Gonzalve
and the fat Gomez inside large clocks and

sends Ramiro up and down stairs carrying the
clocks, admiring his great strength (3). When
Torquemada returns, the men pretend to be
customers. When all the clocks have been
sold, Ramiro promises to call each day,
ostensibly to tell Concepción the time (4).

> **MUSIC** (1) Concepción/Ramiro: *Il reste,
> voilà bien ma chance – Here is my
> opportunity*; (2) Inigo: *Salut à la belle
> horlogère! – Greetings to the lovely clock-
> lady*; (3) Concepción: *Oh! la pitoyable
> aventure! – Oh! the pitiable affair!*;
> (4) Concepción: *Régulier comme un
> chronomètre – As regularly as a clock.*

L'ENFANT ET LES SORTILÈGES
(*The Child and the Spells*), 1920–5
The inanimate objects in this opera are
brought to life by the child's imagination.
SYNOPSIS A naughty Child (mez) (1),
scolded by his Mother (cont), has a temper
tantrum and assaults the Cat (mez), the
furniture, the china, his books, the Clock (bar)
(2), etc. These objects come to life and berate
him, joined by trees he has slashed and wild
animals he has hurt (3). Frightened, the Child
calls for his Mother. An injured Squirrel (mez)
appears and the Child bandages his paw.
Touched by this act of kindness, the animals
join in a chorus (4) and help him call for his
Mother, into whose arms he rushes.

> **MUSIC** (1) Child: *J'ai pas envie de faire
> ma page – I don't want to learn my
> lessons*; (2) Clock: *Ding, ding…Je ne peux
> pas m'arrêter de sonner! – Ding, ding…
> I can't stop myself from chiming!*; (3)
> Chorus: *Ah! C'est l'Enfant au couteaux! –
> Ah! It's the child with the knife!*; (4)
> Chorus/Child: *Il est bon, l'Enfant/Mama! –
> He is good, the Child/Mama!*

ABOVE *L'Enfant et les Sortilèges*, Glyndebourne
1987, with Cynthia Buchan as the Child, Thierry
Dran (Teapot), and Louise Winter (Chinese Cup)

Vaughan Williams

Ralph Vaughan Williams
(1872–1958)

LEFT Ralph Vaughan Williams photographed in his later years

WHERE TO START
Riders to the Sea

WHERE TO GO NEXT
The Pilgrim's Progress

Vaughan Williams deliberately set out to be "an English composer" – whatever that implies – and was responsible with other contemporary composers for the so-called English musical renaissance at the beginning of the 20th century. He was the youngest child of a clergyman in the Gloucestershire village of Down Ampney. His mother was descended from the Darwins and the Wedgwoods. His father died when he was two and his mother took him and his brother and sister back to the family home in Dorking. In 1890 he entered the Royal College of Music, London, and two years later started reading history at Trinity College, Cambridge, but continued his lessons at the RCM. He was awarded Cambridge degrees in both subjects. His first job in 1895 was as organist at St Barnabas, South Lambeth. Two

years later he married Adeline Fisher and they spent an extended honeymoon in Berlin where he was able to see Wagner's *Ring* and to study for three months with the composer Max Bruch (1838–1920).

His earliest compositions were songs and chamber music, and his first success was the song "Linden Lea" of 1901. In 1903 he started to collect folk-songs. He feared that with urbanization they would disappear, and he travelled the country taking down these songs as they were sung to him by local men and women. A year later he was asked to edit the *English Hymnal*. He undertook this work, which took him two years, because he knew that the first music most people heard in those days was in the churches, and he felt that at least it should be good music. By now

his works were being performed, but he was dissatisfied with his progress and felt his music needed "a little French polish", he said in his *Musical Autobiography* (1950). In 1908 he went to Paris to study for three months with Ravel (see p.173). Ravel opened his ears to the new influences of Debussy and the Russian composers. Vaughan Williams absorbed as much as he felt he needed without becoming a clone of his teacher – Ravel described him as "the only one of my pupils who didn't write my music" (*ibid*). When he returned home in March 1908 he seemed to have found his feet as an original composer.

Vaughan Williams was a great believer in music-making with amateurs. In 1905 his sister was paramount in instigating a competitive music festival for the villagers of Leith Hill and she invited her brother to conduct its evening concert and train the choirs. He conducted at every Leith Hill Music Festival from then until 1953, with legendary performances of Bach's *St Matthew Passion*, and his enthusiasm was one of the reasons the festival so successfully established itself. A bronze statue of Vaughan Williams, paid for by public subscription, stands outside the Dorking Halls.

But successful as his choral and orchestral works now were, he was determined to succeed as an opera composer, although there was at that time almost no operatic tradition in Britain and he saw little chance of any opera he wrote being produced in his lifetime. His first opera, *Hugh the Drover* (1910–14), is set in a small market town and includes a boxing match. After the First World War, in which he served in the army, he revised the opera for its first performance in 1924. He wrote a further five operas, including one that occupied him intermittently for 40 years, *The Pilgrim's Progress*, based on John Bunyan's allegory. His earlier one-act opera *The Shepherds of the Delectable Mountains* was incorporated into the larger work, which had its first, rather unsatisfactory, production in London in 1951. It has been

ABOVE *The Pilgrim's Progress*: Richard Whitehouse (Pilgrim, kneeling) watches scenes of depravity at Vanity Fair, produced by Joseph Ward, RNCM, Manchester, 1992

RIGHT *Riders to the Sea*: Maurya (Maria Jagusz) comforts her daughters Cathleen (Elaine Luxton) and Nora (Christine Thompson), RNCM, 1977

criticized as "undramatic", but when seen in a good production, as it was in England and Australia at the end of the 20th century, it is a gripping and impressive theatrical experience.

Sir John in Love (1924–8) is based on Shakespeare's *The Merry Wives of Windsor*. While employed as music director for Sir Frank Benson's Shakespeare company at Stratford-upon-Avon in 1913, Vaughan Williams had arranged the traditional "Greensleeves" for use in *The Merry Wives of Windsor* and in *Richard III*. He now used it in his Falstaff opera, where it is sung by Mistress Ford (and it is from this arrangement that he extracted the popular *Fantasia on "Greensleeves"* in 1934). *The Poisoned Kiss* (1927–9) he described on the score as a "romantic extravaganza with spoken dialogue". It is a comic opera in which all the characters have the names of plants. In 1938 Vaughan Williams first met a young writer and poet after she sent him a scenario for a ballet. She was Ursula Wood, who became very important in his personal life, and as a collaborator in his work. They married in 1953 when he was 80 years old, Adeline having died in 1951. In 1956–7 Ursula Vaughan Williams provided new spoken dialogue for *The Poisoned Kiss*, which strengthened that aspect of it; but delightful though the music is, the libretto is weak and the humour somewhat obvious, and this has mitigated against it.

The opera of Vaughan Williams that has had fairly regular productions is the one-act *Riders to the Sea*, for which the libretto is almost a verbatim setting of J M Synge's 1902 play of the same name. It deals with the life of fisherfolk on the Isle of Arran and is a depressing story. Nevertheless it is one of his important works, with the main character well-developed. The short cast list makes it attractive for smaller opera companies.

On the day he died in 1958, at the great age of 85, Vaughan Williams was working on his seventh opera, *Thomas the Rhymer*. His ashes were interred in Westminster Abbey.

RIDERS TO THE SEA, 1925–32

This short one-act opera was given its first performance in 1937 by students at the Royal College of Music, London. It has since had many productions in England and the USA. Vaughan Williams was always inspired by the subject of man against nature and his music for this opera is strong and evocative.

SYNOPSIS Early 20th century, a village on Arran, an island off the west coast of Ireland: Nora (sop) is shown clothes belonging to a man who has drowned, and she recognizes them as belonging to her brother Michael. She and her sister Cathleen (sop) (1) hide the clothes from their mother Maurya (cont), who has already lost her husband and four sons at sea. Only one son, Bartley (bar), is still alive and he is about to catch a boat across the bay to take horses to be sold at Galway Fair (2). His sisters and mother try to persuade him

not to go, but he is insistent. His mother takes food to him for the journey. When she returns she is distressed and tells her daughters that she has seen Bartley riding to the sea with Michael riding behind him (3). The girls tell her that Michael is dead and she realizes that what she saw was a vision, and that Bartley will also drown (4). Bartley's body is carried in – he has fallen off his horse and drowned. Maurya is almost relieved that the sea cannot hurt her any more (5).

> **MUSIC** (Much of the music is conversational, and these are entry points) (1) Nora/Cathleen: *Where is she now?/She's lying down*; (2) Bartley: *Where is the bit of new rope, Cathleen?*; (3) Maurya: *I've seen the fearfullest thing…* (4) Maurya: *Bartley will be lost now*; (5) Maurya: *They are all gone now.*

Walton

William Walton
(1902–83)

WHERE TO START
The Bear

WHERE TO GO NEXT
Troilus and Cressida

Walton was the second of four children of a choirmaster and organist in Oldham, Lancashire. William's musical talent was obvious from an early age and when he was ten his father saw an advertisement for choral scholarships at Christ Church, Oxford. Mrs Walton took her son for an audition. He was accepted and left Oldham for Oxford, an enormous upheaval for a young boy from the industrial north. He stayed there for the next six years, starting to compose when he was 13. In 1919 Sacheverell and Osbert Sitwell were so convinced that Walton was a musical genius that he was taken to live with the Sitwell family in London for the next 15 years. They introduced him to their artistic friends and took him for his first visit to Italy. In 1921 he began composing *Façade*, "an entertainment" to poems by Edith Sitwell, which had its first performance in 1922.

The overture *Portsmouth Point* (1925) was the first of a series of works which were performed with considerable success and from then until the start of the Second World War in 1939 Walton was Britain's foremost composer. At the time of composition of his First Symphony (1931–5) he met Viscount Wimborne and his wife Alice. She was 22 years older than Walton, but their relationship developed and lasted until her death in 1948. During the war years he composed works for Sadler's Wells Ballet and he was exempted from military service to write music for films considered to be of national importance. These included George Bernard Shaw's *Major Barbara* (1941) and *The First of the Few* (1942), the story of R J Mitchell's designing of the Spitfire aeroplane. He also composed the music for three Shakespeare films directed by

LEFT Susana and William Walton at their home in Ischia in the 1960s

Laurence Olivier, *Henry V* (1944), *Hamlet* (1947), and *Richard III* (1955), the music for *Henry V* being among the greatest scores written for the cinema.

Walton first considered composing an opera in 1941, but it was another six years before a commission from the BBC led to the composition of *Troilus and Cressida*, based not on Shakespeare but on Chaucer. All his life Walton's creativity was spurred on by the success of others, and the stimulus for the composition of this opera was the success of Britten's *Peter Grimes* in 1945 (see pp.181–2). The first performance of *Troilus and Cressida* was at Covent Garden in 1954.

At the suggestion of Peter Pears, Walton was commissioned to write a one-act opera for the 1967 Aldeburgh Festival, which had

been established in 1948 by Benjamin Britten. Walton based *The Bear* on a Chekhov vaudeville and it was a success from the start. One of opera's fascinating "might-have-beens" was the suggestion, not taken up, that Walton compose an opera on Wilde's *The Importance of Being Earnest*.

After the death of Alice Wimborne in 1948, Walton threw himself into his work, including a revision of his highly successful choral work *Belshazzar's Feast*. He then went to Buenos Aires as a delegate to a conference of the Performing Right Society at which it was hoped to persuade Argentina to sign the Berne Convention on copyright. At the conference he met for the first time Señorita Susana Gil Passo, and three weeks later they were engaged. She was 24 years younger than Walton. They married and travelled to Britain in January 1949, but then settled in Italy, in Forio on the island of Ischia in the Bay of Naples, and there they built their home and cultivated the garden. They made regular visits to England, but Ischia remained their home until Walton's death in 1983. There he was

ABOVE Opera North's 1995 production of *Troilus and Cressida*, with Alan Opie as Diomede and Judith Howarth as Cressida

THE BEAR, 1965–7

The Bear, based on a "vaudeville" by the Russian writer Anton Chekhov (1860–1904), is in one act and has a libretto devised by the composer and Paul Dehn (1912–76), a writer and librettist he had met in Ischia and liked. The opera is wonderfully witty and the score contains parodies of Puccini, Strauss, Britten, Offenbach, and others. *The Bear* recaptures some of the carefree light-heartedness of *Façade*, written when he was only 19.

SYNOPSIS Russia, 1888: attractive Madame Popova (mez), a widow, has sworn that she will mourn her husband for the rest of her life. She is cared for by her servant Luka (bass), who urges her to start life afresh (1). He knows her husband was unfaithful and did not deserve her loyalty to his memory. A visitor calls. He is Grigory Smirnov (bar), a huge bear of a man, a landowner to whom her late husband owed money for the oats he purchased for their horse, Toby (2). He demands immediate payment. Popova tells him she is unable to pay immediately and he becomes quite aggressive (3). She accuses him of rudeness (4). Gradually he is attracted to this spirited young widow (5), who admits her husband's infidelities (6). Smirnov challenges her to a duel with pistols to settle their argument. She has no idea how to use a pistol, and as he tries to demonstrate this to her, they realize they have fallen in love.

> **MUSIC** (1) Luka: *It is not just, Madam*;
> (2) Smirnov: *I lent him the sum*;
> (3) Smirnov/Popova: *I need it today, my finances will crash/My bailiff will pay, I haven't the cash*; (4) Popova: *You don't seem to know how to behave*;
> (5) Smirnov: *Madame, je vous pris*;
> (6) Popova: *I was a constant faithful wife.*

able to concentrate on composition without any of the distractions there would have been living in London. He wrote many more works, including the march *Orb and Sceptre* for the Coronation of Queen Elizabeth II in 1953, but he composed no more operas.

TROILUS AND CRESSIDA, 1947–54, rev. 1963, 1972–3

It was always a source of great disappointment to Walton that this opera had such limited success. The libretto by Christopher Hassall (1912–63), a librettist and translator who had written texts for several musicals, has been described as too flowery and diffuse. The score is lovely, but the characters are not sufficiently strong to carry what should be a heroic opera.

SYNOPSIS The Trojan War has lasted ten years. In Troy, the young widow Cressida (sop) knows that her father Calkas (bass) is going to surrender to the Greeks, against the wishes of the Trojan captain Antenor (bar) (1). Troilus (ten), Prince of Troy, defends Calkas's action. Calkas's brother Pandarus (ten) encourages Cressida to respond to Troilus's love (2). She prepares for bed (3). Troilus enters and they spend the night together (4), and as a token of her love she gives him her crimson scarf.

Antenor has been captured by the Greeks. The Greek prince Diomede (ten), who is in love with Cressida, demands that she join her father in Greece in exchange for Antenor. Before she leaves, Troilus gives back to her the scarf as a token of his love and promises to come to her (5). Ten weeks pass with no word from Troilus. Thinking he has deserted her, she agrees to marry Diomede (6). She is unaware that her maid Evadne (mez) has, on Calkas's orders, burnt all Troilus's letters. Troilus and Pandarus arrive at the Greek camp (7). Seeing the crimson scarf on Diomede's helmet, Troilus attacks Diomede, and Calkas stabs and kills Troilus. Diomede demands that Cressida remains in the camp for the pleasure of the Greek soldiers. Rather than submit to this fate, Cressida grabs Troilus's sword and kills herself.

> **MUSIC** (1) Cressida: *Slowly, it all comes back*; (2) Pandarus: *Dear child, you need a little comfort*; (3) Cressida: *At the haunted end of the day*; (4) Troilus: *If one last doubt … remains*; (5) Troilus: *This thing shall be revoked*; (6) Diomede: *This night I shall proclaim it*; (7) Cressida/Troilus: *O Troilus, why did you forget me?/Time and again have I bribed the sentries.*

Tippett

Michael Tippett
(1905–98)

WHERE TO START
The Midsummer Marriage

WHERE TO GO NEXT
King Priam

Tippett composed major works in all genres: orchestral, chamber, instrumental, choral and vocal, and opera. Born in London, his parents (his mother was a suffragette) encouraged him and his brother to be independent in thought and deed. He learned the piano as a child and entered the Royal College of Music, London, in 1923, studied there for five years, and returned in 1930 for two more years. Even as a young man he espoused left-wing politics, studied Jungian psychology, was a conscientious objector (in 1943 he went to prison for breaking the terms of his exemption from the armed services), an avowed agnostic, and a homosexual, and all these characteristics influenced his music. One of his earliest successes, his oratorio *A Child of Our Time* (1939–41), written just after he had undergone dream analysis, is a commentary on the fate of the individual confronted by

totalitarianism, and it movingly uses Negro spirituals as chorales.

By the 1950s Tippett's compositions were gaining ground and he started moving in artistic circles. His music has always caused controversy and divided critical opinion, but undaunted and unperturbed he continued to compose steadily until shortly before his death in 1998.

Tippett's interest in composing opera dates from the 1930s, but he didn't begin his first opera, *The Midsummer Marriage*, until 1946. It was completed in 1952 and had its première at Covent Garden in 1955. He wrote all his own librettos. He wrote four more operas, in which the plots are tenuous and the works are full of symbolism. His aim was to explore the feelings and forces of human nature and to stimulate audiences to explore their own psyche. *King Priam* (1958–61) tells how Priam set in motion the Trojan War. *The Knot Garden* (1966–9) and *The Ice Break* (1973–6) both deal with contemporary questions and confront the issues of man's capacity to love his fellow man. *New Year* (1986–8) contrasts the reality of urban violence with the fantasy of life in a spaceship of the future. Apart from his first opera, the rest have struggled to survive and it is too early to say what their future will be.

THE MIDSUMMER MARRIAGE, 1946–52

Most press reviews of the 1955 première were hostile, mainly directed at the libretto. The music was admired, and by the time of the 1968 Covent Garden production, the opera had become, and has remained, part of the repertoire.

ABOVE LEFT **Michael Tippett** in 1987, the time of composition of his opera *New Year*

SYNOPSIS In a wood at dawn: with their friends, Mark (ten) and his bride Jenifer (sop), daughter of businessman King Fisher (bar), greet the sun on midsummer morning. Dancers emerge, led by Strephon (dancer) and followed by the two Ancients (bass and mez), guardians of the Temple (**1**). Jenifer postpones their wedding to "seek truth" (**2**). Mark goes into a cave and the gates close behind him. King Fisher and his secretary Bella (sop) appeal to the men to help open the gates (**3**). Bella's boyfriend Jack (ten) attempts to do so but desists when a voice (Sosostris) warns him against interfering. Jenifer is dazed by her experiences; Mark sings of earthly passions. Again they part, each to undergo the other's experience. Bella and Jack witness Ritual Dances (**4**), where violent conflict between the sexes is demonstrated, which Bella finds distressing (**5**). King Fisher brings the clairvoyant Sosostris (mez) to sort out the mysteries (**6**). She describes a vision of Mark and Jenifer making love. King Fisher tries to shoot Mark but himself falls dead. As the sun rises, Jenifer accepts Mark's wedding ring (**7**).

> **MUSIC** (**1**) Mark: *I don't know who they really are*; (**2**) Jenifer/Mark: *Today there'll be no wedding/No wedding! Why?*; (**3**) King Fisher: *So you are Mark's fine brood of friends*; (**4**) Orchestra: *Ritual Dances* (some of the best-known music from the opera, heard in the concert-hall as an orchestral suite); (**5**) Jack/Bella: *There Bella, steady/I don't care who they are*; (**6**) Sosostris: *Who hopes to conjure with the world of dreams*; (**7**) Mark/Jenifer: *Jenifer, my darling/O Mark, truth is assumed.*

ABOVE *The Midsummer Marriage* (with John Tomlinson as King Fisher), ROH, London, 1996

Britten

Benjamin Britten
(1913–76)

WHERE TO START
Peter Grimes
Albert Herring

WHERE TO GO NEXT
Billy Budd
A Midsummer Night's Dream

Britten was the first major opera composer born in Britain since Purcell, almost 300 years earlier (see p.33). A new era in British music was born with the production at Sadler's Wells in 1945 of his first opera, *Peter Grimes* (if we exclude *Paul Bunyan*, written for students in the USA in 1941).

The youngest of four children, Edward Benjamin Britten was born in Lowestoft, Suffolk, on 22 November 1913, the Feast Day of St Cecilia, the patron saint of music, so the omens were always good. His father was a dentist and his mother an amateur singer. She gave him his first piano lessons when he was five and he was soon good enough to accompany her. He composed from the age of five and some of the music he wrote when he was ten and eleven found its way into his early published works. In 1923 he started having viola lessons and writing small pieces for strings. When he was ten he went to the 1924 Norwich Festival and heard Frank Bridge (1879–1941) conduct his orchestral suite, *The Sea* (1911). Britten was, in his own words, "knocked sideways".

Bridge was a prolific composer. He followed the developments in music in Europe after the First World War and some of his compositions were influenced by the Second Viennese School (see pp.155–6). Young Britten's viola teacher introduced him to Bridge who took him as a pupil. Bridge's emphasis was on good technique, for which grounding Britten always remained grateful. Bridge took him to concerts and encouraged him to listen to contemporary music such as Stravinsky as well as the classics. As a pacifist, Bridge also influenced Britten's attitude to war.

Britten went to public school in Norfolk in 1928, had piano lessons from the pianist Harold Samuels in London, and continued his lessons with Bridge. His earliest published songs and anthems were written at this time. In 1930 he won a scholarship to the Royal College of Music, London. By now he was attending concerts in London and hearing works by anyone from Mozart to Mahler and he also developed an interest in Purcell and the English madrigalists. His own works were being performed by fellow students at the RCM. He was bitterly disappointed to be refused permission by the College to go abroad to study with Alban Berg in Vienna.

In 1935 Britten met the poet W H Auden (1907–73) and collaborated with him on two short films, *Coal Face* and *Night Mail*, which became classics of their kind. Britten's works were being performed professionally and broadcast, and in 1936 he signed a contract with the publishers Boosey & Hawkes, giving him financial security.

In 1937 he met the tenor Peter Pears. They remained personal and professional partners for the rest of Britten's life. Many of Britten's works were written with his voice in mind and all Britten's operas had major roles for Pears. They settled in a converted windmill in Snape, just outside Aldeburgh, the following year. In early 1939 they sailed for the USA, remaining there for the next three years, during which he composed his first opera, *Paul Bunyan*, for the students at Columbia University, New York, with Auden as librettist. It was for many years regarded as a "musical" suitable only for students, but recent professional productions have shown it to be a well-constructed and delightful work.

Back in England, Britten started work in 1943 on the opera *Peter Grimes*. The idea had taken root in the USA in 1941. He read an article about the poem *The Borough* by George Crabbe. Pears located a copy of the poem and Britten at once saw its possibilities as an opera libretto. The story of the fisherman Grimes, an outsider in society, appealed to Britten, the conscientious objector and homosexual (homosexuality was a serious crime in Britain until 1967). He asked the playwright Montagu Slater to prepare a libretto but it was not an easy collaboration and many alterations were made by the director Eric Crozier during rehearsals. The first night of *Peter Grimes*, 7 June 1945, has passed into operatic history. The opera was a triumph with the critics and the public and was launched on its international path.

In 1947 Britten, Pears, Crozier, and the soprano Joan Cross formed the English Opera Group (EOG) for the performance of new works with the least possible expense. This implied chamber operas, which did not require a large orchestra or chorus. For this group Britten had composed *The Rape of Lucretia*, which had its première at Glyndebourne on 12 July 1946. Two casts alternated at the performances, the title-role being shared by Kathleen Ferrier and Nancy Evans.

Albert Herring was also composed for the EOG to perform at Glyndebourne, and uses the same small orchestral forces, but in this opera the instruments produce a very different sound-world from that in *The Rape*

ABOVE **Benjamin Britten (later Lord Britten of Aldeburgh) on the seashore at Aldeburgh in 1964 – shades of *Peter Grimes***

BELOW Snape Maltings Concert Hall, near
Aldeburgh, converted in 1967 from a
19th-century malthouse

of Lucretia. Eric Crozier wrote the libretto. All the characters in the opera are affectionately parodied and it makes one wish Britten had written more comedy. Not that this was always the feeling. On the opening night, 20 June 1947, John Christie, Glyndebourne's owner, glumly greeted his guests with "This isn't really our sort of thing, you know". Well, it became their sort of thing: a production by Peter Hall for Glyndebourne in 1985 was a total triumph and has remained in their repertory ever since.

In 1948 Britten founded the Aldeburgh Festival and the first opera he wrote for it was *The Little Sweep*, a children's opera, composed in 1949. It forms the second half of an evening which begins with *Let's Make an Opera!*, a play with music in which adults and children prepare to perform an opera they have written. The second half is the opera, which includes choruses involving the audience. It is a wonderful introduction to opera for children.

Britten suggested Herman Melville's 1891 story *Billy Budd* as an operatic subject to Eric Crozier and the writer E M Forster (1879–1970), whose 1941 essay on Crabbe had been instrumental in Britten's choice of *Peter Grimes* for his first triumph. Forster and

Crozier wrote the libretto. It underwent many revisions before the composer was satisfied and he started to compose the music in 1950. Britten originally planned the opera in two acts, but changed this to four acts. This caused too many interruptions to the flow of the action and he revised it to two acts in 1960, which is how it is usually performed. In its scale and content, with the public and the private lives of the characters juxtaposed, it is Britten's Verdian opera. It was not an unqualified success at its first performance at Covent Garden, London, in 1951, but now many would rate it his greatest opera.

King George VI died in February 1952 and his daughter became Queen Elizabeth II. Her cousin the Earl of Harewood (later to be managing director of English National Opera and director of the Edinburgh Festival) suggested to Britten that he write an opera to celebrate the young Queen's coronation the following year. As a subject Harewood suggested the relationship between Queen Elizabeth I and the Earl of Essex. *Gloriana* had its first performance on 8 June 1953 at Covent Garden in the presence of the newly crowned Queen and an invited audience. It was coolly received, the majority of the gala

audience being new to opera of any kind, never mind contemporary opera. And it was criticized as being disrespectful, showing the first Queen Elizabeth as an all-too-vulnerable woman. Later performances in the run had a better reception.

The artist John Piper and his wife Myfanwy were close friends of Britten from 1935. Piper designed the sets for several Britten operas. It was Myfanwy who gave the composer the idea for his next opera. She suggested Henry James's ghost story *The Turn of the Screw* (1898), and the theme of innocence corrupted appealed to Britten. Myfanwy Piper wrote the libretto and Britten made the decision to give the two ghosts – who do not speak in the novel – lines to sing. He felt this was essential for dramatic credibility. It has 15 short scenes linked by interludes and it is scored for chamber orchestra.

Britten's next large-scale opera was *A Midsummer Night's Dream*, the libretto very cleverly adapted from Shakespeare by the composer and Pears for the 1960 Aldeburgh Festival. Each level of characters – lovers, fairies, and rustics – has its own sound-world, given a distinctive timbre by the use of certain instruments. The poetry is beautiful, the music enchanting, evocative, and lyrical. The whole effect is magical; Britten's Shakespeare opera ranks with the best.

Owen Wingrave, another Myfanwy Piper libretto based on Henry James, has never gained the praise nor achieved the popularity of *The Turn of the Screw* and, in my opinion, neither should it. It was written for BBC Television and first relayed in May 1971. Although Britten wrote it for television, he surely intended it as a stage work. It deals with one of his favourite themes, pacifism, in a family with a long military tradition. The pacifist Owen, the last of the Wingraves, is accused by his family of being a coward, and to prove them wrong he volunteers to be locked in a haunted room for the night. When his fiancée goes to him the next morning, he is dead. It

RIGHT Anthony Rolfe Johnson as Grimes and Sam Reed as his apprentice, John, Savonlinna Festival, Finland, 1998

works better in a smaller house, as it did at Glyndebourne, rather than on a large stage such as Covent Garden. No Britten opera can be wholly dismissed, and it has its champions.

Britten's last opera *Death in Venice*, was composed whilst he was ill with heart disease. Myfanwy Piper wrote the libretto, after the 1911 novella by Thomas Mann, and Britten started work on the music in early 1971. In late 1972 he was told he needed an operation to replace a damaged heart valve. He insisted he be allowed to finish the opera first. He wanted to complete it as a tribute to Pears who would sing the main role. He finished the opera in March 1973 and in May he had the operation, during which he had a slight stroke. He was unable to supervise rehearsals or to attend the first performance at the Snape Maltings in June that year. He saw it at Covent Garden later that year and again when it was revived at both Aldeburgh and Covent Garden in 1975.

Britten's never fully recovered from the effects of his operation. His right arm was partially paralysed which made the physical act of composing, of writing the notes on paper, difficult. He was not well enough to attend any of the national celebrations of his 60th birthday in November 1973. Pears persuaded him to revise *Paul Bunyan* and he heard extracts performed at the 1974 Aldeburgh Festival. That year he wrote his first new work since the operation. By now he had a resident nurse who gave him the confidence to compose again and organized his working hours. He attended some performances of his works, but became increasingly weak and frail and needed to use a wheelchair. In June 1976 he was made a Life Peer in the Queen's Birthday Honours, the first musician to receive such an honour, and took the title Lord Britten of Aldeburgh. He died at The Red House, where Pears and he had lived since 1957, two weeks after his 63rd birthday, and was buried in Aldeburgh Cemetery.

The eight operas that are regularly performed – and not just in England – will be described in more detail.

PETER GRIMES, 1944–5

In 1944 Britten played some of the music for this opera to the soprano Joan Cross who was managing Sadler's Wells Opera on tour during the war. She was immediately anxious to stage it to re-open their theatre in London after the war. There was much opposition from some of the company, who found the modern score unsingable and unplayable. Cross persisted and she and Pears sang the two leading roles at the première on 7 June 1945. It was a critical and public triumph and is probably Britten's most popular opera.

SYNOPSIS The Borough, a small fishing town on the East Coast about 1830: an inquest is held into the death of Grimes's young apprentice. The coroner, Swallow (bass), gives the verdict that he died "in accidental circumstances" (1) but the local people suspect that the fisherman Peter Grimes (ten) caused his death.

Grimes's only friends are the widowed schoolteacher Ellen Orford (sop) and the retired merchant skipper Captain Balstrode (bar). Balstrode and the apothecary Ned Keene (bar) have found him a new apprentice, John (silent role), at the workhouse and Ellen offers to accompany the carrier Hobson (bass) to fetch the boy, reprimanding those who criticize her for helping Grimes (2). Grimes explains to Balstrode that he wants to make enough money to marry Ellen. In the local inn, The Boar, run by Auntie (cont) and her two "Nieces" (two sop), Mrs Sedley (cont), the town gossip, is meeting Keene to collect her sedative tablets. Outside a storm is raging and tempers are frayed. Balstrode tries to calm everybody (3). Grimes arrives (4) and Balstrode has to deter the drunken Methodist Bob Boles (ten) from attacking him. Ned Keene causes a diversion by starting to sing a catch (5). Hobson, Ellen, and John, the new apprentice, arrive; John leaves with Grimes.

ABOVE *Peter Grimes*, Finnish National Opera, 2003, with the tenor Jorma Silvasti in the title-role of the fisherman

RIGHT Sarah Connolly (Lucretia) and Christopher Maltman (Tarquinius) in *The Rape of Lucretia*, ENO, London, 2001, produced by David McVicar

Ellen and John listen to the hymns coming from the church (**6**). She finds a bruise on the boy's neck and the townspeople assume that Grimes is beating him and start a witch-hunt. Only Auntie and the Nieces stay behind with Ellen (**7**). Grimes, in his hut on the cliff, thinks of his future with Ellen. He hears the men, led by the Revd Horace Adams (ten), marching towards his hut. He urges John to hurry so they can set sail, and in his rush John falls down the cliff and is killed.

Swallow is chasing the Nieces (**8**) and Mrs Sedley is gossiping as usual. In despair, Ellen knows that once again the Borough will blame Grimes for the death (**9**). Balstrode helps Grimes push his boat out to sea and, to Ellen's distress, advises him to scuttle it. Next morning, as the fisherfolk gather to go about their business, Swallow reports that a boat was seen sinking.

MUSIC (**1**) Swallow: *Peter Grimes, I here advise you*; (**2**) Ellen: *Let her among you without fault cast the first stone*; (**3**) Balstrode/Chorus: *We live, and let live…*; (**4**) Grimes: *Now the Great Bear and Pleiades*; (**5**) Keene: *Old Joe has gone fishing*; (**6**) Ellen/Chorus: *Glitter of waves, and glitter of sunlight*; (**7**) Nieces/Auntie/ Ellen quartet: *From the gutter…*; (**8**) Swallow/Nieces trio: *Assign your prettiness to me/Together we are safe*; (**9**) Ellen/Grimes: *Peter, we've come to take you home/What harbour shelters peace.*

THE RAPE OF LUCRETIA, 1945–6, rev. 1947

After its successful Glyndebourne première, the English Opera Group took *The Rape of Lucretia* on a disastrous tour of the provinces and to Holland, where it was a financial loss. *Lucretia* took longer to establish itself than most of Britten's operas and it is still not exactly a repertory work, although it is produced more often these days.

SYNOPSIS In or near Rome, 500 BC: the Male (ten) and Female (sop) Choruses sketch in the historical background about Tarquinius Superbus seizing power in Rome (**1**). They are on stage throughout the opera and comment on the Christian aspects of the various relationships – although the events enacted took place 500 years before Christ. Tarquinius (bar), son of the above, is in the army camp outside Rome discussing women with his fellow officers Collatinus (bass) and Junius (bar). Six generals have ridden back to Rome to spy on their wives. They report that only Lucretia, wife of Collatinus, has been faithful. The unmarried Tarquinius is determined to prove that Lucretia can also be tempted. His ride to Rome is described by the Male Chorus (**2**).

Lucretia (cont) and her companions Bianca (mez) and Lucia (sop) are at home. They fold the linen and prepare for bed. Tarquinius arrives, claiming his horse is lame. Lucretia offers him a bed for the night and shows him to his room. During the night he goes to Lucretia's room and approaches the bed where she is sleeping (**3**). When he kisses her she wakes and refuses him (**4**). He threatens her with his sword and rapes her (**5**). The next morning the servants, arranging the flowers (**6**), discuss how they heard Tarquinius ride away at dawn. Lucretia appears, almost in a trance. She sends a flower to Collatinus and makes the others into a wreath (**7**). Collatinus returns home with Junius, to find the distraught Lucretia dressed in mourning (**8**). She tells him what happened. Collatinus forgives her, but Lucretia's feeling of guilt is such that she stabs herself to death. The Male and Female Chorus invoke the Christian ethic: Christ is all (**9**).

MUSIC (**1**) Male Chorus: *Rome is now ruled by the Etruscan upstart*; (**2**) Male Chorus: *Tarquinius does not wait*; (**3**) Male Chorus: *When Tarquinius desires, then Tarquinius will dare*; (**4**) Lucretia: *Oh my beloved Collatinus*; (**5**) Male and Female Chorus together: *Here in this scene you see virtue assailed by sin*; (**6**) Lucia/Bianca: *Oh! What a lovely day!*; (**7**) Lucretia: *Flowers bring to every year the same perfection*; (**8**) Collatinus: *Never again must we two dare to part*; (**9**) Male/Female Chorus: *Is all this suffering and pain.*

ALBERT HERRING, 1946–7

Britten had composed the tragic side of life in a fishing community at the beginning of the 19th century. Now he wanted to show its lighter side and he set this opera in the imaginary Suffolk town of Loxford. It used to be said that it was too parochial to travel easily. However, it has been performed in translation in several European countries with great success.

RIGHT For the 1951 world première of *Billy Budd* at the ROH, London, the American Theodor Uppman sang the title-role and Inia Te Wiata was Dansker

SYNOPSIS In a small market town in East Suffolk about 1900, a meeting is being held in the house of the *grande dame* of the town, Lady Billows (sop), to elect a new May Queen. Her ladyship has given a prize of 25 sovereigns. Florence Pike (cont), her housekeeper, gets the room ready for the committee: Supt Budd (bass), Mr Gedge the vicar (bar), the schoolteacher Miss Wordsworth (sop), and Mr Upfold, the Mayor (ten). Lady Billows opens the discussion (1). All the girls nominated are vetoed by Florence Pike on the grounds of some form of immorality. In desperation Supt Budd proposes they have a King of the May, and suggests Albert Herring (ten), son of Mrs Herring (mez), the greengrocer. He is under his mother's thumb and his reputation is unsullied (2). All agree he should be asked.

In the Herrings' shop, the baker's daughter Nancy (mez) and her boyfriend, the butcher's assistant, Sid (bar), tease Albert about being tied to his mother's apron strings and missing all the fun. Sid arranges to meet Nancy later (3). Albert is horrified when Lady Billows and her party arrive and tell him he is to be May King, but with a prize of 25 sovereigns, Mrs Herring insists he

agrees. At the crowning ceremony, Sid spikes Albert's lemonade with rum and gradually Albert becomes tipsy. Lady Billows makes her speech (4). That night Albert arrives home still drunk (5). He decides it is time to sow some wild oats and sets off for the town (6). He hasn't returned the next morning and Mrs Herring calls the police. His crushed May King hat is found and he is presumed dead. The villagers call to express their condolences. They sing a threnody or lament (7), during which Albert walks in. He has spent some of his prize money in a pub, has been with girls, and has had a wonderful time (8). He has also seen another way of life and will no longer be his mother's obedient son.

> **MUSIC** (1) Lady Billows: *Now then, notebook, Florence!*; (2) Budd: *Albert's clean as new-mown hay*; (3) Sid/Nancy duet: *We'll walk to the spinney…*; (4) Lady Billows: *I'm full of happiness to be here in your midst*; (5) Albert: *Albert the Good! Long may he reign*; (6) Albert: *Heaven helps those who help themselves*; (7) Ensemble: *In the midst of life is death*; (8) Albert: *I can't remember everything.*

BILLY BUDD, 1950–1, rev. 1960

An all-male cast (with the then unknown American baritone Theodor Uppman in the title-role), and no romantic interest, were some of the factors which mitigated against *Billy Budd*'s popularity with early audiences. Although several critics appreciated its worth from the beginning, it was not really a success with the public for over 20 years. An outstanding production by Michael Geliot in 1972 for Welsh National Opera put the opera on the international map, where it still resides.

SYNOPSIS On board the *Indomitable* during the French Wars. In a short Prologue, Captain Vere (ten), now an old man, thinks back over his career and especially of the summer of 1797 (1): a boat approaches Vere's ship, returning from a press-ganging operation to find more crew members. The new recruits are questioned by the iniquitous Master-at-Arms, John Claggart (bass). They include the young seaman Billy Budd (bar) who, when he's nervous, has a stammer. He is pleased to be placed in the foretop (2). He leads a chorus of praise for the captain, Starry Vere. A young corporal, Squeak (ten), is used by Claggart to spy on Budd. An old seaman, Dansker (bass), warns Billy to beware of Claggart. Billy finds Squeak apparently stealing from his kit-bag, and a fight breaks out. Left alone, Claggart vents forth his wrath about Billy, threatening to destroy him (3). He goes to see Vere, who

ABOVE *Albert Herring*, Glyndebourne, 1985: Rev. Gedge (Derek Hammond Stroud), Florence Pike (Felicity Palmer), Albert (John Graham Hall), Lady Billows (Patricia Johnson), Mayor Upfold (Alexander Oliver), Mrs Herring (Patricia Kern), Supt. Budd (Richard Van Allan), Miss Wordsworth (Elizabeth Gale)

is busy sending the crew to their action stations to fight the approaching French **(4)**. Claggart tells Vere his worry that Billy is going to rouse the men to mutiny. Vere, in Claggart's presence, questions Billy **(5)**, who is so nervous that he stammers and is unable to explain his thoughts. In sheer frustration he strikes out at Claggart, who falls down dead. Vere knows in his heart that this was an accident, but he feels obliged to court-martial Billy, who is sentenced to death by hanging from the yard-arm. As he awaits his punishment **(6)**, Dansker brings him food and a drink. The men threaten to mutiny on his behalf, and he pleads with them not to do so. The crew assembles to watch Billy's execution. His last words are in praise of Vere: "Starry Vere, God bless you!" But the Captain knows he could have saved Billy. As an old man, he laments his own inaction **(7)**.

> **MUSIC (1)** Vere: *I am an old man…*; **(2)** Billy: *Billy Budd, king of the birds!*; **(3)** Claggart: *Oh beauty, oh handsomeness, goodness!*; **(4)** Chorus of sailors: *This is our moment*; **(5)** Vere: *Master-at-Arms and foretopman…*; **(6)** Billy: *Look! Through the port comes the moon-shine astray!*; **(7)** Vere: *…I was lost on the infinite sea…*

GLORIANA, 1952–3

Written to celebrate the Coronation in 1953 of Queen Elizabeth II, *Gloriana* took a long time to reach the general public and until the 1990s was the only one of Britten's operas not to have been recorded. Rather than "scenes", the action takes place in a series of tableaux. It is slowly gaining ground and has been shown to be considerably more than an *opéra d'occasion*.

SYNOPSIS Late 16th-century England, towards the end of the reign of Queen Elizabeth I: the Earl of Essex (ten) urges Queen Elizabeth ("Gloriana") (sop) to send him as Viceroy to Ireland **(1)**. The Queen visits Norwich, attended by Essex, Sir Robert Cecil

BELOW **A majestic Josephine Barstow as Queen Elizabeth I in** *Gloriana*, **Opera North, 1993, produced by Phyllida Lloyd**

(bar), and Lord Mountjoy (bar), who resent the influence Sir Walter Raleigh (bass) has on the Queen. They watch a Masque (2). Mountjoy's lover is Essex's sister Penelope, Lady Rich (mez). Together with Essex and his wife Frances (mez), Mountjoy and Penelope plan who will succeed the Queen when she dies (3). At a ball in the Palace of Whitehall, the Queen deliberately humiliates Frances, who wears a beautiful gown. The Queen orders all the ladies to change their gowns and herself reappears wearing Lady Essex's dress, which does not fit her (4). Frances is comforted by the others (5). The Queen now appoints Essex to the post he wanted (6), but he fails in his campaign in Ireland. On his return, he bursts unannounced into the Queen's apartment (7) while she is wigless and being dressed. He tries to persuade the citizens of London to rebel, while a Blind Ballad Singer (bass) reports all these happenings to the people in the street (8). Essex is declared a traitor for inciting the people to rebel and is condemned to death. His sister Lady Rich appeals to the Queen to save him (9), but angered by Penelope's attitude to her, the Queen signs his death warrant and proclaims her justification (10).

MUSIC (1) Essex/Queen: *I am the man to conquer Tyrone/On rivalries 'tis safe for kings to base their power*; (2) Chorus of Masquers: *Melt earth to sea, sea flow to air*; (3) Essex/Frances/Mountjoy/Penelope quartet: *On my own ground, with my own voice*; (4) Queen: *Well, ladies, how like you my new-fancied suit?*; (5) Essex/Mountjoy/Penelope trio: *Good Frances, do not weep*; (6) Elizabeth: *My Lord of Essex…* (7) Essex: *Is the Queen up?*; (8) Blind Ballad Singer: *To bind by force, to bolt with bars*; (9) Penelope: *The noble Earl of Essex was born to fame and fortune*; (10) Queen (spoken): *I have ever used to set the last Judgment Day before mine eyes…*

THE TURN OF THE SCREW, 1954

One could justify labelling this as Britten's greatest opera – certainly musically it is the most ingeniously constructed. The Prologue and 15 scenes are linked by 16 interludes that consist of a theme and 15 variations. The part of the Governess is one of Britten's best female roles. The opera was commissioned by the Venice Biennale for 1954 and had its first performance at La Fenice, given by the EOG with the composer conducting.

SYNOPSIS A country house, Bly, mid-19th century: in a short Prologue, a male Narrator (ten) tells how the Governess came to be at Bly (1). The Governess (sop) arrives by coach (2). She has been employed to teach two orphaned children, Flora (sop) and Miles (treble), who are being looked after by the housekeeper Mrs Grose (sop). The Governess has been engaged by the children's guardian, who she must never contact. Mrs Grose and the children anxiously await her arrival and greet her (3). A letter from his school says that Miles has been expelled. In the garden one evening, the Governess sees a man on the tower (4), and later sees him looking through a window. She describes him to Mrs Grose who recognizes him as Peter Quint (ten), the master's former valet. He had a relationship with the children's governess, Miss Jessel (sop), who became pregnant. Miss Jessel died and Quint slipped on an icy road and also died. The Governess realizes that the children, too, can see these ghosts. She gives Miles a Latin lesson (5). The ghosts meet and talk to each other (6). When they vanish, the Governess is frightened of their evil (7). She later sees Miss Jessel in the schoolroom (8). The Governess knows the ghosts are an evil influence on the children, and despite her promise never to trouble him, she writes to their guardian (9). Quint forces Miles to steal the letter which is waiting to be posted (10). Mrs Grose decides to leave and take Flora away with her. The Governess stays behind with Miles (11), determined to defeat Quint's influence on the child. She forces Miles to tell her who it was that

made him steal the letter. As he screams Quint's name, he collapses in the Governess's arms and she realizes that he is dead.

MUSIC (1) Narrator: *It is a curious story*; (2) Governess: *Nearly there. Very soon I shall know what's in store for me*; (3) Mrs Grose: *I'm so happy that you've come, Miss*; (4) Governess: *How beautiful it is… Who is it, who?*; (5) Miles: *Malo… I would rather be…*; (6) Quint/Miss Jessel: *The ceremony of innocence is drowned*; (7) Governess: *Lost in my labyrinth*; (8) Miss Jessel: *Here my tragedy began, here revenge begins*; (9) Governess: *Sir, dear sir, my dear sir…*; (10) Quint: *So! She has written… Easy to take!*; (11) Governess: *All the same, go, and I shall stay.*

A MIDSUMMER NIGHT'S DREAM, 1959–60

The casting of a countertenor as Oberon was inspired, the other-worldly sound of the voice at times becoming quite sinister. Puck is a spoken role, best when acted by a talented and athletic child. The rustics' *Pyramus and Thisbe* play is comic opera of the highest order, and invites the listener to "spot the tunes" in its parodies of Italian opera.

SYNOPSIS Oberon (counterten), King of the Fairies, has quarrelled with his Queen, Tytania (sop), and is plotting revenge. He sends his messenger Puck (boy acrobat/actor, spoken) to collect a magic herb (1) which, if its juice is squeezed into the eyes of Tytania, will make her fall in love with the next person she sees. Hermia (mez) is being forced by her father to marry Demetrius (bar), who loves her, but she is in love with Lysander (ten) and they plan to leave Athens together (2). Helena (sop) is in love with Demetrius, who does not love her (3). Oberon orders Puck to put the herb juice in Demetrius's eyes and to make sure that the next person he sees is Helena (4). The rustics are to perform a play, *Pyramus and Thisbe*, for Theseus, Duke of Athens (bass), and Hippolyta, Queen of the Amazons (cont), to celebrate their marriage. They come to the woods to rehearse. Bottom the weaver (bass-bar) wants to play all the parts. The four lovers have fallen asleep in the woods. Puck finds them (5) and mistakenly puts the herb juice in Lysander's eyes. As soon as Lysander wakes up he declares his love for Helena. So all the lovers are falling in love with the wrong person; Helena and Hermia are having a furious row about it (6), and Oberon orders Puck to sort out the confusion. Tytania arrives with her retinue of fairies (7) and falls asleep. Oberon puts the juice in Tytania's eyes and the first person she sees on waking is Bottom wearing an ass's head. Later Oberon releases Tytania and Bottom from the spell and Bottom joins the other rustics. The four lovers are correctly paired off, Lysander with Hermia

and Demetrius with Helena (8). The rustics prepare to perform (9). Everyone takes their seats in the palace to watch the play, introduced by Quince, a carpenter (bass) (10), after which they all retire. Oberon and Tytania join Puck and the fairies for the final chorus (11), then they too depart, leaving Puck to have the last word (12).

> **MUSIC** (1) Oberon: *My gentle Puck come hither*; (2) Lysander/Hermia duet: *How now my love?/Belike for want of rain*; (3) Demetrius/Helena: *I love thee not, therefore pursue me not/ You draw me, you hard-hearted adamant*; (4) Oberon: *I know a bank where the wild thyme blows*; (5) Puck: *Through the forest have I gone*; (6) Helen/Hermia: *Fie, fie, you counterfeit, you puppet, you/Puppet? Why so?*; (7) Fairies: *You spotted snakes with double tongue*; (8) Helena/ Demetrius/Hermia/Lysander quartet: *And I have found Demetrius/fair Helena/Lysander/sweet Hermia like a jewel*; (9) Bottom: *…I have had a dream…*; (10) Quince: *Gentles, perchance you wonder at this show*; (11) Oberon/Tytania/Fairies: *Now until the break of day*; (12) Puck: *If we shadows have offended…*

DEATH IN VENICE, 1971–3, rev. 1973 and 1974

Britten had for some time had the idea of an opera based on Thomas Mann's *Death in Venice* and in late 1970 he asked Myfanwy Piper to write a libretto. The leading tenor role of Aschenbach is a long and arduous part, and the bass-baritone, who sings seven roles, each with its own character, does not have an easy time either. These parts were sung respectively by Peter Pears and John Shirley-Quirk at the première on 16 June 1973 at Snape Maltings near Aldeburgh. The unearthly Voice of Apollo is sung by a countertenor and the cast also includes non-speaking parts played by dancers as well as the silent role of the boy Tadzio.

SYNOPSIS Munich and Venice, 1911: the writer Gustav von Aschenbach (ten) has a creative block (1). In a cemetery he meets the Traveller (bass-bar) who suggests he travel south (2). Aschenbach decides to go to Venice where it will be sunny. On the boat he meets an Elderly Fop (bass-bar), who joins with the youths on board singing of Serenissima (3). An Old Gondolier (bass-bar) rows him to his hotel on the Lido and then disappears (4). He is shown to his room by the Hotel Manager (bass-bar) (5). He watches guests of all nationalities arriving for dinner and is attracted to a beautiful young boy, Tadzio (silent), the son of a Polish family (6). Aschenbach sees the boy again playing games with his friends on the beach. He plans to leave the hotel, but changes his mind (7). He sits on the beach watching Tadzio play. He hears the Voice of Apollo (8). Achenbach wants to speak to Tadzio, but can't pluck up the nerve to do so. When the boys have all left and he is alone, he admits to himself that he loves the boy. The Hotel Barber (bass-bar) tells Aschenbach that there is cholera in Venice (9) and everyone is advised to leave. Many guests have gone. Aschenbach returns to sit on the beach watching the boys' games. He calls out to Tadzio. Tadzio beckons to him, but there is no response. Aschenbach is dead in his chair.

LEFT One of the supreme interpreters of
Aschenbach, Philip Langridge, in Opera Australia's
2005 production of *Death in Venice*

MUSIC (1) Aschenbach: *My mind beats
on and no words come*; (2) Traveller:
Marvels unfold! … Go, travel to the South;
(3) Elderly Fop: *We'll meet in the piazza*;
(4) Aschenbach: *Mysterious gondola…*;
(5) Hotel Manager: *We are delighted to
greet the Signore*; (6) Aschenbach: *Surely
the soul of Greece lies in that bright
perfection*; (7) Aschenbach: *That's what
made it hard to leave*; (8) Voice of
Apollo: *He who loves beauty worships
me*; (9) Hotel Barber: *Guardate, Signore!
Va bene, Signore?*

Other operas of note

In addition to the operas discussed, in 1957
Britten composed the wholly enchanting
Noye's Fludde (*Noah's Flood*), a one-act
Chester Miracle Play. It was conceived with
children and amateurs in mind and does not
need elaborate staging. Performances in
churches and school halls are ideal. Britten felt
that the more animals that go into the ark
two-by-two the better, giving plenty of scope
for children to be involved both in making
their own animal costumes and taking part
in the work. Adults take the roles of God
(spoken), Noah (bass-bar), and Mrs Noah
(cont), and their sons and daughters-in-law
are played by older children. There are three
hymns that punctuate the action for the

audience or "congregation" to sing and the
whole experience is charming and uplifting.

The three Church Parables were written
especially for churches and had their first
performances in Orford Church, Suffolk,
during Aldeburgh Festivals. Britten wrote
the first of them after a visit to Tokyo in
1958 where he saw the Japanese Noh-play
Sumidagawa (*The Sumida River*) by Juro
Motomasa (1395–1431). He was especially
impressed by the stylized method of
performance, the slow and deliberate action,
and the mixture of chant, speech, and song.
He transferred the scene to his local Suffolk
area, and composed music that grows out of
the plainsong chanted by the monks as they
walk through the church to take their places,
don their robes, and begin the play they are
to present. At the end, they walk back to their
original places in the church.

In *Curlew River* (1964) the part of the
Madwoman who searches for her lost child is
written for a tenor and was originally sung by
Peter Pears. The Madwoman persuades the
Ferryman to take her across the river. He tells
of a boy from near the Black Mountains who,
a year ago, was left to die by his kidnapper. His

grave is revered by the locals. It becomes clear
to the Madwoman that the Ferryman is talking
about her child. Grief-stricken, she joins those
praying at the boy's graveside. Suddenly her
son's spirit appears and his voice (a treble)
reassures his mother, whose madness is lifted.

The Burning Fiery Furnace (1966) is much
more colourful, and tells the bible story of
King Nebuchadnezzar (ten) and the three
men Shadrach (bar), Meschach (ten), and
Abednego (bass) chosen to rule in Babylon.
When they refuse to kneel and worship a
golden image, they are thrown into a furnace.
They survive unharmed and the king
acknowledges that their God is the only God.

For *The Prodigal Son* (1968) Britten turned
to the New Testament story. The Younger Son
asks his father for his share of the inheritance,
to the disgust of the Elder Son. The Tempter
takes the Younger Son to the city and
introduces him to gambling dens and the
pleasures of wine and women. The Younger
Son loses all his money. He returns home and
his father forgives him and kills the fatted calf
to welcome him home. The Elder Son's
objections disappear at his father's prompting
and the brothers are reconciled.

ABOVE **Children in their bird and animal masks and
costumes for the Aldeburgh Festival production of
Noye's Fludde in 1958**

Musgrave

Thea Musgrave
(b. 1928)

WHERE TO START
Mary, Queen of Scots

WHERE TO GO NEXT
Harriet, the Woman called Moses

The Scottish composer Thea Musgrave has lived in the United States since the 1970s. The strong sense of drama in all her music makes it not surprising that her large output includes ten operas. Her musical education was at Edinburgh University, the Paris Conservatoire, privately with Nadia Boulanger (1887–1979), the most influential music teacher of the 20th century, and with Aaron Copland in the USA. She returned to London in 1959. She briefly embraced serialism and also occasionally used electronic music. Tape was used in her chamber opera *The Voice of Ariadne* (1972), based on a short story by Henry James. In 1970 Musgrave became a guest professor at the University of California in Santa Barbara and the following year married the American viola player and opera conductor Peter Mark and eventually settled in the United States.

Historical subjects are one of Musgrave's favourite themes. Apart from *A Christmas Carol* (1979), there is *Mary, Queen of Scots*, described below; *Harriet, the Woman Called Moses* (1984), based on the true story of

Harriet Tubman, an escaped slave who in the 1850s helped 300 others escape to Canada; *Simón Bolívar* (1989–93), about the Venezuelan hero who liberated five South American countries from Spanish colonial rule; and *Pontalba* (2003), concerning the 1803 Louisiana Purchase and the forging of the United States.

Thea Musgrave is often asked about being a "woman" composer. Her reply on one occasion was "Yes, I am a woman; and I am a composer. But rarely at the same time".

MARY, QUEEN OF SCOTS, 1976–7

Musgrave covers the seven years from 1561 when Mary, the Catholic widowed Queen of France, returned to rule Scotland, to when she was imprisoned by Queen Elizabeth of England.

SYNOPSIS Mary (sop) is returning to England (**1**). Her half-brother James Stewart, Earl of Moray (bar), has imprisoned the Catholic Cardinal Beaton (bar), who supports Bothwell (ten). Bothwell and James quarrel. At a ball, Bothwell and James are jealous when Mary dances with Lord Darnley (ten) (a cousin of Mary and Elizabeth) (**2**). Bothwell insults Darnley, to whom Mary is attracted, and she banishes him (**3**). Mary marries Darnley and Bothwell leaves the court. The Lords of the Council are unhappy about the appointment of Darnley's friend Riccio (bass-bar) as the Queen's secretary and even more about Darnley himself as her consort. Mary is pregnant. She sends for her brother to placate the Council, but will not yield to his demands for power (**4**). Finally, seeing him for what he is, she condemns him for the death of Beaton and realizes she will have to rule alone (**5**). Darnley, drunk and incited by James's henchmen, murders Riccio. Mary flees and James tries to turn the people against her by accusing her of complicity in Riccio's murder and desertion of her country. Mary reappears, accuses her brother of arranging the murder to discredit Darnley and herself, and banishes him for life (**6**).

Mary's son is born. James raises an army against her and the people follow him. Mary must protect her son (the future James VI of Scotland and James I of England). She asks Bothwell for help (**7**) and in return for his protection, he seduces her. James forces his way into the palace. Darnley's murder is announced. Bothwell is defeated by James's men. At James's urging, the people demand Mary's abdication in favour of her son, accusing her and Bothwell (now her husband) of Darnley's murder. Her son is taken to safety (**8**) and she flees to England where she is imprisoned for the rest of her life. James is murdered and Mary's son is proclaimed King of Scotland.

MUSIC (**1**) Mary: *No-one, and no-one, and no-one*; (**2**) James: *Mary, it is not politic for you to dance so much with Lord Darnley*; (**3**) Bothwell: *Now powerless, I am sent away*; (**4**) Mary/James: *Good evening brother … I need your support/ Foolish sister! I warned you…*; (**5**) Mary: *Alone, alone, I stand alone*; (**6**) Mary: *James, you are guilty of treason … Do not ever return!*; (**7**) Mary: *Bothwell, my Lord, I am glad to welcome you*; (**8**) Mary: *My son, where is my son?*

ABOVE LEFT **Thea Musgrave**, the Scottish composer resident in the USA

ABOVE *Mary, Queen of Scots*, Virginia Opera Association, 1978, with Ashley Putnam (the Queen) and Jake Gardner (James, Earl of Moray)

Birtwistle

Harrison Birtwistle
(b. 1934)

WHERE TO START
Punch and Judy

WHERE TO GO NEXT
Yan Tan Tethera

Born in Accrington, Lancashire, Birtwistle studied at the Royal Manchester College of Music in the early 1950s and formed the New Music Manchester Group with the composers Peter Maxwell Davies and Alexander Goehr, the pianist John Ogdon, and the conductor Elgar Howarth, an exceptional gathering of musical minds. Birtwistle started to play the clarinet when he was seven, his teacher being the local bandmaster. At the RMCM he studied clarinet and composition, but from 1965 concentrated on composition. The Manchester Group were interested in the avant-garde music emerging from the Continent, and this coloured their own music. Birtwistle experimented with serialism and studied the music of Stravinsky and Webern, both of whom left their mark on his compositions.

After he left the Manchester College, Birtwistle spent a year at the Royal Academy of Music, London, and from 1962 to 1965 taught music at a girls' boarding school. While in the United States in 1966 as a visiting fellow

ABOVE **Harrison Birtwistle**, photographed in 2004

at Princeton University for two years, he wrote his first opera, *Punch and Judy*. On a visit home from the USA in 1967, Birtwistle, Maxwell Davies, Stephen Pruslin, and Alan Hacker formed the Pierrot Players to perform small-scale music-theatre.

The première of *Punch and Judy* was at the 1968 Aldeburgh Festival. It caused a sensation. The libretto was a mixture of the traditional children's play and Greek tragedy, and Birtwistle's music combined Baroque opera and Bach Passions. His next theatre piece, a "dramatic pastoral", was the one-act *Down by the Greenwood Side* (1968–9), based on the medieval *Mummers' Play* and *The Ballad of the Cruel Mother*. Like *Punch and Judy*, it contains much violence and cruelty. It concerns the battle between St George and the Black Knight (both spoken roles). The only singer in the piece is Mrs Green (the Cruel Mother), who tells how she murdered her two children "down by the Greenwood Side", the source of the work's title.

Birtwistle's longest and most complicated opera is *The Mask of Orpheus*. Almost ten

years separate the composition of its two part: Acts 1 and 2 were completed in 1973–5; Act 3 and the electronics date from 1981–84. The opera is an extremely complicated and multi-faceted approach to the myth of Orpheus and Euridice, which makes it almost impossible to provide a comprehensible synopsis. At the end, knowing he will not find Euridice, Orpheus hangs himself. It requires huge forces, and the three main characters are each represented by a singer, a dancer, and an actor. Some of the voices, Apollo for instance, are electronically produced. Apollo is present at the birth of Orpheus and gives him the gifts of speech, music, and poetry. These voices were created at IRCAM, the electronic institute in Paris, and use elongated syllables instead of recognizable words.

In 1984 Birtwistle was commissioned to write an opera for television, and the result was *Yan Tan Tethera*, the title coming from an ancient northern numbering system for counting sheep, and meaning "One, Two, Three". This "mechanical pastoral" is about the jealousy and rivalry between two shepherds,

BELOW *Punch and Judy*, premièred at Aldeburgh, 1968, with John Cameron as Punch and Maureen Morelle as Judy

all settled with the help of the counting incantation of the title. It contains some quite lyrical music and is more easily approachable than his other operas.

The first theatre work that the composer called an "opera" was *Gawain*, premièred at Covent Garden, London, in 1991. Birtwistle had always been fascinated by the medieval story of the Green Man. The Green Knight challenges everyone to strike his neck with an axe, and to then receive a similar blow a year later. Gawain, a knight at Arthur's court, accepts the challenge and severs the Green Knight's head. The Knight picks up his head and arranges to meet Gawain a year later. On his long journey to this meeting, Gawain encounters and is helped by Sir Bertilak and Lady de Hautdesert. The latter gives Gawain a girdle to protect his neck, which he conceals

from her husband. When he meets the Green Knight, the blows of the axe fail. The Green Knight reveals himself as Sir Bertilak. Gawain returns to Arthur's court, accepting himself as a coward for having used the protective girdle.

The Second Mrs Kong was first performed by Glyndebourne Touring Opera, at Glyndebourne, in 1994. The chief characters are King Kong and Pearl, from Vermeer's painting *The Head of a Girl with a Pearl Earring*. The opera starts with part of the film of King Kong, although the composer insists it is "the idea of Kong", an archetypical mythical Kong, the "lost and lonely child of all the world". The work varies from serious drama to absolute farce, with many and varied characters. At the end Kong finds Pearl, but has to accept that they can never be united – he is only an "idea".

Birtwistle's "dramatic tableau" *The Last Supper* (1998–9) continues his interest in myth, ritual, and the seasons. Written in English and Latin, it is set in contemporary times. Ghost, representing the modern people, invites Christ to join us for supper. Eleven disciples enter, led by Peter, and reassemble the fragments of the table. Judas brings a red cloth for the table and tries to defend his action of betrayal. He is shouted down. Christ appears, come to wash away the dust of 20 centuries. He leads them all to the table, Judas included. Christ reaffirms a faith of love and he and the disciples walk into the garden. A vision depicts The Betrayal. Christ asks "Whom do you seek?" and a cock crows. The work is gripping, melancholy, poetic, and lyrical.

The latest Birtwistle opera to be performed is *The Io Passion*, premièred at the 2004 Aldeburgh Festival. There are two roles, the Man and the Woman, each played by two singers and an actor. We follow the story of the two characters, who have been lovers in Greece at the site of the Mysteries of Io. The references to ancient myth look set to continue: at the time of writing, Birtwistle is composing an opera, *The Minotaur*, for Covent Garden in 2008.

PUNCH AND JUDY, 1966–7

At the première of this work at the 1968 Aldeburgh Festival, there was a sensation when Britten and Pears left their box well before the opera ended. It was variously described by the critics as offensive and like a baby's tantrum. It is a work of its time, demonstrating Expressionist features, and now that audiences are more used to the idiom and the music does not sound so strange, it is seen to be a powerful piece.

SYNOPSIS In a prologue, Choregos (bar) opens his Punch-and-Judy booth and comments on the action (**1**). Punch (bar) sings a lullaby to his baby, then throws it in the fire (**2**). When Judy (mez) discovers the body and confronts him, Punch stabs her (**3**). He also kills the Doctor (bass) and the Lawyer (ten). He searches for Pretty Polly (sop), but three times she rejects him. He kills Choregos and a nightmare begins, his victims all coming back in disguises to seek revenge. Punch is put in prison to await execution (**4**). The hangman, Jack Ketch, is the disguised Choregos. Punch tricks Ketch into putting his own neck in the noose and hangs him. Killing the hangman earns him redemption and Pretty Polly now returns his love (**5**). Choregos sings an epilogue (**6**).

MUSIC (**1**) Choregos: *Let the tragedy begin*; (**2**) Punch: *Dance, baby diddy, What shall Daddy go widdy?*; (**3**) Punch: *There's an end of her, by goll!*; (**4**) Punch: *Right tol de riddle doll, I'm the boy to do 'em all*; (**5**) Pretty Polly: *Spring has come, shattering the prism*; (**6**) Choregos: *The tale is told, the damage done.*

Maxwell Davies

Peter Maxwell Davies
(b. 1934)

WHERE TO START
The Lighthouse

WHERE TO GO NEXT
Taverner

Maxwell Davies was part of the New Music Manchester Group (known as the Manchester School), with the composers Harrison Birtwistle and Alexander Goehr, the pianist John Ogdon, and the conductor Elgar Howarth, who all studied composition with Richard Hall at the Royal Manchester College of Music (RMCM) in the early 1950s. Peter Maxwell Davies was born in Salford, Lancashire, in 1934 and showed an early talent for music. His parents encouraged this, arranging for him to have piano lessons and taking him from a very young age to see Gilbert and Sullivan operas. His first compositions date from 1942. He was accepted to study music at both the RMCM and Manchester University and between 1953 and 1956 he pursued parallel courses at these two institutions. He was fortunate in being part of a group of talented students who provided stimulus, each helping the others to study the scores of the post-war European composers who were espousing serial techniques. Maxwell Davies composed works for his fellow-students – John Ogdon played his *Five Piano Pieces* and Elgar Howarth his *Trumpet Sonata* at New Music Manchester Group concerts, and Harrison Birtwistle played his *Clarinet Sonata* at one of the Darmstadt summer courses.

The earliest sketches of both the libretto and the music for his first opera, *Taverner*, were made by Maxwell Davies in 1956. Work was then suspended because he was awarded an Italian government scholarship to study for a year with Goffredo Petrassi (1904–2003) in Rome. From 1959 to 1962 Maxwell Davies was director of music at a grammar school, where he emphasized how important it was for students at all levels of ability to perform

some sort of music, a theory to which he has remained faithful, writing short "operas" suitable for children to perform. He then went to Princeton University in the USA for two years and while there completed the first act of *Taverner*. He taught at the University of Adelaide for a year, returning to Britain in 1967 and forming, with Birtwistle, the Pierrot Players, a group of instrumentalists brought together for the purpose of performing small-scale music-theatre. A number of his works composed for these players demonstrate the radical ideas he was expressing at this time in his career, influenced by such works as Schoenberg's *Pierrot Lunaire*, which gave the group its title. The group survived until about 1971 when Maxwell Davies made his home in the Orkney Islands, first in Hoy, later in Sanday, when it was disbanded and reformed under his sole direction as the Fires of London. For the next 15 years most of the works he composed were played by them and conducted by him. He also commissioned works for them and conducted new works by other composers, especially at the St Magnus Festival, which he founded on Orkney in 1977.

Between 1979 and 1984 Maxwell Davies was artistic director of Dartington Summer School and in the late 1980s he established a summer school for student composers on Hoy, near his Orkney home. He was associate

composer/conductor of the Scottish Chamber Orchestra from 1985 for ten years, composing for the orchestra his ten *Strathclyde Concertos*, each for a different instrument, each linked to projects in schools – again following his belief in the importance of everyone performing music at whatever level of competence they are able to achieve. In 2004 he was appointed Master of the Queen's Music.

In 1969 his first venture into music-theatre was the 30-minute piece *Eight Songs for a Mad King*, which had its first performance in London. Composed for a solo singer and six instrumentalists, and based on the supposed mad ravings of King George III, it contains elements of Baroque music juxtaposed with wildly extravagant modern sounds, and it was praised and castigated in equal measure. His first real opera, *Taverner*, took some years to complete. He began it in earnest in 1962, finished it in 1968 and revised it considerably in 1970 for its Covent Garden première in 1972. It concerns the 16th-century composer John Taverner, who composed sublime music for the church, turned his back on his art, became a persecutor of the Catholic faith, and ultimately was tried for heresy. The opera, incidentally, was based on facts that were thought to be true at the time of composition, but have since been disproved.

More music-theatre followed in 1974 with *Miss Donnithorne's Maggot*, a female equivalent of the *Eight Songs for a Mad King*. Here, a mad jilted spinster is the mezzo-soprano soloist accompanied by the same six instruments (in medieval times, a "maggot" was a whimsical fancy). A chamber opera, *The Martyrdom of St Magnus*, had its first performance in St Magnus Cathedral, Orkney, in 1977. Magnus was Earl of Orkney in the 12th century, a Viking who was, unusually, a pacifist. He was finally murdered by decree of his cousin, Earl Håkon, and was at once canonized. Maxwell Davies saw Magnus as a prisoner of conscience, the opera being a political allegory applicable to the present day.

The most often performed of Maxwell Davies's operas is the one-act *The Lighthouse*, composed in 1979. It is discussed below. His latest opera is *The Doctor of Myddfai*, which was premièred by Welsh National Opera in 1996. It is set in Europe "in the near future" and is full of symbolism and mystical myth, all performed in a creepily sinister atmosphere. Maxwell Davies has said that this is the last opera he will compose. Time will tell.

THE LIGHTHOUSE, 1979

Maxwell Davies wrote his own libretto for this one-act opera based on an incident, said to be true, about the disappearance of lighthouse keepers. It was commissioned for and first performed at the 1980 Edinburgh Festival. It is set in Edinburgh and in a lighthouse, early in the 20th century. The gloomy atmosphere of the North Sea at night makes for a grim work.

SYNOPSIS Three lighthouse keepers have disappeared and in a Prologue a court is hearing evidence from three officers (1). Gradually the officers move into flashback and become the keepers, Officer 1/Sandy (ten), Officer 2/Blazes (bar), and Officer 3/Arthur (bass). The three keepers have been closeted together in the lighthouse for several months and tensions have developed between them. To try to reduce this fraught atmosphere, they sing songs: Blazes starts with a ballad of street violence (2), Sandy sings of making love (3), and Arthur sings a hymn (4). The songs remind them of ghosts from the past, and this depresses them. The fog descends and two bright lights are seen over the dark sea. Each man believes he is being claimed by "The Beast" (5). As "The Beast" approaches the lighthouse, its "eyes" are seen to be the lights of the boat that has come to rescue them. The three officers from the boat search for the lighthouse keepers (6), but find nothing but rats – as they explain in their evidence before the court.

> **MUSIC** (1) Officer 1: *No, Sir, our passage was difficult*; (2) Blazes: *When I was a kid our street had a gang*; (3) Sandy: *Oh, my love, I dream of you*; (4) Arthur: *This be thy God, oh Israel*; (5) Arthur: *The Beast is called out from his grave*; (6) Officers 1/2/3: *We had to defend ourselves/God, what a mess!/Explanations will be difficult.*

Weir

Judith Weir
(b. 1954)

LEFT Judith Weir teaching at the Dartington
Summer School in 1999

WHERE TO START
A Night at the Chinese Opera

WHERE TO GO NEXT
Blond Eckbert

This Scottish composer in all genres came
to the attention of the public with her 1987
opera *A Night at the Chinese Opera*. Weir was
born in Cambridge and while at school in
London she had private lessons from the
composer John Tavener (b. 1944) and played
the oboe in the National Youth Orchestra
of Great Britain. She studied at Cambridge
University (1973–6) and in the United States
at Tanglewood. She taught at Glasgow
University (1979–83) and Trinity College,
Cambridge (1983–5). Between 1988 and
1991 she was composer-in-residence at the
Royal Scottish Academy of Music and Drama
in Glasgow.

Of great influence on her music is the folk-
music of different nations, together with her
belief in the importance of the composer's
role in society. She has devoted a lot of
her time to education in music and feels it
important to communicate with an audience
as well as with performers. Her first opera
owes much to the declamatory style of

Chinese theatre and although the sounds of
Chinese music are there, they are not simply
imitative, but are conveyed in her own musical
style, which owes something to Mozart and
Schubert. Weir is a natural composer for the
stage, even her instrumental music having a
narrative side to it, and she has composed
incidental music for plays at the National
Theatre, London, and the Royal Shakespeare
Company, Stratford.

A Night at the Chinese Opera is so far her
best-known work and is described below.
Her second full-scale opera was *The Vanishing
Bridegroom*, given its first performance in
Glasgow in 1990 by Scottish Opera. Weir
wrote the libretto herself, basing it on old
tales from the West Highlands of Scotland.
Each of its three parts concerns a bridegroom
who disappears – it has quite a creepy
atmosphere. Her third opera, *Blond Eckbert*,
was first produced by English National Opera
in London in 1994. The atmosphere is almost

supernatural, the music is melodic, and the
story gripping. It has received productions in
Europe and is highly thought of. In addition
to the three operas mentioned, Weir has
composed shorter pieces of music-theatre,
including *Armida* (2005), a 50-minute opera
for television that is both a modern take on
a 16th-century love story, and a comment
on contemporary warfare.

A NIGHT AT THE CHINESE OPERA, 1987

Unveiled at the Cheltenham Festival of 1987,
Weir's first large-scale opera was performed
at the Santa Fe Festival in New Mexico two
years later. It was revived in 2006 at the Royal
Academy of Music, London, to unanimous
critical acclaim. Weir wrote the libretto, based
on a 13th-century Yüan Dynasty drama. Much
of this opera, despite the seriousness of the
subject, is very funny indeed, and it is difficult
to know why it has been so neglected since
its première.

SYNOPSIS Late 13th-century China: an
explorer, Chao Sun, is exiled. His son, Chao
Lin (bar), is to construct a canal. Among the
workers are some actors, and the night before
Chao Sun departs, they enact a play, *The Chao
Family Orphan*, in which a wicked General
(actor) **(1)** causes his servant and wife to
commit suicide, leaving behind a baby son.
The General adopts and raises the child. Some
20 years later, the young man discovers his
identity and vows revenge **(2)**. After the play,
Chao Lin finishes the canal, which is highly
praised. An old woman tells of his father's fate
and Chao Lin now also vows revenge – the
play within the play has come full circle.

> **MUSIC** (The greater part of the
> libretto consists of short snatches of
> conversation and it is almost impossible
> to offer entry points. The two indicated
> below may be helpful) **(1)** General: *I am
> general Tu-an-ku*; **(2)** Orphan/Chao Lin:
> *When I meet with my enemy…*

ABOVE Première of *A Night at the Chinese Opera*,
Kent Opera at the 1987 Cheltenham Festival, with
Meryl Drower and Jonathan Best

Adès

Thomas Adès
(b. 1971)

WHERE TO START
The Tempest

WHERE TO GO NEXT
Powder Her Face

Of all the young composers in Britain in the past few years, the one making the greatest impact, especially in opera, despite having so far composed only two, is Thomas Adès. His music is already being performed not only in Britain but also across Europe and in the USA. Adès was born in London, the son of a writer and an art historian. His first obvious musical talent was as a pianist. He studied at the Guildhall School of Music and Drama in London and then at King's College, Cambridge, from where he graduated in 1992 with the highest honours.

In 1993, aged 22, he gave his first public piano recital in London and it seemed that this was the path his career would follow. But whilst still at Cambridge his compositions had started to make their mark. Aged 18 and a student, he composed his *Chamber Symphony* (1990), the first of his works to receive, in

1993, a professional performance. *Living Toys* (1993), a tone-poem for chamber orchestra commissioned by the London Sinfonietta, received widespread critical acclaim and became his most performed work, being heard throughout Europe, the United States, Japan, and Australia. In 2000 Adès was the youngest composer ever to win the Grawemeyer Prize (for his orchestral piece *Asyla*), the largest international prize for composition. Adès was only the third British composer ever to win it since its inauguration at the University of Louisville in 1985 (it was won by Harrison Birtwistle in 1987 for *The Mask of Orpheus* [see p.189] and by Simon Bainbridge in 1997).

But it was his chamber opera *Powder Her Face*, commissioned for and first produced at the 1995 Cheltenham Festival, that brought him real international recognition. It was televised in Britain, quickly released as a recording, and has been produced all round the world. It is based on the life of the notorious and sex-obsessed Margaret, Duchess of Argyll. Her behaviour, revealed in her divorce hearing from the Duke in 1963, was a scandal among the British aristocracy, photographs of her sexual conduct with an unidentified "headless man" being shown in court. The judge described her as a woman who had "started to indulge in disgusting sexual activities…". She died in 1993. The opera covers episodes in her eventful life. Adès portrays her as a 20th-century-style anti-heroine in the line of Salome and Lulu, but there is also pathos in his interpretation. The opera was much more than a mere *succès de scandale*, and commissions started to flow in. Adès is also a more than

ABOVE LEFT **Mary Plazas as the Duchess in *Powder her Face* at the 1999 Aldeburgh Festival, conducted by the composer**

competent conductor and holds high-profile administrative posts. He was music director of Birmingham Contemporary Music Group in 1998–2000 and from 1999–2008 was artistic director of the Aldeburgh Festival.

His second opera, *The Tempest*, is a three-act work to a libretto adapted by the playwright Meredith Oakes from Shakespeare. It was premièred at Covent Garden, London, in early 2004 with the composer conducting, and received almost unqualified critical and public praise. Within its first two years it had successful productions in Europe and at the Santa Fe Festival in New Mexico, and was revived at Covent Garden in 2007. It is described below.

Adès's rise to fame has been meteoric. Not since Benjamin Britten have a young British composer's works been anticipated with such excitement and greeted with such enthusiasm; many would name him as the most promising British composer of the present generation. There is always the danger, as with performers, of the "too-far-too-soon" syndrome with a resulting early burn-out. Adès seems to have the personality and security to cope with the adulation – and the work – and to keep his feet firmly on the ground. It will be very interesting to watch his progress over the next few years.

THE TEMPEST, 2004

Shakespeare's play has spawned much music. John Weldon (1676–1736) wrote incidental music for the play and about 1695 Purcell based a semi-opera on it (although there is reason to wonder if this, too, was by Weldon). In 1873 Tchaikovsky wrote a symphonic-fantasy for orchestra; Sibelius, in 1925, wrote incidental music on a large scale, involving soloists, chorus, and orchestra; and the symphonic prelude *The Magic Island* was composed by William Alwyn (1905–85) in 1953. Operas include *The Magic Island* of 1942 by Heinrich Sutermeister (1910–95), *Der Sturm* (1952–6) by Frank Martin (1890–1974), and *The Tempest* by the American John C Eaton (b. 1935), produced in Santa Fe in 1985.

SYNOPSIS On a remote island, the cries of the victims of a shipwreck after a storm are heard. Miranda (mez), daughter of Prospero (bar), wants to know what has happened (1). Her father explains: his brother Antonio (ten), who usurped him as Duke of Milan, and the King of Naples (ten), have been delivered into his hands by fate (2). Prospero sends his spirit Ariel (sop) to bring the victims to him. Caliban (ten), a monster whose father used to rule the island, claims to be the true heir to its throne, but Prospero rejects his claims (3). Ariel tells Prospero that he has saved the victims, and in return wants his freedom, which Prospero had promised (4). Miranda falls in love with a survivor, Ferdinand (ten), son of the King of Naples. Prospero uses magic to immobilize Ferdinand (5). Observed by Prospero, Caliban greets the new arrivals (6). Ariel does his best to cause confusion. The King and his men search for Ferdinand, who is meanwhile freed by Miranda (7). Miranda and Ferdinand announce their marriage. Prospero no longer wants revenge. He forgives his brother and the King, and grants Ariel his freedom. The wrecked ship is magically restored and the "visitors" anticipate returning home. Prospero snaps his magic wand in two – he no longer needs it (8). Caliban, left alone, wonders if it has all been a dream (9).

MUSIC (1) Miranda: *Oh father, storm and thunder, rain and hail…* (2) Prospero: *I was Milan! I was duke!*; (3) Caliban/ Prospero: *This island's mine, I am king/ You lie, you whine, you waste my time*; (4) Prospero/Ariel: *You made a promise when you were freed/Five fathoms deep your father lies*; (5) Miranda/Ferdinand: *Father don't, oh father, please/I'm paralysed by him*; (6) Caliban: *Friends, don't fear, the island's full of noises*; (7) Miranda/ Ferdinand: *High on the headland, Low in the dry sand*; (8) Prospero: *I'll drown my book, I'll break my stave*; (9) Caliban: *Who was here? Have they disappeared?*

Gershwin

George Gershwin
(1898–1937)

LEFT George Gershwin, one of the earliest American-born composers to achieve fame in the genre of opera

WHERE TO START
Porgy and Bess

Edward MacDowell (1860–1908) and Charles Griffes (1884–1920) were the first two native-born American composers to achieve any sort of international recognition and Charles Ives (1874–1954) was almost 50 years old before his works were performed. None of these composers wrote operas. For a native-born composer of operas, there was a further wait of over 25 years and then, at long last, America struck gold. George Gershwin was born Jacob Gershovitz in New York, the second child of Jewish Russian immigrants. His elder brother Ira (1896–1983) was expected to be the musician in the family. From 1913 George had piano lessons and in 1914 left school and started work as a pianist, plugging songs for a publisher of popular music. He wrote his first song in 1916 and in 1919 his first real "hit", the song "Swanee". For many of his songs Ira was his lyricist and they produced hundreds of songs that have survived the years, such as "I Got Rhythm", "Embraceable You", "The Man I Love", "'S Wonderful", "Lady Be Good", and "Love Walked In".

Gershwin wrote his first Broadway musical (*La, La Lucille*) in 1919. Over the next 14 years there followed *George White's Scandals* (1920–4), *Lady Be Good* (1924), *Oh Kay!* (1926, with lyrics by P G Wodehouse), *Funny Face* (1927), and *Girl Crazy* (1930). He incorporated the new jazz idiom into orchestral works such as *Rhapsody in Blue* for piano and orchestra (1924), *An American in Paris* (1928), and *Variations on I Got Rhythm* (1934). After 1931, Gershwin composed music for films such as *Delicious* of 1931 and *The Goldwyn Follies* of 1938 (Gershwin died from a brain tumour in 1937, while the latter was still filming).

Some of the shows he wrote between about 1925 and 1930, such as *Strike Up the Band* (1927) and *Of Thee I Sing* (1931), warrant the classification of operetta, as opposed to musical-comedy. They satirize aspects of American life and have been likened to the English operettas of Gilbert and Sullivan rather than Viennese operetta. These works of Gershwin use marches, patter-songs, and waltzes, and because of their structure contain fewer "hit songs" than his musicals, although they were still composed for show voices rather than trained opera singers. But trained opera singers were what he had in mind for his only opera, *Porgy and Bess* of 1934–5.

In 1926 Gershwin read *Porgy*, written the previous year by DuBose Heyward, a native of Charleston, South Carolina, and adapted by Heyward and his wife Dorothy as a play. Gershwin wrote to the author suggesting that they might collaborate on a folk-opera based on the novel. Although Heyward agreed to this suggestion, it was not until 1934 that Gershwin's composing and performing commitments allowed him time to begin work. The libretto was written by Heyward and Ira Gershwin. Feeling it would guarantee better audiences, Gershwin chose to première *Porgy and Bess* on Broadway rather than have a full operatic production. The first cast included Todd Duncan as Porgy and Anne Brown as Bess, and Alexander Smallens conducted. *Porgy and Bess* was tried out in Boston and opened in New York in 1935, for a run of only 124 performances (few by the standards of musicals) and was a huge financial loss for its backers. The opera ran into difficulties from the beginning, with criticism of its portrayal of African Americans and accusations of racism rife, especially just after its composition and also during the years of the American Civil Rights and Black Power Movements in the 1950s, 1960s, and 1970s. Ira Gershwin stipulated that only black singers should be allowed to sing the roles and refused to give permission for white casts to perform the opera, particularly during the apartheid years in South Africa.

For many years *Porgy and Bess* was performed more often in Europe, where it was considered a true American opera. The British première was given by an all-black American company that toured Europe and went to the Stoll Theatre, London, in October 1952. The cast was headed by Leontyne Price as Bess and William Warfield as Porgy (they married during the tour). This production was taken to Broadway at the Ziegfeld Theatre and then toured Latin America. When it had its first uncut production in Houston in 1976, conducted by John DeMain and with the score played as Gershwin composed it, the

ABOVE In the 1953 revival of *Porgy and Bess* in the USA, Cab Calloway sang Sportin' Life, with Leontyne Price as Bess

BELOW The crippled Porgy (Willard White) leaves Catfish Row to search for Bess in New York – "Oh Lawd, I'm on my way", Glyndebourne, 1986

work was perceived for the first time in the USA as a true opera, not an upmarket musical. It was an immediate success and in 1985 it finally received a production at the Metropolitan Opera, New York, 50 years after its composition. In Britain it was superbly produced by Trevor Nunn at Glyndebourne in 1986, conducted by Simon Rattle, the cast led by Cynthia Haymon and Willard White. It received a standing ovation at every performance. The production was taken to Covent Garden, London, in 1992 with a largely unchanged cast.

PORGY AND BESS, 1934–5

The story is of African American families living in a Negro tenement, the fictitious Catfish Row, in the slums of Charlestown in the 1930s. Whilst composing the music, Gershwin visited South Carolina to absorb the atmosphere. Probably the most popular aria is "Summertime". For the first time Gershwin was attempting to write for trained opera singers, and he succeeded triumphantly.

SYNOPSIS A Negro tenement in the early 20th century: Clara (sop) sings a lullaby to her baby (**1**), her husband Jake (bar) is helping her, other men are playing crap. Everyone greets the crippled Porgy (bass-bar), who pushes himself around in a goat-cart. Crown (bar) and his girlfriend Bess (sop) arrive and Crown joins the crap game. A fight ensues and Crown kills a man and flees, leaving Bess behind to fend for herself. She is given shelter by Porgy. The victim's widow Serena (sop) is joined by other residents of Catfish Row. Serena cries for her man (**2**) and Bess leads them all in a spiritual (**3**).

Bess slowly grows to love Porgy, who is truly happy for the first time (**4**). Sportin' Life (ten) tries to sell the people drugs, "happy dust", he calls it, but the shopkeeper Maria (cont) discourages him. The annual church picnic is being planned. Porgy is not mobile enough to go and Bess is happy to stay with him (**5**), but Porgy and Maria persuade her to go alone to have some fun. On the island Sportin' Life still attempts to dispense his dope

(**6**). Bess finds Crown hiding there. He wants her to remain with him, and she cannot resist him (**7**). She is later found on the island, delirious, and they all pray for her recovery. She does recover and wants to stay with Porgy (**8**).

In Act 3 Crown has followed Bess and tries to claim her back from Porgy, and in a fight Porgy kills Crown. While Porgy is being questioned by the police, Bess accepts dope from Sportin' Life and leaves for New York. Nobody will give evidence against Porgy and the police are obliged to release him. When he finds that Bess has gone, he sets out to follow and find her (**9**).

MUSIC (**1**) Clara: *Summertime*; (**2**) Serena: *My man's gone now*; (**3**) Bess: *Leavin' for the Promised Land*; (**4**) Porgy: *I got plenty o' nuttin'*; (**5**) Porgy/Bess duet: *Bess, you is my woman now*; (**6**) Sportin' Life: *It ain't necessarily so*; (**7**) Bess: *What you want wid Bess?*; (**8**) Bess: *I loves you, Porgy*; (**9**) Porgy: *Oh, Lawd, I'm on my way*.

Barber

Samuel Barber
(1910–81)

WHERE TO START
Vanessa

WHERE TO GO NEXT
Antony and Cleopatra

Barber was one of the most successful American composers of the early part of the 20th century. His mother was a good pianist and his aunt was the operatic contralto Louise Homer. She was married to the composer Sidney Homer (1864–1953) who encouraged his young nephew's talent and was his mentor for 25 years, greatly influencing his style. Barber had piano lessons and started to compose from an early age, writing an operetta, *The Rose Tree*, when he was ten, to a libretto by the family's Irish cook! When he was 14 he entered the newly opened Curtis Institute of Music in Philadelphia, studying piano, singing (he was a good baritone), and composition. In 1928 he

met a fellow-student, Gian Carlo Menotti (1911–2007), with whom he had a lifelong personal and professional relationship. Barber travelled widely in Europe, especially Italy, and while there absorbed much of the Romantic tradition that is evident in most of his music.

His works started to be published in 1930. His *Symphony in One Movement* (1936) was performed at the opening concert of the 1937 Salzburg Festival – the first performance of a symphonic work by an American composer at the festival. His most famous work is the *Adagio for Strings*, an arrangement (1937) of the second movement of his only string quartet (1936). It resulted in many commissions. Barber's music was – and is, by some critics – regarded as very conservative. He had little time for the trends of the serial composers or the Neoclassicists in the 1920s. He experimented with dissonance and chromaticism a bit in the 1940s, but never to the detriment of tonality. Conservative his music might be, but that is probably what has kept it before the public up to the present time.

Among his considerable output, Barber wrote only a few works for the stage. There were two ballets and two operas – three if one includes the nine-minute *A Hand of Bridge* composed in 1953 and first produced in 1959 at the Spoleto Festival in Italy (founded by Menotti in 1958), which is for four solo voices and chamber orchestra. It concerns the inner thoughts of two couples as they play cards. Barber's first full-scale opera, *Vanessa*, was composed 1956–7 to a libretto by Menotti, who also directed the first production at the Metropolitan Opera, New York, in 1958. It is described below. In 1966 Barber composed *Antony and Cleopatra*, to a libretto by Franco

Zeffirelli after the Shakespeare play. It was commissioned for the opening of the new Metropolitan Opera House in the Lincoln Center. It was not a success then nor when revived in 1975.

VANESSA, 1956–7, rev. 1964
The sets and costumes for the first production of *Vanessa* were elegantly designed by the photographer and designer Cecil Beaton (1904–80). Menotti directed and the cast was superb, the title-role sung by Eleanor Steber, for whom Barber had written his atmospheric 1948 scena, *Knoxville: Summer of 1915*. It was an immediate success in the US, winning Barber the Pulitzer Prize in 1958. Originally in four acts, it was reduced to three in 1964.

SYNOPSIS In her country house in about 1905, Vanessa (sop), with her mother the Old Baroness (mez), and her niece Erika (mez) (1), awaits the return of her lover, Anatol, who deserted her 20 years ago. He has died and his son, also called Anatol (ten), arrives to visit her (2). On the night he arrives he seduces Erika (3). At a ball he pledges his love to Vanessa (4). Erika, pregnant by Anatol, attempts suicide (5), but recovers. Anatol and Vanessa marry and he takes her to Paris. Erika is left to await his return as Vanessa had waited for his father (6).

MUSIC (1) Erika: *Must the winter come so soon?*; (2) Vanessa: *Do not utter a word, Anatol*; (3) Erika/Baroness: *He made me drink too much wine…/The very night you met him?*; (4) Anatol/Vanessa duet: *Love has a bitter core, Vanessa/Anatol*; (5) Anatol: *On the path near the lake*; (6) Erika: *I am truly alone.*

ABOVE LEFT **Samuel Barber photographed in 1955, aged 45**

ABOVE *Vanessa*, **Monte Carlo Opera/Rhin National Opera, 2001. Kiri Te Kanawa (Vanessa), Lucy Schauffer (Erika), Rosalind Elias (Baroness), David Maxwell Anderson (Anatol), David Evitts (Doctor)**

Glass

Philip Glass
(b. 1937)

WHERE TO START
Akhnaten

WHERE TO GO NEXT
The Voyage

In the 1960s a mode of composing known as minimalism developed in the United States of America, of which the chief proponents were Philip Glass, John Adams, Steve Reich, and Terry Riley. It was taken up to varying degrees by the Englishman John Tavener (b. 1944), the Estonian Arvo Pärt (b. 1935), and the Polish Henryk Górecki (b. 1933). Minimalism in music can be simply defined as a repetition of short motifs in a simple harmonic idiom – or, the minimum of material repeated to the maximum hypnotic effect.

Philip Glass's father had a radio repair shop and took home records for his sons to play. Philip soon became familiar with Beethoven and Schubert chamber music and Shostakovich symphonies. By the time he was 12 he had started composing. At 15 he went to the University of Chicago and graduated in Liberal Arts in 1956. He also had lessons at the Juilliard School of Music in New York. He took a full-time course there from 1957 to 1961. In the early 1960s he went to Paris to study with Nadia Boulanger for two years, but he was not tempted by the avant-garde of the Boulez school of composers.

One of the first real influences on his music occurred when he was hired in Paris to transcribe for Western musicians the music of the Indian composer and sitar-player Ravi Shankar (b. 1920) for the film *Chappaqua*. The additive and repetitive processes in the Indian music were crucial in the development of his minimalist style. From Paris Glass travelled to North Africa and India, absorbing their music structure and patterns. On his return to New York he established the Philip Glass Ensemble to play his music, which sounded to many ears more like rock than classical music.

The first full-scale stage work Glass composed was in 1976 in collaboration with the theatre director Robert Wilson, whose mixed-media work has been described as "theatre of visions". *Einstein on the Beach* did not have a libretto as we would understand it. It consisted of drawings and numbers used to train the singers in pitch and rhythm. There were dances, bizarre costumes, monologues, and the audience were invited to walk in and out as they wished during the five-hour performance. His next two theatre works were of a more conventional operatic structure. The first was *Satyagraha* (1980), about Mahatma Gandhi's years in South Africa and used a mixture of fact, fairy-tale, and comic-books, told in music that contained recognizable arias, ensembles, and choruses. The other was *Akhnaten* (1980–3), a study of

LEFT **American minimalist composer Philip Glass in 2005**

the Egyptian pharaohs. It had a mixed reception in Europe and in the USA at the time of its first performances. The production was revised for its London première the following year and was much more favourably received.

Several more theatre works followed, including *The Fall of the House of Usher* (1988), based on the story by Edgar Allen Poe. In 1992 Glass was commissioned by the Metropolitan Opera to write a work to commemorate the 500th anniversary of the landing of Christopher Columbus in America. *The Voyage*, a three-act opera, proved his most controversial work, equally praised and criticized. He later wrote a trilogy of works based on Cocteau films, to be performed by singers and his own ensemble during the projection of the films with the soundtrack removed. These attracted great acclaim. He has collaborated with many writers and pop-singers, his most recent opera collaborations including *Galileo Galilei* (2002) and *The Sound of a Voice* (2003). His compositions have had their own influence on film and television music, which he still writes in addition to theatre and concert pieces.

ABOVE **Glass's *Akhnaten* produced by ENO, London, 1987, with (at the front) Sally Burgess as Nefertiti and Christopher Robson as Akhnaten**

Adams

John Adams
(b. 1947)

WHERE TO START
Nixon in China

WHERE TO GO NEXT
Dr Atomic

This American composer and conductor was one of the foremost American minimalists (see p.157), together with Philip Glass, Steve Reich, and Terry Riley. As a child he studied the clarinet with his father and with the clarinettist from the Boston Symphony Orchestra. He began composition and theory lessons when he was ten and by the time he was 14 his first composition was performed by the local community orchestra, with whom he practised conducting. He studied composition at Harvard University from 1965 to 1972, occasionally performing with the Boston SO as a clarinettist. In 1971 he went to live in San Francisco and quickly became involved with the arts scene there, teaching at the Conservatory and commissioning and performing new works by young composers. In his own compositions he made the decision not to follow the European avant-garde or academic American composers, and integrated American life into his works, one of his earliest being *Shaker Loops* of 1978 for string septet, a work already showing minimalist tendencies with its hypnotic pulsation. The San Francisco SO appointed Adams composer-in-residence from 1982 to 1985, and two works he composed for them, *Harmonium* (1980–1) and *Harmonielehre*, (1984–5) brought him to national attention.

During the 1980s Adams's music developed in two directions at once – lighter works that incorporated the American sounds of big band music, dances, and marches, such as *Grand Pianola Music* of 1982; and the much more sober side of his work such as *The Wound Dresser* (1988) to words by Walt Whitman. In 1983 he was approached by the American director Peter Sellars (b. 1957), who

suggested he might write an opera on the subject of President Nixon's six-day visit to China in 1972 to meet Mao Tse-tung (Chairman Mao). *Nixon in China*, with a libretto by Alice Goodman, had its première in Houston in 1987 and the Houston Grand Opera took the production to Edinburgh, Scotland, a year later. In the few years following, it had over 70 performances, was televised and recorded, and has received other productions since then. Details of the opera are given below.

Adams's second opera, created with the same team (Alice Goodman and Peter Sellars), was also on a contemporary subject, the hijacking of the cruise ship *Achille Lauro* by Palestinian terrorists in 1985, resulting in the murder of a disabled Jewish passenger. *The Death of Klinghoffer* (1989–91) had its first performance in 1991 in Brussels and the same production was also seen in Lyons, Vienna, Brooklyn, and San Francisco. It tackles a very delicate political subject, and although Adams treated it sensitively, it was picketed at its San Francisco performance and has not been performed in the USA since 1992. His next stage work, which he called an "earthquake/romance" was *I was Looking at the Ceiling and Then I Saw the Sky*. It had its first performance (Sellars again) in California in 1995 and then

toured the United States and Europe for five months. The story covers the reactions of seven young Americans, all from different social and ethnic backgrounds, to the 1994 earthquake in Los Angeles. The opera's title is based on a comment from one of the earthquake's victims. The composition uses popular songs performed by pop singers and accompanied by a combination of synthesized tunes and a rock band. The work, nevertheless, is basically minimalist.

His next opera, *Dr Atomic*, had its world première in San Francisco in 2005, to a mixed critical reception. It is based on the physicist J Robert Oppenheimer and the project he led to create the first atomic bomb. The story concentrates on the final hours in July 1945 leading up to the first atomic bomb explosion at the Alamagordo test site in New Mexico. In 2006 Adams's opera *A Flowering Tree* had its world première in Vienna. Inspired in many ways by Mozart's *The Magic Flute* (see p.55), it is based on a southern India folk-tale of the same title and describes a young couple undergoing trials to discover the transfiguring power of love.

Adams has been greatly helped in his composition of operas by his librettists, especially Alice Goodman, and he has been assisted and strongly influenced by the American director Peter Sellars, who gave him the ideas for some of his operas. He continues to compose for the theatre and for the concert-hall, and has expressed the hope that some of his works – such as *A Flowering Tree* and the oratorio *El Niño* – will work equally well in either location. But he has moved further away from minimalism, as it was previously defined, than Reich or Riley. He manages to combine the repetitive rhythmic energy of minimalism with the harmony and orchestral colours of late-Romanticism, and his works, though quite complex, are tonal and emotional and therefore easily accessible – a great relief for audiences struggling with some contemporary music.

NIXON IN CHINA, 1987

The idea for this three-act opera came from Peter Sellars, whose world-première production was toured in the United States, was taken to Edinburgh and Amsterdam, and was televised. It has since been staged by other companies and is the most often performed of Adams's operas so far. It has been hugely successful.

SYNOPSIS China, 1972: Richard Nixon (bar) and his wife Pat (sop) arrive by aeroplane, "The Spirit of '76", at Peking (now Beijing) airport for the President's historic visit to China. He is accompanied by the Secretary of State, Henry Kissinger (bass). They are greeted by Premier Chou En-lai (bass).

Nixon, in his "News" aria **(1)**, is aware that it is prime television time back home and his arrival will be witnessed by the nation. Nixon and Kissinger meet Chairman Mao Tse-tung (ten) and his wife Chiang Ch'ing (sop) and Nixon has a political discussion with Mao and Chou En-lai **(2)**. The first evening in China they are guests at a banquet in the Great Hall of the People **(3) (4)**. Pat Nixon goes sight-seeing the next day, being given a guided tour of a commune and the Summer Palace **(5)**. They are taken to see a contemporary political ballet, *The Red Detachment of Women*, devised by Mao's wife, which Pat Nixon finds very disturbing as fact and fiction become intertwined, demonstrating the cruel

treatment of the women. Chiang Ch'ing talks about her own place in the history of the Cultural Revolution **(6)**. On the last night of their visit, all the characters talk about their past lives, the events that have taken place in the week, and how these will affect each of them in the future.

> **MUSIC** **(1)** Nixon: *News has a kind of mystery*; **(2)** Mao: *We no longer need Confucius*; **(3)** Chou En-lai: *Ladies and Gentlemen, comrades and friends*; **(4)** Nixon: *Mr Premier, distinguished guests*; **(5)** Pat Nixon: *This is prophetic*; **(6)** Chiang Ch'ing: *I am the wife of Mao Tse-tung*.

ABOVE John Duykers (Chairman Mao) and James Maddalena (President Nixon) in the première of *Nixon in China*, Houston Grand Opera, 1987

More Opera Composers of the 20th Century and Beyond

As in other periods, there are late 20th-century and early 21st-century composers who have created at least one opera, but may be better-known for their other works or have, as yet, composed no further operas. The most prominent of these are now discussed.

ITALY After Puccini, there has been no world-dominating Italian opera composer. His successors have been Malipiero, Dallapiccola, Menotti, and Berio. The first two of these have made little impact on opera: **GIAN MALIPIERO** (1882–1973) rebelled against Italian operatic traditions and **LUIGI DALLAPICCOLA** (1904–75) had some influence on younger Italian composers with his one-act work about a political prisoner, *Il prigioniero* (1944–8). **LUCIANO BERIO** (1925–2003) was influenced by serialism and electronics. His best-known opera is *Un re in ascolto* (*A Listening King*), premièred in Salzburg in 1984 and is the story of an old impresario losing control of his "kingdom", ie his theatre. **GIAN CARLO MENOTTI** (1911–2007) was born in Italy but spent most of his adult life in the USA and later in Scotland. He wrote his own librettos (and also two for his partner Samuel Barber). Among his operas that receive

productions are *The Consul* (1949), a classic of its time, about the struggle to obtain a passport in a police state; *The Telephone* (a one-act comedy from 1946); *The Medium* (1945), describing the disastrous effects of attending a séance on the unhinged mind of a woman; and the delightful *Amahl and the Night Visitors* (1951), about a crippled child who is healed during a visit by the Magi. So while not exactly in the operatic wilderness, if we discount Menotti, who can be considered an American rather that an Italian opera composer, Italy has not exactly held its place in the current market.

FRANCE There are two Frenchmen who composed prolifically in all genres: **FRANCIS POULENC** (1899–1963) wrote four operas, two of which receive regular productions. The one-act *La voix humaine* (*The Human Voice*) of 1958 is a tour-de-force for a soprano, who spends 40 minutes alone on stage, on the telephone in a panic, talking to the man who obviously no longer loves her. The three-act *Les Dialogues des Carmélites* (1953) describes the martyrdom of 16 Carmelite Sisters from Compiègne at the time of the French Revolution, their interrelationships, and how they face with courage their execution by

guillotine. Unusually for its time, it is an "old-fashioned" grand opera that Verdi and even Monteverdi would have recognized. **OLIVIER MESSIAEN** (1908–92) wrote only one opera, *Saint François d'Assise* (1983), which is a vast oratorio-like work, lasting four hours and demanding large forces including an off-stage chorus. It depicts St Francis's transition towards a state of spiritual grace at the time of his death.

EASTERN EUROPE BOHUSLAV MARTINŮ (1890–1959) is (after Janáček) the main Czechoslovakian opera composer of the 20th century. One of his early operas is *Julietta: the Book of Dreams* (1936–7), a most descriptive title of this surrealist work, which probes the depths of the human psyche. *The Greek Passion* (1956–7) explores life in a Greek village where the actors take on the personality of the characters in the Passion play they are rehearsing. This governs their attitudes to refugees who arrive in the village. **ZOLTÁN KOLDÁLY** (1882–1967) is second only to Bartók among 20th-century Hungarian composers and was a dominant figure in his country's musical life. His opera *Háry János* (1925–6) should be seen more often. It is really a play with music, spoken dialogue

ABOVE **The final scene of Poulenc's *Les Dialogues des Carmélites*: one by one the Carmelite sisters mount the scaffold for execution by guillotine, Santa Fe, 1999**

being interspersed with songs, choruses, and orchestral interludes. The title-character was a real person who fought in the Napoleonic wars and the opera tells of his adventures. **GYÖRGY LIGETI** (1923–2006) came quite late to opera, composing his only true opera, *Le grand macabre*, in 1972–6 when he turned 50. It is set in "Breughelland", the characters recognizable from Breughel's paintings. It is another surreal work and propounds the theory that we might as well enjoy life because tomorrow we die. At its Stockholm première it was very successful. **KAROL SZYMANOWSKI** (1882–1937) was the outstanding Polish composer of the 20th century. His only important opera, which has elements of oratorio, is *King Roger* (1918–24), based on his own novel. Set in the 12th century, it is about the conflict between the pagan (represented by an unknown Shepherd) and the Christian (personified by Roger).

NORDIC COUNTRIES at last produced some opera composers. The Danish **CARL NIELSEN** (1865–1931) is nowadays recognized primarily as a symphonist, but he wrote two operas, both of which have a strong plot. *Saul and David* (1898–1901) is based on the Old Testament. *Masquerade* (1904–5) has a light-hearted atmosphere, a romantic love duet, and cheerful dance music and in Denmark is regarded as a classic. In Finland **AARNE MERIKANTO** (1893–1958) wrote music considered too avant-garde at the time of composition and *Juha*, now recognized as the first operatic masterpiece by a Finnish composer, was not performed in his lifetime. It uses speech-rhythms reminiscent of Janáček and the orchestration is lush. **JOONAS KOKKONEN** (1921–96) wrote one opera, *The Last Temptations*, concerning a revivalist preacher whose fundamentalism brings him into conflict with the church. The work was popular after its 1975 Helsinki première. **EINOJUHANI RAUTAVAARA** (b. 1928) has so far composed ten operas. Initially influenced by serialism, in the later 1960s his music became more Romantic and

ABOVE **Kaija Saariaho's** *L'amour de loin*, Finnish National Opera, 2004: Hans Christoph Begeman (Jaufré Rudel) and Lilli Paasikivi (the Pilgrim)

he has also used jazz elements. Best-known in his homeland is *Thomas* (1985), about the English bishop who tried to set up a papal state in 13th-century Finland. **AULIS SALLINEN (b. 1935)** is a successful composer of operas that have travelled outside Finland. *The Horseman* (1975) was highly praised at its première at the Savonlinna Festival. *The Red Line* (1978) is about a family of peasants living at starvation level in 1907 after the Russo-Japanese War, and though the subject is depressing the opera is uplifting. *The King Goes Forth to France* (1984), a fantasy on events in English and French history, displays the composer's satirical humour and his compassion. *Kullervo* (1987–8) is based on Finnish myth, and *The Palace* (1994–5) was another Savonlinna première. His latest opera, *King Lear* (2000), was a triumph for the cast but, like much of Sallinen's music, was accused by critics of being "too traditional". The latest Finnish opera composer to be acclaimed is **KAIJA SAARIAHO (b. 1952)**. She made a huge impression with her first opera, *L'amour de loin* (*Love from afar*), based on the life of the 12th-century troubadour Jaufré Rudel and produced at the 2000 Salzburg Festival. *Adriana Mater* (2005) mixes present-day reality and dreams, and had mixed reviews at the Opéra Bastille in Paris in 2006.

GERMANY PAUL HINDEMITH (1895–1963) is not known primarily for his operas, of which he wrote several, but his early three-act *Cardillac* (1926) and *Mathis der Maler* (1934–5, based on the life of the 16th-century painter Mathias Grünewald) are revived from time to time. Still unjustly neglected is **ERICH KORNGOLD (1897–1957)**, son of Julius Korngold, Vienna's most eminent music critic. Erich went to the USA in 1934 and became one of Hollywood's foremost composers of film music. This has unfairly mitigated against his reputation as an opera composer. His masterpiece is *Die tote Stadt* (*The Dead City*) (1917–19), musically halfway between Strauss and Puccini, and performed quite regularly in

Germany, if less often elsewhere. His last opera, *Die Kathrin* (1931–7), has been condemned as "old-fashioned". **VIKTOR ULLMANN (1898–1944)** composed *Der Kaiser von Atlantis* in Theresienstadt concentration camp before his transfer to Auschwitz, where he died. During rehearsals the work was condemned as anti-Hitler and no performance was allowed. After the war it was reconstructed and it has been widely performed and recorded since. **BERTHOLD GOLDSCHMIDT (1903–96)** escaped to England from Nazi Germany in 1935, where he already had a reputation as a promising composer. Of his two operas, the best-known is *Beatrice Cenci*, written to celebrate the

Festival of Britain in 1951. It had its first (concert) performance in 1988 in London and was staged in Magdeburg in 1994. **BERND ALOIS ZIMMERMANN (1918–70)** was raised under the Nazi régime and after the war studied serialism. His only opera, *Die Soldaten* (1958–60), is very anti-military and incorporates the use of film. The most prominent name in 20th-century German opera is Hans Werner Henze (see pp.164–5). Coming to the fore is a pupil of Henze, **DETLEV GLANERT (b. 1960)**. His 13th full-length opera, *Caligula*, had its world première in Frankfurt in 2006, was well received, and was described as mixing beauty and violence in the manner of Strauss's *Salome* and *Elektra*.

ABOVE **In Turnage's** *The Silver Tassie*, **ENO 2000, Gerald Finley created Harry Heegan, seen here with Anne Howells as his mother**

RIGHT *Little Women* by Mark Adamo: Jennifer Aylmer (Amy), Laura A Coker (Beth), Stephanie Novacek (Jo), and Joyce DiDonato (Meg), Houston, 1998 (world première)

BRITAIN The major British opera composers of today have been discussed (see pp.174–95), but a few others are briefly mentioned here. Of the same era as Vaughan Williams and Elgar was **GUSTAV HOLST (1874–1934)**. He wrote about a dozen operas, most of which have been forgotten. The one likely to be seen is the one-act *Savitri* (1908–9) which reflects his interest in Hindu literature. He learned enough Sanskrit to translate the works he read and he wrote his own libretto. **JOHN TAVENER (b. 1944)** has adopted a minimalist style of composition. He has had some success with works for the stage, his chamber opera *Mary of Egypt* (1991) demonstrating his idea of theatre as a devotional ritual. **MARK-ANTHONY TURNAGE (b. 1960)** gained attention when in his early 20s with his opera *Greek* which had an immediate success. Since then he has composed *The Silver Tassie* (1997–9), given its first performance by English National Opera in London in 2000. It is based on Sean O'Casey's anti-war play. It was a triumph with the cast, the audience, and the critics and Turnage was hailed as Britain's foremost living opera composer. His next opera is eagerly awaited.

AMERICA may have been late entering the opera arena, but is making up for it at the present time. At the start of this period was **BERNARD HERRMANN (1911–75)**, an excellent composer of film music, whose opera *Wuthering Heights* (1943–51) had a long gestation and waited for its first performance until seven years after his death, although he conducted a recording of it. It is atmospheric and musically attractive. Born in 1926, **CARLISLE FLOYD**'s second opera, *Susannah*, was given its first performance by students at Florida State University in Tallahassee in 1955. Since its New York première the following year, it has been his most popular and successful opera. *Of Mice and Men* (1969) has also had many performances in the USA and in Europe. Whether one regards **LEONARD BERNSTEIN (1918–90)** as a composer of

operas or musicals is debatable. He called *Trouble in Tahiti* (1952) an opera and *Candide* (1954–6, rev. 1973, 1988–9) a comic operetta. *West Side Story* was designated a "musical". In this day of the "cross over", one must make up one's own mind. *Candide* was one of the last works that the composer conducted in London and it was greeted with rapturous acclaim. **MARVIN LEVY (b. 1932)** composed *Mourning Becomes Electra* to a 1961 commission from the New York Metropolitan Opera, where it had its première in 1967. It was critically acclaimed but the public found the atonality that was then *de rigueur* among American composers very difficult to take. Levy revised the orchestration for a 1998 Chicago production and again for Seattle in 2003, making it more approachable. **JOHN CORIGLIANO (b. 1938)** created a sensation with *The Ghosts of Versailles*, composed in 1980–91 and premièred at the Metropolitan Opera in 1991. It uses the same characters as the Beaumarchais operas of Rossini and Mozart, but in a different era, their ghosts helping Marie Antoinette's ghost come to terms with her execution. Since this time, new American operas have abounded. The same age as Corigliano, **JOHN HARBISON (b. 1938)**

wrote his third opera, *The Great Gatsby*, to a commission from the New York Metropolitan Opera in 1999. It was enthusiastically received, was revived in Chicago in 2000, and at the Metropolitan Opera again in 2002. **TOBIAS PICKER (b. 1954)** has had a series of high-profile successes, starting with *Emmeline* at Santa Fe in 1996, followed by *Thérèse Raquin* (1995–6) for Dallas Opera, and *An American Tragedy* (2005–6) for the Metropolitan Opera. **JAKE HEGGIE (b. 1961)** had *Dead Man Walking* premièred by San Francisco Opera in 2002, and his second opera, *The End of the Affair*, by Houston Grand Opera in 2004, both praised by critics and public. The 2001 Glimmerglass Festival included a production of *Little Women* (1998), composed by **MARK ADAMO (b. 1962)** to his own libretto adapted from Louisa May Alcott's famous children's story. Its first performance had been in Houston three years earlier and it was an immediate success. It has had over 30 performance throughout the USA and received its Southern Australia première in 2007. His next opera, *Lysistrata* (2005), was also a Houston Grand Opera commission and was produced in New York the following year. American opera is clearly alive and kicking.

The Future of Opera

"The Arts allow us to discover who we can be". This was the slogan of an advertiser in the programme of a concert I attended in the USA early in 2007. I find it a clear expression of the importance and value of the arts in society, and it is relevant to the future of opera. Factors that I see as contributing to the future of opera are: (1) the quality of new operas and their ability to travel; (2) a change in attitude to opera as being an "elitist" pursuit; (3) a positive effort to introduce children to opera from an early age; (4) the financial support of the arts generally and opera in particular; (5) a return to the dominance of the music as opposed to the production; (6) the attitude of audiences to the established repertoire.

There is no shortage of new operas, especially in the United States. Since 1987, there have been at least 20 new operas by American composers produced by major

companies such as the Metropolitan, New York, New York City, Chicago, San Francisco, Houston, Santa Fe, and St Louis, and with casts including leading American singers – and countless shorter operas have appeared. New operas have also been produced in Britain, Germany, Finland, and Australia. Various reasons have been given for this burgeoning, especially in the USA. One theory is that there has been a move towards more "accessible" and more melodic music, which is "audience friendly" – and often lacking in musical gravitas. The use of surtitles, so frowned upon by the purists, has made the words equally accessible. The subjects have often been stories already well-known to the audience from books, plays, television, films, or newspaper reports, such as André Previn's *A Streetcar Named Desire*, Tobias Picker's *Thérèse Raquin*, Mark Adamo's *Little Women*, Jake Heggie's *Dead Man Walking*, Thomas Adès's *The Tempest*, and John Adams's *Nixon in China*. There is no shortage of an audience for a first performance. The telling factors are if the work is revived and if it travels to other houses and other countries (as most of those mentioned above have done) or whether the new work vanishes very quickly. Various excuses can be made for failure, but if the music is not good enough, the work will not survive for long, no matter how good the story. No opera has ever survived on its libretto alone – and many operas with weak librettos but great music have lived for hundreds of years.

For a company to stage a new work is a very expensive undertaking, and there will be an understandable reluctance to invest so much money, time, and energy unless there is a reasonable chance of success. Adams's *Nixon in China* was a subject with a worldwide appeal and the music is immediately compelling. New operas have not always been "easy on the ear". Beethoven's *Fidelio*, Wagner's *Tristan und Isolde*, Berg's *Wozzeck*, and Britten's *Peter Grimes* all startled their first listeners, but they rapidly established themselves because their music was great music and people wanted to see and hear them again and again.

And now to that mis-used and misunderstood word "elite". In the Oxford Dictionary it is defined as "the choice part or flower of society". In Roget's *Thesaurus* the definitions are "best, very best, the tops, the pick of the bunch". So Manchester United, Real Madrid, Chicago Bears, Bayern Munich – these are all elite teams. Gaultier, Lagerfeld, Armani, Karan, Oldfield – these are all elite fashion designers. Rolls Royce, Bentley, Ferrari, Aston

ABOVE LEFT Peter Gelb (right), general manager of the Metropolitan Opera, with Plácido Domingo, still in costume after a rehearsal of Tan Dun's new opera, *The Last Emperor*, NY, 2006

BELOW AND RIGHT **A simultaneous relay from the Metropolitan Opera of Puccini's *Madama Butterfly*, being enjoyed by a very large audience in Time Square, NY, 2006**

Martin – these are elite cars. Who would not prefer to watch an elite team play, to wear clothes designed by an elite designer, to drive an elite motor car? Yes, these are expensive choices, because they are "the best". But things can be "elite" and "popular" at the same time. Why is opera condemned as an "elitist pursuit"? Because it is expensive? Seats at major sports events or pop concerts are not cheap, and when one adds the cost of travel, they become even more expensive. Some of us choose cheaper clothes, less expensive cars and holidays, and choose to spend our money going to the opera.

Opera has survived in the UK and the USA despite the fact that we do not raise our children to accept it as a normal form of entertainment, even those of us who love it. Our attitude might be different if we did, as on the European Continent, where there is (or used to be) less tendency to regard it as an "elitist" pursuit. In the UK one is often asked "What is a good opera to take my child to for a first try?" This would not be asked on the European Continent, where parents take children to whatever opera they are going to see. Not long ago I asked a 25-year-old German friend how old she had been when her mother first took her to an opera. Eleven years old was the answer. And what was the opera? *Parsifal*. It would be difficult to think of a less "suitable" introduction to opera for a young child, but she has been addicted ever since. One can argue that she was innately musical, from a musical family who could afford the tickets. Equally one could argue that had she not been exposed to it from such an early age, she may never have known that she liked it. We take our children to the cinema, to musicals, to sports events, to pop concerts, all of these often at great expense. But some countries have no

tradition of taking them to orchestral concerts or operas. In the 18th and 19th centuries, music was a natural part of family life. Many homes had a piano in the parlour and family concerts were the norm. But this was an attitude that changed in the 20th century, possibly as a result of families being riven apart during two world wars and also because of the growth in the record industry and radio, making it much easier to listen to music without the effort of performing it. Some schools make the effort to take pupils to an occasional concert, and most music organizations, orchestral and operatic, have education programmes that they take to schools to arouse interest. Does this work? Maybe. But we should not rely on schools to introduce our children to the arts.

Many impoverished students from non-musical backgrounds find their own way to opera – as I did – by standing in long queues for the cheapest seats for performances by often a non-first rate company. After they finish studying, these same enthusiasts have jobs to worry about, children to raise, babysitting problems – and, as often as not, no spare cash. For a period of 10 to 20 years they may be unable to afford either the time or the money to indulge their love of opera. I heard Joseph Volpe, recently retired as general manager of the Metropolitan Opera, New York, say that he considered a *young* opera audience to be aged 45 or 50. If the love of the art form has been implanted in childhood, they will return to it when they are free to do so – as long as it is there for them to return to. Nowadays they have the advantage of being able to play CDs or watch DVDs in their own homes. Another venture that should appeal to those unable to afford the time or money to travel to opera is the move to relay productions to cinemas. This

was initiated in 2006 by the Metropolitan Opera, New York, three of their productions being seen across the USA and Canada. People unable to go to the opera house were able to see the same productions at a fraction of the price at venues near to where they live. In the UK, Glyndebourne Festival Opera has entered into a similar partnership with a cinema chain and three of its operas were shown during autumn 2007, with seats costing no more than for any other cinema visit. Hopefully, people who consider opera too "elite" or "not for the likes of us" and are therefore wary of attending a performance in an opera house, will be able to try it in a local cinema and may even find they like it!

"The Arts allow us to discover who we can be". The next point of reference is our attitude to opera. If we want to be regarded as a civilized and cultured society, then we – and that means the people who govern us – must find the means to support the arts. Imagine not being able to take your children to an art gallery to see great paintings. To a theatre to see a play by Shakespeare. To a concert to hear a Mozart concerto. Or to an opera house to hear Verdi. Yes, I am aware that whole swathes of the population never go to an art gallery or a play or a concert – but we must never be in a position where the opportunity is not there if they

wish to seize it. Poverty comes in more than one form, and this would surely be cultural poverty and deprivation. So governments must either provide sufficient subsidies or must offer enough incentives to those who are willing to sponsor the arts. In some countries this situation already exists: in the USA the lists of sponsors printed in programmes runs to several pages. They are not all passionately interested in the art form they support, but they are all interested in making that art form available to the largest possible number of people in their city and their country, and many of these sponsors regard it as their local and national duty to help make this happen. Yes, they receive much public acknowledgement and thanks, but why not? They are public benefactors in the same way as were the aristocracy and royalty who supported composers in days of yore, thus enabling them to devote their time to composing instead of having to earn a living – without these patrons, we may have had little music by Mozart, Beethoven, or Tchaikovsky.

The arts are expensive forms of entertainment, but they are also forms of education. Even at a small level, by which I do not mean a "low" level of standards, expenses are high: sets, however simple, have to be constructed, costumes

ABOVE A modern design for Puccini's *Tosca* on the floating stage on Lake Constance, Bregenz Festival, 2007

made or hired, music hired from publishers, pianos hired and tuned, venues rented together with their attendant staff, insurance premiums paid, and artists and their expenses paid (they have to live, too). Rarely can an opera company retrieve more than about a third of its expenses from the box office – unless it raises seat prices to a level where very few people could afford them, and this would defeat the aim. Unless a change occurs in attitudes to sponsorship, such as an inducement for those who may be willing to aid our opera companies in the shape of tax relief, opera companies will continue to struggle. The more effort that has to be put into raising money and cutting back on expenses, the less energy is available for the production of high quality and attractive performances.

For the past 40 years or so, there has been an increasing emphasis on the "production" rather than the music. There are, of course, many directors who are also very musical - Luc Bondy, Peter Hall, Nicholas Hytner, Stefan Janski, Yannis Kokkos, Nikolaus Lehnhoff, Jonathan Miller, Elijah Moshinsky, Trevor Nunn, Peter Stein, Francesca Zambello, Franco Zeffirelli, to name but a few. This does not mean that their productions are "set in stone" and must never vary from the original idea of the creators. Some of their productions have been decidedly innovative (Miller's mafia-based *Rigoletto*, for instance), but they have certain things in common – respect for the work they are directing, consideration for the singers, and the knowledge that many people in the audience are seeing this opera for the first time. The people one sees frantically re-reading the synopsis in the interval, and trying to relate what they read to what is happening on the stage, speaks volumes. Works do not have to be updated and coarse, the libretto shamelessly altered to suit the "concept", in order to be "relevant" to the present day – audiences are perfectly capable of making the analogies for themselves without having it thrust down their throats. And, despite what many modern directors may think, the composers and librettists *did* know better than anyone what it was in their works they wanted to convey to the audience.

And so to my last point: the importance of the standard repertory. It will, I firmly believe, continue to survive. We only have to compare the number of opera companies and opera festivals around the world today with those of 50 years ago. Despite all the financial problems they have to face, opera companies have sprung up outside capital cities.

In some countries this situation has existed for many years – any self-respecting small town in Germany boasted an opera company. The UK now has major regional companies, touring companies, specialist companies performing in very small venues, and an ever-increasing number of opera festivals; in the USA there are listed 135 professional opera companies, and this does not include the opera festivals. A recently published list of the 20 most popular operas in the USA included four each by Puccini, Verdi, and Mozart; two each by Rossini and Donizetti; two French operas (*Carmen* and *Faust*); the inevitable *Cav. & Pag.*; and Johann Strauss's operetta *Die Fledermaus*. In Europe the situation is similar – there are many more companies than there were before the Second World War, and audiences flock to all the major festivals. Audiences will always want to be transported out of their everyday lives into the never-never land of beauty and thrills that make them forget their own problems for a few hours. There will always be an audience for Handel, Mozart, Verdi, Puccini, Wagner, and Strauss. Their works are the best of their kind – shall we say they are elite? But beware – do not be too complacent. The wheels need to be oiled and new tyres fitted from time to time, otherwise there is always the risk that the machine might stop.

ABOVE **A soprano of the younger generation, Anna Netrebko, in *Le nozze di Figaro*, Salzburg**

Opera Houses and Festivals

These are the major companies worldwide. Sometimes the name of the company is the same as the name of the house in which it performs – eg La Scala, Milan, or Metropolitan Opera, New York. Sometimes it is not, such as the Bayerische Staatsoper (Bavarian State Opera), which performs at the National Theatre, Munich. Some festivals concentrate on one composer or one particular genre of opera; others are general opera festivals; others include orchestral and chamber music. Telephone numbers given are usually for the box office, as are email addresses.

Opera Houses/Companies

ARGENTINA
Teatro Colón
Cerrito 618, Buenos Aires 1010
www.teatrocolon.org.ar; tel: +54 (11) 4378 7344
email: boleteria_colon@buenosaires.gov.ar
Opened 1908; horseshoe auditorium; seats 2,478 + 500 standing; March–Dec

AUSTRALIA
Opera Australia
Sydney, Bennelong Point, Sydney 2001, NSW
www.sydneyoperahouse.com
tel: +61 (2) 9250 7777
email: bookings@sydneyoperahouse.com
Opened 1973; shoebox auditorium; seats 1,547 + 22 standing; Jan–March, June–Oct in Sydney; 3–4-month season in Melbourne

State Opera of South Australia
Festival Theatre, King William Rd,
PO Box 1269, Adelaide SA 5001
www.saopera.sa.gov.au; tel: +61 (8) 8226 4790
email: info@saopera.sa.gov.au
Opened 1973; shoebox auditorium; Festival Theatre seats 1,978; two smaller theatres; various seasons

AUSTRIA
Vienna Staatsoper
Opernring 2, 1010 Vienna (Office: Vienna Classic, Wehrgasse 1, 1050 Vienna)
www.wiener-staatsoper.at
tel: +43 (1) 513 15 13

email: order@viennaclassic.com
Opened 1869, bombed 1943, reopened 1955; horseshoe auditorium; seats 1,709 + 567 standing; Vienna Philharmonic Orchestra are members of the Vienna State Opera Orchestra; Sept–June

BELGIUM
Théâtre Royal de la Monnaie
Place de la Monnaie, 1000 Brussels
www.demunt.be; tel: +32 70 23 39 39
email: info@lamonnaie.be
Opened 1819, fire 1855, reopened 1856, renovated 1955–6; horseshoe auditorium; seats 1,179; Sept–June

CANADA
Canadian Opera Company
227 Front Street E, Toronto, ON, Canada M5A 1E8 & Four Seasons Center for the Performing Arts, 145 Queen St W, Toronto, M5H 4G1
www.coc.ca; tel: +1 416 363 66711
email: Info@coc.ca
Company founded 1950; first company to use surtitles, 1983; new theatre 2006; horseshoe auditorium; seats 2,071; Oct–May

CZECH REPUBLIC
Estates Theatre (National Theatre)
Národni Divaldo, Ostrovni Street, Prague 1
www.estatestheatre.cz; tel: +420 224 227 981
email: tickets@czechopera.cz
Opened 1881, destroyed by fire, reopened 1883; horseshoe auditorium; seats 986 (chamber theatre 500); Sept–June

DENMARK
The Opera
Ekvipagemestervej 10, 1438 Copenhagen
www.operaen.dk; tel: +45 3369 6969
email: dktbooking@kglteater.dk
Opened 2005; horseshoe auditorium; main theatre seats 1,492–1,703, small theatre 200; Sept–June

FINLAND
Finnish National Opera
Helsinginkatu 58, PO Box 176, 00251 Helsinki
www.ooppera.fi; tel: +358 9 4030 2211
email: tickets@operafin.fi
Opened 1993; horseshoe auditorium; seats 1,350; Aug–June

FRANCE
L'Opéra National de Paris
Palais Garnier: 8 rue Scribe, 75 009 Paris
Opened 1875; shares programmes with Opéra Bastille; horseshoe auditorium; seats 1,991; Sept–July
Opéra Bastille: 120 rue de Lyon, 75 012 Paris
Opened 1989; shares programmes with Palais Garnier; shoebox auditorium; seats 2,716; Oct–July
Both: www.operadeparis.fr
tel: +33 1 72 29 35 35; email: fnac.com

Opéra de Châtelet
1, Place du Châtelet, 75001 Paris
www.chatelet-theatre.com
tel: +33 1 40 28 28 40; tickets via website
Opened 1862; horseshoe auditorium; seats 2,500; opera and classical music all year round

GERMANY
Deutsche Staatsoper
Unter den Linden 5–7, 10117 Berlin
www.staatsoper-berlin.org
tel: +49 20 35 45 55
email: tickets@staatsoper-berlin.de
Built 1843, rebuilt after fire 1844, destroyed in WW2, rebuilt 1955; horseshoe auditorium; seats 1,354; Sept–July

Deutsche Oper
Bismarckstrasse 34-37, 10585 Berlin
www.deutscheoperberlin.de
tel: +49 (0) 700 67 37 23 75 46
email: info@deutscheoperberlin.de
Opened 1912, destroyed in WW2, reopened 1961; shoebox auditorium; seats 1,885; Nov–May

Komische Oper
Behrenstrasse 55–57, 10117 Berlin
www.komische-oper-berlin.com
tel: +49 30 47 99 74 00
email: info@komische-oper-berlin.com
Opened 1892, partly destroyed in WW2, reopened 1947 under leadership of Walter Felsenstein; horseshoe auditorium; seats 1,208; July–May

Bayerische Staatsoper
Max-Joseph-Platz 2, Munich
www.staatsoper.de; tel: +49 89 21 85 19 20
email: tickets@st-oper.bayern.de

Opened 1818, fire, reopened 1885, destroyed in WW2, reopened 1963; horseshoe auditorium; seats 1,723 + 369 standing; also performs in Prinzregententheater and 1730s Rococo Cuvilliés Theatre; Sept–July

Dresden Staatsoper
Theaterplatz 2, Dresden 8010
www.semperoper.de; tel: +49 (0) 351 49 11 70
email: bestellung@semperoper.de
Opened 1841, designed by Gottfried Semper, destroyed by fire 1869, rebuilt 1878, destroyed in WW2, rebuilt 1985 to original Semper designs; horseshoe auditorium; seats 1,323 Aug–July

HUNGARY
Hungarian State Opera
Magyar Allami Opera House,
Andrassy Street 22, 1061 Budapest VI
www.opera.hu; tel: +36 1 331 2550
email: info@opera.hu
Opened 1884; horseshoe auditorium; seats 1,261 + 82 standing; Sept–June

ISRAEL
Israeli Opera Tel Aviv-Yafo
Tel Aviv Performing Arts Centre,
19 Saul Hamelech Avenue, Tel Aviv 61332
www.israel-opera.co.il; tel: +972 3 692 7777
email: kupa@tapac.org.il
Company formed 1985; present theatre opened 1994; shoebox auditorium; seats 1,500; Nov–July

ITALY
Teatro alla Scala
Piazza della Scala, 20121 Milan
www.teatroallascala.org; tel: +39 02 860 775
email: biglietteria@teatroallascala.org
Opened 1778, renovated, bombed 1943, reopened 1946; horseshoe auditorium; seats 2,105; Dec–July

Opera San Carlo
Via San Carlo 98/F, 80132 Naples
www.teatrosancarlo.it
tel: +39 081 7972 331/412
email: biglietteria@teatrosancarlo.it
Opened 1737, fire 1816, rebuilt same year; horseshoe auditorium; seats 1,450; full-time

Teatro La Fenice
Campo San Fantin, 30124 Venice
www.teatrolafenice.it; tel: +39 041 2424
tickets via website

Opened 1792, reopened after fire 1837, fire 1996, rebuilt to original Rococo design, reopened 2003; horseshoe auditorium; seats 1,176; season variable

NETHERLANDS
Netherlands Opera
Het Musietheater, Waterlooplein 22,
1011 PG Amsterdam
www.dno.nl; tel: +31 (0) 20 625 54 55
tickets via website
Founded after WW2, moved to this theatre 1986; shoebox auditorium; seats 1,594; full-time

PORTUGAL
Teatro Nacional de São Carlos
Rue Serpa Pinto 9, 1200 Lisbon
www.saocarlos.pt; tel: +351 213 612 444
email: reserva.bilhetes@saocarlos.pt
Opened 1793; horseshoe auditorium; seats 1,148; Sept–July

RUSSIA
Mariinsky (Kirov) Opera
1 Teatralnaya Ploshchad, 190000 St Petersburg
www.mariinsky.ru; tel: +7 812 326 4141
email: tickets@mariinsky.ru
Founded 1783, new theatre in 2007; horseshoe auditorium; seats 1,780 + standing; Sept–July

Bolshoi Opera
Ploshchad Sverdlova 1, Moscow
www.bolshoi.ru; tel: +7 (495) 250 73 17
email: sales@bolshoi.ru
Company began 1773, theatre opened 1824; horseshoe auditorium; seats 2,153 + standing; Sept–July

SPAIN
Gran Teatre del Liceu
Rambla dels Caputxins 65, Barcelona 08002
www.liceubarcelona.com; tel: +34 93 485 99 13
email: tiquet@liceubarcelona.com
Opened 1847, fire 1861, rebuilt, fire 1994, rebuilt 1999; horseshoe auditorium; seats 2,292; Sept–July

SWEDEN
Royal Swedish Opera
Kungliga Operan, Jakobs Torg, 4, PO Box 16094, S-103 22 Stockholm; www.operan.se
tel: +46 8 791 44 00; email: biljett@operan.se
Company founded 1773, first theatre opened 1782, new theatre 1899; horseshoe auditorium; seats 1,200; Aug–June

SWITZERLAND
Grand Théâtre de Genève
Bd du Théâtre 11, CH-1211 Geneva 11
www.geneveopera.ch; tel: + 41 22 418 31 30
email: billetterie@geneveopera.ch
Founded 1876, new theatre 1962; shoebox auditorium; seats 1,488; Sept–June

Zurich Opera
Falkenstrasse 1, CH-8008 Zurich
www.opernhaus.ch; tel: +41 44 268 66 66
tickets via website
Founded 1834, present theatre 1891; horseshoe auditorium; seats 1,238; Sept–June

USA
Chicago Lyric Opera
Civic Opera House, 20 N Wacker Drive,
Chicago, IL 60606
www.lyricopera.org
tel: +1 (312) 332 2244 Ext 5600
tickets via website
Founded 1954; shoebox auditorium; seats 3,563; Sept–March

Houston Grand Opera
Wortham Theater Complex, 550 Prairie
Street, Houston, TX 77002
www.houstongrandopera.org
tel: +1 713 546 0240
tickets via website
Founded 1977; seats 2,172; Oct–June

Los Angeles Opera
Dorothy Chandler Pavilion,
135 North Grand Avenue, Los Angeles,
CA 90012
www.losangelesopera.com
tel: +1 213 972 7219
tickets via website
Company formed 1986 (previously LA Civic Grand Opera from 1948); theatre opened 1964; shoebox auditorium; seats 3,086; Sept–April

Metropolitan Opera
Lincoln Center, New York, NY 10023
www.metopera.org; tel: +1 212 362 6000
tickets via website: www.metoperafamily.org
Company formed 1883; new house in Lincoln Center 1966; shoebox auditorium; seats 3,800 + 265 standing; Sept–May

New York City Opera

Lincoln Center, New York, NY 10023
www.nycopera.com; tel: +1 212 721 6500
Booking via website
*Founded 1943, present theatre from 1966 in
Lincoln Center; shoebox auditorium; seats 2,779
+ some standing; Sept–Nov, March–April*

San Francisco Opera

War Memorial Opera House, 301 Van Ness
Avenue, San Francisco, CA 94102
www.sfopera.com; tel: +1 415 864 3330
email: webtickets@sfopera.com
*Founded 1923; shoebox auditorium; seats
3,176 + 200 standing; Sept–May*

Seattle Opera

1020 John Street, Seattle, WA 98109
www.seattleopera.org; tel: +1 206 389 7676
email: tickets@seattleopera.org
*Founded 1963; famous for annual Ring cycles;
shoebox auditorium; seats 3,017; Sept–May*

Virginia Opera

PO Box 2580, Norfolk, VA 23501-2580
www.vaopera.org; tel: +1 866 673 7282
email: info@vaopera.org
*Founded 1974, only U.S. regional opera company
performing in 3 theatres: Edythe C & Stanley
L Harrison Opera House, Norfolk, shoebox
auditorium, seats 1,626; Landmark Theater,
Richmond, shoebox auditorium, seats 3,569; George
Mason University's Center for the Arts, Fairfax,
shoebox auditorium, seats 1,859; Sept–April*

UK

Royal Opera House

Covent Garden, London WC2E 9DD
www.royalopera.org; tel: +44 (0) 20 7304 4000
email: BoxOffice@roh.org.uk
*Handel operas first performed in 1735, fire 1808,
new theatre 1809, reopened as opera house 1847,
fire 1856, new theatre 1858, renamed Royal Opera
House 1892, used as dance hall during WW2,
reopened as opera house 1946, vastly improved
1999; horseshoe auditorium; seats 2,253; Sept–July*

English National Opera

London Coliseum, St Martin's Lane,
London WC2N 4ES
www.eno.org; tel: +44 (0) 870 145 0200
tickets via website
*Vic-Wells Opera formed 1931 at Sadler's Wells
Theatre, moved to Coliseum in 1968, changed name
to ENO 1974; all operas sung in English; horseshoe
auditorium; seats 2,356 + 75 standing; Sept–July*

Opera North

Grand Theatre, 46 New Briggate, Leeds
LS1 6NU; www.operanorth.co.uk
tel: +44 (0) 113 243 9999
email: info@operanorth.co.uk
*Founded 1977 as English National Opera North,
offshoot of ENO, independent as Opera North
1981; based at Grand Theatre, Leeds, and tours to
other cities predominantly in the north of England;
Grand Theatre built 1878, greatly renovated 2006;
horseshoe auditorium; seats 1,550; Sept–June.*

Scottish Opera

39 Elmbank Crescent, Glasgow G2 4PT
www.scottishopera.org.uk
tel: +44 (0) 870 060 6647 (Theatre Royal)
email: via website (each theatre individually)
*Scottish national company formed 1962, based in
Glasgow; tours extensively to Scottish cities and
some in north of England; Theatre Royal opened
1867, two fires, rebuilt 1895; seats 1,497; Sept–June*

Welsh National Opera

Wales Millennium Centre, Bute Place, Cardiff
CF10 5AL
www.wno.org.uk; tel: +44 (0) 29 2063 5000
email: marketing@wno.org.uk
*Company formed 1946; moved to Wales Millennium
Centre (WMC) 2004; tours to many cities in Wales
and England; WMC seats 1,700; Sept–July*

Opera Festivals

AUSTRIA

Bregenz Festival

POB 311, 6901 Bregenz
www.bregenzerfestspiele.com
tel: +43 5574 407 6
email: tickets@bregenzerfestspiele.com
*Spectacular opera productions on a floating stage
with seating round the lake; standard repertoire,
established and young artists; 4 weeks, July–August*

Salzburg Festival

PO Box 140, 5010 Salzburg
www.salzburgfestival.at; tel: +43 662 8045 500
email: info@salzburgfestival.at
*Summer festival founded in 1922 by Richard
Strauss, Hugo von Hofmannsthal, and Max
Reinhardt; emphasis is still on Mozart, with a wide
range of opera productions, orchestral concerts,
recitals, choral concerts, and plays; very high
international standards; 5 weeks, end July–Aug*

FRANCE

Aix-en-Provence

La Boutique du Festival, 11 rue Gaston de
Saporta, 13100 Aix-en-Provence
www.festival-aix.com; tel: +33 4 42 17 34 34
email: billetterie@festival-aix.com
*Founded 1948; international standards; operas, some
in open-air theatre, concerts; 4 weeks, June–July*

GERMANY

Bayreuth Festival

Festspielhügel 1–2, 95445 Bayreuth
www.bayreuther-festspiele.de
tel: +49 921 78 78 0; tickets from Kartenbüro
der Bayreuther Festspiele, Postfach 10 02 62,
D-95402 Bayreuth
*Theatre built by Wagner for performances of his
own works; first festival 1876; still administered by
Wagner family; classical amphitheatre auditorium
seating 1,925; annual festival for 5 weeks in
July–Aug of The Ring (3 cycles) and three
other operas; very long waiting list for tickets*

ITALY

Maggio Musicale

Biglietteria del Teatro Comunale, Corso Italia
16, Florence 50123
www.maggiofiorentino.com
tel: +39 055 213 535
email: tickets@maggiofiorentino.com
*Based at Teatro Comunale; international standard,
operas, concerts, recitals; 8 weeks, May–June*

Pesaro: Rossini Opera Festival

Teatro Rossini, Via Rossini 37, 61100 Pesaro
www.rossinioperafestival.it
tel: +39 0721 3800 294
email: boxoffice@rossinioperafestival.it
*Founded 1980; performs popular and lesser-known
Rossini operas, recitals, concerts; 2 weeks, August*

Spoleto: Festival dei Duo Mondi

Piazza del Duomo 8, 06049 Spoleto
www.spoletofestival.it; tel: +39 0743 220320

email: boxoffice@spoletofestival.it
Founded 1958 by Gian Carlo Menotti (parallel with Spoleto festival, near Charleston, S Carolina, USA, now independent); opera, dance, concerts, recitals; established and rising artists; 2 weeks, June–July

Torre del Lago: Viale Giacomo Puccini

257A 55048 Torre del Lago Puccini (LU)
www.puccinifestival.it; tel: +39 0584 359322
email: ticketoffice@puccinifestival.it
Founded 1930 following Puccini's wishes; open-air theatre, new theatre 1966, another new theatre 2008, seating 3,200; three or four operas; international artists; 4 weeks, July–Aug

Verona: Arena di Verona

Servizio Biglietteria, via Dietro Anfiteatro 6/b, 37121 Verona
www.arena.it; tel: +39 045 8005151
email: ticket@arena.it
Founded 1913, at inspiration of the tenor Giovanni Zenatello; amphitheatre, with huge stage, seats over 16,500; five or six operas in spectacular productions, live animals, etc; 6 weeks, July–Aug

SWEDEN
Drottningholms Slottsteater

Föreställningar, Box 15417, SE 10465 Stockholm; www.dtm.se; tel: +46 8 660 82 25
tickets via website: www.ticnet.se
Jewel of a theatre, built 1766; 1922 wax candles replaced by electric light, new ropes for moving scenery; original stage designs copied and still used; two Baroque operas annually; 2 weeks, May–June, 2 weeks, July–Aug

USA
Aspen Music Festival

2 Music School Road, Aspen, Colorado 81611
www.aspenmusicfestival.com
tel: +1 970 925 9042; tickets via website
Founded 1949; pre-professional and established artists; opera, concerts, chamber music, master classes, etc; various venues, some with free seating on lawns; 9 weeks, June–Aug

Glimmerglass Festival Opera

PO Box 191, Cooperstown, NY 13326
www.glimmerglass.org; tel: +1 607 547 2255
email: tickets@glimmerglass.org
Founded 1975; four productions each season; standard repertory and new operas, established and young performers; 900-seat Alice Busch Theater opened 1997 on shores of Lake Utsega ("Lake Glimmerglass" in James Fenimore Cooper's novels); 8 weeks, July–Aug

Opera Theatre of St Louis

PO Box 191910, St Louis, MO 63119-7910
www.opera-stl.org; tel: +1 314 961 0644
email: boxoffice@opera-stl.org
Founded 1976 by Richard Gaddes (now director of Santa Fe Opera); performs in Loretto-Hilton Center of Webster University; high standards (many now-established American artists began their careers at St Louis); four operas, standard repertoire and new works, sung in English; 5 weeks, May–June

Santa Fe Opera

PO Box 2408, Santa Fe, NM 87504-2408
www.santafeopera.org; tel: +1 505 986 5900/ +1 800 280 4654; tickets via website
Founded in 1957 by John Crosby in New Mexico desert surrounded by mountains; standard repertoire, including many commissions, premières and American premières; high standards with established and rising singers and large apprentice programme; spectacular new theatre opened 1998; shoebox auditorium; seats 2,128 + 106 standing; 8–9 weeks, June–Aug

UK and IRELAND
Aldeburgh Festival

Aldeburgh Music, Snape Maltings Concert Hall, Snape, Suffolk IP17 1SP
www.aldeburgh.co.uk
tel: +44 (0) 1728 687110
email: enquiries@aldeburgh.co.uk
Founded 1948 by Benjamin Britten, Peter Pears, and Eric Crozier as home for English Opera Group; main venue is Snape Maltings Concert Hall, opened 1967, other venues include local churches; opera, often modern and usually in concert performance, concerts, recitals; 3 weeks, June

Buxton Festival

3 The Square, Buxton, Derbyshire SK17 6AZ
www.buxtonfestival.co.uk
tel: +44 (0) 1298 70395
email: info@buxtonfestival.co.uk
Founded 1979; operas, recitals, literary events; rising and established artists; Opera House is a beautiful Frank Matcham 1903 theatre; horseshoe auditorium; seats 937; 2 weeks, July

Edinburgh International Festival

The Hub, Castlehill, Edinburgh EH1 2NE Scotland; www.eif.co.uk; tel: +44 (0)131 473 2000
email: boxoffice@hubtickets.co.uk
Founded 1947; festival of music and drama with strong operatic component by visiting companies using various theatres and concert-halls; restored and renamed Festival Theatre opened 1994; horseshoe auditorium; seats 1,915; 3 weeks, Aug–Sept

Garsington Opera

Garsington Manor, Oxford OX44 9DH
www.garsingtonopera.org; tel: +44(0)1865 361636
email: office@garsingtonopera.org
Founded 1989 by Rosalind and the late Leonard Ingrams at their home, Garsington Manor, made famous by the Bloomsbury set in 1920s; three operas, high standards, young promising singers; temporary purpose-built theatre; seats 500; 4 weeks, June–July

Glyndebourne Opera Festival

PO Box 2624, Lewes, E Sussex BN8 5UW
www.glyndebourne.com
tel: +44 (0) 1273 813813
email: boxoffice@glyndebourne.com
Founded 1934 by John Christie and his wife, the soprano Audrey Mildmay, in grounds of their home; international performers and top-class standards, wide repertoire, five or six operas; new theatre 1994, horseshoe auditorium; seats 1,200 + standing; 14 weeks May–Aug; Glyndebourne Opera on Tour visits various towns each autumn

Longborough Opera Festival

Longborough, Moreton-in-Marsh, Gloucestershire GL56 0QF
www.longboroughopera.com
tel: +44 (0) 1451 830292
email: enquiries@longboroughopera.com
Founded 1991 by Lizzie and Martin Graham in grounds of their home; wide repertoire, focus on Wagner; rising and established singers; shoebox auditorium; enlarged 2008, seats 630; 4 weeks, June–July

Wexford Festival Opera

49 North Main Street, Wexford, Ireland
www.wexfordopera.com; tel: +353 53 91 22144
email: boxoffice@wexfordopera.com
Founded by Dr Tom Walsh in 1952; resurrects three operas unlikely to be seen anywhere else; international casts of rising singers; new theatre 2008, seating 750; 3 weeks, Oct

Glossary

alto lowest female voice, or highest male voice

aria (It.) "air", a solo song in an opera

arioso "like an aria" – a short aria or a section of recitativo accompagnato

atonal no obvious key – the opposite of tonal

avant garde (Fr.) "vanguard" – artists or their works radically different from traditional

baritone male voice between tenor and bass

baryton-Martin named after the singer Jean-Blaise Martin (1768–1837), a light baritone voice usually used in French Romantic opera.

bass the lowest male voice or the lowest part of the music being sung or played

bass-baritone bass voice but with higher and stronger top notes than the average bass

basso continuo (It.) figures indicating which notes a player should play as chords below the harmonies – see *continuo*

breeches (or trousers) role See *travesti*

brindisi (It.) "health" or "toast" – a drinking song

buffo, buffa, (It.) "comic" ("buffoon"), e.g. buffo bass, a comical bass role

cabaletta (It.) used especially in Italian opera to describe the quick final section of an aria

cadenza (It.) a solo passage at the end of an aria

Camerata (It.) "comrade" – the circle of composers who met in Count Bardi's salon in Florence in the 1570s

cantilena (It.) "small song"

castrato (It.) high male voice in the 17th and 18th centuries achieved by castration before puberty

coloratura (It.) "colouring" – a brilliant agile voice capable of rapid and florid ornamentation

conte (Fr.) "tale" or "story"

continuo (It.) Baroque term to indicate the instrument(s) playing the bass line and thus supporting the harmonies above it. This was usually a harpsichord, but could also be a cello or a chitarrone

contralto (alto) (It.) the deepest female voice; also a low-voiced *castrato*

counter-tenor male alto often with a falsetto upward extension – not the same as *castrato*

da capo (D.C.) (It.) "from the head", i.e. from the beginning, describes a 3-part aria, the first part, middle part, then the first part repeated

diva (It.) "divine" – highly celebrated female singer

drame lyrique (Fr.) Romantic opera, without dialogue, and less "grand" than grand opera

ensemble (Fr.) "together" – group of singers or the music they sing, e.g. trios, sextets, etc.

entr'acte (Fr.) "between the acts" – musical interlude between two acts of an opera

Fach (Ger.) "compartment" or "box" – used mainly in Germany to indicate a specialist area of performance or voice category into which a singer falls, e.g. dramatic soprano, light tenor, soubrette

fioritura (It.) "flourish" – vocal ornamentation

formalism accusation by Soviet officials in the Stalin era of emphasis on form as opposed to content, also implying discordant modernism

gamelan form of percussion with metal instruments, traditionally used in Indonesia

Gesamtkunstwerk (Ger.) "total art work" – often applied to Wagner's works combining many art forms

grand opera distinguishes between opera (all sung) and operetta (spoken dialogue). Also describes early 19th century epic operas on historical subjects

guerre des bouffons See *querelle des bouffons*

habanera a slow Cuban dance in a dotted rhythm, as danced by Carmen in Bizet's opera

haute-contre (Fr.) very high tenor voice of the 18th century, mainly in French opera

Helden (Ger.) "heroic", so *Heldentenor,* a powerful tenor voice as heard in the singing of Wagner

intermezzo (It.) an interlude, usually orchestral, between scenes in an opera

IRCAM Institut de Récherche et de Coordination Acoustique/Musique – opened in Paris in 1976 for producing electronic and computer music

Kapellmeister (Ger.) originally the music master in a chapel, but later came to mean any music director

key tonal music is centred round a particular key

Leitmotif/Leitmotiv (Ger.) "leading motif" – a phrase or figure representing a character, object, or idea, especially in Wagner's operas

libretto (It.) "little book" – text of an operatic work

Liebestod (Ger.) "love-death" – the final aria sung by Isolde in Wagner's *Tristan und Isolde,* as she is metaphysically carried from life to join her dead lover

Lied (Ger.) "song" – an "art song" as opposed to a popular song or an operatic aria

lyric soprano/tenor a light, fluent voice

lyrics words to be sung, not spoken

melodrama a sensational drama; but also used in opera to describe spoken text to a musical accompaniment

mezza voce (It.) "half voice" – singing with a soft tone

mezzo-soprano (It.) "half soprano", the voice between *soprano* and *contralto*

Mighty Handful term coined by a Russian critic to describe a group of five composers (Balakirev, Borodin, Cui, Musorgsky, Rimsky-Korsakov) in the mid-19th century who advocated Russian national music

minimalism music which relies on repetition of a single figure or phrase over a long stretch of time. Term arose in the mid-20th century.

monodrama (Gr.) a *melodrama* with one main character

motif (Fr.) a short recurring theme. See *Leitmotif*

music theatre term coined *c.* 1960 to describe a work involving singing, speech, and dancing, suitable for performance in small venues

number opera an opera divided into sections by arias, and so-called because the arias are numbered in the score

opera buffa/seria (It.) comic/serious opera, especially of 18th and 19th century Italy

operetta (It.) 19th century light romantic opera, usually with spoken dialogue, similar to musical comedy

overture "opening" – an orchestral introduction to an opera, usually incorporating tunes from the opera

prelude See *overture*

première the first performance of a work

prima donna (It.) "first lady" – the principal female singer in the cast of an opera

querelle des bouffons (Fr.) in French music history this was the virulent argument between the supporters of French or of Italian opera, and was triggered by the performance in Paris of Pergolesi's *La serva padrona* by a comic Italian opera troupe (the *Bouffons*)

recitative the setting of speech, the music following the rhythms of the spoken word. It can be accompanied by occasional chords on the continuo (*recitativo secco,* i.e. dry recitative) or by the orchestra (*recitativo accompagnato*)

répétiteur (Fr.) musician who coaches and rehearses singers at the piano

rescue opera genre dating from the time of the French Revolution, involving an eleventh hour rescue by an act of great heroism or sacrifice. The most famous is Beethoven's *Fidelio*

Second Viennese School applied to Schoenberg and his followers, especially Berg and Webern, the First Viennese School being the Classical Haydn, Mozart, and Beethoven

serial music refers to the music of Schoenberg and his pupils, in which all 12 semitones in an octave are used in a fixed order and have equal value

Singspiel Ger. ballad opera involving songs and spoken dialogue such as the works of Weill and Brecht

soprano (It.) the highest female voice

soubrette (Old Fr.) "cunning" or "shrewd" – usually refers to knowing servant girls such as Despina in *Così fan tutte* or roles requiring a light soprano voice such as Adèle in *Die Fledermaus.*

spinto (It.) "pushed" and really short for *lirico spinto*, a lyrical voice which can be safely "pushed" when needed, such as in late-Romantic Italian opera

Sprechgesang (Ger.) "speech singing" – a vocal category between singing and speech

tableau (Fr.) "scene" a stage setting, or subdivision of an act in an opera, some operas, especially Russian, consisting of a series of short scenes

tenor the high male voice (but see also *countertenor* and *haute-contre*)

tessitura (It.) "texture" – refers to the range at which a role lies in relation to the voice for which it was written. All the notes of a role may be within the singer's range, but if much of the part lies very high in that range, i.e. the role has a high *tessitura*, it can cause strain and discomfort for the singer

threnody a dirge, a lament for the dead

tonal music using a system of keys, as did all music from the 17th to the early 20th centuries.

travesti (Fr.) "disguised" – a role played by someone in disguise, usually applied to a female singer playing the role of a male

treble a child's singing voice (also the top line in choral music)

trouser role see *travesti*

verismo (It.) "realism", mainly applied to the brutal dramas of the late 19th and early 20th century

vibrato (It.) controlled rapid fluctuation of the pitch which gives a voice (or an instrument) its main expressive quality

Vorspiel (Ger.) "prelude" – similar to overture

zarzuela traditional opera of Spain, combining song, speech, and dance

Index

Picture Credits

Mitchell Beazley would like to acknowledge and thank the following for supplying photographs for publication in this book.

Key a above, b below, l left, r right

2 Yoshio Tomii/SuperStock, 8l Lebrecht Music & Arts/Alamy, 8r Bibliothèque Nationale/akg-images, 9 Imagno/Getty Images, 10 Nigel Norrington/ArenaPAL/TopFoto.co.uk, 11 Ilja Hulinsky/Alamy, 13 Phototake Inc/Alamy, 14l Getty Images,14r, 15r Time & Life/Getty Images, 15l Ira Nowinski/Corbis, 16l Roger-Viollet/TopFoto.co.uk, 16r Marion Kalter/akg-images, 17l Getty Images, 17r Clive Barda/ArenaPAL/TopFoto.co.uk,18l Time & Life/Getty Images, 18r AFP/Getty Images, 19, 20l & 20r Getty Images, 21 Robbie Jack/Corbis, 22l ArenaPAL/TopFoto.co.uk, 22r Getty Images, 23 Time & Life/Getty Images, 24 Artmedia/HIP/TopFoto.co.uk, 26 Civico Museo Bibliografico Musicale, Bologna, Italy/Alinari/The Bridgeman Art Library, 27l Lebrecht Music & Arts, 27r City of Westminster Archive Centre, London/The Bridgeman Art Library, 28a Conservatory of St. Peter, Naples/The Bridgeman Art Library, 28b Tristram Kenton/Lebrecht Music & Arts, 29 Ken Howard/ArenaPAL/TopFoto.co.uk, 30a Stapleton Collection/The Bridgeman Art Library, 30b Bill Cooper/PAL/TopFoto.co.uk, 31r Guy Gravett, 32 Marion Schone/Staatsoper Unter den Linden, Berlin, 33a Lebrecht Music & Arts/Alamy, 33b TopFoto.co.uk, 34l Musée des Beaux-Arts, Dijon/akg-images, 34r akg-images, 35l Bibliothèque de L'Arsenal, Paris/Giraudon/The Bridgeman Art Library, 35r Lebrecht Music & Arts, 36l akg-images, 36r Lebrecht Music & Arts, 37 Ken Howard/ArenaPAL/ TopFoto.co.uk, 38 Clive Barda/ArenaPAL/TopFoto.co.uk, 39 Ullstein Bild/akg-images, 40 Clive Barda/TopFoto.co.uk, 41 Tristram Kenton/Lebrecht Music & Arts, 42 The Holburne Museum of Art, Bath, UK/The Bridgeman Art Library, 44 Lebrecht Music & Arts, 45l Rabatti-Dominigie/akg-images, 45r Theatermuseum, Munich/akg-images, 46l Louvre, Paris, France/Lauros/Giraudon/The Bridgeman Art Library, 46r TopFoto.co.uk, 47 akg-images, 48a Topfoto.co.uk, 48b Archiv für Kunst & Geschichte, Berlin/akg-images.co.uk, 49 Mike Hoban/TopFoto.co.uk, 50l Lebrecht Music & Arts, 50r Mozart Museum, Salzburg, Austria/Lauros/Giraudon/The Bridgeman Art Library, 51 Lebrecht Music & Arts, 52 Heikki Tuuli/Lebrecht Music & Arts, 53 Tristram Kenton/Lebrecht Music & Arts, 54l TopFoto.co.uk, 54r Marilyn Kingwill/ArenPAL/TopFoto.co.uk, 55, 56a Clive Barda/ArenaPAL/TopFoto.co.uk, 56b Ron Scherl/ArenaPAL/TopFoto.co.uk, 57 Clive Barda/ArenaPAL/Top|Foto.co.uk, 58 Beethoven Haus, Bonn, Germany/Lauros/Giraudon/The Bridgeman Art Library, 59a Ron Scherl/ArenaPAL/TopFoto.co.uk, 59b Clive Barda/ArenaPAL/TopFoto.co.uk, 60l Ben Christopher/ArenaPAL/TopFoto.co.uk, 60r Archive für Kunst & Geschichte, Berlin/akg-images, 61l Erich Lessing/Musée du Louvre/akg-images, 61r Private Collecton/Lebrecht Music & Arts, 62 ©Tate London, 2008, 64 Private Collection/© Chris Beetles, London, UK/The Bridgeman Art Library, 65l Roger-Viollet/TopFoto.co.uk, 65r Bibliothèque de l'Opera Garnier, Paris, France Joseph Martin/The Bridgeman Art Library, 66a Alinari/TopFoto.co.uk, 66b Roger-Viollet/TopFoto.co.uk, 67 Mary Altaffer/AP/PA Photos, 68l Amati Bacciardi/ArenaPAL/ TopFoto.co.uk, 68r Mike Hoban/ArenaPAL/TopFoto.co.uk, 69l Civico Museo Bibliografico Musicale, Bologna, Italy/ Alinari/The Bridgeman Art Library, 69r Private Collection/ The Bridgeman Art Library, 70 Clive Barda/ArenaPAL/ TopFoto.co.uk, 71 Roger-Viollet/TopFoto.co.uk, 72 Clive Barda/ArenaPAL/TopFoto.co.uk, 73 TopFoto.co.uk, 74 Private Collection/

Lauros/Giraudon/The Bridgeman Art Library, 75 Private Collection/photo © Bonhams, London, UK/The Bridgeman Art Library, © ADAGP, Paris and DACS, London 2008, 76l Fritz Curzon/ArenaPAL/TopFoto.co.uk, 76r Roger-Viollet/TopFoto.co.uk, 77 Ron Scherl/ArenaPAL/ TopFoto.co.uk, 78l akg-images, 78r Private Collection/Roger-Viollet, Paris/The Bridgeman Art Library, 79 Roger-Viollet/akg-images, 80 Ron Scherl/ArenaPAL/ TopFoto.co.uk, 81 Colette Masson/Lebrecht Music & Arts, 82 Marty Sohl/Metropolitan Opera, 83, 84 Clive Barda/ArenaPAL/TopFoto.co.uk, 85 Marco Brescia/AP/PA Photos, 86 Gianfranco Fainello/ ArenaPAL/TopFoto.co.uk, 87 Clive Barda/ArenaPAL/ Topfoto.co.uk, 88l Nationalgalerie, Berlin/akg-images, 88r Archiv für Kunst & Geschichte, Berlin/akg-images, 89 Laurie Lewis/Lebrecht Music & Arts, 90l Lebrecht Music & Arts, 90r Sue Adler/ArenaPAL/TopFoto.co.uk, 91 akg-images, 92l Ullstein Bild/akg-images, 93 Private Collection/The Bridgeman Art Library, 94 S Lauterwasser/Lebrecht Music & Arts, 95 Mander & Mitchenson/ArenaPAL/TopFoto.co.uk, 96 Sue Adler/ ArenaPAL/TopFoto.co.uk, 97 S Lauterwasser/ Lebrecht Music & Arts, 98 Ron Scherl/ArenaPAL/ TopFoto.co.uk, 99 Clive Barda/ArenaPAL/TopFoto.co.uk, 100 Bradford Art Galleries and Museums, West Yorkshire, UK/The Bridgeman Art Library, 101 Colin Willoughby/ ArenaPAL/ TopFoto.co.uk, 102l akg-images, 102r Pietro Baguzzi/akg-images, 103l Archiv für Kunst & Geschichte, Berlin/akg-images, 103r Robbie Jack, 104a Archiv für Kunst & Geschichte, Berlin/akg-images, 104b Private Collection/Roger-Viollet, Paris/The Bridgeman Art Library, 105 ArenaPAL/TopFoto.co.uk, 106l Conservatory of St. Peter, Naples, Italy/Giraudon/The Bridgeman Art Library, 106r Metropolitan Opera Archives/Lebrecht Music & Arts, 107 Clive Barda/TopFoto.co.uk, 108l akg-images, 108r Robbie Jack, 109a Haags Gemeentemuseum, The Hague, Netherlands/The Bridgeman Art Library, 109b Archives Larousse, Paris, France/Giraudon/The Bridgeman Art Library, 110 Bibliothèque de l'Opera Garnier, Paris, France/Archives Charmet/The Bridgeman Art Library, © ADAGP, Paris and DACS, London 2008, 111l Haags Gemeentemuseum, The Hague, Netherlands/The Bridgeman Art Library, 111r Keith Saunders/ArenaPAL/ TopFoto.co.uk, 112l Bibliothèque de l'Opera Garnier, Paris, France/Archives Charmet/ The Bridgeman Art Library, 112r Sabine Toepffer/Deutsches Theater/Lebrecht Music & Arts, 113a Tretyakov Gallery, Moscow, Russia/ Giraudon/The Bridgeman Art Library, 113b State Central A A Bakhrushin Theatre Museum, Moscow, Russia/ The Bridgeman Art Library, 114l Moscow, Tretjakov Gallery/akg-images, 114r Lebrecht Music & Arts, 115 Time & Life/Getty Images, 116 Moscow, Tretjakov Gallery/akg-images, 117 RIA Novosti, 118 Robbie Jack, 119l Moscow, Tretjakov Gallery/akg-images, 119r Keith Saunders/ ArenaPAL/TopFoto, 120 Smetana Muzeum, Prague, Czech Republic/Roger-Viollet, Paris/The Bridgeman Art Library, 121a Private Collection/photo © Bonhams, London, UK/The Bridgeman Art Library, 121b Robbie Jack, 122 © Samuel Courtauld Trust, Courtauld Institute of Art Gallery/The Bridgeman Art Library, 124 Musée de la Ville de Paris, Musée Carnavalet, Paris, France/Lauros/ Giraudon/The Bridgeman Art Library, 125l Time & Life/Getty Images, 125r Bettmann/Corbis, 126 akg-images, 126b, 127a Debra Hesser/Sarasota Opera, 127b, 128 Museo Teatrale alla Scala/Nimatallah/akg-images, 129 Robbie Jack, 130l S Lauterwasser/Lebrecht Music & Arts, 130r Gianfranco Fainello/ArenaPAL/TopFoto.co.uk, 131 Hulton-Deutsch Collection/Corbis, 132 Civica Raccolta Stampe Bertarelli, Milan, Italy/Roger-Viollet, Paris/ The Bridgeman Art Library, 133l Private Collection/The

Bridgeman Art Library, 133r Metropolitan Opera Archives, 134 Robbie Jack, 135 Museo Teatrale alla Scala, Milan, Italy/The Bridgeman Art Library, 136l akg-images, 136r B Rafferty/Lebrecht, 137 Erich Lessing/akg-images, 138 Sabine Toepffer/Deutsches Theater, 139 British Library, London, UK/ © British Library Board. All Rights Reserved/The Bridgeman Art Library, 140, 142 Clive Barda/ArenaPAL/ TopFoto.co.uk, 143 Guy Gravett, 144 British Library, London, UK/ © British Library Board. All Rights Reserved/ The Bridgeman Art Library, 145 Lebrecht Music & Arts, 145 Marion Kalter/Lebrecht Music & Arts, 146 Lebrect Music & Arts, 147 Ron Scherl/ArenaPAL/ TopFoto.co.uk, 148 Catherine Ashmore, 149 Tony Tree/Lebrecht Music & Arts, 150 Tristram Kenton/Lebrecht Music & Arts, 151 Catherine Ashmore, 152l Mary Evans Picture Library/Alamy, 152r © Leeds Museums and Galleries (City Art Gallery) UK/The Bridgeman Art Library, 153 Lebrecht Music & Arts, 154 Schlesinger Library, Radcliffe Institute, Harvard University/ The Bridgeman Art Library, 156 Private Collection/The Bridgeman Art Library © Succession Picasso/DACS 2008, 157 Pierre Vauthey/Corbis Sygma, 158l Arnold Schoenberg Institute/Lebrecht Music & Arts, 158r Laurie Lewis/Lebrecht Music & Arts, 159 Lebrecht Music & Arts, 160l Bettmann/Corbis, 160r Ken Howard/Santa Fe Opera, 161 JazzSign/Lebrecht Music & Arts, 162 Kurt Weill Foundation/Lebrecht Music & Arts, 163 Bettmann/Corbis, 164l Richard Haughton/Lebrecht, 164r Laurie Lewis/ Lebrecht, 165 Guy Gravett, 166a Time & Life/Getty Images, 166b TopFoto.co.uk, 167 Tristram Kenton/Lebrecht Music & Arts, 168l Moscow, Tretjakov Gallery/akg-images © ADAGP, Paris and DACS, London 2008, 168r Robbie Jack/Corbis, 169l Clive Barda/ArenaPAL/TopFoto.co.uk, 169r Guy Gravett, 170 Bettmann/Corbis, 171l Donald Cooper/Lebrecht Music & Arts, 171r Lebrecht Music & Arts, 172l Getty Images, 172r Time & Life/Getty Images, 173a Roger-Viollet/ TopFoto.co.uk, 173b Guy Gravett, 174a Bettmann/Corbis, 174b Gerry Murray/Royal Northern College of Music, Manchester, 175 Royal Northern College of Music, Manchester, 176a Christina Burton/ArenaPAL/ TopFoto.co.uk, 176b Laurie Lewis/Opera North, 177 Pauline Neild/Clonter Opera, 178l Mike Evans/Lebrecht Music & Arts, 178r Clive Barda/ArenaPAL/TopFoto.co.uk, 179 Brian Seed/Lebrecht Music & Arts, 180 Clynt Garnham/Alamy, 181l Heikki Tuuli/Lebrecht Music & Arts, 181r Matti Kolho/Lebrecht Music & Arts/Alamy, 182 Laurie Lewis/Lebrecht Music & Arts, 183l Guy Gravett, 183r Mander & Mitchenson/ArenaPAL/TopFoto.co.uk, 184 Stephen Vaughan/Opera North, 185 Elisabeth Carecchio/Festival d'Aix, 186 Guy Gravett, 187a Keith Saunders/ArenaPAL/TopFoto.co.uk, 187b Time & Life/Getty Images, 188l Christian Steiner/www.theamusgrave.com, 188r Courtesy of Virginia Opera, 189l M Nicolaou/ Lebrecht, 189r B Rafferty/Lebrecht Music & Arts, 190 Catherine Ashmore, 191 Sisi Burn/ArenaPAL/TopFoto.co.uk, 192 Jon Super, 193a Kate Mount/Lebrecht Music & Arts, 193b TopFoto/ ArenaPAL, 194l Ben Christopher/ArenaPAL/ TopFoto, 194r Clive Barda/ArenaPAL/TopFoto.co.uk, 195 Ken Howard/ Santa Fe , 196l Popperfoto/Alamy, 196r Bettmann/Corbis, 197 Guy Gravett, 198l Gordon Parks/Time & Life/Getty Images, 198r Clive Barda/PAL/ TopFoto.co.uk, 199a AFP/Getty Images, 199b Catherine Ashmore, 200 Nina Large/ArenaPAL/TopFoto.co.uk, 201 Jim Caldwell/ ArenaPAL/TopFoto.co.uk, 202 Ken Howard/Santa Fe Opera, 203 Heikki Tuuli/Lebrecht, 204 Laurie Lewis/Lebrecht, 205 Jim Caldwell/Houston Opera, 206 Mary Altaffer/AP/PA Photos, 207l & r Shannon Stapleton/Reuters/Corbis, 208 Kerstin Joensson/AP/PA Photos, 209 Action Press/Rex Features